CONIECTANEA BIBLICA • NEW TESTAMENT SERIES 16

With best regards

Bruce C. Johanson

BRUCE C. JOHANSON

To All the Brethren

A TEXT-LINGUISTIC AND RHETORICAL
APPROACH TO I THESSALONIANS

ALMQVIST & WIKSELL INTERNATIONAL

ABSTRACT

Johanson, B.C., 1987. To All the Brethren. A Text-Linguistic and Rhetorical Approach to I Thessalonians. **Coniectanea Biblica. New Testament Series 16.** xiv +230 pp. Uppsala. ISBN 91-22-00865-9.

The purpose of the present study is to achieve an as valid as possible reconstructive understanding of the capacity of meaning of I Thessalonians as an act of communication in its initial communicative context. To this end, useful models involving communication, textuality, communicative functions hierarchically arranged, and types of persuasive appeals and strategies have been selectively borrowed from textlinguistics, literary theory and both modern and ancient rhetoric.

By way of a wholistic and text-centered analysis and interpretation of the accessible text-context features, of text-internal part-whole relations, and of situation-related features of intertextuality the following general conclusions are arrived at: (1) The persuasive strategies observed in the text-internal part-whole relations in relation to the accessible text-context features indicate that within the inital communicative context, it is the rhetorical-persuasive function that dominates over other functions, viz., the bulk of persuasive strategies are shown to be directed to solving the issues arising from the exigence reflected in I Thess 4:13—5:11. (2) The integrity and unity of I Thess is substantiated both in view of the overall rhetorical coherence of the text as a persuasive act and on the basis of intercorroborative criteria in the pragmatic, semantic and syntactic text-dimensions indicating a tightly woven, consistently symmetrical composition. (3) At the same time, the text gives evidence of a rich, creative intertextuality of overlapping structures and functions common to ancient Greek letters and to rhetorical-persuasive discourse, as well as to O.T.-Jewish exhortatory discourse appropriate to an anticipated worship-setting of reception. This complex intertextuality is seen as reflecting an intention to provide the text with features appropriate to subsequent, more general contexts of rereading. It also indicates that any simple generic classification of the text cannot be entirely adequate.

The analysis also contributes to the question of text-delimitation of epistolary macrostructure relevant to Pauline and other N.T. letters and provides numerous minor exegetical insights from a text-linguistic perspective.

Bruce C. Johanson. Teologiska institutionen, Uppsala Universitet, Box 1604, S-751 46 Uppsala, Sweden.

© 1987 Bruce C. Johanson
Distributor: Almqvist & Wiksell International, Stockholm
ISBN 91-22-00865-9
Printed by Graphic Systems AB 1987

**Dedicated
to Anne,
to Michael, Christina and Nadia
and to my parents**

διοτι αγαπητοι μοι γεγενησθε

PREFACE

Whenever the N.T. interpreter turns to more or less new methods of analysis in carrying out his or her task, there is always the necessity of providing the reader with an orientation of such new tools. Almost inevitably, such orientations will be regarded as inadequate by the specialists of the new methods and as overly technical and burdensome by the general N.T. exegete. The present undertaking will undoubtedly not escape this dilemma. In order to lighten the general exegete's burden I have tried to keep technical terminology to a minimum.

As is often the case with such investigations, the most effective way to come to grips with the material presented here is to proceed from the introductory in 1.1 to the interpretive analyses and conclusions in Part III and in Part II while referring back to the orientative material in Part I as the need arises. To facilitate such a process of reading I have tried to provide adequate cross-references at strategic points in the presentation.

In view of the lack of availability of many of the Greek accents in the print trains used to print this text, I have elected to leave them out altogether. Justification for this is also found in there being some precedent in N.T. monographs on the Continent and in Scandinavia. Except where otherwise noted, I have followed the text of the 26th edition of the Nestle/Aland **Novum Testamentum Graece**. Also, unless specifically noted, I assume responsibility for the English renditions that are given for the Greek.

While assuming total responsibility for the present selection and presentation of text-linguistic and rhetorical theory and method and the application of these in interpreting I Thessalonians, I wish to express my deep indebtedness to Doc. David Hellholm, Dr. Bertil Wiklander, Doc. Birger Olsson and Prof. Jan Bergman for their inspiration and interest, and especially so to Prof. Lars Hartman for his inspiration, constructive criticism and patient encouragement. A special word of thanks is also expressed to all the members of the N.T. seminar at the University of Uppsala for their many insightful and constructive criticisms as the work on this thesis progressed. I wish to also express my gratitude to the Theological Faculty of the University of Uppsala for the research scholarship which has made it possible to carry through this work to its completion.

With regard to the formatting of the text-body, the document-composition program used was often forced to allow footnotes to flow over onto a subsequent page. Their sequential numbering, however, will hopefully keep the reader sufficiently well-oriented. Finally, while assuming responsibility for the formatting of the text-body, bibliography and indeces, I wish to express special thanks to L. Bruzelius at Uppsala Datacentral for his patient help in solving the many problems that arise in such an undertaking.

March, 1987   B.C. Johanson

CONTENTS

PART I -- Motivation, Method and Theory

1 ORIENTATION ON A TEXT-CENTERED APPROACH 3

  1.1 Introductory 3
      1.1.1 Primary and Subsidiary Aims 3
      1.1.2 The Need for a Text-Centered Approach 3
  1.2 Proceeding from a Communication Model 7
      1.2.1 The Basic Semiotic Dimensions of Texts 7
            1.2.1.1 The Text-Syntactic Dimension 8
            1.2.1.2 The Text-Semantic Dimension 9
            1.2.1.3 The Text-Pragmatic Dimension 10
  1.3 Some Theoretical Observations on Communicative Functions 11
      1.3.1 Establishing the Basic Communication Functions 11
      1.3.2 Some Models Compared and Criticized 12
            1.3.2.1 The Priority of Pragmatics in Modelling
                     Functions 13
            1.3.2.2 Criticism of the Poetic or Literary Function 14
            1.3.2.3 Distinguishing Types and Subtypes of Functions 15
      1.3.3 The Bilateral Nature of Communicative Functions 17
  1.4 Interpreting Communicative Functions of Texts 17
      1.4.1 A Brief Orientation on Text-Interpretation in
           General 17
      1.4.2 Some Text-Context Aspects of Interpreting Functions 21
      1.4.3 Text-Syntagmatic Aspects of Interpreting Functions 23
  1.5 Markers for Hierarchical and Sequential Textual Structure 24
      1.5.1 Metacommunicative Clauses (MC) 26
      1.5.2 Substitutional Markers 26
            1.5.2.1 Substitution on Text-Level 26
            1.5.2.2 Substitution on Abstraction-Level (SA) 27
            1.5.2.3 Substitution on Metalevel (SM) 27
      1.5.3 Thematic Markers (ThM) 29
      1.5.4 Time and Place Co-ordinators (TC, PC) 31
      1.5.5 Renominalization (R) 31
      1.5.6 Connectors (C) 32
      1.5.7 Other Delimitational Characteristics of Pauline
           Style 32
  1.6 Summary of Delimitation-Markers and Related Features 33
  1.7 Orientation on a Model of Rhetorical Analysis 34
      1.7.1 The Basic Character of Persuasion 34
      1.7.2 The Basic Means of Persuasion 36
      1.7.3 G.A. Kennedy's Methodological Proposal 39

	1.7.4	The Status and Critical Use of the Three Rhetorical Genres 39
	1.7.5	Rhetorical Disposition and its Use in Analysing Letters 42
	1.7.6	A Brief Survey of Disposition in Greek Rhetoric 44
		1.7.6.1 Text-Oriented Dispositional Features 44
		1.7.6.2 User-Oriented Dispositional Features 45

PART II -- A Text-Centered Analysis of I Thessalonians

2 RECONSTRUCTING SITUATIONAL FEATURES: SURVEY OF RELEVANT ASPECTS 49
2.1 General Aspects of the Communication Situation 49
2.2 Aspects Relevant to the Rhetorical Situation 52
    2.2.1 The Author-Addressee Relationship 52
    2.2.2 The Status of the Community's Christian Conduct 55
    2.2.3 The Problem Regarding Deceased Christians 55
    2.2.4 The Problem of Tribulations and Suffering 57

3 A TEXT-LINGUISTIC/LETTER-CONVENTIONAL ANALYSIS 59
3.1 The Letter and Its Primary Functional Subsequences 59
    3.1.1 The Letter as a Whole 59
    3.1.2 I Thess 1:1: The Letter-Opening 60
    3.1.3 I Thess 1:2-5:24: The Letter-Body 61
        3.1.3.1 Form-Criticism's Inadequacy in Isolating the Letter-Body 61
        3.1.3.2 Taking the Broader View of the Letter-Body 64
    3.1.4 I Thess 5:25-28: The Letter-Closing 65
3.2 The Primary Subsequences of the Letter-Body 67
    3.2.1 I Thess 1:2-3:13: A Predominant Expressive Function 67
        3.2.1.1 The Significance of Recurrent Thanksgiving-Reports 69
        3.2.1.2 Other Conventional Topics and Phraseology Expressing Goodwill 70
        3.2.1.3 Some General Conclusions on I Thess 1:2-3:13 71
    3.2.2 I Thess 4:1-5:24: A Predominant Conative Function 72
        3.2.2.1 A Criticism of C.J. Bjerkelund's Form-Critical Method 73
        3.2.2.2 Some General Conclusions on I Thess 4:1-5:24 75
    3.2.3 Temporal and Spatial Features of Coherence and Delimitation 75
        3.2.3.1 Temporal and Spatial Features in I Thess 1-3 76
        3.2.3.2 Temporal Features in I Thess 4-5 78

4 A TEXT-LINGUISTIC/RHETORICAL ANALYSIS OF THE LETTER-BODY 81
4.1 Analysis of I Thess 1:2-2:16 and Subsequences 81
    4.1.1 The Delimitation and Coherence of 1:2-2:16 81
    4.1.2 The Rhetoric of 1:2-10 83
    4.1.3 The Delimitation and Coherence of 1:2-10 86

	4.1.4	The Delimitation and Coherence of 2:1-12 87

- 4.1.4 The Delimitation and Coherence of 2:1-12 87
- 4.1.5 The Rhetoric of 2:1-12 89
- 4.1.6 The Connection and Delimitation of 2:13-16 94
- 4.1.7 The Rhetoric and Coherence of 2:13-16 96
- 4.1.8 Some Concluding Observations on I Thess 1:2-2:16 99
- 4.2 Analysis of I Thess 2:17-3:13 and Subsequences 100
  - 4.2.1 Connection, Delimitation, Coherence of 2:17-3:13 and 2:17-20 100
  - 4.2.2 The Rhetoric of 2:17-20 101
  - 4.2.3 The Delimitation and Coherence of 3:1-8 103
  - 4.2.4 The Rhetoric of I Thess 3:1-8 104
  - 4.2.5 The Delimitation, Coherence and Rhetoric of 3:9-13 107
  - 4.2.6 Some Concluding Observations on I Thess 2:17-3:13 108
- 4.3 The Terminal-Transitional Functions of I Thess 3:9-13 109
- 4.4 Analysis of I Thess 4:1-5:24 and Subsequences 111
  - 4.4.1 Text-Syntactic Connection of 4:1-5:24 to 1:2-3:13 111
  - 4.4.2 The Delimitation and Coherence of 4:1-12 112
  - 4.4.3 The Rhetoric of 4:1-12 113
    - 4.4.3.1 Generally Relevant Religious-Ethical Exhortation 113
    - 4.4.3.2 A Credibility-Enhancing Persuasive Function 116
  - 4.4.4 The Delimitation and Coherence of 4:13-5:11 118
  - 4.4.5 The Delimitation and Coherence of 4:13-18 119
  - 4.4.6 The Rhetoric of 4:13-18 119
    - 4.4.6.1 I Thess 4:14: The First Argument 121
    - 4.4.6.2 I Thess 4:15-17: The Second Argument 123
  - 4.4.7 The Delimitation and Coherence of 5:1-11 126
  - 4.4.8 The Rhetoric of 5:1-11 128
    - 4.4.8.1 The Rhetorical Character of 5:1-3 128
    - 4.4.8.2 The Rhetorical Functions of 5:1-3 129
    - 4.4.8.3 The Rhetoric of 5:4-11 132
  - 4.4.9 The Delimitation and Coherence of 5:12-24 136
  - 4.4.10 The Rhetoric of 5:12-24 140
  - 4.4.11 Some Concluding Observations on I Thess 4:1-5:11 143

5 AN ANALYSIS OF MACROSTYLISTIC SYMMETRY IN THE LETTER-BODY 145
- 5.1 Textual Symmetry: Background, Method, Functions 145
- 5.2 Text-Syntactic Symmetry in I Thess 1:2-5:24 147
- 5.3 Text-Symmetry and Macrostructure: Some Observations 152

PART III -- The Interpretation of I Thess as an Act of Communication

6 I THESS: PERSUASIVE ACT OCCASIONED BY A RHETORICAL EXIGENCE 157
- 6.1 I Thess 1:2-3:13: Its Function of Captatio Benevolentiae 157
- 6.2 The Exordium-Like Relation of 1:2-3:13 to 4:1-5:24 160
- 6.3 I Thess 4:1-5:24: Exhortation, Argumentatio and Peroratio 161

	6.4	Interpreting the Rhetorical Situation of the Letter 163

    6.4   Interpreting the Rhetorical Situation of the Letter 163
        6.4.1   The Persuasive Coherence of I Thess as a Whole 163
        6.4.2   The Particular Question of I Thess 2:1-12 164
        6.4.3   The Question of Rhetorical Genre 165
        6.4.4   Some General Concluding Observations 167

7   I THESS: A SINGLE, INTEGRAL, COHERENT ACT OF
        COMMUNICATION 169
    7.1   The Consistency Presupposition and Interpolation
        in I Thess 169
    7.2   The Evidence of Textual and Rhetorical Coherence 170

8   I THESS: CREATIVE ACT IN A PRACTICAL PROCESS OF
        COMMUNICATION 173
    8.1   "The Christian Letter in the Making" 173
    8.2   Intertextuality and a Worship-Setting of Reception 175
        8.2.1   The More Obvious Worship-Appropriate Features
            in I Thess 175
        8.2.2   Other Worship-Oriented, O.T.-Jewish Features
            of Discourse 176
            8.2.2.1   The Sermon in Acts 13 and O.T.-Jewish
                Exhortatory Discourse 180
            8.2.2.2   The Intertextuality of O.T.-Jewish Discourse
                in I Thess 181
        8.2.3   Conclusions on O.T.-Jewish Intertextuality 186
    8.3   General Summary and Conclusions 187

LIST OF ABBREVIATIONS 192

BIBLIOGRAPHY 195

INDICES 222

FIGURES

Figure 1 59
Figure 2 67
Figure 3 79
Figure 4 88
Figure 5 99
Figure 6 109
Figure 7 144
Figure 8 149
Figure 9 150
Figure 10 151

PART I

MOTIVATION, METHOD AND THEORY

Chapter 1

ORIENTATION ON A TEXT-CENTERED APPROACH

1.1 INTRODUCTORY

1.1.1 Primary and Subsidiary Aims

The primary aim of the following study is to achieve an as valid as possible understanding of I Thessalonians, seen as **an act of communication**. To this end, a selective use will be made of insights and analytical means provided by text-linguistics, literary theory and both modern and ancient rhetoric (see 1.2-1.7).

Although not expressed in such terms nor treated in all its relevant aspects, this primary aim is broadly dealt with in previous exegetical treatments of the occasion and purpose of the letter. The present approach intends to contribute a text-centered and dynamical-rhetorical interpretation of the primary and the subordinate communicative functions or purposes of the text (chs. 6 and 8) by way of an investigation of the text-internal, part-whole relations and of the accessible text-context features. In this way an attempt will be made to attain an as reasonable as possible reconstructive grasp of the capacity of meaning of I Thess as an act of communication in its initial communicative context. This is carried out by way of an isolation of the relevant and accessible situational features (see ch. 2) and a concerted analysis of text-delimitation and text-coherence (see chs. 3-5), with attention given to intertextuality (chs. 4, 6, and esp. 8). The integrally related question of the text's unity and integrity is also treated from a text-centered perspective (see ch. 7).

1.1.2 The Need for a Text-Centered Approach

A brief review of various positions of interpretation regarding the occasion and purpose will serve to provide a perspective within N.T. exegesis from which the present approach to the letter may be motivated. There is general agreement that, strictly speaking, the immediate occasion of the letter is the return of Timothy with news of the community's welfare (3:6), and that the contents of the letter reflect various aspects of their welfare and needs as reported by Timothy (see 2.1). When, however, it comes to interpreting communicative purpose(s) from the form and contents of the letter, the interpretive conclusions diverge widely not only with regard to the actual situation that appears to be reflected but also with regard to the relative importance of the various contents within the letter.

Thus, one may ask whether the communicative goal should be described in very general epistolary terms as the renewal of contact in which news and questions are taken up, without any particularly serious degree of urgency involved in the latter,[1] or similarly but more abstractly, whether it should be described as general exhortation and encouragement modelled on precedents of Greek letters and Cynic exhortatory discourse?[2] Or is it necessary for one to see a whole series of more or less urgent issues being addressed, viz., insinuations against the addressors' integrity (2:1 ff.), afflictions of the addressees (3:3 ff.), moral problems (4:3 ff.), idleness (4:11; 5:14), doctrinal difficulties (4:13 ff.), failure in internal discipline (5:12), etc?[3]

Furthermore, for those who locate the primary communicative purpose in the former major part of the letter (chs. 1-3), there are widely diverging views as to whether the purpose was basically the expression of relieved thanksgiving at the good news of the recipients' spiritual welfare in general,[4] or whether it was such thanksgiving combined with an **apologia pro vita sua** (2:1 ff.) and an **apologia pro absentia sua** (2:17 ff.),[5] or whether it was primarily encouragement due to the pressure of affliction (3:3).[6]

As for those who see the primary purpose as located in the latter major part of the letter (chs. 4-5), the purpose has been located in 4:1-12 as general parenesis elaborating a tradition and not being occasioned by the concrete situation,[7] or more particularly in 4:1-2 and 4:10b-12 as general encouragement to "increase more and more" in living a life pleasing to God,[8] or in 4:13 ff. as dissuasion of the recipients from overt suspicion and mistrust of Paul and his gospel due to an apparent incongruency of his teaching on the parousia which did not anticipate the deaths of believers prior to this event.[9] Although not going so far as to see overt mistrust of Paul, a good number of interpreters see the main concrete problem addressed in the letter as located in 4:13 ff., seeing additional instruction or comfort or both as the primary purpose.[10]

---

[1] Thus Vielhauer, 1975, 87. Generally in the same vein see, e.g., Lightfoot, 1904, 51, 62; Zahn, 1906, Vol. I, 154-5; McNeile, 1953, 126-7; Masson, 1957, 7-8; Robert/Feuillet, 1959, Vol. II, 394-5; Guthrie, 1961, 180-1; Schlier, 1972, 11-13; Wikenhauser/Schmid, 1973, 401; Kümmel, 1973, 224; Best, 1977, 15, 180 ff.; Klijn, 1980, 120-1; Koester, 1980, Vol. II, 112-14; Holtz, 1986, 29-31, among others.

[2] Thus Boers, 1975-76; Malherbe, 1983.

[3] Thus, e.g., Milligan, 1908, xxxi-xxxv; Frame, 1912, 9 ff.

[4] E.g., Schubert (1939, 26) who saw chs. 1-3 as an extented thanksgiving replacing the "letter-body." Cf. Funk (1966, 264) who locates the "body" of the letter in 2:1-3:13 and J.L. White (1972, 70-1) who locates the center of this "body" in 2:5-2:16. For criticisms see under 3.1.3.

[5] E.g., Moffat, 1910, 5. See also Marshall, 1983, 10.

[6] E.g., Rigaux, 1956, 57.

[7] Thus Koester, 1982, Vol. II, 55.

[8] Thus Bjerkelund, 1967, 134.

As for those who have analysed the letter rhetorically, they find what corresponds to the **probatio** (argumentation concerning the main issue or issues) in the latter main part of the letter (chs. 4-5), but differ as to whether this encompasses 4:1-5:5 or 4:1-5:22.[11] None of them note a relatively greater degree of urgency as characterizing any one of the various topics treated. At the same time, R. Jewett sees the letter belonging to the epideictic genre in view of the pervasive note of thanksgiving and praise and G.A. Kennedy sees it as belonging to the deliberative genre as "an exhortation to stand fast in the Lord (3:8)."[12]

All of these different "understandings" of the purpose of I Thess obviously cannot be regarded as valid, unless one is willing to wholeheartedly embrace absolute interpretive relativism, the absurd consequence being that communication would be reduced to haphazard chance if not become altogether impossible (see 1.4.1). For the most part, these positions have been arrived at intuitively from the random, more or less explicit references that appear to reflect various aspects of the communicative context and from the form and contents of the letter in general. An attempt to obtain more objective criteria for interpretation may be seen in the form-critical approach to the letters in which conventions shared by Paul's letters with contemporaneous letters and exhortatory discourse are made explicit.

However, in isolating opening, closing and transitional phraseology and some letter topics in common with the private and official letters of antiquity, form-critics have been too limited to a static treatment of such constitutive elements of letters to give an adequate account of how they interact in the overall structures and thus achieve communicative functions in each of the N.T. letters as concrete acts of communication (see ch. 3 and 1.7.5).[13] Furthermore, Paul's letters are too different from the private and the official Hellenistic letters both in length and contents for such common generic features to give an adequate literary background against which to interpret them without also taking other intertextual features into consideration (see ch. 8).

The pragmatic dimension of the text is better accounted for by a rhetorical approach (see under 1.5). However, the rhetorical analyses carried out so far have been content to remain on a very general level. Basic functional text-sequences of the letter have been isolated for the most part in terms of the common **exordium, narratio,**

---

[9] Hyldahl, 1980, 122.

[10] E.g., Baur, 1867, Vol. II., 99; Gregory, 1909, 658; Jülicher, 1931, 59; Knopf/Lietzmann/Weinel, 1949, 80-1; Meinertz, 1950, 83; Marxsen, 1963, 32-3; 1969, 26, 32; 1979, 28-9; Becker, 1976, 46 ff.; Lüdemann, 1984, 214, 220; Plevnik, 1984; among others.

[11] See under 6.1 and 6.3 for summaries and references on this and on the fact of widely differing opinions as to which part of chs. 1-3 constitutes the exordium and which part the narratio.

[12] Jewett, 1984, 14; Kennedy, 1984, 142.

[13] See, e.g., Schubert (1939, 26), Funk (1966, 264) and J.L. White (1972, 70-1), who see the main purpose in chs. 1-3, and Bjerkelund (1967, 130 ff.) and Koester (1982, Vol. II., 55) who see it in 4:1-12, although all approach the letter from a form-critical perspective.

probatio and **peroratio** schema of classical rhetoric without sufficient sensitivity to the particular epistolary and exhortatory or parenetic characteristics that play a part in its structure and communicative function(s). Furthermore, the various proposals regarding these rhetorical divisions have not been justified by explicit, detailed analyses of the text.[14]

Epistolary form-criticism and rhetorical dispositional analyses are of course appropriate and useful tools in the interpretation of texts. But in previous instances of both such more specialized approaches as well as exegesis in general on I Thess there is the deficiency of drawing interpretive conclusions without a sufficiently rigorous and concerted text-centered analysis that makes explicit how the various smaller and larger textual entities function interactively in serving to achieve the overall communicative function(s) of the text. Such a text-centered analysis is necessary in order to be able to judge the extent to which conventional influence has controlled individual expression or to which the individual author has bent and shaped the conventional into something new and appropriate to the situation in hand.[15]

Furthermore, it is possible for more than one typical structure to govern an entire text (see ch. 8), in which case it becomes necessary to be able to show how these interact and how they relate in a hierarchy of dominances.[16] Also, as previously noted, more than one important function may be served by a single text, something that may be more or less encoded in the text or interpreted from its use in a concrete communicative situation (see under 1.4.2). Usually, however, one particular function appears as dominant in a particular communicative context (1.3.3). All these observations point to the need to focus on the text as a whole, the composition of which being seen as directed by a total strategy that determines its structure.[17]

Such an undertaking demands a close reading of the text. To this end text-linguistics provides a useful and appropriate means of analysis in the text-syntactic, text-semantic and text-pragmatic dimensions (see below). With regard to the pragmatic dimension of textual communication, there are factors that speak for the usefulness and appropriateness of using both ancient and modern rhetoric for analysing I Thess. For one thing, modern rhetoric has gained some sharper, more useful insights, standing as it does on the shoulders of of a long tradition, and for another, there is the fact that Paul belonged to a world in which rhetoric was highly conceptualized (see 1.7).

Finally, it may be added here that a close reading, making use of text-linguistics, will also often provide important co-textual insights and motivations for making a particular interpretive judgment regarding the sense of an ambiguous word or grammatical construction (see the analysis in ch. 4).

---

[14] See Jewett 1984, 12-20; Kennedy, 1984, 141-4.

[15] See, e.g., Knierim (1973, 162) on this aspect in his critique of form-criticism.

[16] Thus, Knierim, 1973, 162.

[17] Enkvist, 1983, 66.

1.2 PROCEEDING FROM A COMMUNICATION MODEL

The plethora of text-linguistic models and the veritable jungle of varying technical terminologies makes in necessary to be selective with an eye to what appears to be most useful in achieving the above-mentioned aims.[18] To this end, the aim of making a wholistic interpretation of I Thess as an act of communication makes it necessary to proceed from the perspective of verbal communication.

The particular version of communication model outlined by E. Gülich and W. Raible is subscribed to as one of the most useful for describing the most important, basic textual processes and features of verbal communication.[19] The basic elements represented in the model are encoder/author, decoder/audience, a universe of entities and situations, a text as a linguistic communicative act and a language code presumably more or less shared by the communication partners.

The universe is divided into the entities and situations of the immediate context of communication, referred to by means of textual **deixis** (e.g., "here," "over there," etc.), and the entities and situations outside of the immediate context referred to by means of textual **reference**. With regard to the language **code**, this should not be limited to rules of a linguistic code alone involving **linguistic competence** but should also include rules or conventions of a generic code which involves a **communicative competence**.[20]

1.2.1 The Basic Semiotic Dimensions of Texts

From the perspective of semiotics, H.F. Plett has shown that the syntactic, semantic and pragmatic dimensions of texts, when taken together, provide a useful model for describing a text as a linguistic macrosign used in communication:[21] 1) **Pragmatics** concerns the relations between **signs**, **designata** and **sign-users** 2) **semantics** concerns the relations between **signs** and **designata** and 3) **syntactics** concerns the relations be-

---

[18] See, e.g., Kallmeyer et al. (1974, Vols. I-II), Gülich/Raible (1977), van Dijk/Petöfi (1977) and Dressler (1978) for surveys and critical presentations of various models and their attendant technical terminologies. In the English language, see, e.g., van Dijk (1977) and de Beaugrande/Dressler (1981) and introductions to "discourse analysis," e.g., by Stubbs (1983), Brown/Yule (1983), Hoey (1983). For surveys and samples of text-centered work being carried out on biblical and related literature in Uppsala see Olsson (1985); for the Continent see, e.g, Güttgemanns (1976), Hardmeier (1978, 1986), Sellin (1983-84) and Schenk (1984), and for South Africa see, e.g, Louw (1973) and various articles appearing often in Neotestamentica.

[19] Gülich/Raible, 1977, 21-6; reproduced by Hellholm (1980, 14-17) and in a simpler version in English by Wiklander (1984, 39-45) followed by Olsson (1985, 120). Cp. Kallmeyer et al., 1974, Vol. I, 26 ff.

[20] See, e.g., Hempfer, 1973, 222-3; S.J. Schmidt, 1976, 106; Hardmeier, 1978, 101-9; Ryan, 1979, 307 ff.; Hellholm, 1980, 62-74.

[21] Plett, 1979, 52. Cf. van Dijk, 1981, 266. The distinction of these three semiotic dimensions goes back to Morris, 1938, 6 ff., 13-42.

tween **signs** and **signs**. These three dimensions stand in a hierarchical relationship with pragmatics inclusive of semantics and syntactics and with semantics as inclusive of syntactics.[22] Furthermore, all three dimensions interact intimately in texts so that whenever we focus on one of them in particular in a textual analysis, the other two dimensions can never be entirely excluded.[23]

Since texts are basically characterized by "extension," "delimitation" and "coherence," Plett accordingly describes the syntactic, semantic and pragmatic textual dimensions each in terms of text-extension, text-delimitation and text-coherence.[24] However, one may refer generally to "textual coherence" as the primary criterion of a meaningful text.[25]

1.2.1.1 The Text-Syntactic Dimension

In the text-syntactic dimension the focus is primarily on connection.[26] The combination of two sentences is seen as the minimal requirement of **syntactic text-extension**. Although it has no practical bearing for the subsequent analysis, for theoretical completeness it may be noted that, since text-delimitation cannot be realized on the basis of purely syntactic relations, the maximal limit of syntactic text-extension cannot be fixed. **Syntactic text-coherence** may be achieved by various devices for which there is a great variety of different designations and descriptions within text-linguistics. For the sake of economy and clarity the terminology and categories here are taken from de Beaugrande and Dressler, who refer to types of **junction** (e.g., **and, but, because**, etc.), substitutionary **pro-forms** (e.g., **he, these, thus, do**, etc.), ellipsis, and **recurrence** of words, classes of words sharing the same stem, grammatical surface structures, etc.[27]

---

[22] See Plett, 1979, 52; Breuer, 1977, 26; Hellholm, 1980, 22 ff.; 1986, 25-6; Schenk, 1984, 18-26; Olsson, 1985, 118-20.

[23] Plett, 1979, 52.

[24] Plett, 1979, 52-119. See further Hellholm, 1980, 27-52, and Wiklander, 1984, 97-242.

[25] See Wiklander (1984, 47) with reference to Hirsch (1967, 236 ff.). See also Charolles (1983, 71-97).

[26] For a more detailed discussion, see Plett, 1979, 56-70; Hellholm, 1980, 27-31.

[27] See de Beaugrande/Dressler, 1981, 54-81. For extensive references to and explanations of analogous and different devices with different designations, see, e.g., Plett, 1979, 60-70; Hellholm, 1980, 29-31.

1.2.1.2 The Text-Semantic Dimension

In the text-semantic dimension the focus is primarily on the semantic reference of expressions to some reality,[28] but it also involves relations between the propositions of a text in which semantics more palpably overlaps with syntactics and pragmatics.[29]

Semantic text-coherence is determined by the coreference of textual entities which may be described in terms of shared semantic features. For instance, in a sequence of sentences one may find a distribution of the references **Socrates, Athenian, he,** and **philosopher** all referring to the man called Socrates. A continuity of senses is realized by these references, the semantic features common to all of them being **singular and person.**[30] Since a text involves a selective reduction of reality,[31] there will always be gaps which the addressee will have to fill in by **inferencing** from the explicit references of the text and his or her own common store of knowledge.[32] A particular aspect of the continuity of senses that achieves semantic text-coherence may be seen in the indications in a text of the continuity of "the same possible world," of "the same place and/or...time" and of the "referential identity between individuals" who serve as **dramatis personae.**[33] Besides the continuity of senses based on shared referential features, the process of inferencing mentioned above also involves the links or relations that hold between the propositions of a text, whenever these semantic links are not made lexically explicit.[34]

Semantic text-extension is defined in terms of the referential unity of linguistic elements as they serve to expand themes and subthemes in subsequences.[35] **Semantic text-delimitation** is oriented to the same unity of thematic reference. A change of theme indicates a textual transition. Such points of transition need not, however, coincide with other transitions of a syntactic or pragmatic character, although they often do so. Semantic transitions are often marked by titles, subtitles and transitional formulae. The referential aspect of the semantic dimension allows a text to be constituted by even a single word, e.g., "Poison" on a bottle label.

---

[28] For a more detailed discussion of this dimension see Plett, 1975, 99-107; Hellholm, 1980, 31-42.

[29] See van Dijk, 1981, 23, 165; de Beaugrande/Dressler, 1981, 94 ff.

[30] Cf. Plett, 1979, 104 ff.

[31] Thus Raible (1980, 321-2) in dependence on Husserl (1970, 354 f.) and quoted by Hellholm (1986, 13-14): "Texts are abbreviations; they abridge, they simplify what is to be designated--and they do so by omitting."

[32] de Beaugrande/Dressler, 1981, 101 ff.

[33] See van Dijk, 1977, 93 ff.; further Hellholm, 1980, 40.

[34] de Beaugrande/Dressler, 1981, 73 ff., 101 ff.

[35] Cf. Werlich, 1982, 30 ff.

1.2.1.3 The Text-Pragmatic Dimension

In the text-pragmatic dimension the focus is primarily on the author and audience and the communicative context in terms of textual processes that outside of text-linguistics have their closest analogue in rhetoric.[36]

Pragmatic text-coherence has its basis in the text-user's co-operation in construing a text's meaning from textual and contextual features. Depending on the immediacy of the situative context, a speaker/author will usually provide the hearer/audience with sufficient encoded metacommunicative signals or instructions to sustain relatively successful communication. Besides this, by means of prior knowledge of the appropriate level of information, of the relevant situational factors and of the appropriate generic conventions, one can co-operate in anticipating pragmatic gaps in a text and in inferencing, or obtaining the required knowledge for inferencing, so as to fill in such gaps. Some useful concepts in describing important aspects of this process of co-operation are presented by R.-A. de Beaugrande and W.U. Dressler:[37]

1. **intentionality:** the text-encoder's attitude that a text should be cohesive and coherent and that it should serve his or her intentions of informing someone or of obtaining someone's co-operation in some goal;

2. **acceptability:** the text-decoder's attitude that a text should be cohesive and coherent and that it is useful or relevant for obtaining information or for co-operating in some goal;

3. **informativity:** the extent to which the contents and structures of a particular text are commensurate with the decoder's knowledge level and expectations;

4. **situationality:** those factors which give a text relevancy to a current or recoverable situation of its occurrence; and

5. **intertextuality:** the ways in which the production and reception of texts depend on a knowledge of other texts, both in general with regard to genres and in particular with regard to the ways well-known texts are used and referred to.

Pragmatic text-extension is gauged by the unity of communicative function. This is usually realized by the dominance of a particular function over other coinciding, subordinated functions. While **pragmatic text-delimitation** may be marked by metacommunicative signals at the beginning or end of a text or its subsequences, the standard of delimitation is based on the unity of communicative function that may be ob-

---

[36] For a more detailed treatment see Plett, 1979, 79-99; Hellholm, 1980, 42-52.

[37] de Beaugrande/Dressler, 1981, 7-11, 113-207. It should be noted here that their use of the term "coherence" is limited to the text-semantic dimension and that they use "cohesion" in place of text-syntactic coherence (1981, 3-7, 48-112). Thus, together with the concepts outlined above, cohesion and coherence are referred to as "standards of textuality." For a critical comparison of these standards of textuality with Plett's syntactic, semantic and pragmatic semiotic dimensions see Wiklander, 1984, 47.

served in the predominance of one or more particular types of function. All such pragmatic text-delimitations underlie very important genre-identifying norms.[38]

Finally, it must be observed that where a text may appear to lack syntactic and/or semantic coherence, it is often the case that coherence can be significantly established in the pragmatic dimension, when sufficient contextual knowledge is available to allow the pragmatic gaps to be filled in or the recognition of a previously hidden communicative strategy. As will be noted further on, both redaction and form criticism of the Pauline letters have focussed too exclusively on features of the syntactic and semantic dimensions without giving due attention to the pragmatic dimension. It is this last dimension which is ultimately decisive when analysing a text as an act of communication.

1.3 SOME THEORETICAL OBSERVATIONS ON COMMUNICATIVE FUNCTIONS

The preceding references to the communicative functions of texts need to be enlarged upon here in terms of a model that is useful and appropriate for text analysis. The exceedingly complex and difficult question of how one may most adequately and systematically isolate and describe the basic functions of verbal communication cannot be given a detailed treatment here, given the scope and the aims of the present study. However, a critical orientation is in order. One of the more comprehensive treatments of the topic has been given by J.L. Kinneavy in **A Theory of Discourse** with the subtitle "The Aims of Discourse," and this work will be taken as the point of departure here.[39]

1.3.1 Establishing the Basic Communicative Functions

Kinneavy makes a broad survey of the classification of language functions from various fields of study and schools of thought that have been exercised by this question: geneticists, sign theorists, communication theorists, logical positivists, semanticists, educators, the liberal arts tradition, expressionists, and comparative philologists. Dispite many directly opposing axiomatic commitments in the theories involved, there turns out to be a surprising degree of relative concordance.[40] Thus in a comparison with the various principles of classification of different systems, viz., level of probability, stress on one or another capability of the language, social function, syntactic differentiation, the particular faculty addressed, or a preponderance of reference or emotion, etc., he shows that the basic **referential**, **persuasive**, and **expressive** classes of aims more or less roughly reappear in most of the systems.[41] However, re-

---

[38] Plett, 1979, 86; Hellholm, 1980, 45-6.

[39] Kinneavy, 1971. For other possibilities see the references made in Kinneavy (1971, 51 ff.).

[40] Kinneavy, 1971, 51-8.

garding what he calls the "literary" aim, it is seriously questionable whether he is successful in establishing anything that comes near to a relative consensus.[42]

While it is granted as axiomatic that all discourse is destined for receivers of some sort, Kinneavy points out that the communicative process is, nevertheless, capable of focusing on one of the constituents of the process as primary in a given situation. Thus, a focus or emphasis on the encoder or decoder gives **person** discourse, a focus on reality to which reference is made gives **reference** discourse, and a focus on the discourse product itself is seen as giving **product** discourse. There are, furthermore, two kinds of person discourse; **expressive**, focusing on the encoder, and **persuasive**, focusing on the decoder.[43]

1.3.2 Some Models Compared and Criticized

Kinneavy indicates that his model is similar to those of R. Jakobson and K. Bühler.[44] Apart from the "literary" aim he associates with product discourse, the other three aims are seen as corresponding to Bühler's "symptom-expressive," "symbol-representational" and "signal-appellant" functions.[45] Jakobson uses the terms "emotive," "referential" and "conative" respectively for these three, and "poetic" for the "literary" function. However, he divides the "sign" constituent into "message" and "contact" so as to derive his "poetic" and "phatic" functions respectively. He also adds "code" to the constituents of the speech event so as to derive a "meta-lingual" function.[46]

---

[41] Kinneavy, 1971, 64 ff.

[42] This can be clearly seen from Kinneavy's paradigm (1971, 65) illustrating the various comparable functions arrived at by other theorists.

[43] Kinneavy, 1971, 60, cf. 37-40. Halliday (1973, 22 ff.) arrives at corresponding "ideational," "interpersonal" and "textual" functions.

[44] Kinneavy, 1971, 59. He makes it clear that it was already completed and copyrighted when he became aware of their contributions.

[45] Bühler, 1933, 74 ff; 1934, 24 ff.

[46] Jakobson, 1960 353 ff. According to Hymes (1968, 121), Jakobson later retracted seeing the functions as being "determined" by the constitutive factors, preferring to express the relationship purely in terms of focus or emphasis.

1.3.2.1 The Priority of Pragmatics in Modelling Functions

While Bühler meant his model to be a model of the concrete speech event,[47] there is justification for C.F. Graumann's conclusion that it is suitable in this respect more as a "Gebilde-Modell" than as a 'Handlungs-Modell.'[48] Bühler described the functions of the linguistic sign in terms of its "semantic relations" (also "functions") to the three constituents "sender," "receiver" and "objects and states of affairs." He explicitly refers to the "expressive" and "appellant" functions, derived from the sign's "symptom" and "signal" relations to sender and receiver respectively, as "other forms of representation" ("andere Darstellungsverfahren") and as semantic relations that "limit the **dominance** of the representational function of language."[49] However, he goes on to refer to the representational function only in terms of the external world of reality, in spite of the fact that it must be recognized as including the representation of the "inner life" of the speaker as well.[50] Furthermore, although he referred to sign relations in terms of "semantic functions," he nevertheless explained the expressive and appellant functions pragmatically in terms of a "Kausalverhältniss", and the representational function semantically in terms of a "Zuordnungs- verhältniss".[51]

Thus, Bühler's model of functions, together with all those based on Bühler, cannot be seen as homogenous, since various functions are ultimately based on different types of criteria.[52] Kinneavy's model is superior in that the functions are all approached from the perspective of the communicative process. However, in his apparent desire to avoid the "intentional" and the "affective" fallacies,[53] he limits himself to regarding the "language process" as being "capable of focusing attention on one of its own components as primary in a given situation."[54] This personification of the "language process" can only thinly veil the fact that it is, nevertheless, addressors and addressees who do the focusing through their use of language.[55]

---

[47] Bühler, 1934, 24.

[48] Graumann, 1984, 245. See also Koerner (1984, 14) who notes that Bühler's "sign functions should not be confused with the various functions or uses of language as a whole."

[49] Innis' translation (1982, 153) of Bühler (1933, 79).

[50] Thus Kubczak (1984, 19), who also presents other important criticisms.

[51] Thus Kubczak, 1984, 9.

[52] See Brinker's criticism (1983, 132) of especially Grosse (1976) in this respect.

[53] Kinneavy (1971, 49), referring to Wimsatt/Beardsley (1954, 3-18, 21-39).

[54] Kinneavy, 1971, 59.

[55] Referring to Martin (1959, 33), Kinneavy (1971, 60) relates the receiver in the communicative process to the basic functions in terms of different kinds of acceptances (or rejections). In so doing, he is in fact viewing the functions from the perspective of audience acceptability. As for the perspective of authorial intention,

Thus, it is necessary to make a clear shift here from linguistic structure to communicative act, from a basically intrinsic, semantic perspective to an extrinsic, pragmatic perspective. With regard to Bühler's "symbol-representational" function, E. Coseriu observes that it is essentially an "inner function of the sign" and should be distinguished from a communicative "performance" of this type in acts of informing, reporting, etc.[56] This distinction is reflected in Kinneavy's theory where he breaks the "referential" function down into an "informative use" when the facts of the reality are known and merely relayed, a "scientific use" when the information is systematized and accompanied by demonstrative proofs, and an "exploratory use" when the reality is not known but being sought.[57]

Modelling language functions from the pragmatic perspective of communicative process also makes the communicative context, rather than the explicitly encoded functions of a verbal sign, the ultimate criterion in interpreting its communicative function(s). Although a particular communicative function may be explicitly encoded in or conventionally associated with a particular verbal sign (text), only in communicative interaction within a particular context is it possible to judge whether this verbally encoded or conventional function is directly realized or whether it indirectly serves to realize a different function. This is obvious from the fact of indirect speech acts.[58]

1.3.2.2 Criticism of the Poetic or Literary Function

Coseriu is also critical of Jakobson's extension of Bühler's model by the poetic function.[59] When both Kinneavy and Jakobson refer to the "literary" and the "poetic" function respectively they both refer to this in terms of a focus on the text which is achieved by a special unity of textual structure.[60] This comes to expression in Jakobson's famous definition where "the poetic function projects the principle of equivalence from the axis of selection into the axis of combination," so as to explain all the various kinds of linguistic parallelisms observable.

---

see, e.g., Dimter (1981, 54 ff.) who refers to the referential, expressive and conative functions in terms of "wissen, werten und wollen."

[56] Coseriu, 1980, 67. Similarly, Brown/Yule, 1983, 28.

[57] Kinneavy, 1971, 39. For roughly similar subcategories see Halliday (1973, 59). These subcategories indicate that Kinneavy is oriented to an ontological, epistemological view of reality. With regard to communication in general, however, one must allow for reality to be understood in the broader sense of semiotic, cultural reference to "possible worlds" as in mythical, religious and also science fictional texts. On this see Hellholm (1980, 34) and van Dijk (1977, 29 f.).

[58] See, e.g., Searle, 1975, 59-92; Traugott/Pratt, 1980, 233 ff. See also, e.g., Leech's critique and modification (1983, 37-40) of Searle's observations.

[59] Coseriu, 1980, 59-60.

[60] Kinneavy, 1971, 344, 355; Jakobson, 1960, 358.

This formalistic view that reduces the poetic function to "how" something is said rather than to "what" is said must be rejected, since esthetic discourse also has very much to do with a particular content.[61] Indeed, as P. Hernandi holds, "literature as verbal art relies on the balanced interplay of expressive intensity, representational coherence, persuasive power, **and** verbal elaboration rather than on the marked preponderance of the last mentioned or any other constitutive factor of discourse."[62] However, such a "balanced interplay" may be seen as also desireable in a forensic or deliberative speech, so that it becomes extremely difficult to separate esthetic texts from other kinds of communication even on such a basis.[63] Furthermore, a focus on the text would not appear to inform a communicative function as such, but rather the general language process of creating and receiving texts according to constitutive and regulative norms of textuality (see 1.2). That which serves to distinguish the esthetic from the other functions of texts would appear to lie outside of this model in some kind of deviation from the norms of everyday grammar and textuality guided by the personal and communal esthetic tastes and norms that happen to prevail in a particular socio-linguistic culture at a particular time or period of time.[64]

1.3.2.3 Distinguishing Types and Subtypes of Functions

As for the phatic function added by Jakobson, this is defined in terms of language "primarily serving to establish, to prolong, or to discontinue communication, to check whether the channel works ("Hello, do you hear me?"), to attract the attention of the interlocutor or to confirm his continued attention."[65] It is questionable whether one needs to isolate "channel" from "message" in the "sign" constituent in order to explain this function, since channel has to do with whether the message is oral, written, telegraphic, etc. As Coseriu correctly observes, the phatic function is actually a particular form of the conative (appellant, persuasive) function as an appeal to the addressee to co-operate in a communicative process.[66] As such it may be classified as a subcategory of the conative function and will prove useful in the analysis of textual delimitation since it tends to be especially predominant at the opening, closing and transitional points of texts in greeting formulae, transitional signals, and formulae of

---

[61] Coseriu, 1980, 59-60.

[62] Hernandi, 1976, 380, n. 20. See, e.g., Hempfer (1973, 168) who holds that Jakobson's poetic function actually lies on a higher level of abstraction than the other functions.

[63] See Plett's discussion (1979, 121-3) of the complexity of the problem with regard to the semantic and pragmatic dimensions.

[64] See Plett's discussion (1979, 133-5) and references to the relevant literature.

[65] Jakobson (1960, 355-6) borrows the concept and term from B. Malinowski (1953, 264).

[66] Coseriu, 1980, 63.

acknowledgement, etc.[67] In I Thess this may be illustrated from, e.g., the opening prescript (1:1), the repeated address αδελφοι at major and minor transitional points throughout the letter, and the closing request for prayer, sending of greetings and the wish of grace (5:25-28).

Likewise in the case of the metalingual function, we actually have to do, not with a function of equal rank with what Jakobson calls the emotive, referential and conative functions, but with a subtype of the referential function. In this instance, the "code" or language system is a kind of reality that is **referred** to in metalinguistic utterances aimed at clarifying or talking about the language code, e.g., in the course of foreign-language acquisition.[68]

To these subcategories we may add the "metacommunicative" function as a type of "referential" function.[69] This function is performed by utterances that refer to utterances or texts **as acts of communication**. Gülich and Raible note that metacommunicative references may thematize both one's own act of communication (e.g., "I'm going to tell you a story about...") as well as the communicative act of someone else (e.g., "John said to Mary...").[70] Due to this, one often finds several "levels of communication" respectively embedded in each other in a narrative, starting with the primary level of the actual speaker or writer.

Thus, the basic communicative functions that characterize interpersonal communication may be reduced to basically three under which more specific types of functions may be respectively subsumed.[71] The designations to be used for these three functions will be the terms "expressive," "referential" and "conative" reflecting the respective focus on sender, reality and receiver in any process of communication.

---

[67] See Roloff, 1985, 242.

[68] Jakobson, 1960, 356.

[69] The concept goes back to Watzlawick/Beavin/Jackson, 1967, 51-4. From the preceding observations it must be concluded that one cannot subsume the poetic, phatic and metalinguistic functions all together under "metacommunication" as Stubbs does (1983, 48).

[70] Gülich/Raible, 1977, 26-8; see Harweg (1980, 283 ff.) who rightly calls for a clearer distinction between "metalingual" and "metacommunicative" functions on the basis of the respective distinction between "langue" and "parole." On the interactive character of such utterances see, e.g., Caffi (1984, 458-64) with references.

[71] See Hempfer (1973, 168) who observes the need to distinguish functions on different levels of abstraction.

1.3.3 The Bilateral Nature of Communicative Functions

Theorists are careful to insist that in any given discourse the basic aims of discourse overlap, although it is legitimate to isolate them by way of abstraction for theoretical and analytical purposes.[72] The usual pattern of overlapping aims involves the dominance of one particular aim with the others serving subordinate roles.[73] As Kinneavy points out, though, interference can arise when, e.g., the persuasive aim is too intrusive in the otherwise appropriately predominant referential aim of scientific discourse, etc. Furthermore, he notes that it seems possible for some discourses to be quite appropriate in combining more than one aim in fairly equal measure, although such instances appear to be rare.[74]

1.4 INTERPRETING COMMUNICATIVE FUNCTIONS OF TEXTS

1.4.1 A Brief Orientation on Text-Interpretation in General

In the history of interpretation since the time of the enlightenment it is possible to trace a shift from a focus on the author-text relation to a focus on the text itself, and from this to the recent focus on the text-receptor relation; in other words, from a diachronic, historical preoccupation with sources, authorship, etc., to a synchronic, structuralistic preoccupation with the "auto-semantic nature of texts," and from this to a pragmatic preoccupation with the nature of the process of text-reception.[75]

The focus on the text helped in particular to expose the "genetic fallacy" common among practitioners of the historical-critical method whereby a text's meaning was primarily conceived in terms of its origin.[76] However, structuralism overstated the auto-semantic character of texts, something made particularly obvious by the discovery that text-reception is not merely a passive but also an active process in establishing a text's message.[77] The resulting emphasis on the pragmatic dimension of text-reception has not only given impetus to wholehearted acceptance of subjectivity in interpretation on the part of some,[78] but also to more rigorous efforts to establish ob-

---

[72] Hymes, 1968, 121; Kinneavy, 1971, 61-2; Kubczak, 1984, 18-20.

[73] Cf. Leech, 1983, 61-2.

[74] Kinneavy, 1971, 61-2.

[75] See Lategan, 1984, 3 ff.; Combrink, 1984, 30. See also Hartman, 1979a, 115-21; Olsson, 1980, 110-21.

[76] See Lategan, 1984, 3; Vorster, 1984, 107. Also for reservations regarding the "referential fallacy" see du Plessis, 1984, 80 ff.

[77] On this see esp. Iser, 1976, 107; also Lategan, 1985, 67 ff. See 1.2.1.2-1.2.1.3 on the receptor's activity of inferencing. See, e.g., Kieffer (1972), Hallbäck (1980), Patte (1976; 1983; 1983a) and Malbon (1983) for structuralist orientations.

jectivity in an empirical science of literature on the part of others,[79] as well as a return to the historical problem in a different key.[80] Thus, it is not surprising to find that the various basic polarities and positions of **intuitionism, positivism,** and **perspectivism** observed more generally in theory of interpretation[81] more or less reappear in new clothing and are amenable to roughly the same criticisms.

On the one hand, those who stand at or near the extreme of **intuitionism** pay too little attention to the coercive power of linguistic form and cannot explain why or how one comes to revise an interpretation, while on the other hand, those who stand at or near the extreme of **positivism** tend to claim too much for this coercive force,[82] not being able to account for the polyvalency that arises out of syntactic, semantic or pragmatic ambiguities,[83] nor how one can recognize, e.g., irony, since its presence or absence does not depend on rules and conventions embedded in the text.[84] As for the position of **perspectivism,** this holds that the meaning of a text cannot be the same for any two persons, since each would approach it from different subjective standpoints (psychological version) and/or from different points in cultural time and space (historical version).[85] Should this undeniable aspect of relativity be raised to the position of an axiom in interpretation, the result would be the absurdity of "isolation and silence in our own encapsulated worlds."[86]

The dubiousness of an axiomatic perspectivism is suggested by the fact that verbal communication is not hindered by omnipresent linguistic asymmetry: although no two persons with even the same dialect actually pronounce identical speech sounds, they nevertheless can recognize the same phonemes, words, etc.[87] While the problem of asymmetry becomes more complicated and occasions a greater degree of indeterminacy in relation to more complex textual and extra-textual phenomena, given available data, cognition has been shown to proceed by means of **corrigible schemata** whereby we "set up a range of predictions of expectations which, if fulfilled, confirms

---

[78] See, e.g., Bleich, 1978.

[79] See, e.g., S.J. Schmidt's program, 1980, 1982.

[80] Lategan, 1984, 4-14. On the return to the historical problem see esp. Petersen, 1984, 38 ff.; Vorster, 1984, 106 ff.

[81] See Hirsch, 1975, 298-312.

[82] Though hardly qualifying as a positivist, Eco (1979, 7-11; 1984, 9) sees the text as controlling the reader's understanding via the author's selection of code, style, etc.

[83] On this polyvalency see, e.g., Louw, 1984, 19 ff.; Combrink, 1984, 27 ff.; de Villiers, 1984, 69.

[84] Thus, Hirsch, 1975, 300-5.

[85] For descriptions see, e.g., Hirsch, 1975, 306; Plett, 1979, 80. In a particularly sophisticated version of this position, Fish (1980) tries to overcome the problems of objectivism and subjectivism with the perspectivistic position of the controlling "interpretive community."

the schema but, if not fulfilled, causes us to revise it."[88] Indeed, "the process of understanding is itself a process of validation."[89]

The recent emphasis on text-reception and the pragmatic dimension in general has particularly brought into sharp focus the need to recognize the approximative, reconstructive character of interpretation and the need for a more text-centered focus than has been usually carried out in the historical paradigm.[90] While this position is accepted here, a caution is called for with regard to a text-centered analysis of structure. R.J. Reddick warns against the "illusion" that text-linguists tend to give that they "are somehow reading out the structure of the text without interpreting the text."[91]

As to the pragmatic dimension, recognition that in every text there is an implied author or reader will serve to create a distance from the text and guard against an involuntary identification of the text's situation with that of the non-authorial reader, so as to give rise to invalid, secondary readings.[92] As for authorial communicative intention, it simply "is not an automatic given which exists in the text as part of an objective reality, being immediately available to the perceiving human mind..., but rather something which arises from an organized interaction between empirical features in the text body (involving an interaction between the parts and the whole), various factors external to the text, and mental operations in the mind of the interpreter."[93] In view of this, it is appropriate to approach the task of interpreting a text in terms of attempting to discern its **capacity of meaning** within a particular communicative context.[94]

Following B. Wiklander,[95] the interpretive approach seen to recommend itself in view of these considerations is the **hypothetical-deductive** method in which 1) "the affirmations in the theories set up and brought to test are not considered absolutely certain but **hypothetical**," and where 2) these "affirmations are tested by and founded

---

[86] Lategan, 1984, 13.

[87] Hirsch, 1975, 306 ff. Similarly, e.g., Brown/Yule, 1983, 38 f., following Hymes, 1968, 109-15.

[88] Hirsch (1975, 308-11) referring to Piaget (1954, 57-8). Similarly, e.g., Brown/Yule, 1983, 27 ff., 61 ff., 223 ff.; Leech, 1983, 30 ff. See McKnight's summary (1985, 72-5).

[89] Thus Hirsch, 1975, 311; 1976, 33-4.

[90] See, e.g., Breuer, 1977, 27 ff.; Wuellner, 1978, 13-16; Lategan, 1984, 14; Vorster, 1984, 110, 118-19; de Villiers, 1984, 66 ff.; Wiklander, 1984, 26 ff.

[91] Reddick, 1986, 41.

[92] See Louw, 1984, 18 ff.; Petersen, 1984, 40 ff.

[93] Wiklander (1984, 27) referring to Kittang (1975, 15 ff.) among others.

[94] See Wiklander (1984, 32) and his references to the pertinent literature.

[95] Wiklander (1984, 34 ff.) referring esp. to Føllesdal/Walløe (1977, 52-107) among

upon a procedure of **deduction**." Such a procedure may be seen as roughly analogous to what has been called the hermeneutical "spiral,"[96] and as being commensurate with the above-mentioned mental processes of **corrigible schemata**.

What is ultimately striven after is **validity** which is to be based on the adequacy of the **fit** between the interpretation and the available textual/contextual factors.[97] More specifically, this adequacy of fit will involve such general criteria as 1) the intercorroborating interpretation of the part/whole relations holding within the text, and 2) the capacity of the interpretation to give a more adequate explanation of the relevant textual data than alternative interpretations.[98]

Besides following a reconstructive process from the perspective of text-reception (decoding), the critic or informed non-authorial reader will also reconstruct a text's meaning from the perspective of text-production (encoding).[99] With regard to ancient texts, specialized knowledge will allow the critic, as opposed to the ordinary reader, to make a more appropriate and more adequate processing of textuality and a more adequate recognition of and adjustment to cultural-situational asymmetry.

In this regard it is important to note that the critic or non-authorial reader does not have to do with "completely different cultural contexts,"[100] when interpretatively dealing with conceptual and cultural asymmetry by way of **corrigible schemata**. According to E.A. Nida and R.W. Reyburn, anthropologists frequently point out that "there is far more that unites different peoples in a common humanity than that which separates them into distinct groups," referring to such cultural universals as "the recognition of reciprocity and equity in interpersonal relations, response to human kindness and love, the desire for meaning in life, the acknowledgement of human nature's inordinate capacity for evil and self-deception (or rationalization of sin), and its need for something greater and more important than itself."[101]

These all too brief observations must suffice to indicate that text-interpretation is an undertaking in which it is possible to escape total subjectivity and relativity, on the one hand, but never attain to absolute objectivity, on the other, although every effort should be spent in striving in the latter direction.[102] What is ultimately striven after is **validity**.

---

others.

[96] Thus, Wiklander (1984, 34-5) referring to Føllesdal/Walløe (1977, 94).

[97] Cp. McKnight, 1985, 132.

[98] See Wiklander (1984, 36) with references to the relevant literature.

[99] See Hempfer (1973, 251, n. 387) and esp. Hellholm (1986, 31-2) who refers to these approaches in terms of semasiological and onomasiological processes. See also Schenk, 1984, 27-8.

[100] To tone down the absoluteness of de Villier's distinction (1984, 71).

[101] Nida/Reyburn (1981, 28) quoted by du Toit (1984, 64).

[102] See Kieffer, 1972, 20.

1.4.2 Some Text-Context Aspects of Interpreting Functions

The problem of relative indeterminacy indicated above is reflected in theorists' observations that the interpretation of communicative functions of texts involves a mediation between a recognition of functions made verbally explicit in the text and functions that can be recognized from the context.[103]

Kinneavy endeavors to contrast the relatively more reliable criteria of encoded indications of functions in longer acts of communication with the greater indeterminacy of such short utterances as "The train is coming."[104] This can have an informative, conative, or expressive function, depending on the specific situational context. However, it must be noted that the situational context can be just as vitally important for an appropriate interpretation of communicative aims even in longer texts.[105] A striking example presented by several critics may be seen in Daniel Defoe's **The Shortest Way with the Dissenters** which was not recognized by even its contemporaneous recipients as being ironical until they came to know that the author himself was a dissenter.[106] To give another example, one can imagine a speech of thanks cast in the form of a scholarly paper at some festive occasion of scholars where the dissonance between genre and context creates mild burlesque and allows the normal referential function of the genre to be replaced by an expressive function.[107]

Thus, knowledge of the various elements of a situational context will constrain the interpreter's expectations: what type of addressor and addressee are involved, what situational context, channel, code, and type of communicative event in which a particular genre may be embedded.[108] Such factors may be organized to match a particular type of situational context which helps to eliminate the possible meanings associated with the form or genre of the text and created by inferencing from the semantic representations in the text.[109]

These observations are more pertinent for non-fictional/practical texts than for fictional/esthetic ones. The latter are relatively more autonomous and situationally abstract, while the former are more heteronomous and situationally dependent,[110]

---

[103] See, e.g., Brinker, 1983, 142-4; Leech, 1983, 5-17; Brown/Yule, 1983, 23 ff.; de Villiers, 1984, 66-9; more generally see, e.g., Hirsch, 1967, 238 ff; Kinneavy, 1971, 24, 49-50; Lategan, 1984, 8, 13; Louw, 1984, 18 ff.; Vorster, 1984, 108-11.

[104] Kinneavy, 1971, 49. He does not, however, adequately distinguish between "sentences" and "utterances" in this instance. On this distinction see, e.g., Brown/Yule, 1983, 19 ff.

[105] See Black, 1967, 17; de Villiers, 1984, 69.

[106] Hirsch, 1975, 303; de Villiers, 1984, 69.

[107] The example is borrowed from Hartman, 1983, 134-5.

[108] See Hymes, 1968, 109-15; Brown/Yule, 1983, 38-9.

[109] See, e.g., Hymes, 1968, 105; further, Louw, 1984, 18ff., 23 ff.

[110] See Berger, 1977, 93; Werlich, 1979, 19-20; 1982, 42-45; de Villiers, 1984, 73.

although in various degrees with the encyclopaedia article as probably the least situationally dependent.[111] As J.G. du Plessis argues, the distinction between these two types in terms of their different referential relations to extratextual reality is an important one: In pragmatic texts authors are constrained to represent reality in conformity with the perspectives of a society and of fundamental humanity in order not to suffer disadvantageous consequences, whereas fiction enables one to build these perspectives oneself.[112] Thus, just because all verbal representations of reality involve distortion, this does not mean that all distortions are more or less equal in value.[113]

This observation is particularly pertinent in the case of interpreting ancient nonfictional texts for which evidence of the original context is inaccessible or seriously limited. In those cases where contextual evidence is discernibly encoded in a particular text, the process of interpretive reconstruction may attain a fairly high degree of probability, even if a text simply does not give **direct** access to the mind or intention of the author, to the events or to the actual addressees of the extratextual context.[114]

Although one does not have direct access to the "real" author/addressee components of the situational context, there are the "implicit" author and addressee of the text itself. Besides being implicit in terms of attitudes, expectations, sociolect, etc., they may be explicitly encoded in names, deictic 1st and 2nd person pronouns, etc.[115] Here the question of reconstruction is complicated by the view that they are to be identified **in no way** with the "real" author and reader.[116]

Again, it is important to note that this position has been developed predominantly with regard to narrative fiction,[117] where the implied reader is seen as a literary device instructing a real reader to suspend his or her own feelings and conceptions in order to identify with the implied reader so as to be able to enjoy the narrative to the full.[118] However, such a definitive cleft between the implied and the real author and original addressee must be seen as untenable for persuasive/practical texts. Besides the difference in textual reference noted above, there is the observation that in texts with predominant conative-persuasive functions the addressee's acceptance is **directly**

---

[111] Thus, Leech, 1983, 62.

[112] du Plessis, 1984, 89. See, e.g., Lategan (1985, 87 ff.) who cautions against pressing the distinction too far.

[113] du Plessis, 1984, 89-90.

[114] See Vorster, 1984, 108-11.

[115] See Petersen, 1984, 39 ff.

[116] See, e.g., Chatman, 1978, 146-51; Booth, 1983, 138. For Iser (1972, 279-99;=1974, 274-94) the implied reader is not in the text but rather a textual construct realized by the interaction of a real reader and instructions provided in the text. On this and the pertinent literature see, e.g., Lategan, 1984, 10-12; Fowler, 1985, 10-15.

[117] See Suleiman (1980, 3-45) for a survey.

[118] Thus, e.g., Booth, 1983, 137.

requested either implicitly or explicitly, whereas in texts that are predominantly referential or expressive the acceptance of the addressee is only **indirectly** elicited.[119] Thus, there will be practical, rhetorical constraints of communicative behaviour which constrain the encoded/implied author and addressee from seriously diverging in character from the real author/addressee. Any serious divergence would obviously jeopardize the appropriateness and consequently the co-operation of the addressee in the persuasive process.[120] It is the essence of rhetoric that "a text must reveal its context,"[121] and the high degree of conceptualization of persuasive strategies in ancient and modern rhetorical **inventio**,[122] by a change of direction, offers the modern interpreter an especially valuable tool of criticism for reconstructing a situational context through the type of language games encoded in the text.[123]

Consequently, apart from texts that are seriously undercoded, an informed, non-authorial reader's **reconstruction** of the real author/addressee from the implied author/addressee in pragmatic, persuasive discourse may be regarded as a legitimate and feasible undertaking.[124]

1.4.3   Text-Syntagmatic Aspects of Interpreting Functions

As previously mentioned, in order to achieve an as valid as possible interpretation of the text's capacity of meaning within a particular communicative context, a text-syntagmatic analysis of the text itself should be carried out, viz., an analysis of its hierarchical-sequential "functional text-sequences." Such an analysis is not only necessary when interpreting dominant and subordinate communicative functions, but also by making the "macrostructure" explicit one is able to identify important generic

---

[119] On this see Kinneavy (1971, 60), referring to Martin (1959, 33). Although there are situations that presuppose the avoidance of communicative co-operation (e.g., interrogation of a captured enemy soldier), co-operation constitutes a basic presupposition for the success of any communication. As noted by Black (1965, 16-17), despite mistakes, deceptions and even the occasional collapse of the system, our verbal communication is based on faith in the postulate that there is a correspondence between the characteristics of a discourse and both authorial intention and recipient response.

[120] de Beaugrande/Dressler, 1981, 115. As Perelman/Olbrechts-Tyteca note (1969,20;=1970, 26), "in real argumentation, care must be taken to form a concept of the anticipated audience as close as possible to reality."

[121] Sloan/Perelman, 1979, 799.

[122] See Kennedy, 1963, 10; Lausberg, 1973, 146 ff. (who treats invention too rigidly in terms of the dispositional schema that is most characteristic of forensic speeches); Plett, 1979, 12-16. See further de Beaugrande/Dressler (1981, 124 ff.) where invention is expressed in terms of "planning." Also, Grice's "cooperative principle" (1975, 45) and the "politeness principle" as developed by Leech (1983, 132) in speech-act theory are some important modern contributions to rhetoric, serving as regulative rather than constitutive aspects of discourse.

features.[125] In contrast to "microstructure', i.e. the syntactic-semantic chain of phrases, clauses, and sentences, the macrostructure concerns the larger textual units making up a text as pragmatic-functional and semantic-thematic sequences and subsequences that stand in a hierarchical and sequential relation to each other.[126] The receiver of a text is not provided with a macrostructure, but must construct this consciously or subconsciously from indications in the text. In this, he or she is assisted by signals which have been referred to as "delimitation markers."[127]

With regard to such delimitation markers, Hellholm has taken over and refined the markers identified by E. Gülich and W. Raible on the basis of their theoretical-deductive and textual-inductive research in text-linguistics.[128] In the following section a brief presentation will be made of these markers as they have been adapted for a persuasive text like I Thess. Together with these markers, both letter-generic conventions, conventions of exhortatory discourse and rhetorical conventions and strategies will be made use of in both the delimitational analysis and in interpreting the relations that hold among the sequences and subsequences and how these functional relations can contribute to the interpretation of the communicative function(s) of the letter as a whole (see chs. 3-4, 6, 8).

1.5 MARKERS FOR HIERARCHICAL AND SEQUENTIAL TEXTUAL STRUCTURE

According to Gülich and Raible, text-sequences of a text's macrostructure are normally marked on the surface level of a text by various linguistic signals or groupings of signals provided for the addressee by the author.[129] It has been shown that such delimitation markers may be classified according to whether their predominant function is pragmatic, semantic or syntactic, and consequently that they should be ordered hierarchically with the pragmatic markers holding the highest rank and the syntactic the lowest.[130] The highest ranking text-sequences would thus be marked by the pre-

---

[123] See S.J. Schmidt, 1971, 215-27; Kallmeyer et al., 1974, 70-1; Sloan/Perelman, 1979, 798-99; Wiklander, 1984, 33-4. Plett (1977, 13) holds rhetoric to be interpretable as a grammar of "vernünftigen Handelns."

[124] See Berger, 1977, 91-111.

[125] On this see esp. Hellholm, 1986, 32 ff. See also Berger, 1977, 17-27.

[126] See Hellholm, 1986, 32, note 39. See further van Dijk, 1980.

[127] Hellholm, 1980, 77 ff.; 1986, 32-3, 38 ff.

[128] Gülich/Raible, 1977a, 135 ff.

[129] Gülich/Raible, 1977a, 132-75.

[130] Hellholm, 1980, 78 ff.; 1986, 38 ff. See also Olsson (1974, 13 ff.) where comparable considerations are treated, although the then current emphasis on semantics in Nida (1971, 341-8) and Nida/Tabor (1969) is reflected in his work.

dominantly pragmatic markers and so on down the line.

It appears, however, that this hierarchical index should be used heuristically rather than axiomatically with sensitivity towards an author's possible idiosyncratic use of such markers. Indeed it has been shown by G. Wienold in some instances that an author has used what would be classified as low-ranking markers by the above-mentioned ranking system to mark high-ranking text-sequences and vice versa.[131] Furthermore, the subsequent analysis of I Thess indicates that there are delimitational features of Pauline style that are not accounted for in the types of markers isolated by Gülich and Raible (see 1.5.7 below.).

Since Gülich and Raible's delimitation markers were defined particularly for narrative texts, the specific kinds of delimitation markers found to function in I Thess as a basically non-narrative text will understandably differ to some extent as to type and frequency of occurrence. However, the shift from a narrative to a non-narrative textual analysis in using such markers is justified not only in view of the fact that the communicative model used by Gülich and Raible is conceived for texts in general,[132] but also because their observations regarding text-delimitational markers are informed by other texts than just narrative ones.[133]

Furthermore, the text-delimitation of I Thess, will not rely entirely on such explicit markers due to the fact that they need not always be present for various reasons. One reason for this may be due to the situational context. For example, when it is clear from the situational context who the communicators are, a text need not contain an initial metacommunicative sentence to indicate who is saying what to whom and thereby delimit the text on its primary level of communication.[134]

Other reasons are of a general textual or of a generic nature. On the most general level of abstraction, all texts as acts of communication involve a beginning, a main part or the "body" of the communication, and a conclusion.[135] Depending on the communication situation, the beginning and the end may not even need to be verbalized by way of an introduction and conclusion. In those instances where thy are verbalized, depending on the particular type of communication, e.g., letter, forensic speech, etc., explicit delimitation markers will understandably be unnecessary when certain functional text-sequences can be easily recognized by their conventional, more or less fixed structure and content serving more or less fixed functions, as in the case of the ancient epistolary prescript.[136] Such indications of functional text-sequences, however, have this in common with the more explicit markers, viz.. they are accessed from indications on the surface of the text.

---

[131] Wienold, 1983, 218 ff.

[132] Gülich/Raible, 1977, 21 ff.

[133] Gülich, 1970. Raible, 1972.

[134] See Gülich/Raible, 1977a, 138.

[135] van Dijk, 1980, 196.

[136] See van Dijk, 1980, 196; see section 3.1.2.

1.5.1 Metacommunicative Clauses (MC)

This type of delimitation marker may be illustrated by the utterance "John said this to Mary." As such, an MC will involve a metacommunicative verb of saying, hearing, or writing, etc., and the identification of someone speaking, hearing, etc., so as to focus upon or thematize a concrete act of communication in a communication situation. Thus, it qualifies as being predominantly pragmatic and constitutes the highest ranking marker.[137] Whatever text-sequence is referred to under "John said this to Mary" is to be seen as being thereby **delimited**, whether the MC occurs only once or is reiterated several times in various ways. Iterations of the same MC will be noted as MCit.

An initial MC may, furthermore, be seen as delimiting a primary **level of communication** within which additional levels of communication may be embedded, being signalled by additional subordinate MC. In I Thess other levels of communication besides the first one between the apostles and the Thessalonian believers (1:1) are thematized in reports of thanksgiving and prayer (1:2-3; 2:13; 3:10), in a report of other believers' witness to the genuine character of the apostles' mission and of the addressees' reception of the word (1:9-10) and in reminders of the apostles' previous predictions of tribulation (3:4) and previous ethical instruction (4:1-2, 11). All of these have various persuasive functions and are not hierarchically embedded in relation to each other, but are rather sequentially embedded in the higher ranking functional text-sequences of the primary level of communication. Thus, such instances of subordinate MC will not be considered in the following macrostructural analysis.

Finally, it should be mentioned that the primary level of communication of a text is often not marked by a MC, since this metacommunicative information may be sufficiently apparent from the immediate communication situation. Embedded levels of communication obviously must be signalled by MC.

1.5.2 Substitutional Markers

Regarding the phenomenon of substitution, three levels must be distinguished on which substitutions occur, viz., text-level, abstraction-level and metalevel.[138] The latter two levels are relevant to macrostructural text-delimitation and are best explained in contrast to text-level substitution.

1.5.2.1 Substitution on Text-Level

Substitution on text-level has to do with connection and coherence in the microstructure of a text and involves (among other types) what was referred to as pro-forms in section 1.2.1.1. For instance, in I Thess 1:10 the reference τον υιον is substituted in the next clause by ον: και αναμενειν τον υιον αυτου εκ των ουρανων, ον

---

[137] Gülich/Raible, 1977a, 137 ff.; Hellholm, 1980, 80 ff.; 1986, 38.

[138] Gülich/Raible, 1977a, 141-2; Hellholm, 1980, 84-7; 1986, 39-40; and esp. 1986-87, 80-6.

εγειρεν εκ (των) νεκρων. The expression ον refers **indirectly** to the text-external reality of the person Jesus (object-level) by referring text-internally to and substituting for the expression τον υιον which refers **directly** to the person Jesus. In other words, substitutions on text-level lie in an intermediate position between text-external reference to realities on the object-level and text-internal reference to linguistic elements of the text.

1.5.2.2 Substitution on Abstraction-Level (SA)

In contrast to substitution on text-level, substitution on abstraction-level involves only text-internal reference. Textual units, i.e. clauses, sentences or larger sequences, are referred to and delimited by expressions such as τουτο in 4:15 substituting what is said in 4:15b or 4:15b-17 and τοις λογοις τουτοις (4:18) substituting what is written in 4:13-17 as a basis for the exhortation to mutual comfort (παρακαλειτε αλληλους).

One of the most important distinguishing features of SA, according to Gülich and Raible, is that this type of substitution involves substituting expressions that have a wider range of meaning in relation to that which they substitute.[139] Raible seems to see substitution on abstraction-level as an intermediate level falling between substitution on text-level and metalevel.[140] Hellholm, however, appears to be more correct in seeing abstraction-level substitution as capable of oscillating anywhere from text-level to metalevel without standing on a "pure" metalevel in relation to a substituted text-sequence.[141] An example of text-level substitution may be seen in ποιειτε αυτο (4:10) substituting for the foregoing αγαπαν clause (4:9), while the example in 4:18 given above lies closer to metalevel substitution. The SA is a predominantly semantic marker and should be seen as a lower ranking delimitation marker than the following substitution on metalevel.

1.5.2.3 Substitution on Metalevel (SM)

As distinct from substitution on text-level, which serves the microstructure, substitution on metalevel functions macrosyntagmatically to delimit text-sequences of the macrostructure of a text. Like substitution on abstraction-level, substitution on metalevel has only text-internal reference. Such substitutions may be manifestations of various generic concepts (e.g., **joke, short story, proverb**, etc.) or of whole texts or their subordinate text-sequences in terms of external features of organization (e.g., chapter, section, etc.) or in terms of content-related features (e.g., vision, instruction, comparison, etc.).[142] As such they may be realized as nouns or as clauses or sentenc-

---

[139] Gülich/Raible, 1977a, 142; Raible, 1972, 150 ff.

[140] Raible, 1972, 13 ff.

[141] See Hellholm, 1986-87, 86.

[142] Hellholm, 1980, 84 ff.; 1986, 39-40; 1986-87, 85; Gülich/Raible, 1977a, 141-2.

es that occur at the beginning or at the end of the text-sequences they delimit. As in the case of MC, SM may also occur iteratively at intervals within such text-sequences. This is a form of redundance that serves to keep the addressee informed of the particular communicative function the ongoing text is intended to serve.[143] Instances of iteration will be noted as SMit.

The distinctive characteristic of SM markers is that they refer to and delimit whole texts or their subordinate text-sequences "as constituents of a communication process."[144] Expressing this in another way, van Dijk notes that sentences like **"I'll give you some good advice"** or **"This is a promise"** serve to "express the illocutionary force of the discourse as a whole."[145] He also sees the descriptive use of speech act predicates such as **"He warned me...,"** **"She promised me...,"** etc., as functioning in the same way.[146] In such instances involving metacommunicative verbs it is clear that SM and MC may coincide. In distinction to MC, however, SM do not necessarily involve a point of reference to the addressor and addressee, time and place, etc., so as to thematize a communicative situation or level of communication.

Two other points of importance must be mentioned here. Firstly, Hellholm has observed that several text-sequences delimited by various SM may stand in both sequential and hierarchical relations.[147] Such sequential and hierarchical relations will be noted here by 1SM, 2SM; 1.1SM, 1.2SM and 2.1SM, 2.2SM, etc. Secondly, Hellholm has observed what he refers to as 'surrogate' SM, e.g., "I saw" as a surrogate for 'vision.'[148] This may be further illustrated by the expression "once upon a time" in place of "this is a fairy tale." Instead of the term "surrogate," it is preferred here to use the direct/indirect distinction and to note the indirect (surrogate) SM as SMind.

There are often important subordinate functional text-sequences that are not marked by such explicit markers. A case in point is the epistolary prescript which is recognized instead from its conventional collocation of syntactic, semantic and pragmatic features. For the sake of a complete notation, such functional text-sequences will be given an appropriate designation followed by (SMinf) for **inferenced SM**, as, e.g., for I Thess 1:1: Prescript (1.1SMinf).[149]

An example of SM in I Thess is $\tau\eta\nu$ $\epsilon\pi\iota\sigma\tau o\lambda\eta\nu$ (5:27), delimiting the whole letter, and an example of SMind is the report of thanksgiving in 1:2 serving as an indirect expression of goodwill, followed by SMind/it in 2:13 and in 3:9 (where it is a rhetorical question), so as to delimit 1:2-3:13 (see 3.2.1).

---

[143] Grosse, 1976, 101-2.

[144] Gülich/Raible, 1977a, 141: "als Bestandteil eines Kommunikationsprozesses."

[145] van Dijk, 1977, 245.

[146] van Dijk, 1977, 245.

[147] Hellholm, 1986-87, 85.

[148] Hellholm, 1986, 47 ff.

[149] See 3.1.2 below.

1.5.3 Thematic Markers (ThM)

A type of marker not included in Gülich and Raible's set of delimitational markers is designated here as the Thematic Marker. In their insistence on the "formal" delimitation of "functional" text-sequences in narrative texts they avoid the thematic aspect.[150] The present study, however, deals with a non-narrative text in which the question of compositional integrity is important. Thus, to some degree it will be necessary to make the semantic macrostructure explicit.

In I Thess significant text-sequences are explicitly marked, usually at the beginning, by theme-indicating words, clauses or sentences.[151] For texts in general T. van Dijk has observed that while such explicit indications of the theme are not necessary, they are often given for emphasis or to facilitate comprehension.[152] A thematic marker may be seen as governing a text-sequence thematically in so far as the propositions of that text-sequence "satisfy" it **directly** or **indirectly**.[153] Such a marker may be seen as activating a "chunk" of knowledge, referred to in terms of a "frame" in text-linguistics, which organizes "certain properties of objects, courses of event and action, which **typically** belong together."[154] Such a frame will then aid the addressee in the process of inferencing the semantic coherence of a text-sequence.

Since most of the ThM in I Thess fall into or close to certain particular patterns of the "explicit semantic sentence" analysed by E. U. Grosse, it will be useful to refer to his description in explaining and illustrating such sentences here.[155] Explicit semantic sentences are constituted by what he calls a "Metapropositional Base" (MB), e.g., "I promise," "It is possible," etc., and a "Proposition" (P), e.g., "that he will come tomorrow." Such sentences may be realized variously. Some of these possible realizations are illustrated here from I Thess:

1. In one pattern of such sentences the MB and P constitute two separate entities with the Proposition element realized variously as follows:

   a) As a that-clause: (MB) αυτοι...ακριβως οιδατε (P) οτι ημερα κυριου ως κλεπτης εν νυκτι ουτως ερχεται (5:2).

   b) As an infinitival clause: (MB) ου θελομεν (P) υμας αγνοειν...περι των κοιμωμενων. (4:13).

---

[150] Gülich/Raible, 1977a, 133 ff.

[151] Louw (1982, 116-17) notes that such explicit thematic markers may occur initially, medially or finally in the particular text-sequence they govern.

[152] van Dijk, 1977, 136 ff., 150; 1980, 27.

[153] van Dijk, 1977, 138.

[154] van Dijk, 1977, 159 ff.

[155] Grosse, 1976, 95 ff.

c) As a nominal phrase: (MB) μνημονευετε (P) τον κοπον ημων και τον μοχθον (2:9).

2. The MB and P may be partly incorporated in each other:

   a) The subject of the that-clause may be drawn forward as the accusative object of the MB: (MB) αυτοι γαρ οιδατε...; (incorporated P element) την εισοδον ημων την προς υμας (P) οτι ου κενη γεγονεν (2:1).

   b) The P may be incorporated in the MB by way of a substituting pronoun: (incorporated P) τουτο (MB) εστιν θελημα του θεου, (P) ο αγιασμος υμων (4:3)

3. The complete fusion of the MB and P: (MB,P) αυτος δε ο θεος υμας ολοτελεις (5:23).

Grosse observes that the particular type of MB realized by a specific metapropositional expression may be established by means of paraphrase.[156] In view of the deliberations on communicative functions above, it should be added that such paraphrase constitutes a process of interpretation which must take the co-text and context into consideration. In the following analysis the type of MB represented by a metapropositional expression will be reduced in this way to the referential (MBref), the expressive (MBexpr) or the conative (MBcon) type. Where MB focus on themes that govern text-sequences, they may be seen as playing an important role in the interpretation of the communicative function(s) of such text-sequences as indicators of dominant or subdominant communicative functions. In some instances they may coincide with SM, e.g., ερωτωμεν and παρακαλουμεν in I Thess 4:1, 10; 5:1, 12, 14.

In I Thess the ThM may occur merely as a clause or sentence or as a simple semantic sentence (MB+P), as in most of the examples given above, or as a complex semantic sentence in which the general theme of the initial proposition is specified in some way in the proposition of an immediately subsequent semantic sentence. This may be illustrated by the complex ThM in 5:1-2. The general eschatological theme of "the times and the seasons" is presented in (P1) περι δε των χρονων και των καιρων...υμιν γραφεσθαι (MBref) ου χρειαν εχετε (5:1). This general theme is then narrowed down to the more specific aspect of the sudden unexpectedness of the "day of the Lord" which informs the discussion of the adressees' eschatological status in the rest of the text-sequence up to 5:11: (MBref) αυτοι γαρ ακριβως οιδατε (P1.1) οτι ημερα κυριου ως κλεπτης εν νυκτι ουτως ερχεται (5:2). The notation ThM(P1.1) will be given in such an instance to indicate the relative relations of the propositions involved.

Finally, it is important to note that major ThM (1ThM; 2ThM, etc.) may mark out superior text-sequences within which subordinate ThM (1.1ThM, 1.2ThM; 2.1ThM, etc.) may in turn mark out subordinate text-sequences. The indication of subordinate ThM does not specify whether the theme expanded in the subordinate text-sequence satisfies the superior theme signalled by the superior ThM directly or only indirectly.

---

[156] Grosse, 1976, 75. See Brinker (1983, 132) for a criticism of Grosse's complex typology. See 1.3.2.1.

Furthermore, there are instances where, e.g., two text-sequences with explicit ThM actually constitute a larger text-sequential unity for which a more general governing theme may be inferenced from the explicit ThM and the contents in general. For the sake of a complete notation such inferenced governing themes will be represented here as (ThInf) for **inferenced theme** and allowed to represent sequential and hierarchical thematic sequences together with ThM thus: 1ThInf, 2ThM and 1ThInf, 1.1ThM, etc.

1.5.4   Time and Place Co-ordinators (TC, PC)

Delimitation markers of these types indicate time or change of time and location or relocation with regard to a sequence of actions or events. They are referred to as "episode-markers" by Gülich and Raible as well as Hellholm.[157] They may be distinguished further as **absolute** markers (TCab, PCab) when they delimit a text-sequence already established by other high-ranking markers and as **relative** markers (TCrel, PCrel) when delimiting text-sequences subordinate to those delimited by TCab or PCab. When either of these markers are repeated within a delimited text-sequence by referring to the same time or place, they are referred to as **iterative** markers (TCit, PCit). As illustrated from I Thess, $εγενηθημεν$ $(εν)$ $υμιν$ (1:5) serves as the first PCab followed by several PCit: $εισοδον$ $εσχομεν$ $προς$ $υμας$ (1:9), $την$ $εισοδον$ $ημων$ $την$ $προς$ $υμας$ (2:1), $εγενηθημεν...εν$ $μεσω$ $υμων$ (2:7). Then $απορφανισ-θεντες$ $αφ'$ $υμων$ (2:17) serves as PCrel and $εν$ $Αθηναις$ (3:1) as another PCrel, etc.

1.5.5   Renominalization (R)

By way of a noun or proper name, this marker serves to reintroduce a person in a text who has been referred to previously by a pronoun. Such a renominalization usually occurs at or near the beginning of a new text-sequence. As both a type of recurrence within the text and a reference to the person, this marker is of a semantic-syntactic nature and ranks below the predominantly semantic markers.[158] The only instances in I Thess are $Τιμοθεον$ (3:2) and $Τιμοθεου$ (3:6).[159]

---

[157] Gülich/Raible, 1977a, 143; Hellholm, 1980, 191-3; 1986, 41. Cf. Olsson, 1974, 14.

[158] Gülich/Raible, 1977a, 144-6; Hellholm, 1980, 94-5; 1986, 41-2.

[159] $Παυλος$ (2:18) appears to be motivated by pragmatic rather than text-delimitational considerations (see 4.2.2).

1.5.6 Connectors (C)

This type of marker is primarily syntactic and is of the lowest rank.[160] In I Thess λοιπον ουν (4:1) and δε (4:13) are examples of this type of marker on the level of text.

1.5.7 Other Delimitational Characteristics of Pauline Style

Apart from the foregoing delimitational markers, there are certain characteristic indications of transition and delimitation that will be taken into consideration in the following comments on the macrostructure. Such indicators may be seen as supplementing and strengthening the observations of text-delimitation arrived at by means of those more universal types of markers delineated above.

The use of the vocative αδελφοι at the beginning of a new text-sequence is quite characteristic of Paul's style.[161] This repeated address has a primarily phatic function, besides expressing the apostles' attitude towards the addressees and thus appealing to their common bond. As a device of maintaining continued contact, it occurs naturally at those places where there is a particular thematic or subthematic transition (e.g., 1:4; 2:1, 9, 17; 4:1, 10b, 13; 5:1, 12, 14). However, it also appears to have a purely emphatic use (e.g., 2:14 and 3:7) where it does not seem to occur at an important thematic transitional location in the text.

Another characteristic of delimitation noted by P. Schubert is the "eschatological climax."[162] While he noticed this characteristic in particular as a phenomenon of delimitation marking what he considered to be the end of the Pauline thanksgiving paragraphs (I Cor 1:8, Phil 1:10f., II Thess 1:10), in I Thess it proves to be a rather common occurrence at the close of text-sequences of different ranks in general. This phenomenon seems to predominate in I Thess 1-3 (cf. 1:10; 2:12, 16, 19; 3:13) although θεον τον (και) διδοντα το πνευμα αυτου το αγιον εις υμας in 4:8 may also qualify as one, as does the wish-prayer in 5:23.

Another stylistic characteristic of composition serving to indicate text-delimitation is, e.g., **inclusio**. It involves the phenomenon of important words, phrases or clauses that occur at the beginning of a text-sequence being repeated at or near the end of it. While such phenomena will be taken into consideration sporadically in the following comments on the macrostructure, they will be given primary treatment in ch. 5.

---

[160] See Gülich/Raible. 1977a, 147, 156 f.; Hellholm, 1980, 95; 1986, 42.

[161] It occurs fourteen times in I Thess, placing its occurrence here among the most dense in the NT epistles. In Rom, e.g., it occurs ten times and in I Cor, twenty-one times.

[162] Schubert, 1939, 4 ff.

1.6 SUMMARY OF DELIMITATION-MARKERS AND RELATED FEATURES

For convenience, the markers and related features of text-delimitation are summarized here in the order of their relative rank of importance, ranging from the predominantly text-pragmatic to the predominantly text-syntactic.

1) The Predominantly Text-Pragmatic Markers:

MC	METACOMMUNICATIVE CLAUSE
MCit	Iteration of the governing MC
SM	SUBSTITUTION ON METALEVEL
SMit	Iteration of the governing SM
SMind	Indirect SM
SMinf	SM inferenced for a functional text-sequence
1SM, 2SM	Sequential SM of equal rank
1SM, 1.1SM	Hierarchical SM of higher and lower rank

2) The Predominantly Text-Semantic Markers:

SA	SUBSTITUTION ON ABSTRACTION-LEVEL
SAit	Iteration of the governing SA
ThM	THEMATIC MARKER
ThM(P1)	ThM with specific proposition that contains the governing theme of a text-sequence
Complex ThM	ThM consisting of two or more sequential explicit semantic sentences (MB+P) in which the general theme of the first proposition (P1) is specified in the next proposition (P1.1)
ThInf	A governing theme not marked by an explicit ThM, but inferenced for a text-sequence
1ThM, 2ThM	Sequential ThM of equal rank
1ThM, 1.1ThM	Hierarchical ThM of higher and lower rank
(MB)	Metapropositional Base in ThM
(MBref)	Referential type of MB
(MBexpr)	Expressive type of MB
(MBcon)	Conative type of MB
(P)	Thematic proposition in ThM
(P1), (P1.1)	Propositions with superior and subordinate themes in a complex ThM

PC, TC	PLACE AND TIME CO-ORDINATORS
PCab, TCab	Absolute PC, TC
PCrel, TCrel	Relative PC, TC
PCit, TCit	Iterative PC, TC

3) The Predominantly Text-Syntactic Markers:

    R   RENOMINALIZATION
    C   CONNECTOR

1.7 ORIENTATION ON A MODEL OF RHETORICAL ANALYSIS

In order to investigate the persuasive dimension of I Thess both modern and ancient rhetorical theory will be drawn upon in the subsequent analysis. A justification for this approach lies not only in the consideration that there appears to be a basic or "deep" human rhetoric universal to mankind, but also the fact that Paul lived in a culture where rhetoric was very much alive and highly conceptualized.[163] It is quite within reason to assume that Paul had some degree of competence regarding Greek rhetorical conventions, besides conventions of Greek letter-writing.[164] He may have acquired such competence formally or through a natural course of observation and imitation through exposure to oratory as an everyday phenomenon of the Hellenistic world he lived in.[165] Regarding the question of whether or not his use of rhetoric was conscious or unconscious, Kennedy makes the pertinent observation that even in the case of natural rhetoric, although not conceptualized, it is usually conscious: "The speaker knows what he wants to say and he is aware of topics, formulae, or patterns of discourse, but he would not be able to give a systematic description of his method, at least not without considerable thought and prompting."[166]

1.7.1 The Basic Character of Persuasion

In the present study "persuasion" is taken as a subtype of the conative function,[167] rather than as its equivalent.[168] Following J. Fafner, the "persuasive" function of language should be ranged beside the "coercive" (orders) and "rogative" (questions) subtypes of the conative function.[169] He basically argues that the persuasive use of

---

[163] Kennedy, 1980, 6-8, 130.

[164] Thus, Kennedy, 1980, 130. Also, e.g., H.D. Betz, 1974-75, 353-79; 1979, 14 ff.; Wuellner, 1976, 330-51; 1979, 177-88; Hübner, 1984, 242-50.

[165] See Kennedy, 1984, 9. See also Scroggs (1976, 271 ff.) following Davies (1955, 1) on seeing an interpenetration of the "Jewish" and the "Greek" in Paul. It may be questioned, however, whether this was entirely "unconscious."

[166] Kennedy, 1980, 7.

[167] Following Fafner, 1977, 72-7.

[168] As, e.g., Kinneavy, 1971, 37 ff., 211 ff.

[169] Fafner, 1977, 73-4.

language presupposes the freedom of the addressee to act, whereas coercive discourse presupposes the addressee's co-operation on the basis of the speaker's coercive power and rogative discourse presupposes co-operation on the basis of social norms of verbal behaviour. For the purposes of analysing texts that are not strictly argumentative it is preferable to use "persuasive" for this function of communication rather than "argumentative," since the latter term tends to associate too narrowly with the purely rational.[170]

As such a subtype, persuasion may be defined as a use of language that presupposes persuasive situations that only arise "on the occasion of divergences with regard to experience, opinion and understanding."[171] In a similar vein, L.F. Bitzer has defined a "rhetorical" situation "as a complex of persons, events, objects and relations presenting an actual or potential exigence which can be completely or partially removed if discourse, introduced into the situation, can so constrain human decision or action as to bring about the significant modification of the exigence," with exigence taken to generally mean something "other than it should be."[172] While his concept of the rhetorical situation has been hotly debated, it is still basically useful, given his own and others' subsequent modifications of it.[173] Especially important is his own move away from a static to a more dynamic view of persuasion as an interactive process,[174] so that with Fafner one can speak of the implicit "dialogical nature" of persuasive discourse.[175]

Another modern theoretician, G.R. Miller, has put forward the proposal that the modifying function of persuasion can be further subdivided into "response-shaping" and "response-reinforcing" processes besides the more universally accepted "response-changing" process.[176] However, from his discussion it follows that the response-shaping process is basically akin to the educating/learning process, and the response-reinforcing process is most often exemplified in sermons and political speeches where the aim is to reinforce currently held convictions so as to make them more resistant to change.[177] The latter category is seen here as useful for defining religious-ethical exhortatory discourse or parenesis as a subcategory of the **conative** function so as to be distinguished from the response-changing process most commonly regarded as the essential characteristic of persuasion.[178] Thus, persuasion or rhetoric

---

[170] Similarly, Brooks/Warren, 1979, 40.

[171] Fafner, 1977, 42: "i tilfaelde af divergens med hensyn til oplevelse, mening og forståelse."

[172] Bitzer, 1968, 6 ff.; cf. 1980, 23.

[173] See Brinton (1981, 247, n. 2) for the relevant literature.

[174] Bitzer, 1980, 21. See also E.E. White (1980, 7-20) and Scott (1980, 39-60).

[175] Fafner, 1977, 43 ff.

[176] Miller, 1980, 15 ff.

[177] Miller, 1980, 16-21.

[178] On the character of parenesis or religious-ethical exhortation see the discussion un-

is used here in the narrower sense of persuasive strategies that serve primarily a response-changing process.[179]

This view of rhetoric is to be distinguished from two other major views of rhetoric which also have long traditions. These are the stylistic view, reducing rhetoric to techniques of ornamentation,[180] and a comprehensive view of it that broadens it into covering all the techniques and rules of textual composition both spoken and written. This broader view encompasses many and various approaches and overlaps considerably with the modern field of text-linguistics.[181]

1.7.2 The Basic Means of Persuasion

Besides the inartificial proofs of direct evidence, the basic types of artificial persuasive appeals isolated in both ancient and modern rhetoric are the intellectual (**logos**), the credibility (**ethos**) and the purely affective (**pathos**) types.[182] While there has been a tendency to regard the **ethos** type of appeal as a milder form of the **pathos** type so as to include both under affective appeals,[183] it is more useful to keep them apart, both in theory and in analysis.[184] The probable character of reasoning in rhetoric, as distinct from scientific demonstration, places considerable value upon the good sense and moral character of the speaker, so as to justify taking these aspects of the **ethos** type of appeal into account.[185] Furthermore, audiences are also influenced by a speaker's non-moral attributes of personality and by appeals to the emotions, so that any adequate account of persuasion must take these factors into consideration.[186]

---

der 4.4.3.2 and 8.2.3.

[179] See Kinneavy (1971, 211-28) for a more detailed and substantial defence of this view of rhetoric.

[180] See Kinneavy's discussion and references (1971, 213-14).

[181] Regarding the rhetorical background and tradition of this view see Kinneavy's discussion and references (1971, 215-18). See also Halloran, 1976. Its beginnings are connected with Isocrates, Cicero and Quintilian, while, e.g., Burke (1950), Richards (1965), Perelman/Olbrechts-Tyteca (1969, 1970) and Brooks/Warren (1979) may be mentioned as different important modern representatives. Regarding its relation to text-linguistics see de Beaugrande/Dressler (1981, 15 ff.) and Breuer (1974). Cp. Wiklander, 1984, 33-4.

[182] See Aristotle, Rhet 1.2.3 ff.; further Lausberg, 1973, 140 ff.; Kennedy, 1963, 90 ff.; Kinneavy, 1971, 236-53; Dockhorn, 1977, 263. Betz (1979, 24) is too restrictive in limiting a written text's persuasive capacity to "only" rational arguments.

[183] For an appraisal of this tendency in Cicero and Quintilian see Sattler, 1947, 62-3; for modern reflections of this see, e.g., Fafner, 1977, 36-8; Plett, 1979a, 4-6; Burgoon/Bettinghaus, 1980, 141-53.

The **ethos** type of appeal is seen as basically involving three elements:[187] 1) "good sense" ($\phi\rho o\nu\eta\sigma\iota\varsigma$), which at times may overlap with the **sensus communis**, 2) "moral character" ($\alpha\rho\epsilon\tau\eta$), and 3) "goodwill" ($\epsilon\upsilon\nu o\iota\alpha$), which has both moral and non-moral dimensions.[188] On the moral side, goodwill is defined as wishing and seeking what is good for the addressees for their own sakes rather than the speaker's, and on the non-moral side, it involves such characteristics as the speaker having ties of resemblance with the audience, being able to be beneficial in some way, praising their good qualities, seeing the good in them, taking them seriously, etc.[189] In short, the **ethos** type of appeal advances the credibility of the speaker so as to induce the audience to trust him or her.[190]

As for the **pathos** type of appeal, this involves appeals to positive or negative feelings such as anger or mildness, love or hatred, fear or confidence, shame or shamelessness, gratitude or ingratitude, pity or virtuous indignation, and emulation or contempt.[191] As M. H. Wörner has made clear, Aristotle did not try to formulate a comprehensive psychology of emotions but rather treated those basic feelings which cause men to change their opinions with regard to their judgments.[192] Furthermore, for the appeal to a particular emotion to be possible and appropriate the speaker must necessarily know the mental disposition that leads to a particular emotion, the type of people towards whom the emotion is typically directed, and the type of occasion that typically gives rise to the emotion. Without the presence in a rhetorical situation of the people and the grounds that justify such an emotion, it will not be possible for the speaker to make any appropriate or successful appeal to that emotion.[193] In fact, attempts to arouse emotions that are not commensurate with the situation serve to awaken mistrust. Wörner goes on to point out that emotions are connected to assumptions, opinions and conceptions, that they are characterized by the basic opposition of pain or pleasure in relation to such assumptions so as to involve positive and

---

[184] See Sattler, 1947, 55-65; Kinneavy, 1971, 218-63.

[185] Thus, Sattler (1947, 57) on Aristotle's conception of ethos, which is to be distinguished from sophistic rhetoric's view of it "as a technique by which one may persuade audiences to accept proposals which are morally indefensible."

[186] Thus, Sattler (1947, 57-8) on Aristotle.

[187] Aristotle, Rhet 2.1.5. See esp. Sattler, 1947, 58-9; also Fafner, 1977, 37.

[188] See Sattler, 1947, 59.

[189] Aristotle, (Rhet 2.1.7) states that these things must be inferred from the classification of the emotions (see Rhet 2.4.1 ff.).

[190] Aristotle, Rhet 1.2.3 ff.; further Kennedy, 1963, 90-2; Kinneavy, 1971, 238-41; Wörner, 1984, 43-64.

[191] Aristotle, Rhet 2.4 ff.

[192] Wörner (1981, 60-61) referring to Rhet 2.1.8.

[193] Wörner, 1981, 62 ff.; see Aristotle, Rhet 2.1.9.

negative evaluations, and that such evaluations dispose the person experiencing a particular emotion to co-operate or not to co-operate in a speaker's goal. In sum, it turns out that, allowing for the relative status of assumptions and evaluations, **pathos** appeals have a quite sensible as opposed to an irrational role to play in persuasion: "Es ist vernünftig, affektiv betroffen zu sein."[194]

As for the **logos** type of appeal, as mentioned above, this involves a logic of probability rather than of demonstration.[195] Aristotle presented two basic types of quasi-logical proofs or appeals, viz., **examples** used in inductive argument and **enthymemes** used in deductive argument.[196] While some kind of syllogism stands behind an enthymeme, it is rarely presented in full. As in everyday speech, a premis and/or the conclusion may be left unexpressed, being mutually understood by the communication partners.[197] Furthermore, the mutual understanding of such premises and conclusions presupposes points of agreement between the communication partners which may rest on shared socio-cultural norms and/or religious convictions and not necessarily on scientifically demonstrable facts. An element of relativism is involved here which may also be discerned in the rhetorical topics seen as attempts to isolate the kinds of arguments that appear to be plausible to a particular audience.[198] In view of this factor of relativity and of the informal, prominently religious-theological basis of arguing in I Thess, the term "quasi-logical" will be used in a broad sense to cover those arguments that generally appeal to the intellect.[199] For the same reason, "appeal" is preferred to "proof." Finally, the fact that implicit premises and conclusions are left to be filled in by the addressee once again underlines the processual, implicitly dialogical character of persuasive discourse.

From these remarks it is clear that rhetoric is approached here from the dimension of text-pragmatics, or in rhetorical terms, from **inventio**, and is not reduced to rhetorical stylistics dealing primarily with figures and tropes in the syntactic-semantic dimensions of texts.[200] However, in those instances where such devices are dealt with, the focus will be on their pragmatic functions.[201] With the shift to include the pragmatic dimension in text-linguistics, the common cause with rhetoric as persua-

---

[194] Thus, Wörner, 1981, 78. Cp. Fafner, 1977, 37 ff.

[195] See Aristotle, Rhet 1.1.11; Cope, 1877, vol. I, 19. See further Kinneavy, 1971, 250 ff.; Dockhorn, 1977, 264-66. In view of this probabilistic character the term "appeal" will be used instead of "proof."

[196] Rhet 1.2.8 ff. See Fafner, 1977, 35; Kennedy, 1984, 16 ff.

[197] See Kinneavy, 1971, 251; Berger, 1977, 88-9; Fafner, 1977, 35-6; Kennedy, 1984, 16.

[198] Thus, Kinneavy, 1971, 247-9.

[199] Thus, "quasi-logical" is used in an even broader sense than, e.g., by Perelman/Olbrechts-Tyteca (1969, 193 ff.;=1970, 259 ff.).

[200] For a survey of the different conceptions of rhetoric see esp. Kinneavy, 1971, 212 ff.; Kennedy, 1980, 4-5.

[201] See Plett (1977, 141-7) and Snyman's discussions (1984, 94-103) in this respect.

sive discourse comes into focus.[202]

1.7.3 G.A. Kennedy's Methodological Proposal

In a recent contribution to rhetorical analysis of N.T. texts, G.A. Kennedy presents the following methodological procedure.[203] First, one should determine the **rhetorical unit** to be analysed. Second, it is necessary to define the **rhetorical situation** in terms of the exigence involved.[204] Third, the rhetorical unit may be analysed in terms of classical **stasis theory**, i.e. the basic issue or central question involved. Fourth, the analysis should determine the **species of rhetoric** or rhetorical genre to which the rhetorical unit belongs, i.e. the forensic, deliberative or epideictic genre. After these "preliminary matters" the critic should turn to an analysis of the **arrangement of material** in terms of the subdivisions of the discourse, the persuasive effects of these parts, and how they work together in achieving or not achieving a unified purpose in meeting the rhetorical situation. This will involve a line-by-line analysis of arguments in the light of assumptions, topics, formal features, and **devices of style**.

In general, Kennedy's proposal is basically sound in as much as it approaches the text and its various aspects from the pragmatic perspective of **inventio**. As he himself observes, one cannot rigidly follow such a schematic sequence of tasks. The definition of the rhetorical situation and the basic issue or issues involved is closely bound up with an interpretive analysis of part/whole relations that presuppose text-delimitation very much at the beginning of a spiral-like process of interpretation. Modern text-linguistics, as described above, provides a particularly useful tool giving such text-delimitational analysis a greater degree of precision. However, there is the question of the universality of the three classical species or genres of rhetoric to be taken up in the following discussion.

1.7.4 The Status and Critical Use of the Three Rhetorical Genres

It is questioned here whether the rhetorical genres as defined by Aristotle are of a sufficiently general and inclusive character to be so universally applicable as Kennedy and many others appear to allow.[205] It was the forensic (judicial), deliberative (political) and epideictic (ceremonial) genres as systematized by Aristotle that became a standard part of Greco-Roman rhetoric.[206] He defined these three genres in **Rhet**

---

[202] See, e.g., Plett, 1977, 11 ff.; Breuer, 1977, 25 ff.; Spillner, 1977, 93-108; de Beaugrande/Dressler, 1981, 15 ff.; and Enkvist, 1983, 65-79. In Biblical studies this is reflected in, e.g., Wuellner's (1978, 16 ff.) work on James, Wiklander's (1984, 33-4) work on Isaiah, and Olsson's (1986, 125-7) work on III John.

[203] Kennedy, 1984, 33-38.

[204] This is based on Bitzer's earlier definition (1968, 6) of a rhetorical exigence.

[205] See, e.g., Berger (1984, 1038 ff.) on this whole question.

1.3.1-5 both in terms of their distinctive types of audience and their distinctive functions, topics and temporal foci. In forensic oratory the functions are either accusation or defense, the topics are the just or the unjust, and the temporal focus is on the past. In deliberative oratory the functions are either exhortation or dissuasion, the topics either the expedient or the harmful, and the temporal focus is on the future. In epideictic oratory the functions are praise or blame, the topics are the honorable or the disgraceful, and the focus is on the present. While the functions, topics and temporal foci that are characteristic of one genre can appear in another one, in such instances they are seen as being accessory and serving subordinate persuasive roles.

The anomalous character of Aristotle's classification has long been recognized with regard to the types of audience characterized for each genre.[207] While forensic and deliberative types of orations are seen as addressed to arbiters ($\kappa \rho \iota \tau \alpha \iota$), the epideictic type is delivered to spectators ($\theta \epsilon \omega \rho o \iota$). In Rhet 2.18.1 the clarification is made that while all persuasive speech is directed towards a judgment ($\kappa \rho \iota \sigma \iota \varsigma$), in the case of forensic and deliberative speeches addressed to arbiters (assembly members or judges in court) a controversy ($\alpha \gamma \omega \nu$) is involved which requires an arbiter in the proper sense of the word. By contrast, in speeches of the epideictic genre the spectator is merely treated like an arbiter.[208]

Aristotle's classification was an attempt to cover the existing fields of oratory of his day and consequently it can only be defended from those circumstances.[209] Thus, regarding the forensic and deliberative genres, these must be seen as rooted in the political and judicial types of rhetorical contexts of his time. As such, they will only be useful in categorizing speeches that reflect more or less the same types of rhetorical contexts. With regard to epideictic, the generality of the audience of this genre and its varying celebrative contexts (funerals, festivals, sophistic exercises, etc.) led to divergence and confusion among subsequent theorists, and ultimately it became a repository for all types of speeches and other literary forms that could not be subsumed under the other two genres.[210]

D.A.G. Hinks perceptively observes that in an age not accustomed to sermons and where protreptics were most often heard in a political assembly, Aristotle had neglected the type of speech which could be both hortatory and delivered to spectators,[211] e.g., as in much religious discourse. E. Black has also convincingly argued

---

[206] See, e.g., Kennedy, 1963, 85.

[207] See Hinks, 1936, 172 ff.

[208] On this see Hinks, 1936, 174. Likewise, in Rhet ad Alex 1440b,13 epideictic is regarded as not addressing any controversy.

[209] Hinks, 1936, 174; Kinneavy, 1971, 227. Cf. Kennedy, 1963, 87.

[210] See Kennedy, 1984, 73-7; 1963, 152 ff.; Hinks, 1936, 174. What is the basic function of epideictic? Is it the praise of beauty (Lausberg, 1973, 130), the reinforcement or the gaining of adherence to traditional, universal values (Perelman/Olbrechts-Tyteca, 1969, 50-1;=1970, 67-8), the inducement of partisanship (Berger, 1977, 53), or the display of the luminosity of noble acts and thoughts (Rosenfield, 1980, 132 ff.)?

that there is a type of rhetorical genre that lies outside of Aristotle's theory: "The genre is one in which the evocation of an emotional experience in the audience induces belief in the situation to which the emotion is appropriate instead of following as a consequence of belief in the situation."[212] Such a rhetoric follows procedures that do not find their end in judgment, but rather inculcate new convictions by obliterating the audience's capacity for making judgments,[213] e.g., in much commercial advertising.

While shorter passages may be found where epideictic occurs as the display of the "luminosity of noble acts and thoughts"[214] (e.g., I Cor 13) or more practically in praise or blame as accessory persuasive devices (e.g., I Thess 1:6-8; 2:15-16), it is questionable whether any letter of Paul as a whole could be adequately classified as epideictic without a radical redefinition of the term.[215] This is due to the fact that when he wrote to Christian communities as relatively new socio-religious minority groups of mixed ethnic composition and with newly accepted beliefs and ethical standards that generally collided with those of the surrounding society at large, there was almost unavoidably some exigence, actual or potential, external or internal, general or specific, that would give a real as opposed to a merely apparent agonistic dimension to his letters with varying degrees of urgency.

At the same time, with Paul in the role of a religious authority addressing religious audiences with regard to shared interests (whether conflicting or not) in pertinent beliefs and practices, the **ultimate** persuasive goal will almost inevitably be to strengthen continued adherence to the Christian gospel, whatever specific exigence(s) may occasion a particular letter.[216] In other words, one has to do with a basically different audience-role than those of the legal judge, the political deliberator, or the spectator who does not need to take any particular decisive stand. The concern for continued adherance discloses a future focus in common with the deliberative genre, but the topics are not the mundane concern with the politically expedient or harmful but rather with salvation as revealed in the gospel. While forensic, deliberative and epideictic characteristics may appear more or less prominently in such discourse, depending on the particular exigence(s) occasioning Paul's letters, it is doubtful whether any of them can be adequate generic categories strait across the board.[217]

---

[211] Isocrates' Panegyricus is given to illustrate such a genre by Hinks, 1936, 174. See further, Berger, 1984, 1045.

[212] Black, 1965, 118.

[213] Black, 1965, 109.

[214] Rosenfield's definition, 1980, 132.

[215] This is actually what happens when Wuellner (1976, 330 ff.) takes over Perelman/Olbrechts-Tyteca's (1969, 47-51;=1970, 62-68) modern definition of it as strengthening adherence to values so as to be able to classify Romans as epideictic.

[216] This comes to explicit expression in, e.g., I Thess 3:8: οτι νυν ζωμεν εαν υμεις στηκετε εν κυριω.

[217] One that probably comes close to doing so is the forensic genre for Gal, as analysed by H.D. Betz (1979, 14-15, 24 ff.). Kennedy's criticism (1984, 144 ff.)

Consequently, with regard to all three genres, when Kennedy states that "although these categories specifically refer to the circumstances of classical civic oratory, they are in fact applicable to all discourse,"[218] this must be seen as a questionable methodological presupposition.[219] Historically conditioned genres are being treated as though they were universal, ahistorical types. While there will undoubtedly be common features that meet on a higher level of generality, a genre finds its definition in terms of a characteristic grouping of distinctive features that are usually appropriate to a particular type of communicative context. Furthermore, fundamental differences in the distinctive features and their grouping will generally serve to identify different genres and not necessarily hierarchically related genres and subgenres.[220]

1.7.5 Rhetorical Disposition and its Use in Analysing Letters

In the process of conceptualizing rhetoric it appears that from early times in Greek rhetoric to the present day, it has been necessary to guard the pragmatic character of rhetorical **dispositio** from an organic view of it wherein certain set units such as the **exordium, narratio, argumentatio** and **peroratio**, besides other units and subsections, were insisted upon in every speech.[221] Aristotle explicitly attacked such an organic view and defended the pragmatic character of disposition in **Rhet** 3.13.1-4. Depending on the needs of the situation, he allowed that the **prooimion (exordium)** and the **epilogos (peroratio)** could be dispensed with. In fact, the minimally necessary parts of a speech did not even include a narration but could consist of statement **(prothesis)** and proof **(pistis, argumentatio)**.[222] The contention between those insisting on the organic view of **dispositio** and those holding more to the pragmatic view was very much alive even in the first century A. D., as may be seen between the respective schools of Apollodorus of Pergamum and Theodorus of Gadara.[223]

---

of Betz as well as his own classification of Gal as deliberative is not based on a sufficiently rigorous reconstruction of the rhetorical exigence in the letter.

[218] Kennedy, 1984, 19.

[219] Kennedy actually (1984, 104) recognizes something different than the usual rhetorical genres when he describes the Gospel of Mark as "radical Christian rhetoric, a form of "sacred language" characterized by assertion and absolute claims of authoritative truth without evidence or logical argument." See Black (1965, 91-131) for a balanced criticism of Aristotle on the topic of genre and in relation to rhetorical criticism in general.

[220] On this whole problem see esp. Hellholm (1986). See also, e.g., Knierim (1973), Hartman (1983) and Berger (1984, 1036 ff.).

[221] See Black, 1965, 70 ff.; for a survey of the various proposed units of rhetorical disposition see Lausberg, 1973, 148-9.

[222] See 1.7.6.1 below.

With regard to letters, when it is recognized that bridging a separation between communicative parties (απουσια/παρουσια) is the fundamental function of the letter,[224] it becomes obvious that a letter-situation and a rhetorical situation can overlap.[225] Consequently, one cannot be bound to limit the letter-situation so narrowly, e.g., with Demetrius (**De eloc** 4.229-31), to that of maintaining friendship (φιλοφρονησις), so as to exclude any overlap with rhetorical situations that call forth characteristic rhetorical conventions and strategies.[226] On the other hand, in view of the conflicting pragmatic/organic conceptions of rhetorical disposition noted above, one should be particularly cautious not to approach the analysis of epistolary disposition strictly from an organic conception of rhetorical disposition.[227] While the particular pragmatic functions characteristically associated with **exordium, narratio, argumentatio,** and **peroratio** have indeed been more or less clearly discerned as fulfilled by specific text-sequences both in secular Greek letters,[228] as well as in some of Paul's letters,[229] I Thess appears to be less amenable to such precise and consistent delimitations (see under ch. 6). Consequently, an attempt will not be made to impose the four-part rhetorical disposition strictly on this letter, but rather the correspondences in the various text-sequences to pragmatic functions typical of such dispositional parts will be pointed out. Such a procedure has the advantage that the rhetorical functions of epistolary features may be accounted for without drowning their distinctive epistolary character.[230]

---

[223] Kennedy, 1963, 335.

[224] Thus Koskenniemi, 1956, 38; Doty, 1969, 193. It is apparent from Sykutris discussion (1931, 187-8) that it is precisely this aspect which makes it difficult to draw a sharp line between letters and rhetorical discourse.

[225] Thus Hübner, 1984, 245.

[226] See Demetrius, De eloc 4.225, 229, 232 respectively.

[227] It has become common for N.T. exegetes to analyse even subordinate text-sequences within Paul's letters in terms of the four-part rhetorical disposition. Thus, e.g., Berger (1977, 43-5) on Gal 3:1-14 and Bünker (1984, 51-71) on I Cor 1-4 and 15. Against this organic approach it must be protested that ancient rhetoric was obviously aware of providing longer treatments of specific topics within a discourse with appropriate opening and closing remarks without casting the whole section in the four-part dispositio. See, e.g., Rhet ad Alex 1439a,20-40.

[228] See, e.g., Goldstein's analyses (1968) of Demosthenes' letters.

[229] See Wuellner on Rom (1976, 330-51), Church on Phlm (1978, 17-33), and H.D. Betz on Gal (1974-75, 353-79; 1979), with some critical adjustments by Hester (1984, 223-33) and Hübner (1984, 242-50) with regard to Betz, and Hughes

1.7.6 A Brief Survey of Disposition in Greek Rhetoric

In view of the foregoing consideration, a brief review of the characteristic functions and strategies of the common parts of the rhetorical **dispositio** will be useful here. Since later rhetorical handbooks tended to concentrate on the forensic type of speech, special attention will be given to Aristotle's **Rhetorica** and to the **Rhetorica ad Alexandrum**, both of which give a more balanced treatment of the other genres as well.[231] The various relations and functions of the main dispositional parts in Greco-Roman rhetoric in general are given exhaustive treatment by H. Lausberg.[232]

When surveying typical characteristics observed for the main dispositional parts of speeches in ancient rhetorical theory, it is useful to divide them into those involving predominantly internal text-oriented features, on the one hand, and those involving predominantly user-oriented or pragmatic types of persuasive features, on the other.

1.7.6.1 Text-Oriented Dispositional Features

With regard to the former text-oriented features, the **exordium** commonly serves in all three genres to signal the main subject to be expanded in the speech as a whole.[233] In epideictic, however, it may be foreign to the speech[234] and in deliberative oratory **exordia** are uncommon since the subject is often known in advance.[235]

The **narratio**, if it is not reduced to a mere statement of the case without a preceding introduction,[236] serves as a more specific orientation and forms the basis of the **argumentatio** by providing background information, if necessary, and a summary of the facts to be argued. Depending on the number of facts to be narrated and the addressees' familiarity with them, the **narratio** may be included in the **exordium**, or scattered throughout the divisions of the speech, or set out as a separate section by it-

---

(1983) on II Thess. Kennedy's analyses (1984, 141-56) of I Thess, Gal and Rom are disappointingly superficial due to an inadequate treatment of the exigence in each case.

[230] See, e.g., Plett's exemplary discussion (1979, 16-19) in this respect.

[231] Anaximenes is most likely the author of the Rhet ad Alex and will be referred to as such here. See, e.g., Wendland, 1905, 62-3; Kennedy, 1963, 114-15; Goldstein, 1968, 100.

[232] Lausberg, 1973, 150-240.

[233] Rhet 3.14.6; Rhet ad Alex 1436a,31-38.

[234] Rhet 3.14.5.

[235] Rhet 3.14.12.

[236] Rhet 3.13.4.

self.[237]

The text-oriented relation of the **peroratio** is basically that of recapitulation of the main points of the speech.[238]

1.7.6.2 User-Oriented Dispositional Features

With regard to the pragmatic or user-oriented types of persuasive features, the characteristic aims of the **exordium** are to arouse the attention or interest of the audience or the opposite, and to obtain goodwill for the speaker or arouse their indignation towards the opponent.[239] All such aims are referred to by Aristotle as "remedies" by contrast to the subject-indicating function and are taken as common to all three genres according to the needs of the moment. Thus, when he notes that praise, blame, exhortation, dissuasion and appeals to the audience are sources of epideictic **exordia**, the same may be taken to potentially have a general application.[240] Furthermore, he lays it down as a general rule in this part of the speech that one should clear oneself of disagreeable suspicion, whether this has been openly expressed or not.[241] Anaximenes refers to this in terms of anticipation.[242]

As for the **narratio**, it is used to report or remind the audience of past events, arrange and exhibit present facts or forecast what is going to occur.[243] When commenting on forensic oratory, Aristotle notes that the narrative should be presented in terms of moral character and should draw upon what is emotional.[244] And when commenting on the deliberative, he notes that the reminder of past things can help the hearers to take better counsel for the future.[245]

Regarding the **argumentatio**, the primary purpose is to present arguments that will persuade the addressee regarding the issue. After presenting the uninvented proofs of witnesses' evidence, documents, etc., one should present the invented proofs.[246] Aristotle is at particular pains to encourage the use of logical arguments,[247] working ei-

---

[237] Rhet ad Alex 1438b.15-28; 1442b,28-32.

[238] Rhet 3.19.1; Rhet ad Alex 1444b,21-30.

[239] Rhet 3.14.7; Rhet ad Alex 1436a,33-39.

[240] Rhet 3.14.4.

[241] Rhet 3.15.1.

[242] Rhet ad Alex 1437a,1 ff.

[243] Rhet ad Alex 1438a,3 ff.

[244] Rhet 3.16.8-10.

[245] Rhet 3.16.11.

[246] Rhet ad Alex 1442b,33 ff.

ther inductively from examples or deductively from **enthymemes**.[248] Kennedy points out that while Greek oratory was more logical than in the case of religious discourse, it contained nevertheless a good deal of appeal to current values and opinions with logical arguments often only introduced to give a semblance of reason. By contrast, in religious discourse the premises of arguments are usually based on divine authority, often mediated by scriptural quotation, and on personal intuition.[249] Regarding exhortation and dissuasion Anaximenes makes the observation that if the narration carries immediate conviction, the proofs were to be omitted and the policies just stated should be merely confirmed on the basis of justice, legality, expediency, etc.[250]

Finally, the **peroratio** is seen as serving basically to once again appeal to goodwill and excite the emotions of the hearer.[251]

---

[247] Rhet 3.17.1 ff.

[248] Rhet 3.17.5.

[249] Kennedy, 1980, 120 ff.; 1984, 17-18.

[250] Rhet ad Alex 1439a,7-10.

[251] Rhet 3.19.1 ff.

PART II

A TEXT-CENTERED ANALYSIS OF I THESSALONIANS

Chapter 2

RECONSTRUCTING SITUATIONAL FEATURES: SURVEY OF RELEVANT ASPECTS

The following survey of general aspects of the communicative situation (2.1) is placed here in advance of the analyses of textual structures and persuasive strategies in order to make explicit my presuppositions regarding the basic situational elements. This is important since they serve as guiding constraints in the interpretation of the persuasive strategies in particular. As for the aspects relevant to the rhetorical situation (2.2), they are presented here at the outset not only to help the reader anticipate the various aspects which have a potential bearing in this respect, but also to orient such aspects briefly in the perspective of N.T. exegesis. While the presentation of these aspects is obviously made from the viewpoint of the interpretive conclusions of the present study, in some instances arguments directly contributing to the interpretive conclusions are presented here for the sake of convenience rather than in the subsequent analyses.

2.1   GENERAL ASPECTS OF THE COMMUNICATION SITUATION

In the opening address the references to the three senders and to the church thematize the immediate participants of the communicative context: Παυλος και Σιλουανος και Τιμοθεος τῃ εκκλησια Θεσσαλονικεων εν θεω πατρι και κυριω Ιησου Χριστῳ. The **nomen gentilicium** Θεσσαλονικεων also indicates a wider Greek geographical and social context.

The addition of "in God the Father and the Lord Jesus Christ" indicates the interrelation of "this-worldly" and "other-worldly" dimensions.[252] Thus, God and Christ may also be seen as encoded communicative participants in the textual world. Their participation in this wider dimension of the communicative context is seen as being concretized in manifestations of the Holy Spirit (1:5-6; 4:8; 5:19-20) both in the senders' mediation of the gospel (1:5; cf. 2:4, 12, 13) and in the effective working of God's word in the lives of the addressees (1:6, 8; 2:13). Thus, the textual world is informed by the conceptual universe(s) of the Christian gospel of salvation,[253] a salvation grounded in the death and resurrection of Jesus Christ and to be consummated at

---

[252] As Rigaux remarks (1956, 351), "Il n'y a pas de dialogue en dehors d'eux." See van Dijk (1977, 29 f.) and Hellholm (1980, 34) on the semiotic, cultural character of reference to "possible worlds" in texts.

[253] Similarly Patte (1983, 130), although he takes it too easily for granted that the conceptual universes of Paul and his addressees were free of any conflict (see 4.4.6 and 4.4.8).

his parousia (1:10; 4:14-17; 5:9-10). As mediators of this gospel, the senders are all designated as "apostles" (2:7).[254]

From the contents of the letter we can gather that the situation in general was that of a community of fairly recent converts who had suffered (1:6; 2:14) and probably continued to suffer (3:3-4) for their faith and who had been deprived prematurely of their spiritual mentor Paul (2:17-18; cf. Acts 17:5-10).[255] While W. Marxsen does not see any reflection of Acts 17:5-10 in I Thess, Ph. Vielhauer is probably more correct in seeing an oblique reflection in 2:17:[256] $\alpha\pi o\rho\phi\alpha\nu\iota\sigma\theta\epsilon\nu\tau\epsilon\varsigma$ $\alpha\phi'\upsilon\mu\omega\nu$ $\pi\rho o\varsigma$ $\kappa\alpha\iota\rho o\nu$ $\omega\rho\alpha\varsigma$. The choice of language here together with the repeated references to the addressors' desire and efforts to return in 2:17-18 and 3:10 intimate that the departure was premature, even when one accepts a somewhat longer stay by Paul in Thessalonica than the three Sabbaths mentioned in Acts 17:2.[257]

The new community appears to have consisted almost totally of Gentiles (1:9; 2:14; cf. Acts 17:4). On the basis of I Thess 1:9; 2:14; and 4:3 ff. Vielhauer appears to be correct in distinguishing them as "Götzendienern" from the "Gottesfürchtigen" of Acts 17:4.[258] In support of this there is evidence that the discrepancy between Acts 17:4 and I Thessalonians was noticed fairly early. The Western variant reading harmonizes by introducing $\kappa\alpha\iota$ twice so as to include a third category of pagan Greeks thus: $\sigma\epsilon\beta o\mu\epsilon\nu\omega\nu$, $\kappa\alpha\iota$ $E\lambda\lambda\eta\nu\omega\nu$ $\pi\lambda\eta\theta o\varsigma$ $\pi o\lambda\upsilon$, $\kappa\alpha\iota$ $\gamma\upsilon\nu\alpha\iota\kappa\epsilon\varsigma$ $\tau\omega\nu$ $\pi\rho\omega\tau\omega\nu$ $\kappa\tau\lambda$. instead of the generally accepted reading $\sigma\epsilon\beta o\mu\epsilon\nu\omega\nu$ $E\lambda\lambda\eta\nu\omega\nu$ $\pi\lambda\eta\theta o\varsigma$ $\pi o\lambda\upsilon$ $\gamma\upsilon\nu\alpha\iota\kappa\omega\nu$ $\tau\epsilon$ $\tau\omega\nu$ $\pi\rho\omega\tau\omega\nu$ $\kappa\tau\lambda$. (17:4).[259]

While economics should probably not be made too much of in establishing the earliest Christians' social identity,[260] the Thessalonian community together with the other Macedonian believers were in general characterized by "extreme poverty" (η $\kappa\alpha\tau\alpha$ $\beta\alpha\theta o\upsilon\varsigma$ $\pi\tau\omega\chi\epsilon\iota\alpha$ $\alpha\upsilon\tau\omega\nu$) according to II Cor 8:2. Exceptions may have been constituted by a few like Jason and some "leading women" (Acts 17:4-5).[261] Although Luke appears to have a tendency towards a special interest in the high social standing of Paul's converts,[262] one should not be too sceptical in this respect. G.

---

[254] On this see Schnackenburg (1970, 287-303, esp. 302-3) who notes that at the beginning the concept of an apostle was not carefully defined, so that one should not play off the "charismatic" and "institutional" concepts against each other.

[255] Following, e.g., Vielhauer (1975, 88-9) and Suhl (1975, 96-102), an early date (ca. 50/51 A.D.) for I Thess is assumed here. See, e.g., F. Watson (1986, 60) for a criticism of Lüdemann's (1984, 201 ff.) arguments for placing I Thess as early as ca. 41 A.D.

[256] Marxsen, 1979, 15; Vielhauer, 1975, 83.

[257] See Rigaux, 1956, 24-5; Best, 1977, 4-5; Lüdemann, 1984, 177.

[258] Vielhauer, 1975, 83.

[259] See Bruce, (1952, 325) for the variant reading given in full.

[260] Judge, 1980, 212 ff.

[261] See Rigaux, 1956, 26-7.

Theissen among others has made a good case from Pauline sources, particularly I Corinthians, that a minority from the upper social classes was a common constituent in the composition of the communities raised by Paul.[263]

After the addressors, and Paul in particular, had made several thwarted attempts to return (2:18), Timothy was sent alone (2:18, 3:1-5). I Thess appears to be Paul's response to the report that Timothy brought back from this visit (3:6-7). It is thus reasonable to see the concerns and themes of the letter as reflecting Paul's prior knowledge of the community's strengths and weaknesses, their spiritual morale and their attitude to the addressors as updated by Timothy's report. A word of caution, however, is appropriate here regarding περι δε as belonging to epistolary style[264] or as indicating the beginning of replies by Paul to a list of inquiries in a prior letter sent by the addressees on the analogy of I Cor 7:1, 25; 8:1; 12:1 and 16:1.[265] There is ample evidence that περι, frequently combined with δε, μεν, etc., and some meta-communicative expression of writing, speaking, hearing, etc., is a fairly common characteristic of thematic sentences regularly used to introduce the topic of a new paragraph or section in Greek texts in general.[266]

Finally, regarding the nature of those "we" references which refer specifically to Paul and his co-senders Silvanus and Timothy, R.F. Collins gives a reasonable interpretation when he finds that the singular in 2:18, 3:5 and 5:27 represents a conscious choice Paul made when he wanted to zero in on himself, and that the plural throughout the rest of the letter is also conscious.[267] G. Lyons' suggestion of all such "we" references being actually autobiographical is not as appropriate as he would hold,[268] since they continue quite consistently in 4:1-2, 6, 10-11, 13, 15; 5:12, 14 and 25, where autobiography is obviously absent.[269]

---

[262] See, e.g., Cadbury, 1955, 43; and more recently Plümacher, 1972, 22 ff.

[263] In particular see Theissen (1974, 232-72) with Malherbe's evaluations and additional contribution (1977, 71 ff.).

[264] As Rigaux (1956, 91) holds.

[265] Thus, e.g., Faw, 1952, 217 ff.; Hurd, 1976, 900.

[266] A spot check on specific works by such different authors as Aristotle, Isocrates, Josephus, and Diogenes Leartius gave the following examples and instances: Aristotle, Poet. 6.1: περι δε τραγῳδιας λεγωμεν (see also 15.1; 19.7; 23.1; 25.1; 25.15); Isocrates, Panegy 15: περι μεν ουν των ιδιων ταυτα μοι προειρησθω. περι δε των κοινων, οσοι μεν κτλ. (see also 34, 66, 157; further Panath 33, 35, 70, 105, 119, 126, 130, 191); Josephus, Cont Ap 2.291: περι των νομων ουκ εδεησε λογου πλειονος (see also 1.47, 57, 69, 145, 251, 279; II.1, 199, 262, 276, 287); Diogenes Leartius 8.67: περι δε του θανατου διαφορος εστιν αυτου λογος (see also 1.116; 2.12; 3.78; 8.41, 74; 10.117). The usage is obviously of a more general, textual nature. Cf. Bradley, 1953, 242.

[267] Regarding the switches to the first person singular, Collins (1980-81, 351-53;=1984, 178-80) notes that in 2:18 and 3:5 the changes serve to express

2.2   ASPECTS RELEVANT TO THE RHETORICAL SITUATION

Against this general background the following observations are pertinent regarding more specific considerations that bear upon the reconstruction of the **rhetorical** situation (see 1.7.1). The presentation here presupposes conclusions drawn from the subsequent analyses and is intended to orient these conclusions generally within N.T. research on I Thess.

2.2.1   The Author-Addressee Relationship

The "apologetic" character of 2:1-12, where Paul appears to put up a defence against charges of insincerity, self-interest and dishonest motives in his proclamation of the word, has given rise to views of a problematic relation between Paul and the Thessalonian believers. This, however, is difficult to account for in view of Timothy's news reported in 3:6 in which it is explicitly stated that the addressees continued to regard the addressors with goodwill: Αρτι δε ελθοντος Τιμοθεου προς ημας αφ' υμων και ευαγγελισαμενου ημεν την πιστιν και την αγαπην υμων και οτι εχετε μνειαν ημων αγαθην παντοτε, επιποθουντες ημας ιδειν καθαπερ και ημεις υμας.

If there had been any serious misgivings that had become explicit in open accusations on the addressees' part against the senders, such an unqualified reminder in 3:6 would breach what H. P. Grice refers to as the "maxim of **quality**" of the "co-operative principle."[270] Such a breach would raise an implicature of ironical insult rather than serve the maintenance of goodwill which is otherwise dominant in I Thess 1-3 (see 3.2.1). The combined references to good news of the addressees' faith and love and of their goodwill is an indication that the "maxim of **approbation**" (minimizing dispraise and maximizing praise of the addressee) of the "politeness principle" elucidated by G. N. Leech[271] is the most prominent regulative rhetorical feature here. If the politeness "maxim of **agreement**" (minimizing disagreement and maximizing agreement between addressor and addressee) is also at work, this is possible

---

Paul's personal and emotional involvement and in 5:27 it underscores the authority of Paul in relation to the believers. See Best (1977, 26-29) for a similar conclusion and an overview of relevant literature.

[268] Lyons, 1985, 179-80.

[269] For those who see it in more general terms as actually referring more to Paul than to all three senders, see, e.g., Dobschütz, 1909, 68; Frame, 1912, 90; Marxsen, 1979, 53.

[270] See Grice (1975, 45) who isolates regulative maxims of 1) quantity, i.e. giving the right amount of information, 2) quality, i.e., not saying what is known to be false or lacking adequate evidence, 3) relation, i.e., being relevant, and 4) manner, i.e., being perspicuous. See further, e.g., Brown/Yule, 1983, 31 ff.; Leech, 1983, 7 ff.

[271] See Leech, 1983, 132.

within the bounds of a seriously potential rather than an open, concrete, disruptive state of disagreement between addressors and addressees.

What appears to be a clash between 2:1-12 and 3:6 would of course be alleviated if one could point to a faction within the community agitating against the addressors or a group outside whose accusations could be reflected in the negative characteristics rejected in 2:1 ff. Theories have been put forward suggesting inside factions constituted by Judaizers, Gnostics, or spiritual enthusiasts, on the one hand, and outside agitators such as the Jews, on the other, without achieving any consensus.[272] Against these various views, E. Best offers the objections that there is no reference to controversy over the law, there is nothing to suggest a distinct antagonistic group within the community, nor is there any stress on the need for unity.[273] Also unconvincing is E. von Dobschütz' psychological explanation that the apology arose out of a deep depression on Paul's part when he considered how the new converts might have thought of him after his leaving them, so to say, in the lurch.[274]

M. Dibelius presents another possibility in noting that it was common for wandering sophists and philosophers to disclaim underhanded motives in propagating their messages, so that no specific provocation needs to be sought for Paul's defence here.[275] A. J. Malherbe in particular has supported this view by drawing attention to numerous Cynic parallels in language and motives in common with 2:1-12.[276] In view of the presence of most of these motives in O.T.-Jewish literature (see under 6.4 and 8.2.2.2) in relation to prophets or teachers, it is unlikely that one can draw any definite conclusions from them, either for Paul's specific dependence on Cynic convention or for concrete accusations of "false prophecy" lying behind this defence.[277] Given Paul's mixed heritage as a Hellenistic Jew, the connection may lie on a higher level of generality, viz., the common general type of teacher/learner communication situation. Besides this, it is also explicitly proposed as a general rule in rhetoric that a rhetor should clear himself of disagreeable suspicion, whether this is openly expressed or not.[278]

---

[272] For Judaizers see, e.g., Baur, 1867, vol. II, 344; for Gnostics see, e.g., Schmithals, 1965, 123 ff., 127; for spiritual enthusiasts see, Lütgert, 1909, 64 ff.; Jewett, 1972, 202 ff.: 1984, 32; and for outside Jews see, e.g., Milligan, 1908, xxxi-xxxii; Frame, 1912, 90 ff.

[273] Best, 1977, 16. See his arguments in 16-22.

[274] Dobschütz, 1909, 107. Against this Dibelius (1937, 10-11) notes that the rhetorical structure in 2:1 ff. indicates agitation instead.

[275] Dibelius, 1937, 11. See also, e.g., Bornkamm, 1971, 63-4.

[276] Malherbe, 1970, 203-17.

[277] Horbury (1982, 492-508), inspite of recognizing an overlap in the type of terminology used in praise and blame of both Hellenistic philosophers and O.T. prophets, tries to establish such a reflection of "false prophecy" behind the passage. Cf. Henneken (1969, 98 ff.) who sees the language of this passage as indicating that Paul viewed himself in terms of a prophet of the end-time, rather than as a "messianic" prophet as Denis (1957, 245-318) would hold.

While these observations may explain the general nature of Paul's so-called defence,[279] they do not account for the perceptible agitation and what appears to be a concerned insistence visible in the repetitive ου...αλλα antitheses in 2:1-8. Was there not after all some aspect of the situation of the addressees that would make the apologetic tone of the reminders of the initial conduct of the addressors particularly appropriate here?

N. Hyldahl has felt that the apologetic tone of 2:1-12 seems to indicate that there was also a "darker side" to the news brought by Timothy.[280] This "dark side" of the relationship is found to have been occasioned by eschatological considerations. The fact that some of the Christians in Thessalonica had died without experiencing the parousia, a problem that Paul approaches carefully and treats delicately in 4:13-18, is seen as having caused the community to doubt the honesty of Paul and the reliability of the gospel itself.[281]

Against this view, it is held here that although the question of the Christian dead was indeed a serious problem (see below), the explicit sentiments expressed in 3:6, as analysed above, do not allow us to see it as occasioning the **open** mistrust suggested by Hyldahl. On the other hand, it is fairly probable that it created a climate for **potential** mistrust, so that this and the current pressure of tribulations (see below) may be seen as contributing to a perceptibly more than ordinary degree of intensity of pastoral concern on the part of Paul in 2:1 ff. Such a situational climate also goes against G. Lyons' recent conclusion that Paul's use of autobiographical references in I Thess 1-3 have a **primarily** parenetic function, rather than an exordial-like function preparatory for the treatment of any issues in I Thess 4-5 (see ch. 7 below).[282]

Consequently, the apologetic character of 2:1 ff. should probably be seen as not reflecting any specific, explicit charges originating from the addressees. However, besides the context of Greek sophistic conventions and the wider one of Greek rhetoric in general, it is not unlikely that more immediate factors contributed to the intensity of pastoral concern in the passage. One outside group not mentioned above which quite naturally could have taunted the believers with such charges is the Thessalonians' own countrymen (συμφυλεται, (2:14) who persecuted them (see 4.1.4.2). While relations between the addressors and the addressees were probably still relatively positive, such taunts could take on serious dimensions in view of the problems and perplexities experienced by the addressees.

---

[278] See under 1.7.6.2.

[279] Thus Best, 1977, 22.

[280] Hyldahl, 1972-73, 253.

[281] Hyldahl, 1972-73, 254; 1980, 122.

[282] Lyons, 1985, 175 ff., 218 ff.

2.2.2 The Status of the Community's Christian Conduct

It would appear that the repeated references to the good (3:6) and even exemplary character of the Thessalonian believers' Christian life (1:6-7) make it unlikely that the reminder of Paul's previous instructions (4:1-12) were aimed at **correcting** any concrete, current ethical breaches in the life of the community.[283] This is supported in particular by the fact that the topics of these reminders are gathered under and introduced by the superior theme το πως δει υμας περιπατειν και αρεσκειν θεω...ινα περισσευητε μαλλον to which is added the comment καθως και περιπατειτε (4:1).[284]

2.2.3 The Problem Regarding Deceased Christians

From 4:13-18 it is clear that some of the members of the believing community had died and that this apparently constituted a particular problem for those who remained. Various theories have been put forward to explain the nature of the problem, such as 4:13-18 being occasioned by a gnostic denial of the resurrection,[285] or as the relative advantage of living Christians over those who had died, in that the Christian dead could be thought to suffer a disadvantage, either by the resurrection occurring after the parousia,[286] or by their missing out on the blessedness of an intermediate messianic kingdom.[287] It has also been seen as being occasioned by the inability of the Thessalonian believers to apply the contents of Paul's teaching on the resurrection and the parousia to the concrete events of their fellow Christians' deaths.[288] G. Lüdemann has recently convincingly criticized each of the foregoing views and argued in favour of another previously championed view, viz., that due to the intensity of Paul's expectation of the imminent parousia (4:15), he had not instructed the converts about a future resurrection of Christians.[289]

---

[283] Against, e.g., Klijn, 1980, 121.

[284] See, e.g., Conzelmann/Lindemann, 1980, 192 (See 4.4.3 below).

[285] E.g., most recently by Schmithals (1965, 116-19), Jewett (1972, 181-232) and Harnish (1973, 24 ff.).

[286] E.g., Frame, 1912, 164; Wilke, 1967, 122.

[287] E.g., Schweitzer (1931, 88-100) followed recently by G. Friedrich (1976, 242 ff.).

[288] Thus, e.g., Dobschütz, 1909, 189; Luz, 1968, 321 ff.

[289] Lüdemann, 1984, 205-38. This view was previously held by, e.g., Bornemann, 1894, 188; Niel, 1950, 90; Oepke, 1953, 142; Henneken, 1969, 76-8; Marxsen, 1969, 33-5; 1979, 26, 65; Becker, 1976, 46-54; Conzelmann/Lindemann, 1980, 52; Cavallin, 1983, 54-63; and Holtz, 1986, 187.

This last position is criticized independently by N. Hyldahl and J. Plevnik in view of the primary focus on what they have referred to as the "gathering" or "assumption" of dead believers in 4:14-17 rather than on the resurrection itself, on which the addressees must have received some general instruction.[290] According to Plevnik, initial instruction on the parousia was probably given in terms of only the assumption of believers in view of the expectation of its imminence. Consequently, the deaths of fellow believers would have naturally caused consternation. This background explains their grief, the focus on assumption and the need for an authoritative word bringing in the unelaborated reference to the resurrection of the righteous dead to explain how their assumption was possible.[291] However, Hyldahl's view that there arose open internal mistrust that Paul's instruction on the parousia and even the gospel constituted lies and deception[292] tends to overstate the situation in view of 3:6 in particular.

The recent position of C.L. Mearns is a somewhat more radical modification of that of J.C. Hurd.[293] The Thessalonian letters and I Corinthians are all seen as reflecting a general situation where the fact of believers' deaths was forcing Paul to change to a futurist view of the parousia from an almost exclusively realized eschatology, wherein the parousia was identified with the appearance of the risen Lord.[294] An important link in Mearns' argument is what he sees as a tactic on Paul's part in both Thessalonian letters in which his initial references to the parousia play down the futurist aspect in the use of tentative and ambiguous language so as to prepare for the subsequent conspicuous presentations of a futurist view.[295] However, with regard to I Thess, Mearns' exegesis appears to display more of his own subtle effort than Paul's to downplay a futurist aspect in 1:10 in particular.[296]

---

[290] Hyldahl, 1980, 121 ff.; Plevnik, 1984, 276 ff.

[291] Plevnik (1984, 279-80) supports this interpretation by referring to Lohfink's survey and analysis (1971, 55-70) of "assumption" in the O.T., Jewish and Greco-Roman worlds of thought where assumption is not something that happens to the dead but only to persons who are very much alive.

[292] Hyldahl, 1980, 122.

[293] Mearns, 1980-81, 137 ff.; Hurd, 1965.

[294] Mearns, 1980-81, 139, ff.

[295] Mearns, 1980-81, 142 ff.

[296] Mearns, 1979-80, 143. See Best (1977, 84) who notes the emphatic position of the attributive participle in $\tau\eta\varsigma\ o\rho\gamma\eta\varsigma\ \tau\eta\varsigma\ \epsilon\rho\chi o\mu\epsilon\nu\eta\varsigma$.

2.2.4 The Problem of Tribulations and Suffering

As noted above, the addressees had suffered when they first received the word εν θλιψει πολλη μετα χαρας πνευματος αγιου (1:6). The parallel references to "receiving the word" and "becoming imitators" in both 1:6 and 2:13-14 speak for the references to "tribulation" in 1:6 and "suffering" (επαθετε) in 2:14 as referring to the same experiences at the beginning of their faith. That these sufferings had continued is intimated by the reference εν ταις θλιψεσιν ταυταις in Paul's explanation of why they were so anxious to send Timothy to strengthen and encourage them (3:3): το μηδενα σαινεσθαι εν ταις θλιψεσιν τουταις. Although θλιψεσιν ταυταις textually corefers with the preceding references to sufferings of the past, it is quite likely that a "deictic" reference to the present situation is also included.[297]

An indication that the tribulations were a continuing reality lies in the generalizing scope of the argument following upon the general reference to "these tribulations."[298] Instead of going on to relate Timothy's return after this summarizing reference, Paul takes the occasion to remind the addressees that such tribulations are their common destiny (3:3b) and that the addressors' predictions of such sufferings had come to pass: και γαρ οτε προς υμας ημεν, προελεγομεν υμιν οτι μελλομεν θλιβεσθαι, καθως και εγενετο και οιδατε (3:4). The aorist tense of εγενετο should not be pressed here as an indication of the tribulation referred to as being past and over. When referring to events, γινεσθαι is commonly used with the ingressive sense "arise" or "come about."[299] This ingressive sense appears most appropriate here. Given the preceding reference to previous predictions of coming tribulation, for the argument it is sufficient to confirm that it had arisen (see 4.2.4 below).

Furthermore, in view of the "destined" characterization of the tribulation, it is quite likely that Paul associated the tribulation and suffering of the addressees and himself with the so-called Messianic or eschatological woes,[300] so that he hardly had in mind a period of persecution after which the community would return to normality.[301] Further indications that the situation of the converts' faith was seen in a wider eschatological context by Paul may be observed in 2:19-20. Here the believers' preservation until the parousia is expressed in terms of "his own eschatological victory," and in 3:5 the tempter's danger (μη πως επειρασεν υμας ο πειραζων) to their

---

[297] Marxsen (1979, 54) does not capture this deictic reference when he only sees it as indicating that Paul "die Vergangenheit aus seiner jetzigen Sicht darstellt."

[298] Against, e.g., Holtz (1986, 127-8) who holds that Paul was referring specifically to his own tribulations. Furthermore, in view of the preceding references to the addressees' tribulations, normal expectations of textual reference would require a clearer distinction by way of ημων/μου instead of ταυταις.

[299] Bauer, 1952, 157.

[300] See Meeks (1983, 691-2) who alludes to Dan 12:1; Jub 23:13 f., 22; II Bar 70:2 f., 5, 8-10; IV Ezra 5:1-12; 13:30 f.; 14:16 f.; Mark 13:7 f.; and Rev passim, as evidence for this idea.

[301] Thus, e.g., Best, 1977, 135. This "destined" character of tribulation speaks in favour of a collective "we" (καιμεθα) here, against, e.g., Holtz (1986, 128).

faith is expressed in language that may have associative connections with the great πειρασμος of the final times.[302]

Thus, not only does Paul report their past concern over the tempter's power (3:5), but also "now" when writing the letter, although comforted by the good news brought back by Timothy, he expresses concern that they should "stand fast in the Lord" (3:7-8) and that he and his fellow-workers may be able to return to visit them and supply "what is lacking" in their faith (3:10). One should also observe that Paul focusses twice on the addressees' initial spiritual fortitude and success in relating to tribulation (1:6-7; 2:14) and that his report of the reason for sending Timothy (3:3a) becomes an occasion for a renewed argumentative reminder of the character of Christian suffering.

These features may be taken to mirror the fact that even though the Thessalonian believers were bearing up well, their faith nevertheless was under some pressure. In view of the fact that they had experienced tribulation and suffering from the beginning (1:6; 2:14), it is unlikely that it is their experience of these sufferings alone that occasions the particularly pointed reminder in 3:3b-4.

The following analyses as a whole are seen as supporting the view that it was the deaths of fellow Christians before the parousia that constitutes the primary exigence to which the various persuasive strategies of the letter as a whole are directed. This is seen as having cast a potentially dangerous shadow over their hope and faith. As a consequence, there was the danger of their questioning the actual nature of their sufferings, the sincerity and reliability of Paul and his co-workers and ultimately even the validity of the gospel itself (see ch. 6).

---

[302] Thus, Collins, 1984, 220-21;=1978-79, 260-61.

Chapter 3

A TEXT-LINGUISTIC/LETTER-CONVENTIONAL ANALYSIS

3.1 THE LETTER AND ITS PRIMARY FUNCTIONAL SUBSEQUENCES

While the emphasis in the subsequent analysis of text-delimitation and coherence is on pragmatic and semantic aspects, it will be necessary to bring in syntactic considerations also, given the close interdependence of these three dimensions of texts. Also the preceding deliberations on the communicative context will not play such an important role in the immediately subsequent sequential-hierarchical analysis as in the rhetorical analysis that follows later (see ch. 4). This is due to the fact that in what immediately follows the focus is more on interpreting predominances of communicative functions in terms of general epistolary conventions. Also, more generally textual temporal and spatial features with a bearing on text-delimitation and coherence will be taken up.

3.1.1 The Letter as a Whole

The address in 1:1a constitutes an MC which serves to delimit the letter as a whole: Παυλος και Σιλουανος και Τιμοθεος τη εκκλησια Θεσσαλονικεων εν θεω πατρι και κυριω Ιησου Χριστω. It establishes the primary level of communication by identifying the addressors and the addressees of the letter as a whole in what is taken here as an elliptical construction (see 3.1.2 below). Besides the address thematizing the letter as an act of communication, there are MC iterations in 4:9, 5:1 and 5:27. The last instance thematizes the letter as as an act of reading to the addressees: ενορκιζω υμας τον κυριον αναγνωσθηναι την επιστολην πασιν τοις αδελφοις. Here the delimiting anaphoric reference την επιστολην qualifies as 1SM. Thus, these markers establish the letter itself as the primary functional text-sequence on the highest ranking level. This primary level with its delimitation markers may be symbolized as follows in Figure 1:

LEVEL I

I Thess 1:1-5:28

MC; 1SM

Figure 1

3.1.2   I Thess 1:1: The Letter-Opening

The epistolary prescript itself should be seen as the first functional text-sequence on the next level below that of the letter as a whole. Notationally it may be represented as 1.1SMinf. It is delimited by its **essentially** conventional structure, content and predominant phatic function.

Regarding structure and content, the Pauline address consists basically of the identification of both the addresser(s) and the addressee(s) in the third person and in the nominative and dative cases respectively.[303] It may be expanded in various degrees with references to God and Christ or other material relevant to the context or message of the letter itself (cf. Gal 1:1-2). The Pauline greeting usually consists of the basic formulation χαρις υμιν και ειρηνη απο θεου πατρος ημων και κυριου Ιησου Χριστου which may also be expanded by other confessional and doxological material (cf. Gal 1:3-5). This greeting has its most reduced form in I Thess: χαρις υμιν και ειρηνη (1:1b).[304]

The syntactic coherence of both the address and the greeting involves the ellipses of explicit verb forms. According to L.H. Hoek, ellipses may be restored from the context, the co-text or the decoder's knowledge of the language code.[305] Seeing the presence of an elliptical metacommunicative verb in the the address finds linguistic support from the earlier form of the Greek prescript: ο δεινα τω δεινι ταδε λεγει. As for the subsequently most common Greek prescript ο δεινα τω δεινι χαιρειν the imperatival infinitive supplies the verbal element.[306]

In the Pauline formulation the different grammatical subjects of the address (Παυλος και Σιλουανος και Τιμοθεος) and of the greeting (χαρις...και ειρηνη) demand different verbs as being understood and as such constitute a deviation from the normal Greek pattern. Thus, for the address itself one should inference some such verb as γραφουσιν, (cf. 4:9; 5:1). As to the greeting, one may inference some such verb-form as ειη or εστω, as suggested by B. Rigaux.[307] Both the address and the greeting should be seen then as separate utterances connected asyndetically, with an element of semantic coherence established by co-reference between εκκλησια and υμιν.

---

[303] Roller (1933, 54 and 417-18, note 230) divides the address into superscriptio and adscriptio with the greeting designated as salutatio. See esp. Conzelmann (1975, 19-24) for a full discussion with relevant bibliographical references. Cf. Rigaux, 1956, 345 ff.

[304] See Schenk (1984, 83) for arguments and references supporting seeing it as an abbreviated form here rather than a first stage in a development of the Pauline prescript. I Thess is after all only the earliest extant letter we have and not necessarily the first missionary letter written by Paul.

[305] Hoek, 1981, 56 ff.

[306] For these examples see Koskenniemi, 1956, 156. Against Blass/Debrunner (1961, 196; 1979, 390) who see χαιρειν itself as elliptical, see Moulton (1908, 179) and Robertson (1934, 944).

[307] Thus Rigaux, 1956, 352. Cf. πληθυνθειη in I Pet 1:2, II Pet 1:2 and Jude 2.

Regarding the pragmatic coherence of the prescript in terms of communicative functions, the explicit function of the address, as mentioned, is metacommunicative and the explicit function of the greeting is expressive.[308] However, given the primary concentration of the prescript on establishing communication as a whole, these two utterances are best interpreted as implicitly serving a predominant phatic function.[309]

3.1.3   I Thess 1:2-5:24: The Letter-Body

H. Koskenniemi held that the three basic parts of the Greek letter were "the prescript, the actual letter-body and the closing clause" and compared them to a personal meeting with the prescript corresponding to the opening greeting and the closing clause to the departing farewell.[310] F.X.J. Exler, O. Roller, and more recently Ph. Vielhauer also held to the same basic three-part division.[311] This three-part division with the "letter-body" as the middle part stands in contrast to the position of P. Schubert, J.T. Sanders, R.W. Funk, J.L. White and W.G. Doty, who see the letter-body as a more specifically informative section beginning at the close of the thanksgiving section and immediately succeeded either by parenesis or the letter-closing.[312]

3.1.3.1   Form-Criticism's Inadequacy in Isolating the Letter-Body

In spite of Funk's explicit denial, it appears that the concept of the Pauline letter-body subscribed to by himself, Sanders, White and Doty amounts to what is left after one has subtracted prescript, opening thanksgiving, parenesis and a closing doxology, personal greetings and benediction. He denies this on the grounds that "style and sequence analyses have enabled one to identify tight, closely argued sections, which regularly manifest the closest interrelation of theological and practical concerns, and

---

[308] The metacommunicative function of the address is also shared by the inscription, (αποδος) τῳ δεινι παρα του δεινος, written on the outside of the scroll, as well as by the subscriptio of the manuscripts, Προς Θεσσαλονεκεις α', though the latter functions more as a "title" identifying the text for subsequent readers.

[309] Vielhauer (1975, 65) disassociates the address from the inscription with regard to the function of "presentation" ("Vorstellung"), connecting it more integrally to the letter itself. This would correspond to the phatic function.

[310] Koskenniemi, 1956, 155.

[311] Exler, 1923, 101 ff.; O. Roller (1933, 54-5) refers to "einen Eingangsgruss in der "Salutations" formel, worauf dann der eigentliche Briefinhalt, der "Kontext" folgt und an dessen Schlusse als "Eschatokoll" wiederum ein Gruss,..."; Vielhauer (1975, 65) uses "Kontext" in the same way as Roller.

[312] Schubert, 1939, 5, 7, 24; Sanders, 1962, 348-62; Funk, 1966, 263 ff.; J.L. White, 1972; 1984, 1742-50; and Doty, 1973, 27-47.

which customarily form the body of the letter."[313] In I Thess he sees 2:1-3:13 as the letter-body.[314] However, it may be argued that 4:13-5:11 would satisfy Funk's criteria even better, since the contents of 2:1-3:13 are certainly less theological by comparison. But 4:13-5:11 is excluded from consideration, obviously because the parenetic section it is a part of has already been "subtracted."[315]

More recently, under the rubric "The Central Section," H. Boers starts off by noting that "the body as main purpose of the letter probably also includes the thanksgiving, the apostolic parousia and the exhortation."[316] However, instead of going on to show how these elements are functionally interrelated so as to indicate the main purpose of the letter, he deletes 2:13-16 as a later interpolation,[317] claiming that this give I Thess a more "normal" structure. Then, the remaining thanksgiving (1:2-10), apology (2:1-12) and apostolic parousia (2:17-3:13) indicate that the apology is the "central section,"[318] this is not taken to mean that it conveys the main purpose. Rather, the inner connection of these three sequences is seen as disclosing "the purpose of the letter," viz., **philophronesis**.[319]

In his treatment of "the exhortation section" he approves of Bjerkelund's general description of the purpose of the letter as Paul's desire "to express to the congregation his joy about them and his satisfaction with them--and furthermore to spur them on to a way of life pleasing to God."[320] However, he rejects Bjerkelund's conclusion that the "body" of the letter is constituted by 4:1-5:11 in representing him as not quite able to formulate the purpose of the letter in such a way that the $ευχαριστω$ section stands as an introduction to the $παρακαλω$ section.[321] On the contrary, Bjerkelund explicitly states that "mit dieser Auslegung erhölt die Danksagung in Kapitel 1-3 die auch für die übringen Briefe des Apostels übliche Function, einleitend zu dem Corpus des Briefes hinzuführen."[322] With minor reservations, Boers adopts D. G. Bradley's thesis of general parenetic **topoi** in 4:1-5:22, with the situation-specific aspect of

---

[313] Funk, 1966, 263-4; cf. Doty, 1973, 43.

[314] Thus also Sanders, 1962, 355-6; J.L. White, 1972, 70-2; and Doty, 1973, 43.

[315] Berger (1984, 1336) also criticizes this type of patternism.

[316] Boers, 1975, 145. The apostolic parousia refers to I Thess 2:17-3:13 and designates a form that Funk (1967, 249-68) believed he could isolate. However, it is not so much a "form" as a common letter topic as Mullins (1973, 350-58) has convincingly shown.

[317] Boers (1975-76, 145) basically accepts the arguments of Pearson (1971, 79-94) in this respect.

[318] Boers, 1975-76, 152.

[319] Boers, 1975-76, 153.

[320] Boers' (1975-76, 158) translation of Bjerkelund (1967, 134).

[321] Boers, 1975-76, 156.

[322] Bjerkelund, 1967, 134.

4:13-18 relativized by seeing the problem treated in a "semi-independent" way.[323] He follows A. J. Malherbe in classifying I Thess as a parenetic letter, adding that it has "two characteristic main parts, philophronesis and parenesis."[324]

Although Boers observes functional coherence for 1:2-3:13 and 4:1-5:22 on their highest levels of generality, it is held here that he is unable to overturn Bjerkelund's position on the functional relation between these two major sequences on the basis of convincing criteria. It is not enough to refer to the generality of parenetic **topoi** without a closer investigation of the text-pragmatic features in the text that indicate the relations between the text-sequences and reflect aspects of the situational context (see 4.4 and ch. 6).

The conclusions of other form critics are quite disparate. P. Schubert considered that 1:2-3:13 was an extended "thanksgiving" and that in the absence of a "main body" of doctrinal and practical information this functioned as the body with the parenetical section of 4:1-5:22 following as the "conclusion."[325] C.J. Bjerkelund, as already noted, argues that 1:2-3:13 has the same introductory function that the "thanksgiving" has in the other letters of Paul and that the παρακαλω formula in 4:1 introduces the "Corpus" of the letter, viz., 4:1-5:11, with 4:1-2 and 4:10b-12 as the point of the whole letter.[326] H. Koester also sees 1:2-3:13 as basically exordial, but curiously limits the body to 4:1-12, stating that parenesis constitutes the body proper of the Pauline letter-form.[327]

All these views have in common a basic idea of the "letter-body" as normally being a sequence in which the major concern of the letter comes into particular focus. W.G. Doty defines it as "the actual part of the Pauline letter in which Paul dealt with issues most directly and at length."[328] This is basically a rhetorical concept which comes to expression in the **argumentatio** of the rhetorical disposition.[329] Consequently, the form-critical criteria as developed by Sanders, Funk and White are inadequate for delimiting it, since the criteria they use are limited to predominantly syntactic-semantic features of texts.

That which is lacking in the form-critical approach is a concerted focus on the pragmatic dimension of each Pauline and other N.T. letter so as to not merely establish the coherence and delimitation of the primary functional subsequences, but more importantly to show how **all** of the subsequences of a letter functionally interact and co-operate in achieving its communicative purpose(s). While Koester and Bjerkelund are less amenable to this criticism than the others mentioned, they nevertheless do not go far enough in this direction (see ch. 6).

---

[323] Boers (1975-76, 156-8) referring to Bradley (1953, 238-46).

[324] Boers (1975-76, 158) referring to Malherbe (1972, 16-18).

[325] Schubert, 1939, 16-24, esp. 25-26.

[326] Bjerkelund, 1967, 134.

[327] Koester, 1982, Vol. II, 55.

[328] Doty, 1973, 34.

[329] See Wuellner's criticism (1976, 334) in this respect.

3.1.3.2 Taking the Broader View of the Letter-Body

With regard to the broader view of the letter-body mentioned above, a major question has to do with finding criteria for deciding whether Paul's initial expressions of thanksgiving and prayer should be seen as belonging generally to "letter-opening" conventions, as White explicitly argues,[330] or as belonging to or opening the "letter-body," as Exler and Roller held.[331] The latter view may also be inferred for Koskenniemi, who clearly states that the **valetudinis** formulae (e.g., ερρωσθαι and υγιαινειν) "have their place in the letter **after** (my italics) the prescript."[332] Furthermore, he correlates Paul's initial expressions of thanksgiving and prayer with the **proskynema** formula and notes that, while this formula was most often connected with the **valetudinis** formulae, it could itself also occur independently immediately after the prescript, and also elsewhere "im Kontext des Briefes."[333] Thus, he was generally in agreement with Exler.[334]

On the other hand, Schubert, Sanders, Funk and White include the thanksgiving material more closely with the prescript under letter-opening conventions and see the letter-body as being introduced by formulae of **request/appeal/injunction, disclosure, joy, astonishment, compliance** or **hearing/learning**.[335] Against this, however, T.Y. Mullins has convincingly shown that all such formulae, including expressions of thanksgiving, can occur at initial, medial and final positions in Hellenistic letters so as to serve transitional functions in general.[336]

For a solution it is necessary to turn to the pragmatic dimension. As noted above, in the prescript the primary focus is on opening and establishing communication and involves the predominance of the phatic function of communication together with more subordinate metacommunicative and expressive functions. The subsequent analyses in 3.2 below show I Thess 1:2-3:13 and 4:1-5:24 to be primary functional subsequences in which textually embodied expressive and conative communicative functions predominate respectively so as to distinguish these text-sequences from the

---

[330] J.L. White, 1972, 1.

[331] Exler, 1923, 101 ff.; Roller, 1933, 65.

[332] Koskenniemi, 1956, 131: "die im Brief ihren Platz gleich hinter dem Präskript hat." Only a shorter parallel form, declining in use from the 1st century on, is noted as being syntactically connected to the prescript (133).

[333] Koskenniemi, 1956, 139, 144.

[334] Cf. Exler, 1923, 101 ff. When using Koskenniemi in criticism of Exler, J.L. White (1972, 1) generally misrepresents Koskenniemi in stating that the latter suggests that such formulae are connected integrally with the opening of the letter rather than with the opening of the letter-body.

[335] See Doty, 1973, 34-5; J.L. White, 1971, 93.

[336] Mullins, 1972, 380-90, esp. 386 ff. He goes too far, however, in denying a theme-related function and allowing only an expression of the writer's attitudes. They correspond basically to the MB element in Thematic Markers defined text-linguistically in 1.4.3 above.

preceding prescript. As for letter-closing in 5:25-28, there is a distinct return to a predominance of the phatic function again (see 3.1.4 below).

Thus, what comes between the prescript and the letter-closing should be taken as the letter-body which embodies the message (taken in a broad sense) of the letter as a whole. As a functional text-sequence it will be noted here as "Letter-Body" (1.2SMinf). As for the task of analysing where in this letter-body the major concern of the letter comes into focus, a combined text-linguistic and rhetorical analysis will provide the appropriate means for interpreting the functional relations that hold between the major text-sequences in relation to the situational context. This broader concept of the letter-body also makes it possible to better account for the versatility of the letter schema to package not only the more general, practical epistolary correspondence but also texts more specifically shaped, e.g., as rhetorical speeches,[337] philosophical discourse,[338] or even apocalypses, as in the case of Revelation.

3.1.4 I Thess 5:25-28: The Letter-Closing

With 5:25 the predominating focus shifts from a concentration on the persuasive aims regarding the addressees' "Christian life" (see 4.1.1) to that of personal contact between the communicating partners so that the wish-prayer in 5:23-24 is seen as a part of the section closing the letter-body and 5:25-28 is taken to be the letter-closing:
Αδελφοι, προσευχεσθε (και) περι ημων. Ασπασασθε τους αδελφους παντας εν φιληματι αγιω. Ενορκιζω υμας τον κυριον αναγνωσθηναι την επιστολην πασιν τοις αδελφοις. Η χαρις του κυριου ημων Ιησου Χριστου μεθ'υμων.

While the closing wish of grace (5:28) most naturally corresponds to the closing clause, e.g., ερρωσθε, of Greek letters and unmistakably serves to ultimately close the letter,[339] it nevertheless is preceded by a number of utterances with which it shares the same predominating phatic function of communication. The transition in 5:25 is typically marked by Paul's use of αδελφοι. The subsequent request for prayer, the request to greet all the brethren with a holy kiss and the adjuration to read the letter to all of them focus more directly on interpersonal relations. Thus, not only is there a thematic shift at 5:25 (see 4.4.9), but also a shift from a predominantly persuasive-exhortational (see 3.2.2 and 4.4) to a predominantly phatic communicative function.[340] The transition is, however, not abrupt, but has soft features in that the

---

[337] See, e.g., Goldstein, 1968, 97-181.

[338] See, e.g., Malherbe, 1977.

[339] Koskenniemi, 1956, 151 ff.; Thus also Roller (1933, 69-70) for the Hellenistic letter, but for I Thessalonians he clearly argues that what is referred to here as the wish-prayer in 5:23 serves to close the letter-body (165). Also, J.L. White, 1983, 442.

[340] This delimitation supports the judgments of, e.g., Lightfoot, 1904, 90 ff.; Dobschütz, 1909, 232-3; Roller, 1933, 165; Rigaux, 1956, 602 ff.; Wikenhauser/Schmid, 1973, 403; Friedrich, 1976, 251; and Marxsen, 1979, 73. Among those who take 5:23-28 as the letter closing see, e.g., Dibelius, 1937, 1; Kümmel, 1973, 220; Wiles, 1974, 63 ff.; Vielhauer, 1975, 84; Best, 1977, 242 ff.

request for prayer follows naturally upon Paul's immediately preceding wish-prayer for the addressees.[341]

These observations are seen as justifying a departure from Koskenniemi in taking more than the closing-clause as the letter-closing. However, he was not far from this position when he noted that the greeting using such formulae as $ασπασασθε$, $επισκοπου$, etc., "most often formed a separate section at the end of the letter."[342] As Doty notes, the Pauline and other early Christian letters were less bound to the closing conventions of Hellenistic letters than to other formulaic conventions. He finds the most common constituents of the Pauline letter-closing to be **greetings**, **doxology** and **benediction**.[343]

While the language of the wish-prayer, the request for prayer, the reference to the holy kiss and the final wish of grace all contribute to make the letter appropriate for public reading to the believers most likely gathered together for worship (see 8.2), the quite practical adjuration that the letter be read to all the brethren in 5:27 and the use of the typical $ασπασασθε$ letter-formula in the midst of these utterances cautions against describing these utterances too explicitly in "liturgical" terms as G. P. Wiles appears to do.[344]

This functional text-sequence is noted here as "Letter-Closing" (1.3SMinf) and the second level of subsequences made up of the prescript, letter-body and letter-closing may be symbolized as follows in Figure 2:[345]

---

[341] If the $και$ placed in brackets is original, it seems more natural to take it as indicating reciprocity in relation to Paul's immediately preceding wish-prayer, rather than supplementation in relation to the admonition $αδιαλειπτως προσευχεσθε$ in 5:17 as suggested by Metzger, 1971, 633.

[342] Koskenniemi, 1956, 148.

[343] Doty, 1973, 39, 43. However, when Doty classifies the wish-prayer of I Thess 5:23 as a "doxology" in his paradigm of the formal parts of Paul's letters (1973, 43), this is obviously inappropriate. On the wish-prayer form see Wiles, 1974, 29 ff.

[344] Wiles, 1974, 63 ff., 68 ff. The designation "liturgical" associates with fairly rigid conventions of language used in worship, which the admixture of purely epistolary formulae and references goes against here.

[345] Lee/Lee (1975, 39) come to a similar delimitation on the basis of a primarily text-semantic analysis built up from the relations of subordinate semantic units.

LEVEL II

I Thess 1:1	1:2-5:24	5:25-28
Prescript (1.1SMinf)	Letter-Body (1.2SMinf)	Letter-Closing (1.3SMinf)

Figure 2

3.2 THE PRIMARY SUBSEQUENCES OF THE LETTER-BODY

3.2.1 I Thess 1:2-3:13: A Predominant Expressive Function

This first functional text-sequence within the letter-body is delimited by a predominance of the verbally explicit expressive function of communication. Besides explicit expressions of love (2:7-8, 11), concern (2:17; 3:1, 5) and joy (2:19-20; 3:9) over the addressees, this comes particularly into focus in the thanksgiving/prayer-report in 1:2 ff., ευχαριστουμεν τω θεω παντοτε περι παντων υμων μνειαν ποιουμενοι επι των προσευχων ημων, αδιαλειπτως μνημονευοντες, κτλ., the thanksgiving-report in 2:13, και δια τουτο και ημεις ευχαριστουμεν τω θεω αδιαλειπτως, οτι κτλ. and in the expression of thanksgiving in the form of a rhetorical question including a prayer-report in 3:9-10, τινα γαρ ευχαριστιαν δυναμεθα τω θεω ανταποδουναι περι υμων..., νυκτος και ημερας υπερεκπερισσου δεομενοι κτλ.

It is important to emphasize the observation here that such instances, both elsewhere in Paul's letters[346] and here in 1:2 ff. and 2:13, are "reports" of thanksgiving and not "thanksgivings," as commonly taken for granted.[347] This is obvious from the third-person reference to God and the usual addition of παντοτε, the latter missing only in Rom 1:8. P. Schubert observed a double focus on the author and addressee together with this third-person reference to God in contrast to a more liturgically appropriate ευχαριστω σοι, ω θεε as evidence for the particularly epistolary form and function of the thanksgiving-reports without explicitly recognizing them as

---

[346] See Rom 1:8 ff.; I Cor 1:4 ff.; Phil 1:3 ff.; Col 1:3 ff.; and Phlm 4 ff. Cp. Eph 1:15.

[347] Form-critics from Schubert (1939, 7 ff.) to Doty (1973, 31 ff.) refer to them as "thanksgivings" as do the commentaries in general. O'Brian (1977,12) refers to D. J. McFarlane's unpublished dissertation (The Motif of Thanksgiving in the New Testament, M.Th. thesis, St. Andrews University, 1966) were it is pointed out that the Pauline thanksgivings were recitals rather than wishes. See also Hartman (1985, 20). For the previous use of "prayer-report" to designate the prayer elements often incorporated into or following after the so-called "thanksgivings" see Wiles (1974, 7 ff.) who follows Harder (1936, 26) and others' "Gebetsbericht."

reports.³⁴⁸

From the perspective of linguistics, the construction ευχαριστω σοι would qualify as a performative formulation which makes "explicit what action it is that is being performed in issuing the utterance."³⁴⁹ However, with the replacement of the second by the third-person reference after potentially performative verbs like ευχαριστω the "self-naming" performative function has been replaced by that of a reporting function.³⁵⁰

As for the instance in 3:9, its formulation as a rhetorical question heightens the intensity. When transformed into the declarative mode, the hyperbolic intensity achieved by the rhetorical-question formulation finds its parallel in the somewhat milder hyperbolic intensity expressed by παντοτε (1:2) and αδιαλειπτως (2:13). To illustrate this transformation in English, it may be rendered as "We cannot give sufficient thanks to God concerning you for all the joy," etc., or simply "We give superabundant thanks to God concerning you for all the joy," etc. The additions of "sufficient" and "superabundant" are needed to reflect the hyperbolic intensity achieved by the rhetorical question. This is also an instance of a "report" of thanksgiving, as indicated by the syntactically dependent prayer-report (3:10): νυκτος και ημερας υπερεκπερισσου δεομενοι, κτλ.

J.P. Audet, J.M. Robinson and Kl. Berger have no doubt modified Schubert's thesis of the primarily "Hellenistic" background as influencing Paul's usage.³⁵¹ Nevertheless, Schubert's observation of the particular formulation in Paul's letters as being suited to the epistolary use of these utterances must still be seen as primary and any liturgical functions as secondary and based on linguistically associated meaning. In all of the non-epistolary examples drawn from Qumran, contemporary Jewish and early Christian prayers, whether begun by an expression of blessing or thanksgiving, God is addressed directly in the second person and not referred to in the third person.

The following observations may be made regarding these practical communicative utterances which are typical of the opening sequence of the Pauline letter-body. **Firstly**, as "reports" they may be classified as MC which thematize previous acts of verbal communication, viz., actual acts of giving thanks to God in prayer. **Secondly**, as "reports" of thanksgiving or of thanksgiving and prayer made for the addressees or for some aspect of the addressees' activity or life, they must be seen as **linguistically indirect** expressions of goodwill.³⁵² **Thirdly**, Paul's common use of the thanksgiving/

---

348 Schubert, 1939, 37-8.

349 Austin, 1975, 69. For a good survey and refinement of the "performative" concept see Partridge (1982, 13 ff., 40 ff.) who defines performative utterances in terms of having verbs in the first-person and present tense (simple-present in English) which may be identified by the criteria of having "an act-component, a saying-component and an explicitness-component" (40).

350 Thus, Partridge (1982, 19). He is in basic agreement (cf. 138-9) with Leech (1983, 189) who refers to the "performative utterance" as "a self-naming utterance which has the force indicated by its main verb."

351 Audet, 1958, 371-99; 1959, 643-62; Robinson 1963, 124-58; 1964, 194-235; Berger, 1974, 219-24. Cf. Schubert, 1939, 184-5.

352 See Koskenniemi (1956, 144-5) who quotes the thanksgiving/prayer-report of Phlm

prayer-reports should not be taken to indicate that they are so conventional as to be devoid of palpable communicative intent. In accordance with the climate of interpersonal relations in a particular communicative situation he can abandon it, as with the θαυμαζω of ironical surprise in Gal 1:6, or exchange it for the somewhat more impersonal ευλογητος ο θεος formula in II Cor 1:3.[353] While the latter has been shown to be generally interchangeable with thanksgiving expressions,[354] its formulation lacks the more explicit philophronetic force realized by the explicit focus on the addressee, usually made explicit by περι/υπερ υμων in the thanksgiving-reports. **Fourthly,** these thanksgiving-reports have been shown to have basically two formulaic realizations with ευχαριστω/ευχαριστουμεν immediately governing either a οτι clause or one or more participial clauses.[355] **Fifthly,** the particular text-initial sequences they open or in which they dominate have such clearly identifiable exordial characteristics that N. T. critics often refer to them as **prooimia**.[356]

Given these characteristics of indirect communicative function and of epistolary convention, such utterances may be seen as instances of indirect substitutions on meta-level serving to signal the the dominant philophronetic function of I Thess 1:2-3:13. Thus, I Thess 1:2-3 is represented here as 1.2.1SMind, the latter two occurrences being iterations.

3.2.1.1   The Significance of Recurrent Thanksgiving-Reports

Due to the iterations of reported thanksgiving and prayer, the so-called "thanksgiving" section in I Thess 1:2-3:13 has been seen as abnormally long. This has given rise to various interpretations with 1:2-3:13 seen as a "thanksgiving" serving as some kind of surrogate for an otherwise absent "letter-body,"[357] or simply as an extended "thanksgiving" with some part of 4:1 ff. constituting the "letter-body,"[358] or as the present text being the result of the redaction of more than

---

4 under proskynema formulae to which he ascribes this type of function, i.e. philophronesis.

[353] Thus, Schubert, 1939, 8, 34-5, 50, 183-4.

[354] See Audet, 1958, 371-99; 1959, 643-62; Robinson, 1963, 124-58; 1964, 194-235. They indicate the general interchangeability of ευλογειν, ευχαριστειν and εξομολογειν and their related adjectival and nominal forms in prayers and hymns directed to God.

[355] Schubert, 1939, 35.

[356] See, e. g., Vielhauer, 1975, 84 ff.; Conzelmann/Lindemann, 1980, 188 ff. The rhetorical analysis below will confirm the validity of this observation.

[357] Thus, e.g. Schubert, 1939, 25-6; J.L. White, 1972, 70-2; and Boers, 1975, 152-3, with various arguments respectively.

[358] Thus, e.g., Bjerkelund, 1967, 134; Koester, 1979, 38 ff.; 1982, vol. 2, 55.

one originally separate letters.[359] Furthermore, as already mentioned, I Thess 2:13-16 has been seen as a later interpolation, partly on the basis of the iterated thanksgiving-report in 2:13.[360]

F.O. Francis has shown that both in Jewish-Hellenistic and in Hellenistic letters there is a stylistic tendency to repeat expressions of thanksgiving, blessing and rejoicing in the opening period.[361] Though not mentioned by Francis, II Macc 1:11-17 provides a striking example of the general equivalence of thanksgiving and blessing expressions and of this stylistic type of repetition in that this exordial sequence opens with a thanksgiving-report and closes with a blessing forming an **inclusio**: opening (1:11), $εκ\ μεγαλων\ κινδυνων\ υπο\ του\ θεου\ σεσωσμενοι\ μεγαλως\ ευχαριστουμεν\ αυτω\ κτλ.$, closing (1:17), $κατα\ παντα\ ευλογητος\ ημων\ ο\ θεος,\ ος\ παρεδωκεν\ τους\ ασεβησαντας$. Correspondingly, in I Thessalonians the combination of reported **thanksgiving and prayer** in 1:2 and 3:9-10 provides a striking **inclusio**, with the latter close enough to the end to serve this macrostylistic function, even if not exactly at the end.[362]

Besides this instance of **inclusio** delimiting 1:2-3:13, the particular feature of stylistic repetition serving text-coherence in the thanksgiving expressions in 1:2 and 2:13 and in the joy expressions in 2:19-20 and 3:9 is substantiated in the following analyses in chs. 4-5.

3.2.1.2   Other Conventional Topics and Phraseology Expressing Goodwill

The basic philophronetic function of the thanksgiving/prayer-reports has already been noted. In conjunction with this it is significant to observe another iteration that parallels to some extent the previously mentioned **inclusio** of the thanksgiving/prayer-reports of 1:2-3 and 3:9-10, viz., that of $μνειαν\ ποιουμενοι$ and $μνημονευοντες$ in 1:2-3 being echoed by $εχετε\ μνειαν$ in 3:6. In contrast to M. Dibelius,[363] who asserts the epistolary rarity of such expressions as $μνειαν\ ποιεισθαι$, not only does H. Koskenniemi find this expression to be common in the Ptolemaic papyri but

---

[359] Thus, e.g., Schmithals (1964, 295-315, revised in 1965, 175-200;=1972, 239-74) who basically sees 1:1-2:12 and 4:3-5:28 as one letter and 2:13-4:2 as the other. See Collins (1979, 85-106; 1984, 114-35) for a survey and preliminary criticism of Schmithals and others' redactional theories. For a recent redaction theory see Pesch, 1984.

[360] For a survey and criticism of such views see Collins (1979, 68-85, 95-106; 1984, 97-114, 124-35). Also, see ch. 6 below.

[361] Francis, 1970, 111-17. See, e. g., Josephus, Ant 8.50-54.

[362] The same pattern has also been noted for Phlm 4-7 which opens and closes with a thanksgiving-report and an expression of joy respectively. Thus, Francis (1970, 112-13) who, nevertheless, shares Schubert's view of I Thess 1:2-3:13 being the letter-body.

[363] Dibelius, 1937, 2-3.

also that it is the equivalent of μνημονευειν in epistolary usage.[364] Furthermore, regarding the expressions μνειαν ποιεσθαι, μνημονευειν and μνειαν εχειν he states that this remembrance motive "gehört zu den allerfestesten Bestandteilen der Brief-Phraseologie," that it appears from the earliest beginnings on down to Christian letters in 400 A.D. and that its function is philophronetic in both its more religious usage (cf. 1:2-3 above) and its more general usage (cf. 3:6).[365]

Besides this typical epistolary phraseology, Kl. Thraede has drawn attention to the απων-παρων phraseology in what he refers to as the παρουσια motive in I Thess 2:17.[366] Paul's use of απορφανισθεντες is shown to be an emotional paraphrase for the απoντες formula, as indicated by the subsequent expression προσωπω, ου καρδια. In this προσωπον-καρδια opposition he finds a reflection of the epistolary **oculi-mens** convention.[367] Finally, there is what he calls the **pothos** motive, viz., the letter-writers' expression of desire to see/visit the addressee, as exemplified in περισσοτερως εσπουδασαμεν το προσωπον υμων ιδειν εν πολλη επιθυμια. διοτι ηθελησαμεν ελθειν προς υμας κτλ. (2:17b-18a), in επιποθουντες ημας ιδειν καθαπερ και ημεις υμας (3:6c), and in δεομενοι εις το ιδειν υμων το προσωπον (3:10b).[368] To these we may in fact add 3:11: αυτος δε ο θεος και πατηρ ημων και ο κυριος ημων Ιησους κατευθυναι την οδον ημων προς υμας.

3.2.1.3   Some General Conclusions on I Thess 1:2-3:13

All of these observations establish the text-pragmatic coherence of 1:2-3:13. They also indicate that the distinctive epistolary features of at least I Thess cannot be so completely submerged under what Kl. Berger refers to as the predominant features of "apostolische Rede" which he regards as the basic generic category of Paul's letters.[369] In general agreement with H. Boers, an appropriate designation for the specific type of expressive function that is apparently predominant in the passage is "goodwill" or **philophronesis**.[370] Another important function subordinate to this is the referential function of "reminder" apparent from various expressions like οιδατε (2:1; 3:3), καθως οιδατε (1:5; 2:2, 3:3), μνημονευετε (2:9), etc., whereby the

---

[364] Koskenniemi, 1956, 146.

[365] Koskenniemi, 1956, 147.

[366] Thraede, 1970, 95-7. In view of Mullins' criticism (1973, 350-58) it is unlikely that one has to do with a parousia "form" in 2:17-3:13 as Funk has tried to demonstrate (1967, 249-68).

[367] Thraede (1970, 96) gives among other examples the oculi/animus instance in Cicero, Fam 15.16.2.

[368] While recognizing this motive as an epistolary commonplace, Thraede (1970, 96-7) does not see any reflection of conventional phraseology in these utterances.

[369] Berger, 1974, 201.

[370] Boers, 1975-76, 147. Cf. Koskenniemi (1956, 35 ff.) on this function.

addressees were reminded of various aspects of the initial gospel event. Given the fact of Timothy's visit, the references to the senders' attempts to make a return visit (2:17 ff.) are also most likely references to things already known by the addressees, as was of course Timothy's visit itself. As with the reminders in 1:5 and 2:1 ff., these references provide the occasion for expressions of the author's loving concern for and goodwill towards the addressees. For the persuasive appeals served by these expressive and referential features see 4.1.2-4.2.6 below.

3.2.2   I Thess 4:1-5:24: A Predominant Conative Function

This latter major functional text-sequence within the letter-body is quite obviously characterized by the predominance of the verbally explicit conative function of communication expressed variously throughout the passage. It comes to expression in the admonitions regarding αγιασμος (4:3-8),[371] in the announcement of new information to be provided (ου   δε υμας αγνοειν, 4:13), and in the recurrence of imperatives (4:18; 5:11, 13, 14-22) and of hortatory subjunctives (5:6, 8).[372] Above all, it comes into focus in the ερωτωμεν υμας και παρακαλουμεν expression opening the section in 4:1 and various iterations of this as παρακαλουμεν δε υμας (4:10), ερωτωμεν δε υμας (5:12) and παρακαλουμεν δε υμας (5:14).

From the many examples cited by H.A. Steen it is quite clear that both ερωτω and παρακαλω, occurring separately or in combination, were extremely common conative verbs used in Hellenistic letters.[373] Steen refers to them as epistolary "clichés" and describes them from both a grammatical and a rhetorical perspective. He cites ancient rhetors and grammarians' observations that the use of the pure imperative was considered to have a blunt, harsh character and notes how this was attenuated by various types of periphrasis both in orations and in letters.[374] Two basic formulations become apparent in Steen's four constructions, within which the N.T. instances isolated by C.J. Bjerkelund can also be included:[375] 1) Steen's first three types of construction actually involve three different formulations of the subsequent proposition, viz., an imperatival (cf. I Thess 5:14), an infinitival (cf. I Thess 5:12), or a ινα/οπως clause (cf. I Thess 4:1), all governed by the same use of the first singular or plural person, present, indicative of παρακαλω, ερωτω, or both terms in conjunction.

---

[371]   As Rigaux observes (1956, 502), whether one follows Dibelius (1937, 20) in taking the infinitives απεχεσθαι, etc., in this passage as imperatival or as explicative as Rigaux himself does (500), the sense remains the same.

[372]   In the exhortation ωστε παρακαλειτε αλληλους εν τοις λογοις τουτοις, in 4:18, the SM τοις λογοις τουτοις delimits 4:13-17 so that by way of the imperative the otherwise predominantly informative aim of this passage becomes subordinate to the overall dominant conative aim of 4:1-5:24.

[373]   Steen, 1938, 133-8, 150-1.

[374]   Steen, 1938, 123-5.

[375]   Bjerkelund, 1967, 13-17. For examples from the epistolary papyri Bjerkelund (35 ff.) also refers to Steen.

2) His fourth type, not represented in Pauline usage, involves the passive aorist participle παρακληθεις or ερωτηθεις followed by an imperatival clause. Both of these basic types may occur with or without the explicit occurrence of such elements as δε/ουν, σε/υμας, or πατερ/αδελφε/κυριε, etc., or some combination thereof.

3.2.2.1 A Criticism of C. J. Bjerkelund's Form-Critical Method

Since the sense of such verbs as παρακαλω/ερωτω contribute to the signalling of the type of communicative act constituted by 4:1-5:24, it is necessary to consider the significance of Bjerkelund's form-critical analysis of παρακαλω sentences. He insists on the "epistolary" character of the particular "form" of such sentences and thereby imports the urbane sense of "request" in every instance where the form occurs in Paul's letters, as opposed to the religious-ethically oriented sense of "exhort."[376] From scattered references this "form" turns out to be παρακαλω ουν/δε υμας/σε with the verb in sentence-initial position.[377] However, out of the nineteen examples he gives from Paul alone, only eleven have this sort of formulation.[378] It should be observed here that the presence or absence of connectives such as δε, ουν, etc., depends on the immediate co-text, while σε/υμας must be understood as implicit even if not made explicit, given the explicit conative force of the verbs involved. While the sentence-initial position of the verb is the general rule, Steen gives at least one example where it falls at the end of the sentence.[379]

However, wherever there are clear examples of παρακαλω used with the sense "exhort" ("ermahnen") or "encourage" in N.T. letters (e.g., I Tim 2:1; 6:2) or in non-epistolary, Hellenistic literature, Bjerkelund is at pains to use whatever formal deviations there are from the παρακαλω ουν υμας "form" or the sentence-initial position of the verb to disqualify such instances as evidence for a comparative hortatory sense in Pauline παρακαλω sentences.[380] On the other hand, in support of the non-hortatory, petitionary sense he feels free to draw upon examples in decrees and political petitions addressed to kings in which the verbal elements παρακαλει, παρακαλων, etc., are used, but in which the particular form he has isolated is absent.[381] This procedure is unacceptably arbitrary.

In actual fact, the "form" that Bjerkelund has isolated amounts to no more than the basic formal characteristics of the "performative" use of verbs like παρακαλω and ερωτω. This formulation arises out of the more general need to make a request or express one's will explicitly in accordance with the general constraints of the language code. This involves the use of explicit conative verbs in the first singular or

---

[376] Bjerkelund, 1967, 32, 110 -11, 188.

[377] Bjerkelund, 1967, 22, 76-8, 83, (or with αδελφοι added) 188.

[378] Bjerkelund, 1967, 13-17.

[379] Steen, 1938, 133: αλλα ταχειον ποιησαι παρακαλω (Oslo 60, 7).

[380] See Bjerkelund, 1967, 32, 76-8, 83-4.

[381] Bjerkelund, 1967, 65-72.

plural person and in the present indicative, with the content of the request, plea, etc., either understood from the context or made explicit in a subsequent proposition. Such a usage has the function of both making explicit and categorizing the "illocutionary" force of the utterance in which it occurs.[382] In other words, performative verbs both explicitly **say** and **describe** what they **do**.[383] This observation as well as the fact that the conative force is also commonly expressed in participial form in letters clearly show that the "form" Bjerkelund isolates cannot be understood as being "epistolary" ("briefliche") as such.[384]

On the other hand, as G.N. Leech observes, the use of explicit performatives in everyday speech is something highly unusual and occurs when a language user is in particular need of clearly defining the type of speech act he or she is making.[385] This need may be seen to be particularly required in letters in the absence of face-to-face communication where the force of, e.g., an imperative can be inferred from immediate contextual and paralinguistic factors. Consequently, it is the **typical occurrence** of such performatives and other verbally explicit indications of illocutionary force that should be seen as characteristic of letters rather than the "form" of explicit performatives as being epistolary in character.

As observed in speech-act theory of linguistics, **command, request, beg, counsel**, etc., are performative verbs which not only intend to cause the hearer to do something but also reflect a wide variation in the degree of intensity of urging.[386] In this regard, Bjerkelund has made a substantial contribution in establishing the neutral degree of intensity associated with παρακαλω as a "dignified and urbane expression of urging, in which both commanding and subservience are absent."[387] As he observes, this conclusion is supported by Paul's own explicit contrast between επιτασσω and παρακαλω in Phlm 8-9 when making a personal request with regard to the practical matter of the slave Onesimus.[388]

However, as noted above, it is questionable when he specifies the sense of the verb as a "dignified **request**" for Paul's παρακαλω sentences in general, in view of the religious-ethical contents so introduced in texts such as Rom 12:1 ff.; I Thess 4:1, 10b; 5:14, etc. While such contents may be seen to give reason for taking παρακαλω in the sense of "exhort" here,[389] its combination (4:1) and alternation (5:12, 14) with ερωτω advises against going quite so far in this direction. Rather, in view of Steen's

---

[382] Leech (1983, 181 ff.) refers to its "metalinguistic" function by which it is self-descriptive. However, since a focus on "utterance" rather than on "sentence" is involved, it would be more correct to call it a "metacommunicative" function.

[383] Cf. Partridge, 1982, 18 ff., 40, 138-9.

[384] Bjerkelund, 1967, 111, 189.

[385] Leech, 1983, 181.

[386] See, e.g., Searle, 1975a, 355; Partridge, 1982, 89 ff.

[387] Bjerkelund, 1967, 110.

[388] Bjerkelund, 1967, 118.

[389] As, e.g., Luth, KJV, RV, RSV, NTSB, render it.

general observation of a rhetorically attenuating function of such expressions and Bjerkelund's documentation of the neutral, dignified force of παρακαλω, and in view of the specifically exhortatory discourse these verbs introduce here, it appears that both verbs should be taken to have a neutral, dignified sense best represented by "urge" and "appeal" in English: "we urge you and appeal to you" (4:1, JB).

Bjerkelund cannot avoid the significance of these religious-ethical contents thus introduced in I Thess by otherwise correctly noting that the focus is on περισσευητε μαλλον both here and in 4:10b.[390] In these instances, περισσευειν has the substitutionary function of a pro-verb so that the religious-ethical contents of both περιπατειν και αρεσκειν θεῳ (4:1) and αγαπαν αλληλους (4:9) are unavoidably integral semantic aspects of the contents of both παρακαλω sentences.

3.2.2.2 Some General Conclusions on I Thess 4:1-5:24

Thus, while the performative παρακαλω/ερωτω expressions are typical of private and official epistolary style, it is wrong to use their "performative" form to import the sense of "request" for παρακαλω from mundane epistolary contexts into religious-ethical contexts in Paul's letters. Rather, one should see here an integration of the conventions of epistolary petition with the conventions of exhortatory discourse (see 8.2.2.2). While the performative expressions of the clause ερωτωμεν υμας και παρακαλουμεν in 4:1 (with iterations in 4:10b, 5:12, 14) qualify as 1.2.2SM delimiting 4:1-5:24 as a basically conative functional text-sequence, the distinctly religious-ethical exhortation in 4:1-12 (see 4.4.3) and 5:12-24 (see 4.4.10) and the dissuasion-consolation in 4:13-5:11 (see 4.4.6 and 4.4.8) preclude a typical epistolary function of petition as the particular type of conative function governing the whole passage. Rather, the overarching, predominant function of the whole passage is best described on the most general level as "conative."

Finally, whereas it was necessary in 1:2-3:13 to guard against Berger's tendency to neglect the distinctly epistolary by emphasizing the non-epistolary characteristics, here it has been necessary to guard against Bjerkelund's tendency to suppress non-epistolary in favor of epistolary features.

3.2.3 Temporal and Spatial Features of Coherence and Delimitation

In taking up temporal and spatial features of textual coherence and delimitation here, it must be made clear that these features contribute primarily to the semantic-syntactic text-coherence of the passages in question. As such they supplement the primarily text-pragmatic observations made above. Their value for the question of delimitation is limited basically to delimitations within 1:2-3:13 and between 1:2-3:13 and 4:1-5:24 and not between these sequences and the prescript and letter-closing.

When one speaks or writes, the relative temporal perspective of the various utterances that make up the text is usually anchored in the speaker or writer's **now**, although this may also include being anchored in public time.[391] This present time of

---

[390] Bjerkelund, 1967, 130-1

the speaker's utterance functions as an axis of orientation for both the speaker and the addressee and is the primary point of orientation for the verbal tense system and other temporal markers such as temporal adverbs, modal auxiliaries and other expressions.

While the temporal orientational system is basically binary with the "now" oriented to the speaker and the "then" oriented away from the speaker, the "then" subsumes both the past and the future so as to give what has ordinarily been understood as a three-part past/present/future system.[392] In describing these temporal aspects of a text one could also avoid the general past/future terminology and refer instead to an author-antecedent or an author-subsequent focus relative to the author's present.

As implied in 1.5.4 above, temporal and spatial features in texts are generally closely associated. In many situations the "now/then" temporal deictics are often closely aligned with "here/there" spatial deictics.[393] In the case of I Thess the spatial deictics are relevant only for the delimitation of 1:2-3:13 and subsequences.

3.2.3.1 Temporal and Spatial Features in I Thess 1-3

Throughout 1:2-3:13 the author's present comes to expression in various expressions of goodwill in the thanksgiving/prayer-reports (1:2-3; 2:13; 3:9-10), the expressions of joy (2:19-20; 3:8-9), and the expressions of remembrance (1:2-3; 3:6b). It is also realized in the various expressions of reminder, $ειδοτες$, $οιδατε$, $μνημονευετε$, etc. (1:3, 5;2:1, 2, 5, 9, 10, 11; 3:4), that occur.

However, everything that is commonly referred to as tense is not necessarily oriented to the author's present. For instance, when Paul defends the character of the apostles' $παρακλησις$ and asserts that $ουτως$ $λαλουμεν$ with regard to their being approved by God to be entrusted with the gospel, such a statement is a generalization that is not specifically anchored in the author's present.[394] On the other hand, such generalizations as are involved in the thanksgiving/prayer-reports ($ευχαριστουμεν...παντοτε...αδιαλειπτως$) serve to focus the present attitude of the addressers towards the addressees and as such focus on the author's present in the text.

Relative to this author-present axis there is a dominant author-antecedent focus that generally distinguishes 1:2-3:13 from 4:1-5:24. The latter part of the complex 1ThM noted in 4.1.1 below introduces the theme of the addressees' "election": (MBref) $ειδοτες$ (R1.2) $την$ $εκλογην$ $υμων$ (1:4). Their "election" is then treated historically in terms of the initial gospel event involving the addressers and addressees: $οτι$ $το$ $ευαγγελιον$ $ημων$ $ουκ$ $εγενηθη$ $εις$ $υμας$ $εν$ $λογω$ $μονον$ $αλλα$ $και$ $εν$ $δυναμει$ $κτλ$. (1:5 ff.). This event of the more distant past is repeatedly referred to in primarily the aorist tense and commented upon in 1:4-2:16. Then subsequent events of the more recent past, starting with the time after the senders' founding of the Thessalonian church, are again referred to in the aorist tense, viz.,

---

[391] See Traugott/Pratt, 1980, 277-79; Bull, 1960, 7-8.

[392] Thus, Traugott/Pratt, 1980, 278.

[393] Traugott/Pratt, 1980, 275-7.

[394] For such a distinction see Traugott/Pratt, 1980, 279.

references to unsuccessful attempts to make a return visit (2:17 f.) and to Timothy's visit and return with good news (3:1 ff.), which is described as having brought comfort ($\pi\alpha\rho\epsilon\kappa\lambda\eta\theta\eta\mu\epsilon\nu$) to the senders (3:7).

The preceding reminders of past events culminate in 3:8, $o\tau\iota$ $\nu\upsilon\nu$ $\zeta\omega\mu\epsilon\nu$ $\epsilon\alpha\nu$ $\upsilon\mu\epsilon\iota\varsigma$ $\sigma\tau\eta\kappa\epsilon\tau\epsilon$ $\epsilon\nu$ $\kappa\upsilon\rho\iota\omega$, which expresses both satisfaction and implicit concern (see under 4.2.4). It constitutes a transitional point to a final, combined expression of thanksgiving and joy in 3:9. The conditional clause, $\epsilon\alpha\nu$ $\upsilon\mu\epsilon\iota\varsigma$ $\sigma\tau\eta\kappa\epsilon\tau\epsilon$ $\epsilon\nu$ $\kappa\upsilon\rho\iota\omega$, may be seen as anticipating the transition to a predominant focus on the future together with the prayer-report (3:10) and the petitions of the wish-prayer (3:11-13). Here the author's present is expressed in $\delta\epsilon o\mu\epsilon\nu o\iota$ (3:10) and in the wishes expressed in the optatives (3:11-13), while the focus is on the future in the references to a future visit and to the addressees' continued religious-ethical development.[395] Thus, although the "visit" theme includes these verses within the text-sequence of 2:17-3:13, the focus on author-present and author-subsequent time as well as on the religious-ethical contents anticipates the following sequence of 4:1-5:24 and indicates the transitional character of the sub-sequence 3:9-13 (see 4.3).[396]

As for the spatial features in this passage, there is the initial PCab realized in 1:5c by $\epsilon\gamma\epsilon\nu\eta\theta\eta\mu\epsilon\nu$ ($\epsilon\nu$) $\upsilon\mu\iota\nu$ in connection with the initial gospel-event. This is iterated variously until one comes to a PCrel realized in 2:17 by $\alpha\pi o\rho\phi\alpha\nu\iota\sigma\theta\epsilon\nu\tau\epsilon\varsigma$ $\alpha\phi'\upsilon\mu\omega\nu$ indicating the event of departure (see 4.1.1 and 4.2.1). This is followed in turn by the PCrel $\kappa\alpha\tau\alpha\lambda\epsilon\iota\phi\theta\eta\nu\alpha\iota$ $\epsilon\nu$ $A\theta\eta\nu\alpha\iota\varsigma$ (3:1) and $\epsilon\lambda\theta o\nu\tau o\varsigma$ $T\iota\mu o\theta\epsilon o\upsilon$ $\pi\rho o\varsigma$ $\eta\mu\alpha\varsigma$ $\alpha\phi'\upsilon\mu\omega\nu$ (3:6) marking the events of Timothy's subsequent departure and return in visiting the addressees (see 4.2.3). This progression of relative spatial correlations is also paralleled by the series of TCrel markers $\alpha\pi o\rho\phi\alpha\nu\iota\sigma\theta\epsilon\nu\tau\epsilon\varsigma...\pi\rho o\varsigma$ $\kappa\alpha\iota\rho o\nu$ $\omega\rho\alpha\varsigma$ (2:17), $\mu\eta\kappa\epsilon\tau\iota$ $\sigma\tau\epsilon\gamma o\nu\tau\epsilon\varsigma$ (3:1), and $\epsilon\lambda\theta o\nu\tau o\varsigma$ (3:6). Together with the PCrel these help mark out the progression of main events after the initial gospel-event for which no explicit TCab is expressed, events which lead up to the event of the letter itself.

This sequence of PCab followed by PCrel and TCrel types of markers contribute to the coherence of 1:2-3:13 and to its delimitation as a whole from 4:1-5:24 which is not characterized by any such narrative-like sequence of events. They also contribute to the delimitation of the subsequences 1:2-2:16 and 2:17-3:13. The former is characterized by a **"there** with you" focus and the latter by an "away from you" focus in which there may be an implicit progression to a more specific **"here** away from you" focus implicit in $\nu\upsilon\nu$ $\zeta\omega\mu\epsilon\nu$ $\kappa\tau\lambda$. (3:8).

---

[395] Patte (1983a, 130; 1983, 89, 103) fails to acknowledge the future focus here. His somewhat rigid association of the past and future with the warranting level obviously gets into trouble at this point, for what would such future references warrant with regard to the expression of present will or wanting on the dialogic level?

[396] Rigaux (1956, 493) tends to associate the transition to a future perspective too exclusively with 4:1 ff. With this future outlook already anticipated in 3:8 ff., the transition is less "artificial" than he judges it to be.

3.2.3.2   Temporal Features in I Thess 4-5

In contrast to this predominant focus on the past in the sequence of 1:2-3:13 as a whole, there is a predominant author-subsequent or future focus in 4:1-5:24.[397] Here the author's present is realized by the expressions of urging and exhortation (4:1, 10b; 5:12, 14), of reminder (οιδατε, 4:2) of not really needing to write on a particular topic (4:13, 15) and of wanting to inform the addressees on a particular topic (4:13, 15). It is also expressed by the imperatives (4:18; 5:11, 13b, 14-22) and the hortatory subjunctives (5:6, 8), insofar as these express the will of the author.

Otherwise, these imperatives and hortatory subjunctives focus on activities, relationships and attitudes to which the addressees are being urged and which thus have an author-subsequent perspective. This future focus is also realized in the ινα clauses urging the addressees to progress more and more in leading a life that is pleasing to God (4:1), to live decorously (4:12), and not to grieve as those without hope (4:13). It is also realized in the infinitival clauses that describe the ethical behaviour that the addressees must continue to adhere to in accordance with divine will and previous instruction (4:3-11). Besides this predominant focus, there are, of course, intermittent references to past events such as past instruction (4:1, 2, 11) and the death of Jesus Christ (4:14; 5:10).

The closing wish-prayer gathers the preceding religious-ethical and eschatological topics in summarizing petitions for the complete sanctification and preservation of the addressees at the parousia (5:23). The author-subsequent futurity and the ultimate divine source of this sanctification and preservation are finally expressed in the closing utterance: πιστος ο καλων υμας, ος και ποιησει (5:24).

These semantic-syntactic considerations not only serve to support the previous pragmatic evidence of coherence and delimitation for these two major text-sequences, but will also be useful later on in the consideration of intertextual features of the body of I Thessalonians (see ch. 8). Thus, I Thess 1:2-3:13 and 4:1-5:24 may be seen as constituting a third level of sequential-hierarchical text-sequences which may be represented as follows in Figure 3:[398]

---

[397] Generally noted by, e.g. Rigaux, 1956, 493, Ellingworth/Nida, 1976, 73; Marxsen, 1979, 26.

[398] Lee/Lee (1975, 39) arrive at these same major delimitations in their primarily semantic analysis.

LEVEL III

I Thess 1:2-3:13	4:1-5:24
1.2.1SMind, PCab Prominence of Explicit Expressive Function. Predominant Present-Past Perspective.	1.2.2SM, C Prominence of Explicit Conative Function. Predominant Present-Future Perspective.

Figure 3

Chapter 4

A TEXT-LINGUISTIC/RHETORICAL ANALYSIS OF THE LETTER-BODY

The following is a text-linguistically and rhetorically informed analysis of the coherence and delimitation of subordinate text-sequences within 1:2-3:13 and 4:1-5:24. Among other things, this will serve to provide a more rigorously text-centered basis for interpreting the rhetorical character and purpose(s) of the letter in view of the totality of functional relations observable among these sequences and their subsequences. While the primary focus will be on the pragmatic dimension in terms of rhetorical strategies, supporting observations of text-semantic and text-syntactic indications of coherence and delimitation will also be brought in. In view of the rhetorical emphasis, the communicative context and more specifically the rhetorical situation will play a more prominent role here than in the preceding analyses of 2.2.2 above.

4.1 ANALYSIS OF I THESS 1:2-2:16 AND SUBSEQUENCES

4.1.1 The Delimitation and Coherence of 1:2-2:16

I Thess 1:2-2:16, as the first major subsequence of 1:2-3:13, is delimited by the theme of "election" introduced by the last member, 1ThM(P1.2), of the complex thematic marker 1ThM: (MBexpr) ευχαριστουμεν τω θεω παντοτε (P1) περι παντων υμων (MBexpr) μνειαν ποιουμενοι επι των προσευχων ημων, αδιαλειπτως μνημονευοντες (P1.1) υμων του εργου της πιστεως και του κοπου της αγαπης και της υπομονης της ελπιδος κτλ., (MBref) ειδοτες (P1.2) την εκλογην υμων (1:2-4).[399] In this complex ThM the thematic focus narrows from "all of you" (P1) to the theme of the "practical outworking of your faith, love and hope" (P1.1), and from this to the theme of "your election" (P1.2).

---

[399] Koskenniemi (1956. 146) shows that μνειαν ποιεισθαι and μνημονευειν are used synonymously in conventional epistolary usage and gives examples from the first century where they are virtually technical terms for remembrance in prayer. This speaks strongly for taking μνημονευοντες here as a recurrence of the preceding μνειαν ποιουμενοι. In this way αδιαλειπτως may be taken as naturally modifying μνημονευοντες. Thus, the report of thanksgiving and of "prayer-remembrance" culminates naturally in the solemn expression εμπροσθεν του θεου και πατρος ημων, giving 1:2-3 a relative unity of its own. Cf. Rigaux (1956, 361-2), Lightfoot (1909, 12) and Wiles (1974, 8) who similarly see a relative unity here, although not on the same basis.

This reference to the practical outworking of the addressees' Christian life in P1.1 may be seen as thematically focusing the entire message of 1:2-5:24, both regarding the past (1:4 ff.) and the future (4:1 ff.). The frequency of the faith-love-hope triad in the N. T. suggests that it served as a "sort of compendium of the Christian life" in the early church.[400] That the stress is not on the graces as such here, but on their actualization in the addressees' every-day life and activity, is particularly indicated by the accompanying triad of "work," "labour" and "patient endurance." The three graces are respectively related to each of these aspects by way of subjective genitives.[401] In support of seeing this complex triad as constituting a general reference to the addressees' "Christian life," it may be observed that it easily qualifies as an instance of a complex **synecdoche** which, among other types of substitutional devices, involves the representation of the whole through a part.[402] Here the work-labour-endurance elements may be seen as representing the "life" aspect and the faith-love-hope elements as representing the "Christian" aspect of the general concept "your Christian life."

The subsequent theme of election in P1.2, emphasised by the parenthetical address αδελφοι ηγαπημενοι υπο (του) θεου, is specified further in the following οτι clause in the historical dimension by way of the two primary aspects of the initial gospel-event: 1) the apostles' mediation of the gospel: οτι το ευαγγελιον ημων ουκ εγενηθη εις υμας εν λογω μονον αλλα και εν δυναμει και εν πνευματι αγιω και (εν) πληροφορια πολλη, καθως οιδατε οιοι εγενηθημεν (εν) υμιν δι' υμας, and 2) the addressees' reception of it: και υμεις μιμηται ημων εγενηθητε και του κυριου, δεξαμενοι τον λογον εν θλιψει πολλη μετα χαρας πνευματος αγιου. From the reference to the addressees' reception of the gospel with their "tribulation" and "joy of the Holy Spirit" (supplying the content of the imitation),[403] Paul launches into a praise of their exemplary faith (1:7-8) which leads back again to a reiteration of the two aspects of the initial gospel-event: 1) οποιαν εισοδον εσχομεν προς υμας, 2) και πως επεστρεψατε προς τον θεον κτλ. (1:9 f.). These two aspects subsequently become the themes that are expanded respectively in 2:1-12 and 2:13-16. The former one is focused on in the 1.1ThM of 2:1: (MBrep) αυτοι...οιδατε (P) την εισοδον ημων την προς υμας οτι ου κενη γεγονεν, and the latter one in the 1.2ThM of 2:13: (P) δια τουτο (MBexpr) και ημεις ευχαριστουμεν τω θεω (P) οτι...εδεξασθε ου λογον ανθρωπων αλλα καθως εστιν αληθως λογον θεου.

In connection with various aspects of the initial gospel-event treated in 1:2-2:16 there is the striking lexical recurrence of the verb γινεσθαι in 1:5, 6, 7; 2:1, 5, 7, 8, 10, 14 which contributes to the coherence of the sequence in the text-syntactic dimension.[404] Beginning with 2:17 ff. there is a transition to the "visit" theme noted in

---

[400] Thus Hunter, 1961, 33-5. For a discussion giving arguments for its pre-Pauline character and literature on the topic see esp. Conzelmann, 1975, 229-30.

[401] See, e.g., Wiles, 1974, 178-80.

[402] See Plett, 1979a, 72-3.

[403] See, e.g., Frame (1912, 82), Best (1977, 77), and Pobee (1985, 69) who take δεξαμενοι as an aorist of identical action rather than of antecedent action in relation to εγενηθητε.

4.2.1 below. This delimitation is corroborated further by spatial markers. The initial gospel-event introduced under the theme of "your election" is accompanied by an absolute spatial co-ordinator, PCab, realized by εγενηθημεν (εν) υμιν (1:5c).[405] This is reiterated by εισοδον εσχομεν προς υμας (1:9); την εισοδον ημων την προς υμας (2:1), and εγενηθημεν...εν μεσω υμων (2:7). A transition to the text-sequence of 2:17-3:13 is marked by the PCrel απορφανισθεντες αφ' υμων (2:17).[406]

4.1.2 The Rhetoric of 1:2-10

The report of thanksgiving and remembrance of the addressees in prayer (1:2-3) opens the passage with an **ethos** appeal: they have the addressees' spiritual welfare at heart. In 1:4 ειδοτες...την εκλογην υμων gives the cause for the thanksgiving/prayer-report. It is a major exegetical problem as to whether the subsequent οτι clause is to be taken epexegetically ("that," "how that") or as causal ("for," "because").[407] If it is epexegetical, Paul must be seen as mentioning their election with a view to specifying it in terms of the manner and circumstances in which it initially came about. If it is causal, then Paul must be seen as primarily interested in arguing that the addressees were indeed elected by God. In his rhetorical analysis, G. A. Kennedy follows the latter alternative, taking 1:4 ff. as an **enthymeme**.[408]

However, J.B. Lightfoot's observation regarding the idiomatic character of ειδεναι τι οτι, used universally in the N.T. with the epexegetical sense, must be taken seriously here.[409] Furthermore, the focus in 1:5 ff. is not on the presence of the Holy Spirit as proof of divine election, but rather as one indication (besides "power" and "much conviction") of the genuine character of the senders' proclamation of the gos-

---

[404] This phenomenon was already noted previously by Schubert, 1939, 19-20.

[405] On first sight εις υμας in οτι το ευαγγελιον ημων ουκ εγενηθη εις· υμας εν λογω μονον κτλ. (1:5a) would seem to qualify as the first explicit PCrel. However, with ευαγγελιον being a nomen actionis (Friedrich, 1964, 729), it is more likely that εγενηθη does not have the sense of "came," as rendered in most translations, but rather the sense of "happened," "came about" with the preposition taken referentially rather than locatively: "our proclamation of the gospel did not come about for you only in words," etc. Similarly, e.g., Friedrich (1976, 211-13), Masson (1957, 19-20), Dobschütz (1909, 70) as against, e.g., Marxsen (1979, 33, 36-7), Best (1977, 64, 74), Rigaux (1956, 373-4).

[406] Lee/Lee (1975, 37) arrive at the same delimitation of 1:2-2:16 on the basis of thematic content alone.

[407] Regarding this problem see, e.g., Dobschütz (1909, 70), Frame (1912, 78) and Marxsen (1979, 34) who hold to a causal sense, while, e.g., Lightfoot (1904, 12), Dibelius (1937, 4), Rigaux (1956, 272-73) and Best (1977, 73) hold to an epexegetical sense.

[408] Kennedy, 1984, 142; see 1.5.1 above. See also Lyons (1985, 189) who speaks in terms of "proofs."

pel: το ευαγγελιον ημων ουκ εγενηθη...εν λογω μονον αλλα και εν δυναμει και εν πνευματι αγιω και (εν) πληροφορια πολλῃ (1:5).⁴¹⁰ As noted, το ευαγγελιον ημων specifies την εκλεκτην υμων in terms of its historical realization. Besides the more objective testimony (δυναμις, πνευμα αγιον) to the genuine character of their mediation of the gospel, there is the more subjective testimony of their own "great conviction":⁴¹¹ πληροφορια πολλῃ. The pro-modifier οιοι in the subsequent reminder of the senders' character (καθως οιδατε οιοι εγενηθημεν (εν) υμιν δι' υμας) requires this subjective denotation for πληροφορια πολλῃ over against an objective one such as "abundance of every kind,"⁴¹² since it would otherwise have nothing in 1:5a with which it could reasonably corefer.⁴¹³ Thus, the senders' knowledge of the addressees' election as historically realized in the initial gospel-event not only gives the cause for the thanksgiving/prayer report but also constitutes a "reminder" of the genuine character of the senders themselves and their part in the gospel-event. This clearly constitutes an **ethos** appeal.⁴¹⁴

In 1:6 Paul proceeds to describe the character of the addressees' part in the initial gospel-event: και υμεις μιμηται ημων εγενηθητε και του κυριου, δεξαμενοι τον λογον εν θλιψει πολλῃ μετα χαρας πνευματος αγιου. The previous reference "what sort of men we were among you for your sakes" prepares for the theme of imitation here, although the imitation is not only of the missionaries but also of the Lord. This feature plus the emphatic pronoun in και υμεις marking the transition to focus on the addressees speaks for taking the και as both conjunctive and ascensive: "and indeed you on your part." The reference to imitation has an indirect parenetic function as observed by A.J. Malherbe.⁴¹⁵ At the same time, the inclusion of the senders with the Lord as examples for imitation should be seen as aimed at strengthening the addressor-addressee ties via a **pathos** appeal to the emotion

---

⁴⁰⁹ Lightfoot, 1904, 12. To give a more detailed account of this, there appear to be two types of the construction ειδεναι τι οτι. Type I: In I Cor 16:15, II Cor 12:3-4 and I Thess 2:1 the τι element is the subject of the οτι clause drawn forward as the accusative object of the ειδεναι element. Type II: In Rom 13:11 and here in I Thess 1:4-5 the τι element is constituted by a word or nominal phrase representing a general concept or idea which is then specified in the οτι clause. The same construction occurs with other verbs of mental perception. All such instances belong to type II mentioned above: γινωσκειν (II Cor 8:9; Phil 2:22), αγνοειν (Rom 11:25) and βλεπειν (I Cor 1:26). This last instance serves as a striking parallel: Βλεπετε γαρ την κλησιν υμων, αδελφοι, οτι ου πολλοι σοφοι κατα σαρκα, κτλ. Both here and in I Thess 1:5 the οτι is best rendered as "how that" rather than simply "that."

⁴¹⁰ The ου...αλλα και formulation is climactic rather than adversative. See Holtz (1986, 46, n. 84).

⁴¹¹ Thus, e.g., Dobschütz (1909, 71) and Best (1977, 75-6) as against, e.g., Rigaux (1956, 377-8) and Holtz (1986, 47).

⁴¹² Against Rigaux' (1956, 375, 377-8) stylistic argument, Paul can clearly mix subjective and objective realities in tripartite accumulations, as in Rom 13:13, I Cor 1:26 and Gal 5:26.

of "emulation" towards those in possession of emulative characteristics.[416]

The addressees' imitation is qualified specifically in terms of the great tribulation they endured with the joy of the Holy Spirit. This particular experience then provides the context and the basis (ωστε) for the subsequent amplification of the addressees' spiritual status and progress by way of the more explicit **laudatio** in 1:7-8: ωστε γενεσθαι υμας τυπον πασιν τοις πιστευουσιν εν τῃ Μακεδονιᾳ και εν τῃ Αχαιᾳ. αφ' υμων γαρ εξηχηται ο λογος του κυριου ου μονον εν τῃ Μακεδονιᾳ και (εν τῃ) Αχαιᾳ, αλλ' εν παντι τοπῳ η πιστις υμων η προς τον θεον εξεληλυθεν, ωστε μη χρειαν εχειν ημας λαλειν τι. The denial of needing to say anything heightens the praise and prepares for the explanatory allusion in 1:9-10 to the witness given (presumably by the other believers in Macedonia and Achaia) regarding the character of both the senders and the addressees' participation in the initial gospel-event:[417] αυτοι γαρ περι ημων απαγγελλουσιν οποιον εισοδον εσχομεν προς υμας, και πως επεστρεψατε προς τον θεον απο των ειδωλων δουλευειν θεῳ ζωντι και αληθινῳ και αναμενειν τον υιον αυτου εκ των ουρανων, ον ηγειρεν εκ (των) νεκρων, Ιησουν τον ρυομενον ημας εκ της οργης της ερχομενης. Thus, the praise continues **ab nostra persona**, a persuasive strategy typical of **exordia**.[418] At the same time, such a reference to the witness or opinion of others is mentioned by Aristotle as a strategy of **ethos** appeals.[419]

Besides this more explicit praise that pervades 1:6-10, there is also implicit praise of the practical outworking of the addressees' faith, love and hope in the initial prayerful remembrance (1:3). While appropriate praise of the audience is a typical means of **ethos** appeal, the specific context of tribulation (1:6b) gives the praise an additional persuasive dimension, viz., that of a **pathos** appeal to the emotion of confidence as opposed to that of fear. Whether actually current or an ever-present threat,

---

[413] Similarly, e.g., Dobschütz, 1909, 71-72.

[414] Cf. Aristotle, Rhet 3.16.5., where references to anything indicating the rhetor's virtue are appropriate in the narratio.

[415] Malherbe, 1983, 246.

[416] See Aristotle, Rhet 2.11.1-7, although one must supply Christian contents to the emulative characteristics. For Aristotle they are, among other things, ανδρια, σοφια, αρχη (2.11.5); for Paul here it is specifically bearing tribulations with the joy of the Holy Spirit.

[417] See Best (1977, 85-87) for comments and references to the pertinent literature regarding those exegetes who see pre-Pauline confessional material or summary of Gentile-oriented preaching material reflected here.

[418] See Lausberg (1973, 157) on this rhetorical aspect. The return in 1:9 to the double "we/you" focus on the gospel-event initiated in 1:5-6 speaks strongly in favour of seeing an inclusive "we" in περι ημων. An exclusive reference to the senders in this "we" raises unnecessary difficulties with unlikely solutions for which see, e.g., Dibelius (1937, 6) and Holtz (1986, 54).

[419] Rhet 3.17.16; cf. Wörner, 1984, 59.

tribulation would be bound to engender fear. Likewise, the prospect of eschatological wrath could also be a source of fear. Thus, the reference to Jesus' salvation from the approaching wrath in the concluding eschatological climax may be taken as another **pathos** appeal to confidence. Finally, the use of the inclusive "we" to express solidarity with regard to mutual participation both in the gospel event (1:9a) and in the eschatological consumation of salvation (1:10c) serves as another means of **ethos** appeal.

It may be observed here that there is a prominence of the **pathos** type of appeal in 1:2-10 in distinction to the subsequent text-sequence where inartificial and quasi-logical types of appeal are particularly prominent (see 4.1.3.2).

4.1.3 The Delimitation and Coherence of 1:2-10

With regard to the coherence and delimitation of 1:2-10 the following features have relevance. The presentation of the witness of others in 1:9-10 has the function of summarizing and emphasizing the two aspects of the gospel-event introduced in 1:5-6 (to be respectively treated in 2:1-12 and 2:13-16). This may be seen in the general conceptual recurrence between $εισοδον$ $εσχομεν$ $προς$ $υμας$ and $το$ $ευαγγελιον$ $ημων...εγενηθη$ $εις$ $υμας$ (1:5) and between $επεστρεψατε$ $προς$ $τον$ $θεον$ and $δεξαμενοι$ $το$ $λογον$ (1:6), with the pro-modifiers $οποιον$ and $πως$ summarizing the qualitative character asserted for each of these aspects of the initial gospel event.[420] Furthermore, the renewed focus in 1:9b-10 on the addressees's entry and progress in the Christian faith strikingly echoes the similar focus in the prayer-report in 1:3. This echo is apparent in the general triadic conceptual recurrence that serves as a general frame for the whole text-sequence:

1. The addressees' $εργου$ $της$ $πιστεως$ may be seen as echoed in $πως$ $επεστρεψατε$ $προς$ $τον$ $θεον$ $απο$ $των$ $ειδωλων$,

2. their $κοπου$ $της$ $αγαπης$ as echoed in $δουλευειν$ $θεω$ $ζωντι$ $και$ $αληθινω$, and

3. their $υπομςνης$ $της$ $ελπιδος$ as echoed in $αναμενειν$ $τον$ $υιον$ $αυτου$ $εκ$ $των$ $ουρανων$.

Finally, the reference to salvation from the eschatological wrath qualifies as an eschatological climax, a sequence-terminating feature of style particularly common in this letter (see 1.4.7).[421]

---

[420] The conceptual recurrences support taking $πως$ in the sense of "how" rather than "that" as against Best (1977, 81-2).

[421] Lee/Lee's subdivision (1975, 31) of 1:2-10 into four semantic paragraphs (1:2; 1:3; 1:4; and 1:5-10) of equal rank does not justify the overall unity they otherwise ascribe to the passage.

4.1.4 The Delimitation and Coherence of 2:1-12

In 2:1-12 the topic of the senders' participation in the gospel-event, as introduced in 1:5 and 1:9a, is given sustained treatment with the transition to the new subsequence marked in 2:1 by 1.1ThM, (MBrep) αυτοι...οιδατε (P) την εισοδον ημων την προς υμας οτι ου κενη γεγονεν, and by the address αδελφοι. Connection with the preceding text-seqence is explicitly realized by γαρ, taken here to merely express continuation,[422] and by the lexical and conceptual recurrence of εισοδον...προς υμας in 2:1 and 1:9a.[423] This general reference to the senders' missionary visit is textually expanded through partial conceptual recurrence by the following more particular references: επαρρησιασαμεθα...λαλησαι προς υμας το ευαγγελιον (2:2), ουτε...εν λογω κολακειας εγενηθημεν κτλ. (2:5), εγενηθημεν ηπιοι εν μεσω υμων (2:7),[424] εκηρυξαμεν εις υμας το ευαγγελιον του θεου (2:9), παρακαλουντες υμας και παραμυθουμενοι και μαρτυρομενοι κτλ. (2:12). Finally, the reference to God's call into his glorious kingdom may also be seen as constituting an eschatological climax terminating the sequence.

It is possible to see 2:1-12 as subdividing into two further subsequences of 2:1-8 and 2:9-12 with 1.1.1ThM, (MBref) μνημονευετε...(P) τον κοπον ημων και τον μοχθον, and the address αδελφοι marking the transition to the latter subsequence. In 2:1-8 the character of the senders and their gospel is presented for the most part antithetically by way of denials of negative characteristics and assertions of positive characteristics. This is presented by way of striking grammatical recurrences following the ου...αλλα pattern, with one or more negative clauses followed by one or more positive clauses, as illustrated in Figure 4:

---

[422] For this type of usage where it can function much like δε see Bauer (1979, 152). The difficulty of finding any causal or explanatory connection with what precedes leads Lightfoot (1904, 18) and others to propose an explanatory connection to the train of thought in the author's mind. See Best, 1977, 89.

[423] In view of this lexical recurrence it seems best to take εισοδον in 1:9a also to mean "entrance" in the sense of "visit" rather than of "welcome" as suggested by Bauer (1979, 233). Thus, e.g., Rigaux (1956, 388-9).

[424] E.g., Westcott/Hort (1985) and Nestle/Aland (1979) prefer the reading νηπιοι instead of ηπιοι preferred by Nestle/Aland (1963), Kilpatrick (1958), Aland et. al., (1966, 1968). Besides the latter reading rendering better sense in view of the co-text, the former one is easily explained as being occasioned by dittography. For a review of literature dealing with the problem see Collins, 1984, 7-8.

NEGATIVE	POSITIVE
την εισοδον ημων την προς υμας οτι ου κενη γεγονεν (1)	αλλα...επαρρησιασαμεθα λαλησαι προς υμας το ευαγγελιον κτλ. (2)
η γαρ παρακλησις ημων ουκ εκ πλανης ουδε εξ ακαθαρσιας ουδε εν δολῳ (3)	αλλα καθως δεδοκιμασμεθα υπο του θεου πιστευθηναι το ευαγγελιον, ουτως λαλουμεν (4)
ουχ ως ανθρωποις αρεσκοντες (4)	αλλα θεω τω δοκιμαζοντι τας καρδιας ημων (4)
ουτε γαρ ποτε εν λογῳ κολακειας εγενηθημεν...ουτε εν προφασει πλεονεξιας...ουτε ζητουντες εξ ανθρωπων δοξαν, κτλ. (5-6)	αλλα εγενηθημεν ηπιοι εν μεσω υμων, κτλ. (7-8)

Figure 4

In 2:9-12 the antitheses are absent and only positive characteristics are presented. The subtheme of the senders' "labour and toil" is expanded in the reminders of their self-support so as not to be a burden (2:9), supplying proof of their holy, righteous and blameless behaviour (2:10), like that of a father towards each of his children, urging them to live a life worthy of God (2:11-12).[425]

Other indications of this delimitation are certain parallel sequential features to be seen in the verbs of reminder (οιδατε, μνημονευετε) coupled with the αδελφοι address (2:1 and 9a) followed by arguments serving **ethos** appeals regarding the reliable character of the senders (2:2 ff.; 2:9b ff.). Each development of thought following these arguments leads to a simile, viz., ως...τροφος (2:7), ως πατηρ (2:11) respectively in each subsequence.

---

[425] While Lee/Lee (1975, 31-2) observe the delimitation of 2:1-8 and 2:9-12, their purely semantic criteria cannot account for the fact that the reminder of how the addressors had worked (2:9 ff.) is still supporting the proposition in 2:1 regarding their visit not being without genuine character.

4.1.5 The Rhetoric of 2:1-12

The text-sequence 2:1-12 is characterized by a predominance of the quasi-logical type of artificial appeal and the inartificial type of appeal to direct evidence. The latter type of appeal is made to the addressees as witnesses[426] and is expressed implicitly in such metapropositional clauses as $αυτοι$ $οιδατε$ (2:1), $καθως$ $οιδατε$ (2:2, 5), $μνημονευετε$ (2:9), $καθαπερ$ $οιδατε$ (2:11), as well as explicitly in $υμεις$ $μαρτυρες$ $και$ $ο$ $θεος$ (2:10), where divine witness is also appealed to, as also in $θεος$ $μαρτυς$ (2:5). The sustained use of the $ου...αλλα$ formulation in 2:1-8, noted above, underlines the argumentative tone. The contrasts signaled thereby are not formally expressed by balancing expressions or clauses, but rather the positive clause or clauses introduced by $αλλα$, along with other parenthetically introduced positive clauses, contain the various arguments supporting what is denied in the preceding negative clause or clauses.[427] As is common in informal argumentation, the presentation of logical or quasi-logical appeals is not systematic, nor are all the premises made formally explicit.[428] Thus, they must be reconstructed here as reasonably as possible. Furthermore, the quasi-logical appeals in 2:1-12 do not stand in isolation of one another, but in such a way as to manifest a loose interdependence.

The general proposition to be argued for, $την$ $εισοδον$ $ημων$ $την$ $προς$ $υμας$ $οτι$ $ου$ $κενη$ $γεγονεν$, is presented in the opening thematic clause. In view of the parallelism created by the recurrent $ου...αλλα$ formulation, the specific denials in the negative clauses and the arguments discernable in the positive clauses in 2:1-12 indicate that $ου$ $κενη$ should be taken as referring not to the **results** but to the **character** of the senders' visit in terms of their motives and behaviour in mediating the gospel: "empty" in the sense of "wanting in purpose and earnestness" rather than "fruitless" (NEB), "a failure" (TEV), "ineffectual" (JB), or "in vein" (RSV).[429] The perfect tense of the main verb $γεγονεν$ would on first sight appear to speak in favour of the latter renditions. But the fact that the same verb is also used in the aorist in subsequent coreferring clauses ($εγενηθημεν$, 2:5, 7, 10) advises against insisting too strictly on the perfect as affirming an existing result.[430]

---

[426] On artificial and inartificial types of appeals see Aristotle, Rhet 1.2.2.

[427] Consequently, one cannot strictly classify the $ου...αλλα$ formulations as typical instances of correctio defined as the rejection of an opposing position by way of a balanced distinction between semantically contrary words or expressions. See, e.g., Lausberg, 1963, 123; Plett, 1979, 47.

[428] See Aristotle, Rhet 2.22.3.

[429] In agreement with, e.g., Lightfoot (1904, 18) and Marshall (1983, 62-63), although Marshall makes some allowance for both senses, and opposed to, e.g., Rigaux (1956, 400-1), Lee/Lee (1975, 31, 41), Ellingworth/Nida (1976, 19-20), Best (1977, 89), and Holtz (1986, 66-7). Those who prefer the sense "empty of power" (e.g., Frame, 1912, 91; Lyons, 1985, 192-3) appeal to 1:5 and 2:13. The immediate co-text, however, rules this out. Besides, "power" is only one particular aspect referred to in 1:5 and implied in 2:13.

[430] The encroachment of the perfect on the aorist was a development already current in Paul's day with fairly clear instances of this elsewhere in II Cor 2:13; 11:25

Thus, it is the senders' **ethos** that is explicitly argued for, giving the passage the character of an apology (see 2.2.1 and 6.4) This is clear from the initial argument supporting the genuine character of the senders' gospel visit. When it is recognized that the whole of 2:2 constitutes an argument in support of what is denied in 2:1, the disjunctive αλλα ("on the contrary") ceases to be problematic.[431] The antithetical style plus the fact that Paul is reminding of (καθως οιδατε) rather than reporting the previous mistreatment in Philippi speaks in favor of taking προπαθοντες και υβρισθεντες to be concessive besides being temporal.[432] Thus, one may take 2:2 as containing an explicit premise, viz., **inspite** of suffering both antecedent and attendant hardships, they were courageous in God to preach the gospel to the addressees: αλλα προπαθοντες και υβρισθεντες, καθως οιδατε, εν φιλιπποις επαρρησιασαμεθα εν τω θεω ημων λαλησαι προς υμας το ευαγγελιον του θεου εν πολλω αγωνι. The argument appears to be based on probability,[433] with common sense supplying an appropriate, implicit premise: when persons persist in an activity that incurs a high degree of personal hardship, the probability of some other motivation than self-interest is increased, provided there is an absence of any sufficiently compensating personal profit. That some such premise would not be foreign to the addressees' world of thought is supported by Aristotle's observations that people in general find it hard to believe that a person does anything deliberately without it serving self-interest,[434] and that the penalty being less than the profit **or the contrary** provides a common argument from which to exhort or dissuade, accuse or defend.[435] In the present passage the senders' divine motivation is suggested in επαρρησιασαμεθα εν τω θεω ημων.

Before explicitly eliminating two basic types of personal profit that commonly serve self-interest, viz., personal δοξα from men (2:6-7a) and personal economic benefit (2:9), an argument for the senders' divine approval is presented in 2:4 in support of the denials of unworthy motives for their preaching (2:3). The ellipsis of the verb in η γαρ παρακλησις ημων ουκ εκ πλανης ουδε εξ ακαθαρσιας ουδε εν δολω occasions an ambiguity. Does παρακλησις ημων refer the the senders' preaching in general or specifically to their preaching at Thessalonica?[436] The ellipsis may be

---

and 12:17 (see Blass/Debrunner, 1961, 177; 1979, 343; Moulton/Turner, 1963, 81 ff.). Another possibility is Lightfoot's (1904, 18) suggestion that the perfect in I Thess 2:1 may imply that the senders' sojourn in Thessalonica was recent.

[431] Following, e.g., Lightfoot (1904, 19) as against Rigaux (1956, 401) and Ellingworth/Nida (1976, 20) The latter find αλλα in 2:2 problematic, since they expect but fail to find a balancing element in form or content that contrasts with κενη taken in the sense of "fruitless."

[432] Similarly, e.g., Dobschütz, 1909, 84; Rigaux, 1956, 402; Holtz, 1986, 67.

[433] See Aristotle, Rhet 1.2.14; 2.25.8 ff. See further, e.g., Kennedy, 1963, 30-1, 89-90; Perelman/Olbrechts-Tyteca, 1969, 255-60;=1970, 334-50; Siegert, 1985, 59.

[434] Rhet 3.6.9.

[435] Rhet 2.23.21.

supplied by ειναι or γινεσθαι in the present tense by way of coreference with λαλουμεν (2:4),[437] or in a past tense by way of coreference with επαρρησιασαμεθα λαλησαι προς υμας το ευαγγελιον του θεου (2:2) as a particular aspect of the general event την εισοδον ημων την προς υμας (2:1).[438] The fact that the specific denials of error, uncleanness and deceitful means (2:3) and the denial in general of speaking to please men (2:4b) are all supported by the same argument of divine approval (2:4a) indicates an argumentative unity in 2:3-4. This favours the former alternative with the whole of 2:3-4 taken as focusing on the senders' gospel appeal in general.[439]

The argument regarding divine approval is obviously an appeal to authority,[440] viz., their divine approval in being entrusted with the gospel (2:4a): αλλα καθως δεδοκιμασμεθα υπο του θεου πιστευθηναι το ευαγγελιον, ουτως λαλουμεν. As in 2:2, this may be seen as an explicit premise introduced by adversative αλλα. The implicit premise here would appear to be some general recognition that entrusting something valuable to someone usually indicates some appropriate degree of approval of that person.[441] Within the relative framework of shared presuppositions, this premise could be included under "signs," although hardly under "necessary signs" (τεκμηρια) as defined by Aristotle.[442] The senders' being entrusted with the gospel and the gospel's value are apparently presupposed, indicating that these were expected to be mutually accepted factors.

The comparison announced by the καθως...ουτως formulation has been taken as limited to relating reality to reality: since it is a reality that they were "chosen" by God, thus it is a fact that they preach.[443] The focus, however, is on their divine "approval." The relation between the first and the second comparative clauses further bears out this qualitative aspect. Syntactically, both clauses relate to the same verb λαλουμεν, but logically they stand in a dependent, causal relation: their divine

---

[436] For the use in early Christian literature of παρακαλω/παρακλησις to refer to religious discourse in a broad sense of "exhort/exhortation" see II Cor 5:20, Luke 3:8, Acts 2:20 and Heb 13:22. For a recent discussion of the various semantic aspects covered by these terms see Franck (1985, 30 ff.).

[437] Thus, e.g., Dobschütz, 1909, 86-7; Dibelius, 1937, 7; Rigaux, 1956, 406.

[438] Thus, e.g., Masson (1957, 25-6), although he does not discuss this.

[439] On the sense of παρακλησις here, see Schmitz' definition (1968, 795) as "the wooing proclamation of salvation in the apostolic preaching."

[440] On this type of appeal see, e.g., Perelman/Olbrechts-Tyteca, 1969, 305-10;=1970, 410-17; Siegert, 1985, 65-6.

[441] Henneken (1969, 101-3) shows from both the LXX and Hellenistic "Kanzliesprache" that δεδοκιμασμεθα υπο του θεου indicates an act of divine authorization.

[442] Rhet 1.2.14 ff.

[443] Thus, Rigaux (1956, 408) who takes δεδοκιμασμεθα as having a nuance of "election" (409).

approval serves as an argument that they do not speak as those who please men but rather as those who please God:[444] ουχ ως ανθρωποις αρεσκοντες αλλα θεω τω δοκιμαζοντι τας καρδιας ημων. The connection is strengthened by the lexical recurrence of δεδοκιμασμεθα/δοκιμαζοντι, inspite of the difference in meaning as "approve" and "scrutinize" respectively.[445] Some such supporting premise as divine omniscience appears to be intimated by the reference to God who scrutinizes (general present) their hearts. Thus, the senders' gospel visit is defended from the character of their preaching in general as authenticated by God's approval.

Another series of denials is introduced by explanatory γαρ in 2:5-7a: ουτε γαρ ποτε εν λογω κολακειας εγενηθημεν, καθως οιδατε, ουτε εν προφασει πλεονεξιας, θεος μαρτυς, ουτε ζητουντες εξ ανθρωπων δοξαν ουτε αφ' υμων ουτε απ' αλλων, δυναμενοι εν βαρει ειναι ως Χριστου αποστολοι. The first two denials of "flattering speech" and a "cloak of greed" are respectively supported by an appeal to the witness of the addressees and of God. The third denial of "seeking glory from men" is backed up by the argument of their having relinquished the right of insisting on special respect and authority as "apostles of Christ."[446] This explicit premise assumes some such implicit premise that the act of sacrificing rights belonging naturally to a position of authority in order to benefit those who fall under that authority may be seen as a "sign" of earnestness and goodwill.[447] That which is subsequently asserted in the positive clauses, introduced again by adversative αλλα, stands in a closer contrast to this third denial of glory-seeking than to the first two denials. Rather than insisting on their special status and thereby seeking glory from the addressees or any others, they had become "gentle" (ηπιοι) among them like a children's "nurse" or "nursing mother,"[448] caring for them and ready to share even their "hearts" (ψυχας) with them,[449] because the addressees had become so beloved: αλλα εγενηθημεν ηπιοι εν μεσω υμων, ως εαν τροφος θαλπῃ τα εαυτης τεκ-

---

[444] Similarly, e.g., Holtz, 1986, 72.

[445] On these terms see Best, 1977, 95-6.

[446] The recurring pattern of denial-followed-by-argument supports εν βαρει ειναι to be taken as referring to the authority and respect due to the office of apostle rather than to the right of exacting economic support. Similarly, e.g., Frame (1912, 99), Rigaux (1956, 417-18) and Holtz (1986, 78) as against, e.g., Lightfoot (1904, 24) and Milligan (1908, 20-21) who see Paul playing on both senses here.

[447] On the argument from sacrifice see, e.g., Perelman/Olbrechts-Tyteca, 1969, 248-55;=1970, 334-43; Siegert, 1985, 59.

[448] On the Cynic background of the nurse image here see Malherbe, 1970, 211-14. On parallels in O.T.-Jewish Literature, see 8.2.2.2 below. He also notes (1983, 242) that Paul intensifies the image by comparing the senders' behavior to that of a nurse towards her own children (τα εαυτης τεκνα) and not merely those under her charge.

[449] See, e.g., Frame (1912, 102) and Rigaux (1956, 422) for this sense here and for arguments against taking μεταδουναι...ψυχας as a synonym for δουναι την ψυχην, contra, e.g., Lightfoot (1904, 26) who sees an instance of zeugma here.

να, ουτως ομειρομενοι υμων ευδοκουμεν μεταδουναι υμιν ου μονον το ευαγγελιον του θεου αλλα και τας εαυτων ψυχας, διοτι αγαπητοι ημιν εγενηθητε. The syntax may be complicated but the message is clear: they loved the addressees and had behaved accordingly.[450] While the **ethos** appeal is apparent, such a reminder also naturally acquires the character of a **pathos** appeal to the emotion of loving affection.[451]

As noted above, the rest of the passage in 2:9-12 drops the contrastive formulation of 2:1-8, but continues to present positive appeals supporting the denial of the visit having been κενος (2:1). It should be observed here also that the use of γαρ to open a new phase of argumentation in 2:3, 5, 9 serves not so much to relate the subsequent argument closely to the preceding one as to relate each of the argumentative units generally to the main proposition in 2:1.[452]

A renewed call to remembrance, basically parallel to that in 2:1, opens this subordinate text-sequence and focuses on the fact that the senders had been self-supporting when preaching the gospel, so as not to burden the addressees: μνημονευετε γαρ, αδελφοι, τον κοπον ημων και τον μοχθον· νυκτος και ημερας εργαζομενοι προς το μη επιβαρησαι τινα υμων εκηρυξαμεν εις υμας το ευαγγελιον του θεου. As mentioned above, this fact plus that of not having sought glory from men (2:6-7a) supports the argument implied in 2:2 that the endurance of hardships when preaching the gospel was not motivated by self-interest.

Following A.J. Malherbe, this reminder of their not having been burdensome (επιβαρησαι) to the addresses may be seen as making a natural transition to the image of father (2:11), linked by the invocation of the addressees and God as witnesses to the holy, righteous and blameless behaviour of the senders. He notes that ancient moralists of a pessimistic bent often refer to money as taking precedence over family relationships, with children betraying parents and parents becoming "demanding (βαρυτεροι) of their children."[453] Furthermore, the reference to having been like a father towards each one (ενα εκαστον, 2:11) and the description of their hortatory activity (παρακαλουντες υμας και παραμυθουμενοι και μαρτυρομενοι, κτλ., 2:12) would come across as an **ethos** appeal based on their having acted responsibly in the interests of the addressees. Finally, there is a **pathos** appeal to confidence discernable in the closing reference to God's calling them into his kingdom and glory (2:12).

It may be observed that, in general, inartificial and quasi-logical appeals are more prominent in 2:1-12 than in 1:2-10 or in 2:13-16 (see 4.1.2.1 and 4.1.4.2).

---

[450] On the difficulty of establishing the meaning of ομειρομενοι see, e.g., Rigaux (1956, 421). The co-text would support some sense of caring interest here. Thus, e.g., Holtz, 1986, 83.

[451] See Aristotle, Rhet 2.4.2 ff.

[452] See Denniston (1954, 64-5) on the use of γαρ to successively introduce arguments that have the same reference.

[453] Malherbe, 1983, 243.

4.1.6 The Connection and Delimitation of 2:13-16

In 2:13 Paul returns to focus on the second aspect of the gospel-event already introduced and developed in 1:6-8 and 1:9b-10:[454] και δια τουτο και ημεις ευχαριστουμεν τω θεω αδιαλειπτως, οτι παραλαβοντες λογον ακοης παρ' ημων του θεου εδεξασθε ου λογον ανθρωπων αλλα καθως εστιν αληθως λογον θεου, κτλ. This shift of focus back to the addressees' part in the initial gospel-event is made particularly clear by lexical and partial lexical recurrence when Paul returns to the topics of the addressees' reception of the word (δεξαμενοι τον λογον, 1:6; εδεξασθε...λογον, 2:13) and their imitation (υμεις μιμηται...εγενηθητε, 1:6; υμεις...μιμηται εγενηθητε, 2:14).[455] The transition to the subsequence of 2:13-16 is marked in 2:13 by 1.2ThM, which is taken here as basically consisting of (MBexpr) και ημεις ευχαριστουμεν τω θεω αδιαλειπτως, (P) οτι...εδεξασθε ου λογον ανθρωπων αλλα καθως εστιν αληθως λογον θεου. The development of thought in the passage (treated below in 4.1.4.2) leads up to a judgement utterance of eschatological wrath (2:16c). This constitutes another instance of the so-called eschatological climax serving to conclude the text-sequence as a whole.

Since connection with what precedes involves some ambiguities that are seized upon by those who argue for 2:13-16 being an interpolation,[456] it will be necessary to give particular attention to this question in what follows. The question of connection has centred especially around δια τουτο και in the clause και δια τουτο και ημεις ευχαριστουμεν. While the initial και may reflect Semitic influence, in Pauline use it usually also serves to indicate a "division of medium importance," marking both transition and continuation.[457] C.F.D. Moule is followed in taking the second και as being emphatic and as logically modifying the verb, with its position before ημεις observed to be a displacement characteristic of Pauline style.[458]

---

[454] This thematic schematization disqualifies Marxsen's proposal (1979, 47) that 2:1-16 is a single text-sequence unified by the persecution motive and lacking a major transition at 2:13. In 2:1-12 the persecution motif only appears in 2:2 and is not thematically expanded as such. See Dibelius (1937, 13) who also notes the schematic treatment of the sender's activity in 1:4-5 and 2:1-12 and of the addressees' activity in 1:6-10 and 2:13-16, although he does not include the repeated reference to the senders' activity in 1:9a.

[455] Pearson (1971, 91) notes these lexical parallels among others as evidence of a redactor using Pauline words and phrases to provide a putative "Pauline" framework for a new message. However, see ch. 7 where such conclusions are shown to be most dubious.

[456] On this see Boers, 1975, 151.

[457] Thus, Ellingworth/Nida, 1976, 37.

[458] Moule, 1963, 167. It has been taken in the sense of "also" with ευχαριστουμεν, indicating this as a reiteration of the initial thanksgiving-report (e.g., Dobschütz, 1909, 103; Dibelius, 1936, 11), or with ημεις, which raises the difficulty of seeing a reciprocation to thanksgiving expressed by someone else (e.g., Frame, 1912, 106-7, following Harris, 1898, 161-80). It has also been taken in a weakened sense emphasizing ημεις and rendered as "we on our part" (e.g.,

As for the phrase $\delta\iota\alpha$ $\tau o\upsilon\tau o$, this has been taken to refer anaphorically, cataphorically or both.[459] When taken anaphorically it has been seen as referring variously to God's call (2:12b), the senders' exhortation (2:12a), the thought in 2:1-4 or in 2:1-12 as a whole or even more generally to all that has been previously mentioned about the addressees and addressors that merits thanksgiving.[460] In view of the ambiguity suggested by this plethora of interpretations, some prefer to take it cataphorically as referring to the contents of the subsequent $o\tau\iota$ clause.[461] However, since all the other instances of $\delta\iota\alpha$ $\tau o\upsilon\tau o$ in Pauline usage are fairly clearly anaphoric,[462] it is advisable to resort to considering a cataphoric reference only when an anaphoric one cannot be shown to make reasonable sense.

First of all, it should be noted that connection with the preceding text-sequence does not rest on $\kappa\alpha\iota$ $\delta\iota\alpha$ $\tau o\upsilon\tau o$ alone. In the subsequent $o\tau\iota$ clause reference to the addressees' mediation of the word of God ($\pi\alpha\rho\alpha\lambda\alpha\beta o\nu\tau\epsilon\varsigma$ $\lambda o\gamma o\nu$ $\alpha\kappa o\eta\varsigma$ $\pi\alpha\rho'$ $\eta\mu\omega\nu$ $\tau o\upsilon$ $\theta\epsilon o\upsilon$) is explicitly mentioned in relation to the main point, viz., that the addressees' received it as truely God's word and not that of men ($\epsilon\delta\epsilon\xi\alpha\sigma\theta\epsilon$ $o\upsilon$ $\lambda o\gamma o\nu$ $\alpha\nu\theta\rho\omega\pi\omega\nu$ $\alpha\lambda\lambda\alpha$ $\kappa\alpha\theta\omega\varsigma$ $\epsilon\sigma\tau\iota\nu$ $\alpha\lambda\eta\theta\omega\varsigma$ $\lambda o\gamma o\nu$ $\theta\epsilon o\upsilon$, 2:13c).[463] Coreference with preceding references to the addressors' part in the gospel visit especially focused upon in 2:1-12 remains whether one attaches $\pi\alpha\rho'$ $\eta\mu\omega\nu$ to $\pi\alpha\rho\alpha\lambda\alpha\beta o\nu\tau\epsilon\varsigma$ or to $\alpha\kappa o\eta\varsigma$ (2:13b).[464] Furthermore, the antithetical formulation $o\upsilon$ $\lambda o\gamma o\nu$ $\alpha\nu\theta\rho\omega\pi\omega\nu$...$\alpha\lambda\lambda\alpha$...$\lambda o\gamma o\nu$ $\theta\epsilon o\upsilon$ not only echoes that in 2:1 ff., but there is also a connection involving coreference between $\lambda o\gamma o\nu$ $\alpha\nu\theta\rho\omega\pi\omega\nu$ and all the preceding negative characteristics expressed or implied and included under $\kappa\epsilon\nu\eta$ in 2:1-12.[465]

Besides indicating a general text-semantic connection, these observations focus on features that show that for a satisfying anaphoric connection to be served by $\delta\iota\alpha$ $\tau o\upsilon\tau o$, the reason to be understood should be something more than the mere fact of the addressees' mediation of the gospel, since this is already referred to in 2:13b.

Lightfoot, 1904; Rigaux, 1956, 437; and Best, 1977, 110).

[459] For summaries see, e.g., Dobschütz (1909, 103) and Rigaux (1956, 437). O'Brian (1977, 154) would have it to be both anaphoric and cataphoric.

[460] See Rigaux (1956, 437) who holds the last-mentioned view. Frame's view (1912, 106) regarding 2:1-4 rests on taking these verses to principally argue that "the gospel is not human, as the Jews alleged, but divine." The analysis in 4.1.4.2 comes to quite a different conclusion. As for the possibility of reference to God's call (2:12b), e.g., Lightfoot (1904, 30) correctly observed that this immediately preceding dependent clause is not sufficiently prominent.

[461] Thus, e.g., Boers (1975, 151) and Ellingworth/Nida (1976, 37-8). Boers sees this cataphoric reference as giving support to Pearson's theory (1971, 79-94) of 2:13-16 being a later interpolation.

[462] The relevant occurrences are found in Rom 1:26; 4:16; 5:12; 13:6; 15:9; I Cor 4:17; 11:10, 30; II Cor 4:1; 7:13; 13:10; Col 1:9; and Phlm 15, besides Eph 1:15; 5:17; 6:13 and II Thess 2:11.

[463] The accusatives in $\lambda o\gamma o\nu$ $\alpha\nu\theta\rho\omega\pi\omega\nu$ and $\lambda o\gamma o\nu$ $\theta\epsilon o\upsilon$ are taken as predicatives here with, e.g., Dobschütz (1909, 105) and Frame (1912, 108). This involves seeing an ellipsis of $\alpha\upsilon\tau o\nu$ after $\epsilon\delta\epsilon\xi\alpha\sigma\theta\epsilon$, something that is facilitated by the

Also, the reason should be something less than all the previously mentioned things about both addressees and addressors that are worthy of thanksgiving (1:2-2:12), since the antithetical formulation of the addressees' reception of the gospel is explicitly related to the addressors' part in mediating it. This indicates that the reason is more narrowly connected with this latter aspect.

In view of these considerations and of the distinct argumentative unity in 2:1-12 regarding the earnest and purposeful character of the addressors' gospel visit, there is much to say for the view that it is this sequence of thought that is generally referred to by the substituting expression τουτο, functioning as a SA. The connection expresses a personal sentiment rather than a logical relation: In view of the fact that the mediation of the gospel was not a "vain" event springing from unworthy motives on the part of the addressors, gratitude is expressed that it was not received as merely "the word of men."[466] It is specifically the earnest and purposeful character of the addressors' mediation of the gospel that best explains the antithetical formulation in the οτι clause.

4.1.7 The Rhetoric and Coherence of 2:13-16

The focus on the receivers' reception of the word in 2:13 is carried forward by the added observation that God's word had proved to be active in them:[467] ος και ενεργειται εν υμιν τοις πιστευουσιν. Support for this is then presented in the subsequent reference to the suffering that had come to them (2:14), introduced by explanatory γαρ. That suffering was considered to be an identifying mark of Christian believers may be inferred from the imitation motif in 1:6 where the content of imitation is to be seen, not in the reception of the word, but in εν θλιψει πολλη μετα χαρας πνευματος αγιου (see under 4.1.1). It may also be inferred from Paul's reminder of the arrival of predicted suffering in 3:4.[468] Thus, a quasi-logical appeal may be seen here supporting the genuine character of the addressees' Christian experience of the gospel.

---

conceptual recurrence (whether partial or complete) that holds between this verb and παραλαβοντες. Consequently, taking the accusatives to be predicative does not depend on a "receive/accept" distinction of senses between these verbs, contra, e.g., Rigaux, 1956, 440.

[464] See, e.g., Lightfoot (1904, 319) for the former option and, e.g., Dibelius (1937, 11) for the latter.

[465] These observations discount the view held by, e.g., Rigaux (1956, 440) and Best (1977, 111) that ανθρωπων refers specifically to Paul and his companions.

[466] Similarly, Lightfoot (1904, 30) and Milligan (1908, 27-8), although without the arguments presented here.

[467] On ος relating to λογος see Holtz, 1986, 99.

[468] On suffering as a mark of Christian identity, see Meeks, 1983, 692; Pobee, 1985, 107 ff.; and Holtz, 1986, 102-3.

The reference to this suffering is expressed in terms of their having imitated the churches in Judea in suffering comparable things from their fellow countrymen as those churches had from the Jews:[469] υμεις γαρ μιμηται εγενηθητε, αδελφοι, των εκκλησιων του θεου των ουσων εν τη Ιουδαια εν Χριστω Ιησου, οτι τα αυτα επαθετε και υμεις υπο των ιδιων συμφυλετων καθως και αυτοι υπο των Ιουδαιων. From this complex comparison the author launches into what would qualify rhetorically as "blame" or **vituperatio** (2:15-16): των Ιουδαιων, των και τον κυριον αποκτειναντων Ιησουν και τους προφητας και ημας εκδιωξαντων και θεω μη αρεσκοντων και πασιν ανθρωποις εναντιων, κωλυοντων ημας τοις εθνεσιν λαλησαι ινα σωθωσιν, εις το αναπληρωσαι αυτων τας αμαρτιας παντοτε. εφθασεν δε επ' αυτους η οργη εις τελος. The abrupt transition from the topic of 2:14 to the attack in 2:15-16 qualifies the latter as an instance of **digressio** which was observed to commonly serve the rhetorical functions of **laus** or its opposite, **vituperatio**.[470]

The attack on the Jews here hardly qualifies for the characterization of Paul as "holding an unacceptable anti-Semitic position,"[471] but is aimed at Jews only as they had been and continued to be hostile towards and obstructive of the gospel.[472] As W. Marxsen has pointed out, an anti-Semitic interpretation can only be held when 2:15-16 is disconnected from its context.[473] In view of the preceding comparison, the accusations and pronouncement of judgement are not aimed without reservation at the Jews alone. Indeed, apart from the accusations of killing Jesus and persecuting Paul and company, insofar as the addressees' persecuting countrymen also attempted to hinder the gospel, the accusations of "displeasing God" and "opposing all men" and the same condemnation of "wrath" would be readily perceived as implied for them also.[474] It is a well-established fact of public discourse that a speaker must often adjust what he says to a potential audience beyond that of the immediate one in view.[475] Thus, it is a reasonable possibility that Paul resorted to this indirect expression of "blame" in order to spare the Thessalonian believers from any serious consequences in the event that the letter should fall into the wrong hands. Such a direct attack on Jews hostile to the gospel would hardly have occasioned as serious a problem in Thessalonica as it would if made directly on Gentile fellow country-

---

[469] The emphatic υμεις and the renewed address αδελφοι serve to stress this particular aspect of the topic, while 2:13, connecting as it does with what precedes, has a more transitional function.

[470] See Lausberg, 1973, 187, 542, 544; Wuellner, 1979, 179-81. Lee/Lee's semantic analysis (1975, 32) cannot account for 2:15-16 which is simply ignored.

[471] Thus, e.g., Best (1977, 122) on 2:16c.

[472] Thus, e.g., Marxsen, 1979, 49; Donfried, 1985-86, 245 ff.; Lyons, 1985, 205 ff.; Holtz, 1986, 103.

[473] Marxsen, 1979, 48 ff.

[474] Similarly, Marxsen, 1979, 49.

[475] See, e.g., Perelman/Olbrechts-Tyteca, 1969, 18-9;=1970, 24-5.

men.[476]

In the comparison in 2:14 $των$ $ιδιων$ $συμφυλετων$ and $των$ $Ιουδαιων$ represent the general ethnic environments to which the Thessalonian and the Judean believers respectively belonged and which had provided them with their respective social identities. Here $συμφυλεται$ appears to indicate a closer relationship than the common translation "countrymen" expresses, viz., those belonging to the same $φυλη$ or "tribe."[477] The Gentile composition of the addressees (1:9-10) and the comparative relation to $Ιουδαιων$ support some such more or less ethnic reference as opposed to a purely local interpretation that includes Jews.[478] Acceptance of the Christian faith and way of life brought about a "cognitive dissonance" in the respective communities, so that both groups of believers were exposed to suffering persecution and social isolation.[479] In their tribulations, the addressees are made aware by this comparison that they are not alone, but share in the solidarity of a wider community of faith.

The **pathos** appeal appears to be prominent in the passage. The natural source of fear, viz., social isolation and persecution, is turned into a means of appealing to confidence, when it is understood as an indication that God's saving word is active in the lives of the addressees. The comparison between the two groups of believers, although expressed in terms of immitation, serves more as a **pathos** appeal to group solidarity (i.e., confidence) than to emulation as in 1:6. This appeal to confidence is further strengthened by the blame and judgement against their persecutors implied in the subsequent **vituperatio**.[480] There is an inverse parallel here to the **pathos** appeal in 1:10 regarding the eschatological wrath:[481] There believers (inclusive $ημας$) will escape the "wrath," here it is inevitable for the opponents of the gospel who oppress the believers.[482]

---

[476] This gives a reasonable explanation for the digression bringing in the reference to the Jews. See Marshall (1983, 5) who finds a lack of a satisfying explanation among other commentators who observe this comparison between the persecuters.

[477] Thus, Meeks (1983, 691) referring to Latte (1941, 994-1011).

[478] Thus, e.g., Dobschüutz, 1909, 109-10. While $ιδιων$ may be accorded a weakened force following a tendency in Koine, Milligan (1908, 29), followed by Rigaux (1956, 443), bases his "local" interpretation more on Acts 17:5, 13 than on the evidence in I Thess.

[479] See Meeks, 1983, 690 ff.

[480] Thus, Marxsen (1979, 50) who rightly notes that Paul is not thereby trying to turn them against their persecutors.

[481] A connection between the references to wrath in 1:10 and 2:16 supporting an eschatological sense in the latter is also seen by, e.g., Dobschütz (1909, 108, 116), Rigaux (1956, 453), and Holtz (1986, 108).

[482] The prophetic, or more precisely, the proleptic character of the aorist $εφθασεν$ appealed to by, e.g., Dobschütz (1909, 117) and Rigaux (1956, 452) is given further support in a forth-coming article by the present author. Holtz (1986, 108),

4.1.8 Some Concluding Observations on I Thess 1:2-2:16

The foregoing observations indicate that the return to a focus on the addressees' reception of the word in 2:13 ff. may be seen as a natural development of thought following upon 2:1-12. At the same time, by means of the reiteration of thanksgiving-reports (1:2; 2:13) and references to the reception of the word (1:6; 2:13), to imitation (1:6; 2:14) and to eschatological wrath (1:10; 2:16), all involving lexical recurrence, the author also indicates a strategy of ring-composition: A=1:2-10, B=2:1-12 and A'=2:13-16. Although the train of thought in 2:13-16 certainly gets a different development than in 1:2-10, the recurring expressions and motifs contribute formally to the creation of this circular structure. This is further substantiated from rhetorical-pragmatic considerations. While the **ethos** type of appeal is apparent throughout 1:2-2:16, it is made more explicit in 2:1-12 and is supported by inartificial and quasi-logical appeals that are especially prominent in 2:1-12. On the other hand, the prominence of the **pathos** type of appeal in 1:2-10 is paralleled by a corresponding prominence of this type in 2:13-16. This correspondence is particularly apparent from the **vituperatio** in 2:15-16 which balances the **laudatio** in 1:7 ff., where both this explicit praise and explicit blame respectively follow upon the parallel references to the addressees having become $\mu\iota\mu\eta\tau\alpha\iota$ (1:6; 2:14).

Thus, a fourth, fifth and sixth level of hierarchical-sequential text-sequences may be observed for 1:2-2:16, which may be represented as follows in Figure 5:

LEVEL IV

I Thess 1:2-2:16

1ThM(P1.2); PCab

LEVEL V

1:2-10	2:1-12	2:13-16
(as above) Prominence of Pathos Appeals	1.1ThM; C Prominence of Inartificial and Quasi-Logical Appeals	1.2ThM; C Prominence of Pathos Appeals

LEVEL VI

2:1-8	2:9-12
(as above)	1.1.1ThM; C

Figure 5

---

e.g., most recently denies this proleptic character.

4.2 ANALYSIS OF I THESS 2:17-3:13 AND SUBSEQUENCES

4.2.1 Connection, Delimitation, Coherence of 2:17-3:13 and 2:17-20

Having brought the treatment of the initial gospel-event to a climactic close with the vituperative digression in 2:15-16, the author moves to the more recent past in 2:17 ff. Together with the renewed address $αδελφοι$ and transitional $δε$, the PCrel/TCrel $απορφανισθεντες αφ' υμων προς καιρον ωρας$ marks the transition, as does the change to the "visit" theme expressed in $εσπουδασαμεν το προσωπον υμων ιδειν$. While these markers signal the transition from what precedes, they delimit 2:17-20 and not 2:17-3:13. Regarding 2:17-3:13 as a whole, the overall "visit" theme, represented as 2ThInf, must be inferred from the references to past attempts to return (2:17 f.), to the sending of Timothy (3:1 ff.) and his return (3:6) and to the continued desire to return in the future (3:9 ff.). Thus, these references contribute to the text-semantic coherence and indirectly to the delimitation of the passage as a whole.[483] An eschatological climax marks its conclusion in 3:13.

As for the delimitation of 2:17-20, the theme of past efforts to make a return visit, viz., 2.1ThM ($εσπουδασαμεν το προσωπον υμων ιδειν$) is clear enough, even though it is not formulated as an explicit semantic sentence (MB+P). The aorist tense of $εσπουδασαμεν$ does not allow it to function as a direct metapropositional expression commenting on the proposition realized by the infinitival clause. Besides $απορφανισθεντες αφ' υμων$ being a PCrel, the temporal reference $προς καιρον ωρας$ together with $απορφανισθεντες$, taken here as a temporal participle, also functions as a TCrel delimitation marker: "shortly after having been orphaned" or "after having been orphaned...for a short time."[484] The aorist tense of the participle "implies a single action and not a continued state" suggesting that the "short period" is over.[485] Timothy's visit can be seen as terminating this initial separation, even though the separation continued for the others.

The coherence of 2:17-20 is most apparent in the text-pragmatic dimension. As shown below, the insistence on previous attempts to make a return visit is expressed in highly emotive language.[486] This expression of the senders' sincere concern for the addressees becomes explicit in 2:19-20, where the use of specifically eschatological language qualifies the utterances as a sequence-concluding eschatological climax.

With regard to the question of connection to the preceding material, $ημεις δε$ is usually given a text-transitional explanation with $δε$ taken as transitional rather than adversative, and $ημεις$ serving to signal the change of thematic focus rather than a contrast with $υμεις$ (2:14) or the Jews (2:15-16).[487] However, in view of the

---

[483] Lee/Lee (1975, 32 ff., 37) miss these semantic recurrences of the visit theme and thereby place the subsequences 2:17-20; 3:1-5; 3:6-10; and 3:11-13 on the same level with 1:2-2:16.

[484] This translation is justified by the sequence of actions implied by $απορφανισθεντες αφ' υμων$ and $εσπουδασαμεν το προσωπον υμων ιδειν$. On this relation of a dependent participle to a finite verb see Moule, 1959, 99 ff.

[485] Thus, Best, 1977, 124.

[486] See, e.g., Ellingworth/Nida, 1976, 46.

observations made in 4.1.4.2 on 2:14-16 above and in view of the sentiments expressed in 2:17-20, insisting on the efforts to return and on the senders' special esteem of the addressees, ημεις δε may also express a very general contrast between the senders in their solidarity with the addressees and the oppressors of the new faith, both Jews and the addressees' own countrymen with whom previous solidarity had been disrupted.

4.2.2   The Rhetoric of 2:17-20

The **pathos** appeal to loving affection is apparent in the emotionally charged expressions surrounding the initial reference to the endeavors to make a return visit: ημεις δε, αδελφοι, απορφανισθεντες αφ' υμων προς καιρον ωρας, προσωπω ου καρδια, περισσοτερως εσπουδασαμεν το προσωπον υμων ιδειν εν πολλῃ επιθυμια. This is clear from the choice of απορφανισθεντες in place of the epistolary commonplace απο ντες and from προσωπω ου καρδια. Also, προς καιρον ωρας, as a part of the participial clause "after having been orphaned from you **for a short while**," intensifies εσπουδασαμεν by indicating that the eager efforts to return were made shortly after the departure itself.[488]

Further intensification is added by περισσοτερως and εν πολλῃ επιθυμια, as well as by διοτι ηθελησαμεν ελθειν προς υμας, repeating the visit theme and emphasizing that the endeavor to return was grounded in the senders' goodwill.[489] This is followed by a change to the first person singular and an explicit reference to having made repeated attempts:[490] εγω μεν Παυλος και απαξ και δις. While this change could be seen as no more than the boiling up of intense personal feelings,[491] it is a reasonably fair conjecture that it also reflects a response to the addressees' disappointment, either intuitively anticipated or reported by Timothy that Paul himself had not been able to return to them. As such, it would reflect a further note in the chord of self-defence already struck in 2:1 ff., anticipating any potential doubt as to Paul's subsequent sincere interest in them as their spiritual father.[492] In view

---

[487] Thus, e.g., Rigaux, 1956, 457; Ellingworth/Nida, 1976, 46; Best, 1977, 124, Marxsen, 1979, 52. Frame (1912,117) relates it extra-textually as responding to an insinuation that Paul did not wish to return.

[488] This interpretation is anchored in the grammatical relations in the text noted above and as such stands on firmer ground than the often repeated psychologizing speculation that προς καιρον ωρας indicates that Paul is confident the separation will not be long, for which see, e.g., Dobschütz, 1909, 120; Rigaux, 1956, 458-9; Ellingworth/Nida, 1976, 47.

[489] Thus, Dobschütz (1909, 122), taking διοτι=δια τουτο οτι.

[490] See L. Morris, 1956, 205-8.

[491] Thus, e.g., Best, 1977, 126; Collins, 1980-81, 351,=1984, 178.

[492] The return to the 1st per. pl. in the subsequent clause "Satan hindered us" supports taking εγω as coextensive with ημεις (ηθελησαμεν), contrary to, e.g.,

of this, the explicit recurrence of Paul's name here should not be seen as a text-delimiting instance of renominalization (see 1.4.5), but as occasioned by pragmatic considerations.

The reference to being hindered by Satan is an argument that may be seen as being supplied by Paul's spiritual intuition.[493] An indirect **ethos** appeal may be served by this insofar as it should actualize the addressees' sense of being allied with the senders in a cosmic struggle between good and evil. At the same time, it removes personal blame from Paul for not returning personally.

After the unelaborated remark that Satan had hindered their attempts to return, the emotionally charged language used in referring to these attempts intensifies in the purely expressive language conveying the senders' positive feelings towards the addressees by way of a rhetorical question followed by a reiterative affirmation (2:19-20): $\tau\iota\varsigma\ \gamma\alpha\rho\ \eta\mu\omega\nu\ \epsilon\lambda\pi\iota\varsigma\ \eta\ \chi\alpha\rho\alpha\ \eta\ \sigma\tau\epsilon\varphi\alpha\nu o\varsigma\ \kappa\alpha\upsilon\chi\eta\sigma\epsilon\omega\varsigma\ -\ \eta\ o\upsilon\chi\iota\ \kappa\alpha\iota\ \upsilon\mu\epsilon\iota\varsigma\ -\ \epsilon\mu\pi\rho o\sigma\theta\epsilon\nu\ \tau o\upsilon\ \kappa\upsilon\rho\iota o\upsilon\ \eta\mu\omega\nu\ I\eta\sigma o\upsilon\ \epsilon\nu\ \tau\eta\ \alpha\upsilon\tau o\upsilon\ \pi\alpha\rho o\upsilon\sigma\iota\alpha;\ \upsilon\mu\epsilon\iota\varsigma\ \gamma\alpha\rho\ \epsilon\sigma\tau\epsilon\ \eta\ \delta o\xi\alpha\ \eta\mu\omega\nu\ \kappa\alpha\iota\ \eta\ \chi\alpha\rho\alpha$. The Thessalonians' being the "hope," "joy" and "crown of boasting" of the addressors at the parousia should be seen from the perspective of a satisfied "nursing-mother" (cf. 2:7) or "father" (cf. 2:11), rather than as an indication of calculated reward,[494] with "crown" striking a note of eschatological victory.[495] "Joy," expressed in both the rhetorical question and the subsequent responding statement, provides the keynote, which is not only personal and subjective, but also eschatological and cosmic.[496]

The emotional language, the repetitions, the rhetorical question and its response all contribute to expressing a great deal of intensity in these lines, an intensity already felt in the preceding antithetical character of 1:5, 2:1 ff and 2:13 as well as in the vituperative digression in 2:15-16. The predominance of a **pathos** appeal to loving affection in 2:17-20 as a whole is obvious. Insofar as the addressees' participation in the senders' eschatological victory is implied, a **pathos** appeal to confidence may also be discerned here. Finally, **ethos** appeals are also present in the references to repeated efforts to return, to the opposition by Satan and in the goodwill in general expressed towards the addressees.

Lightfoot, 1909, 37. The $\mu\epsilon\nu$ may be taken as emphatic rather than adversative, as convincingly argued by Dobschütz, 1909, 123.

[493] Rigaux (1956, 462) correctly notes the futility of speculating on any specific circumstances giving rise to this argument. On the nature of religious rhetoric see Kennedy, 1984, 6; 1980, 121.

[494] Similarly, e.g., Lightfoot, 1909, 38; Best, 1977, 127-28.

[495] Collins (1978-79, 261;=1984, 221) describes 2:19-20 in terms of Paul's "own eschatological victory."

[496] Thus, Ellingworth/Nida, 1976, 46.

4.2.3 The Delimitation and Coherence of 3:1-8

The next subsequence within 2:17-3:13 is 3:1-8. Here it must be pointed out that the dominant theme "Timothy's visit" governs 3:1-8, although it is not formulated in an explicit semantic sentence (MB+P), but must be inferenced from what turns out to be the initial aspect of it in the sending of Timothy (επεμψαμεν Τιμοθεον, 3:2) and the final aspect of it in the return of Timothy (ελθοντος Τιμοθεον προς ημας αφ' υμων, 3:6). Consequently, the thematic delimitation of 3:1-8 may be represented as 2.2ThInf, being subordinate to the overall "visit" theme. Then, as verbally explicit and thematically subordinate expressions επεμψαμεν Τιμοθεον (3:2) and ελθοντος Τιμοθεον (3:6) may be respectively represented as 2.2.1ThM and 2.2.2ThM, delimiting the subsequences 3:1-5 and 3:6-8.

The transition at 3:1 is marked by TCrel, μηκετι στεγοντες, and PCrel, καταλειφθηναι εν Αθηναις (3:1), and by the transition from the previous text-sequence by the change to the theme of sending Timothy (2.2.1ThM) in 3:2. Connection with the preceding sequence is realized in particular by διο, which at the same time may be taken to refer to the whole thought sequence of 2:17-20 and thereby also delimit this previous text-sequence as a SA. In 3:5 the first part of the sequence 3:1-8 is rounded off by an explicit reiteration of the theme of sending Timothy, with the lexical recurrence of μηκετι στεγοντες...επεμψαμεν (3:1-2) in μηκετι στεγων επεμψα (3:5) contributing to the coherence and delimitation of the subsequence 3:1-5 as an instance of **inclusio**: δια τουτο καγω μηκετι στεγων επεμψα εις το γνωναι την πιστιν υμων, κτλ. These references to sending Timothy and to the pastoral motivations for doing so serve to frame an argument in 3:3-4 regarding the destined character of eschatological tribulation and the fulfillment of the senders' predictions that it would come (see 4.2.4).

In 3:6 the author moves from the initial stage in the event of Timothy's visit to its conclusion by Timothy's return with good news of the addressees' faith and love and their continued goodwill towards the senders: αρτι δε ελθοντος Τιμοθεου προς ημας αφ' υμων και ευαγγελισαμενου ημιν την πιστιν και την αγαπην υμων και οτι εχετε μνειαν ημων αγαθην παντοτε, επιποθουντες ημας ιδειν καθαπερ και ημεις υμας (3:6). Together with 2.2.2ThM, the transition is marked by transitional δε (C), by ελθοντος...προς ημας αφ' υμων as a PCrel, by ελθοντος as a TCrel,[497] and by Τιμοθεου as a renominalization (R). As previously noted (see 3.2.3.1), the temporal progression from the more distant past (1:4 ff.) to the more recent past (2:17 ff.) culminates in the explicit focus on the author's "now" in 3:8:[498]

---

[497] It is questionable whether αρτι can qualify as part of the TCrel here, since, however one may take it, it does not directly correlate with preceding indications of time. According to Lightfoot (1904, 44) it should not be taken to correlate to the author's present, as generally assumed, with the sense "a short time ago." Rather, it should be correlated to the event of the senders' having been comforted (3:7) with the sense of "a short time before." He motivates this by the observation that παρακληθημεν provides the point of time to which everything in the passage is related. Likwise Dobschütz (1909, 139), giving Matt 9:18 and Rev 12:10 as parallels for this "Attic" usage.

[498] Thus Rigaux, 1956, 480. Best (1977, 142) notes that νυν can also have the logical sense of "this being so," but he concedes that the temporal and logical senses are not really distinct here.

οτι νυν ζωμεν εαν υμεις στηκετε εν κυριω. From here on in the text the author's temporal perspective is basically present-future.

4.2.4 The Rhetoric of 3:1-8

The addressors' decision to send Timothy is also expressed in emotional terms that betray a **pathos** appeal to loving affection. Due to their thwarted attempts to return and due to their special care for and goodwill towards the addressees, they came to a point where they could no longer bear the separation and sent Timothy at the expense of his being left alone in Athens:[499] Διο μηκετι στεγοντες ευδοκησαμεν καταλειφθηναι εν Αθηναις μονοι και επεμψαμεν Τιμοθεον κτλ. An **ethos** appeal is implicit in the fact that being left alone implies a sacrifice on the part of the senders for the benefit of the addressees. In general, as D.E. von Dobschütz observed, the previous references to unfulfilled efforts to return would provide weak evidence of goodwill by themselves, and Paul consequently moves on to stronger evidence of this in reminding the addressees of how Timothy was sent to visit them.[500]

An **ethos** appeal is also apparent in the description of Timothy as τον αδελφον ημων και συνεργον του θεου, whereby it is intimated that Paul and his co-workers were arrayed with God over against Satan in the cosmic conflict (cf. 2:18; 3:5). Further **ethos** appeals are observable in Paul's references to the motivations for sending Timothy, viz., pastoral aims and concern, εις το στηριξαι υμας και παρακαλεσαι υπερ της πιστεως υμων το μηδενα σαινεσθαι εν ταις θλιψεσιν ταυταις (3:2b-3a),[501] reiterated in different terms at the close of the sequence: εις το γνωναι την πιστιν υμων, μη πως επειρασεν υμας ο πειραζων και εις κενον γενηται ο κοπος ημων (3:5).[502]

The reference "that no one be disturbed by these tribulations,"[503] prepares the way for a pointed treatment of the topic of suffering tribulations in 3:3b-4. Here the reiteration of οιδατε frames this subsequence at its opening and close in a way that serves to both delimit it and give emphasis to the importance of what is said: αυτοι γαρ οιδατε οτι εις τουτο κειμεθα· και γαρ οτε προς υμας ημεν, προελε-

---

[499] With Collins (1980-81, 351-2;=1984, 178-9) the plural μονοι is taken to indicate not that Paul was "all alone" but that he and his companion(s) were "lonely" in Timothy's absence. See also Rigaux (1956, 76-80) and Best (1977, 26-29) for arguments favouring taking the 1st person plural as a genuine plural here and elsewhere in I Thessalonians.

[500] Dobschütz, 1909, 129.

[501] On the sense of σαινεσθαι see Rigaux (1956, 369-71) who follows Chadwick (1950, 156-8) in assigning it a sense of mental or inner perturbation as against the senses of "shaken" or "beguiled." Bammel's interpretation (1981, 98) of it as entering a state of εκστασις is not convincing.

[502] See Lyons (1985, 212-14) for a detailed discussion of the parallels.

[503] On what is possibly referred to by the expression ταις θλιψεσιν ταυταις see under 2.2.4 above.

γομεν υμιν οτι μελλομεν θλιβεσθαι, καθως και εγενετο και οιδατε.

In spite of this, many commentaries devote little attention to the passage, and those which do treat it theologically with insufficient explicit attention given to it as persuasive discourse relative to the initial addressees. Consequently, the futuristic, predictive aspect of the periphrastic construction μελλομεν θλιβεσθαι is usually played down in favour of it having a sense of 'necessity' parallel to εις τουτο κειμεθα immediately preceding it.[504] However, with εις τουτο κειμεθα taken as the general proposition or position to be supported or reconfirmed by persuasive means, it makes less sense for μελλομεν θλιβεσθαι to be taken as generally reiterating εις τουτο κειμεθα rather than as expressing the futuristic, predictive character of the addressers' previously repeated predictions which were subsequently confirmed by concrete experience.[505]

In other words, 3:4 contains an argument of a distinctly prophetic character used to support the position in 3:3b. The argumentative connection is reflected by γαρ and the thematic connection obviously by partial lexical and semantic recurrences in 3:3-4 (θλιψεσιν-τουτο-θλιβεσθαι-εγενετο). The addressees are reminded of the teaching they had received on the destined character of eschatological tribulations (3:3b) followed by a further reminder of the addressers' repeated predictions that such sufferings will come and of the confirmation of these predictions in their concrete experience.[506] This prophetic fulfillment would serve as a quasi-logical appeal insofar as both communication partners accepted the validity of this type of argument.[507] Furthermore, the addressees themselves could be appealed to as witnesses (οιδατε). Thus, such appeals would serve to help reconfirm the addressees' understanding and acceptance of tribulations as an integral element of their Christian eschatological status as well as to appeal in favour of the addressers' reliable character (**ethos**).[508]

The use of inclusive "we" in κειμεθα and μελλομεν expresses the solidarity of the senders with the addressees in undergoing such afflictions (**ethos/pathos**). It also intimates what is explicitly stated in 3:7, viz., that the senders are themselves also undergoing affliction. This would serve to mitigate potential mistrust that Paul's continued absence reflected a reticence on his part to share or expose himself to sharing the sufferings that followed from his converts' adherence to the gospel he preached (**ethos**).

---

[504] Thus, e.g., Lightfoot, 1904, 42-3; Dobschütz, 1909, 136; Rigaux, 1956, 473; Best 1977, 136.

[505] The use of μελλομεν rather than εμελλομεν indicates that the οτι is most likely introducing direct speech. On the periphrastic future construction of μελλειν + inf., see, e.g., Robertson (1934, 882), Moulton/Turner (1963, 89), and Blass/Debrunner (1961, 181; 1979, 288).

[506] On the predictive-prophetic character of this utterance see Aune (1983, 259) who sees analogies to this type of prophecy in Acts 20:23; 21:4, 10-11.

[507] See, e.g., Deut 18:22; further, Aune (1983, 56, 91) on both O.T. and Greco-Roman predictive elements of prophetic discourse.

[508] In favour of the view that the addressees were most likely still undergoing tribulations, see under 2.2.4.

In 3:5 the change to the first person once again may be seen to reflect Paul's emotional involvement and relative superiority over his companions.[509] At the same time, it may also reflect an effort to accentuate his own personal concern for the addressees, so as to anticipate any potential mistrust of his goodwill due to his own absence. Besides the reminder itself that Timothy was sent, the expression of concern that their labour should not have been in vain also contributes to creating an **ethos** appeal, insofar as such an expression is taken to mark the speech of responsible men who are not merely out to make an immediate but transient impression. Also, the indirect reference to the opposition of the tempter to Paul's work once again (cf. 2:18) serves as an **ethos** appeal.

As for the report of Timothy's good news (3:6), this issues in an explicit reciprocal expression of goodwill ($\kappa\alpha\iota$ $\eta\mu\epsilon\iota\varsigma$ $\upsilon\mu\alpha\varsigma$) and an expression of reciprocal comfort or encouragement in distress and affliction: $\delta\iota\alpha$ $\tau o\upsilon\tau o$ $\pi\alpha\rho\epsilon\kappa\lambda\eta\theta\eta\mu\epsilon\nu$, $\alpha\delta\epsilon\lambda\phi o\iota$, $\epsilon\phi'$ $\upsilon\mu\iota\nu$ $\epsilon\pi\iota$ $\pi\alpha\sigma\eta$ $\tau\eta$ $\alpha\nu\alpha\gamma\kappa\eta$ $\kappa\alpha\iota$ $\theta\lambda\iota\psi\epsilon\iota$ $\eta\mu\omega\nu$ $\delta\iota\alpha$ $\tau\eta\varsigma$ $\upsilon\mu\omega\nu$ $\pi\iota\sigma\tau\epsilon\omega\varsigma$ (3:7). Just as Timothy had been sent to comfort/encourage the addressees in their tribulations ($\pi\alpha\rho\alpha\kappa\alpha\lambda\epsilon\sigma\alpha\iota\ldots\theta\lambda\iota\psi\epsilon\sigma\iota\nu$ $\tau\alpha\upsilon\tau\alpha\iota\varsigma$, 3:2), the addressors had also been subsequently comforted/encouraged by Timothy's good report ($\pi\alpha\rho\epsilon\kappa\lambda\eta\theta\eta\mu\epsilon\nu\ldots\alpha\nu\alpha\gamma\kappa\eta$ $\kappa\alpha\iota$ $\theta\lambda\iota\psi\epsilon\iota$, 3:7).

Immediately subsequent to the report of Timothy's good news (3:7) and prior to the closing thanksgiving/prayer-report (3:9-10), the movement of author-other time in the text intersects the axis of author-present time (see 3.2.3) where the addressors' satisfaction (**pathos** appeal) is expressed conditionally: $o\tau\iota$ $\nu\upsilon\nu$ $\zeta\omega\mu\epsilon\nu$ $\epsilon\alpha\nu$ $\upsilon\mu\epsilon\iota\varsigma$ $\sigma\tau\eta\kappa\epsilon\tau\epsilon$ $\epsilon\nu$ $\kappa\upsilon\rho\iota\omega$ (3:8). Besides Paul's unusual use of $\epsilon\alpha\nu$ with the indicative,[510] the fact that a consistent relation cannot be taken for granted between the form and meaning of objective present conditions ($\epsilon\iota$ + ind. pres.) and hypothetical future conditions ($\epsilon\alpha\nu$ + subj.)[511] makes the sense of this utterance depend heavily on the surrounding co-text. On first sight, the conditional clause would appear to reflect a real present condition in relation to the preceding mention of Timothy's good news.[512] But the immediately subsequent mention of deficiencies (3:10) and the treatment of such in especially 4:13-5:11 gives it a more eventual, future sense and thereby an implicitly exhortatory element of appeal.[513] It may well be that this un-

---

[509] See esp. Rigaux, 1956, 474; also, e.g., Lightfoot, 1904, 43; Milligan, 1908, 39; Best, 1977, 137; Collins, 1980-81, 352;= 1984, 179.

[510] Though this has been regarded as a solicism, the usage was gaining ground in the 1st century and has the overwhelming authority of the manuscripts here. See Lightfoot, 1904, 45-6. Elsewhere in Paul's letters there is the somewhat questionable example in I Cor 13:2.

[511] On this see especially Moule (1963, 149); also Robertson (1934, 1008).

[512] See, e.g., Best (1977, 143): "if, as indeed you do." Similarly, Dobschütz, 1909, 143. Rigaux (1956, 481) notes that it is presented as such: "du moment que, en sorte que, puisque." Milligan (1908, 41) and Ellingworth/Nida (1976, 61-2) see the indicative as bringing out the writer's confidence of fulfillment.

[513] Lightfoot (1904, 45-6) notes hesitation in view of the incompleteness of faith (3:10): "if so be ye stand fast." Likewise, Frame, 1912, 132. The implicit parenetic appeal noted by, e.g., Dobschütz (1909, 143) and Rigaux (1956,481) fits

usual Pauline use of εαν with the indicative was not so much an accidental slip into less careful usage as an accommodation to the need to express both satisfaction and pastoral concern: while the use of the subjunctive would have been inappropriate in view of the addressees' progress, the use of the weaker εαν is more fitting in view of the subsequently mentioned deficiencies.

4.2.5 Delimitation, Coherence and Rhetoric of 3:9-13

The transition to 3:9-13 is not only anticipated by the temporal shift signaled by the TCrel νυν (3:8), but also by the thematic shift from Timothy's visit to the senders' present, continued desire to visit the addressees, introduced in the complex thematic sentence of 2.3ThM: (MBexpr) τινα γαρ ευχαριστιαν δυναμεθα τω θεω ανταποδουναι (P1) περι υμων (MBexpr) επι παση τη χαρα η χαιρομεν δι' υμας εμπροσθεν του θεου ημων (cont. MBexpr) νυκτος και ημερας υπερεκπερισσου δεομενοι (P1.1) εις το ιδειν υμων το προσωπον και καταρτισαι τα υστερηματα της πιστεως υμων (3:9-10).[514] As for the γαρ, Rigaux is followed here in seeing this as an instance of its use in questions where it is generally inferential rather than immediately explanatory, corresponding to the French "donc" and usually left untranslated in English.[515] While there is continuation of the sentiment of 3:8, the particularly strong reiteration of thanksgiving and joy in the form of a rhetorical question here (cf. 1:2; 2:13; 2:19-20) also indicates a general relation to all that has been previously said.[516] This together with the related thematic shift and the change to a predominantly present-future perspective (see 3.2.3.1) provides strong evidence for seeing the next subsequence as opening at 3:9.[517]

With regard to both the delimitation and coherence of 3:9-13, the theme of the present desire of the senders to make a future visit, expressed in the prayer-report (3:10), is clearly continued in the initial petition of the following wish-prayer: αυτος δε ο θεος και πατηρ ημων και ο κυριος ημων Ιησους κατευθυναι την οδον ημων προς υμας (3:11).[518] The references to **past** desires and efforts for a return vis-

---

more naturally with this more eventual, future sense.

[514] While, e.g., Lightfoot (1904, 47), Frame (1912, 135) and Dibelius (1937, 18) take δεομενοι as attaching to χαιρομεν, the connection is in fact looser than this. Dobschütz (1909, 146) is followed here in his preference to see the participle as functioning more like a finite verb much as in 2:12.

[515] Rigaux, 1956, 482. Also reflected in Dibelius' translation, 1937, 18. Cf. Blass/Debrunner, 1961, 235-6.

[516] Thus Rigaux (1956, 482) and Holtz (1986, 136).

[517] This delimitation has been previously adopted by, e.g., Hurd (1972, 27) and Wiles (1973, 177, 184) against most other exegetes who see no major transition here, as, e.g., Lightfoot, 1904, 3; Dobschütz, 1909, 144-6; Frame, 1912, 133; Kümmel, 1973, 220; Schlier, 1972, 48 ff.; Lee/Lee, 1975, 33; Vielhauer, 1975, 84; Best, 1977, 138-45; and Holtz, 1986, 32.

it together with expressions of joy and a concluding eschatological climax in 2:17-20 form a parallel to the references to **present** desire for a return visit combined with expressions of joy and a concluding eschatological climax in 3:9-13. This serves to frame the sequence dealing with Timothy's visit in 3:1-8 (see 4.2.6).

The **pathos** appeal to loving affection in 3:9-13 is prominent. This may be seen in the elaborate expression of thanksgiving and joy (3:9) and in the expression of intense desire to return (3:10; 3:11). Such expressions of goodwill also serve as **ethos** appeals. Furthermore, both **pathos** and **ethos** appeals are apparent in the petition for the increase of mutual Christian love and for the addressees' steadfastness and unblamable holiness before God at the parousia: υμας δε ο κυριος πλεονασαι και περισσευσαι τῃ αγαπῃ εις αλληλους και εις παντας και ημεις εις υμας, εις το στηριξαι υμων τας καρδιας αμεμπτους εν αγιωσυνῃ εμπροσθεν του θεου και πατρος ημων εν τῃ παρουσια του κυριου ημων Ιησου μετα παντων των αγιων αυτου, (αμην). In the latter clause the affective appeal is to the emotion of confidence. Thus, although 3:11-13 constitutes a formal unit as a wish-prayer, these text-semantic and text-pragmatic features of thematic extention and predominant affective appeals indicate that it combines with 3:9-10 to constitute 3:9-13 on a higher level of delimitation. Further evidence of this is to be seen in the parallels between 2:17-20 and 3:9-13 framing 3:1-8.

4.2.6 Some Concluding Observations on I Thess 2:17-3:13

Combined with the foregoing observations based on semantic and pragmatic criteria, there is the particularly strong supporting text-syntactic evidence of a pattern of lexical or partial lexical recurrence between 2:17-20 and 3:9-13 that indicates a strategy of ring-composition similar to that noted in 1:2-2:16 above. There is the recurrence of the visit theme in το προσωπον υμων ιδειν (2:17), εις το ιδειν υμων το προσωπον (3:10), and in (ελθειν) προς υμας (2:18), (την οδον ημων) προς υμας (3:11), of the joy motif in χαρα (2:19-20), χαρα ᾑ χαιρομεν (3:9), and of the judgement and parousia motifs in the eschatological climaxes marking the close of both text-sequences: εμπροσθεν του κυριου ημων Ιησου εν τῃ αυτου παρουσιᾳ (2:20), εμπροσθεν του θεου και πατρος ημων εν τῃ παρουσιᾳ του κυριου ημων Ιησου (3:13).

A further indication of a circular development may be seen between the metaphor of Satan "hindering" the senders' return (και ενεκοψεν ημας ο σατανας) in 2:18 and the first petition of the wish-prayer that their way may be "made straight" to the addressees (κατευθυναι την οδον ημων προς υμας, 3:11).[519] In other words, the temporal and thematic progression in the passage occurs in such a way as to create both a linear and a circular development. Temporally and logically the progression is linear, but thematically and rhetorically-pragmatically the progression is circular.

---

[518] This observation supplements those of Rigaux (1956, 485) that the close connection between 3:10 and 3:11-13 goes against Frame's (1912, 17) taking the latter as a separate text-sequence of equal rank with 1:2-3:9. See also Wiles, 1973, 184.

[519] Thus, Lightfoot, 1904, 48.

As in 2:17-20, there is a prominence of **pathos** appeals and an absence of any quasi-logical appeals in 3:9-13. By contrast, although **pathos** appeals are clearly present in 3:1-8, there is a particular focus on tribulations suffered by both parties where a combined inartificial and quasi-logical appeal is made particularly prominent (3:3-4). At the same time, as in 1:2-2:16, the **ethos** type of appeal is apparent throughout 2:17-3:13. Not only is this strategy of ring-composition present here and in 1:2-2:16, but it will be shown to also inform 4:1-5:24.

Thus, also here (cf. 4.1.5 above) a fourth, fifth and sixth level of sequential-hierarchical text-sequences may be observed. The text-sequence 2:17-3:13 with its subsequences and basic criteria of delimitation may be represented as follows in Figure 6:

LEVEL IV

I Thess 2:17-3:13

2ThInf

LEVEL V

2:17-20	3:1-8	3:(8)9-13
2.1ThM; PCrel; TCrel; C Prominence of Pathos Appeals	2.2ThInf Prominence of Inartificial and Quasi-Logical Appeal	2.3ThM; TCrel; C Prominence of Pathos Appeals

LEVEL VI

3:1-5	3:6-8
2.2.1ThM; PCrel TCrel; C	2.2.2ThM; PCrel TCrel; C

Figure 6

4.3   THE TERMINAL-TRANSITIONAL FUNCTIONS OF I THESS 3:9-13

G.P. Wiles has especially drawn attention to the unity of 3:9-13 and to the fact that the initial prayer-report (1:2b-3) culminates in the prayer-report of 3:10 with the latter giving the occasion of the letter, viz., Paul's "frustrated longing to visit the Thessalonians and help them in their time of crisis."[520] Furthermore, as analysed in 3.2.1

---

[520] Wiles, 1973, 177, 184. Although he finds 3:9-13 to be a distinct unity as a text-sequence (184), the very fact that one has to do with "reports" of prayer

above, apart from the form of the rhetorical question in 3:9-10, which achieves a heightened intensity, this expression of thanksgiving must be seen as a reiteration of the preceding reports of thanksgiving. As a combined unit with the formally dependent prayer-report, it parallels the initial thanksgiving/prayer-report (1:2-3) in particular, so as to form an **inclusio** for the whole of 1:2-3:13 (see 3.2.1.1). The motifs of faith and love (cf. 1:3) are clearly focused on again in 3:10 and 3:12, with hope finding an echo in the reference to the addressees' hearts being established in unblamable holiness before God at the parousia (3:13). Thus, the subsequence 3:9-13 has the function of not only concluding the sequence of 2:17-3:13, as just demonstrated, but also the larger sequence of 1:2-3:13.

On the other hand, not only does this subsection close the first major section, it also prepares for what follows in 4:1-5:24. The topics of "holiness" (4:3, 7; 5:23) and of continued growth in brotherly "love" (4:9-10) and of the **parousia** (4:13 ff.; 5:2 ff.) are all anticipated in 3:12-13.[521] Furthermore, since Paul could not return as yet, it is fair to conclude that the letter itself was intended to serve the need "to supply what is lacking" in the addressees' faith, mentioned in the prayer-report (3:10).[522] It would appear to be more this need that provides the occasion of the letter than Paul's frustration over not being able to return himself, although this was also undoubtedly a factor. In antiquity a letter's status as the representative of its writer was so high that it could be used to carry out a judge's decision in legal proceedings or partner's terms in contractual proceedings with binding effect in their absence.[523] Thus, it is most reasonable to see the subsequent admonitions and instruction in 4:1-5:24 or some particular part of it as officially serving to fulfill the goal $καταρτισαι$ $τα$ $υστερηματα$ $της$ $πιστεως$ $υμων$ in the absence of Paul and company.[524]

This observation necessitates a closer look at the sense of $υστερημα$ in this context. It can mean "deficiency" here in either the neutral sense of "need" or in the negative sense of "defect," implying a failure. The question is whether Paul is referring negatively to defects on their part or more neutrally to needs that arise out of their general or specific circumstances as newly converted believers.[525] E. Best leaves it with the unspecified sense of "deficiencies" with the subsequent reminders of previous moral instructions (4:1 ff.) and new eschatological instructions (4:13 ff.), cate-

---

goes against his view that the rhetorical question of 3:9-10 is evidence of this being "an actual offering of prayer to God" on the basis of parallels to such rhetorical questions in the Psalms. Ps 116:12 is given as a parallel (186).

[521] On this see, e.g., Dobschütz, 1909, 154; Rigaux, 1956, 485 ff.; Marxsen, 1979, 56-7.

[522] "Faith" here should be taken in the broad sense expressed by Best (1977, 145): "the response of the whole being to God."

[523] See, e.g., Doty, 1973, 16.

[524] Thus, e.g., Holmberg, 1978, 82-3; Marxsen, 1979, 26, 57. Best (1977, 145), however, sees this connection between $υστερηματα$ and 4:1 ff. to be presumable but not certain.

[525] See, e.g., Bauer (1979, 849) for the former option and, e.g., Marxsen (1979, 56) for the latter.

chetical admonitions (5:12 ff.) interpreted as indicating that both moral failures and inadequacies due to the brevity of Paul's stay are involved.[526]

In view of the fact that Paul frequently uses the expression $αναπληρουν$ $το$ $υστερημα$ (I Cor 16:17; II Cor 9:12; 11:9; Phil 2:30), the singular use of $υστερημα$ with $καταρτισαι$ here speaks in favour of the more negative sense of some defect.[527] The subsequent analyses indicate that these deficiencies are to be located specifically in 4:13 ff. However, the nature of the problem calls for corrective measures without reproof.

4.4 ANALYSIS OF I THESS 4:1-5:24 AND SUBSEQUENCES

4.4.1 Text-Syntactic Connection of 4:1-5:24 to 1:2-3:13

The delimitation and coherence of 4:1-5:24 as a major text-sequence on the same level as 1:2-3:13 has been carried out above in 3.2.2 and 3.2.3.2. With regard to the relation between these major text-sequences the connective combination $λοιπον$ $ουν$ deserves particular attention here.

A common interpretation holds that $λοιπον$ "is not just an ordinary transitional particle but specifically a **locutio properans ad finem**,"[528] and that in I Thess this supports taking 1:2-3:13 as constituting the "body" of the letter containing "all the primary information that Paul wished to convey."[529] However, in view of the length and contents of 4:1-5:24, other exegetes have been more cautious and take it as marking the transition to the exhortatory section.[530]

The latter position finds support in M. Thrall's arguments for taking the combination $λοιπον$ $ουν$ as being generally inferential with the particles reinforcing each other much in the same way as the $αρα$ $ουν$ combination.[531] However, the examples she takes from Epictetus' **Discourses** only illustrate a close inferential transition between one statement and another.[532] There are, in fact, clear instances where $λοι$-

---

[526] Best, 1977, 144-5.

[527] Thus, Holtz, 1986, 137-8.

[528] Thus Schubert (1939, 26), referring to Dobschütz (1909, 155) and Bultmann (1910, 101). Likewise, e.g., Lightfoot (1904, 51) and Frame (1912, 141-2) take it in the sense of "for the rest" and as marking the "conclusion" of the letter.

[529] Thus Schubert (1939, 25-6), referring to Dobschütz (1909, 155) and followed by, e.g., J.L. White (1972, 70), Boers (1975, 153) with modifications, and Longenecker (1984-85, 89).

[530] Thus, e.g., Rigaux, 1956, 495-6; Ellingworth/Nida, 1976, 73; Marxsen, 1979, 57; Holtz, 1986, 151.

[531] Thrall (1962, 28), following Jannaris' (1898, 429-31) observation that $λοιπον$ in Hellenistic Greek served as a connecting particle much like $ουν$ with the general inferential sense of "then," "therefore" or "well then."

που is used in Epictetus' **Discourses** to mark a **text-sequential transition** where the connection is a loose inference to what is said in general in a preceding section as a whole.[533] Furthermore, with regard to letters, C.J. Bjerkelund notes examples where both λοιπον and λοιπον ουν mark the transition to the petition or request that constitutes the main communicative purpose of the letter.[534]

Whether the transition thus marked is being made to a "conclusion" following the main message, to a text-sequence within the main message or to the sequence containing the main message, is a question that must give priority to text-pragmatic, rhetorical considerations. Here in I Thess 4:1 the evidence is seen to support taking λοιπον ουν as generally inferential ("then" or "and so") in relation to 1:2-3:13 in view of its exordial-like character. Thus it seems to mark a major text-sequential transition to the text-sequence containing the main message of the letter (see ch. 6).

4.4.2 The Delimitation and Coherence of 4:1-12

The transition to the text-sequence 4:1-12 is marked in 4:1-2 by the combined connective particles λοιπον ουν, the address αδελφοι plus the complex thematic marker 3ThM: (MBcon) ερωτωμεν υμας και παρακαλουμεν εν κυριω Ιησου (P1) ινα περισσευητε μαλλον (i.e. καθως παρελαβετε παρ' ημων το πως δει υμας περιπατειν και αρεσκειν θεω, καθως και περιπατειτε). (MBref) οιδατε (P1.1) τινας παραγγελιας εδωκαμεν υμιν δια του κυριου Ιησου. The theme of P1 is expressed in a rather tortuous sentence, but may be readily reduced to "that you progress more and more in living a life pleasing to God according to the instructions received from us." The proposition in P1.1 in 4:2 (τινας παραγγελιας εδωκαμεν υμιν) emphasizes the subordinate modifying element καθως παρελαβετε παρ' ημων in 4:1 so as to specify P1, not in terms of an ethical subtheme, but specifically in terms of the previously given instructions.[535] The general theme in P1 is expanded in the topics of being holy, i.e. avoiding sexual impurity (4:3-8), brotherly love (4:9-10a), and quiet living, minding one's own affairs, manual labour and decorous conduct generally (4:10b-12).[536] This gives 4:1-12 an overall semantic coherence.

The proposition in P1.1, τινας παραγγελιας εδωκαμεν υμιν, κτλ., is actually a MC **directly** and **exophorically** thematizing previous communicative events of instruction. At the same time there is an **indirect, endophoric** reference to the present

---

[532] Thrall, 1962, 28. Among the inferential examples given, there is even an instance of the combination λοιπον ουν itself in Epictetus, Dss 2.19.33.

[533] Dss 1.18.21; 1.30.5; 2.1.8; 2.8.15; 2.14.9; 3.24.88. In 1.18.21 it occurs in the analogous combination of ειτα λοιπον. Furthermore, the combination λοιπον ουν itself also occurs in Bell 2.390 where it clearly marks a text-sequential transition in Agrippa's speech reported by Josephus.

[534] Bjerkelund, 1967, 128.

[535] As Rigaux notes (1956, 499), παραγγελιας εδωκαμεν as a paraphrase of παρελαβετε was a common Hellenistic turn of phrase.

[536] Similarly, e.g., Marxsen (1979, 59); also implied in Lee/Lee (1975, 33, 37).

text by way of substitution on the abstraction and the metacommunicative levels. The expression τινας refers to specific contents, obviously supplied in 4:3-12, and thus qualifies as a SA. The character and function of 4:3-12 is indirectly indicated by παραγγελιας, which qualifies this expression as 1.2.2.1SMind. The indirect reference here is realized by an implicit comparison which is made explicit in the parallel, iterative MC expressions καθως παρελαβετε παρ' ημων (4:1), καθως και προειπαμεν υμιν και διεμαρτυραμεθα (4:6), and καθως υμιν παρηγγειλαμεν (4:11). These expressions of reminder throughout 4:1-12 give the sequence pragmatic coherence and contrast it with the introduction of new information signalled in 4:13.

Finally, that the partial lexical recurrence of παραγγελιας (4:2) in παρηγγειλαμεν (4:11) functions as a delimiting **inclusio** is strengthened by the cluster of lexical elements αδελφοι, υμας, παρακαλουμεν, περισσευητε μαλλον in 4:1 recurring in 4:10 as παρακαλουμεν, υμας, αδελφοι, περισσευειν μαλλον and by the lexical recurrence of περιπατειν/περιπατειτε in 4:1 and περιπατητε in 4:12.

4.4.3 The Rhetoric of 4:1-12

4.4.3.1 Generally Relevant Religious-Ethical Exhortation

The validity of what was being exhorted is not argued for by way of any lengthy discussion, but divine authority is appealed to, as may be seen in such expressions as παρακαλουμεν εν τω κυριω Ιησου (4:1), τινας παραγγελιας εδωκαμεν υμιν δια του κυριου Ιησου (4:2),[537] τουτο γαρ εστιν θελημα του θεου, κτλ. (4:3), τοιγαρουν ο αθετων ουκ ανθρωπον αθετει αλλα τον θεον τον διδοντα το πνευμα αυτου το αγιον εις υμας (4:8) and αυτοι γαρ υμεις θεοδιδακτοι εστε εις το αγαπαν αλληλους (4:9).[538] As Kennedy notes, the appeal to divine authority, characteristic of Judeo-Christian rhetoric in religious discourse, is analogous to **ethos** in classical rhetoric and is often bolstered by a **pathos** appeal to fear of future punishment among other things.[539] Such a **pathos** appeal is apparent in 4:5c:

---

[537] Against Bjerkelund (1967, 132; 140; 213, note 25) 4:1-2 cannot be taken as occurring ad hoc in relation to what follows, as demonstrated above, and the prepositional phrases εν κυριω Ιησου and δια του κυριου Ιησου in 4:1-2 should be taken as indicating the ultimate source of the exhortations and thereby the authority behind them and not as merely expressing the urgency of the exhortations (189). See especially Rigaux' comments on these prepositional phrases (1956, 499-500). Further, Malherbe, 1983, 250.

[538] For a concept elsewhere in Paul comparable to θεοδιδακτοι Rigaux (1956, 517) notes διδακτοις πνευματος in I Cor 2:13. This connection is supported by the fact that the gift of the Holy Spirit has just been mentioned preceding this in 4:8. Malherbe (1983, 253-4) finds that Paul may have coined the term in conscious rejection of something that is self-taught (αυτοδιδακτος), a feature especially vaunted by the Epicurians. However this may be, he is surely correct in rejecting Koester's view (1979, 39) that "taught by God" serves to emphasize the recipients' independence of the senders' instruction. The evidence of 4:1-2 and the emphasis in 2:1-12 on Paul as God's spokesman weighs too heavily against such a reading.

διοτι εκδικος κυριος περι παντων τουτων.

The admonitions in 4:3-8 are aimed against the dangers of sexual impurity of some sort.[540] The transition to this subsequence is marked in 4:3 by γαρ, functioning much like transitional δε, and by 3.1ThM: (MBref) τουτο...εστιν θελημα του θεου, expressing necessity by reference to God's will, with (P) as the noun phrase ο αγιασμος υμων. Also, the lexical recurrences of αγιασμος/αγιασμω in 4:3-4 and αγιασμω in 4:7 may be seen as having the general delimiting effect of an **inclusio**.[541] The fact that the addressees were predominantly Gentile in origin and that Gentile standards in sexual matters in general were seen by Jews and Jewish Christians as decidedly inferior can serve to explain why Paul selects this particular topic for reminder here. Concrete failures on the part of the addressees in this respect are hardly likely to be reflected here in view of the fact that he has just said that they are actually living in a way pleasing to God in 4:1.[542] As A.J. Malherbe has pertinently pointed out, that which particularly distinguished even the more elevated Hellenistic philosophical thought on ethical standards from Jewish and Christian thought was that Jews and Christians always began with God. This general background provides a likely explanation for the prominence of Paul's theological warrants in his references to divine authority (4:3, 8), judgement (4:6b) and calling (4:7): "Paul is concerned with the sanctified rather than the rational life."[543]

As for brotherly love, there is apparently no need to write anything other than the exhortation that they should abound more and more in this (4:9-10), which leads to brief reminders to live quietly, mind their own business and work with their hands in order to live decorously in the eyes of outsiders and not to be in need of anything (4:11-12). The transition to this topic is marked by transitional δε and 3.2ThM: (MBref) ου χρειαν εχετε, referring to lack of necessity in view of the circumstances of the addressees, and (P) as περι...της φιλαδελφιας...γραφειν υμιν. This hardly appears to be a typical instance of the rhetorical device called **praeteritio** used to create irony or avoid a topic due to lack of time, to the addressees' acquaintance with it, or to its being disadvantageous in some way.[544] The subsequent explanation

---

[539] Kennedy, 1980, 121.

[540] For the purposes of the present analysis it will not be necessary to take up the specific exegetical problems involved in 4:4-6. For literature on the problems of the passage see Collins, 1982-83a, 420-29;=1984, 326-35. Cp., e.g., Koester (1979, 42-3) and Donfried (1985-86, 341-42) as recent instances supporting the position of references to both sexual behaviour (4:3-5) and business relations (4:6).

[541] Thus also Malherbe, 1983, 250-1; Collins, 1982-1983a, 424;=1984, 330.

[542] While καθως και περιπατειτε (4:1) is missing in a large number of mss., it is nevertheless backed by the strongest external evidence. See Rigaux, 1956, 500; Metzger, 1971, 632; Marxsen, 1979, 58; Holtz, 1986, 153. Collins (1982-1983a, 421;=1984, 327) observes a consensus that 4:3-6 is without concrete motivation in the community.

[543] Malherbe, 1983, 150-51. See further Nock, 1933, 218-20. See also Koester (1979, 42-3) on the Jewish-Hellenistic background of this exhortation and the Christianized concept of sanctification.

that the addressees were divinely taught in this respect would appear to allow the device to be explained as an instance of avoiding a topic due to the addressees' acquaintance with it. In view of what follows, however, the strategy is more subtle than this. Both the disclaimer of needing to write on brotherly love and the subsequent references to their knowledge and practice of this serves more as an acknowledgment that would disarm any misapprehension that his exhortation to increase more and more should reflect disapproval rather than encouragement.

Most commentators take the admonitions of 4:11 as being directed at concrete instances of actual deficiencies, although they differ regarding the background.[545] In view of the emphasis on the admonition to abound in brotherly love, one can hardly speak of any particular focus on the subsequent admonitions which are loosely tacked on by way of $και...και...και$. Furthermore, the subsequent $καθως υμιν παρηγγειλαμεν$ shows that they are reminders of previous instruction.[546] There is actually nothing in the text that explicitly supports seeing concrete failures over against seeing only potential dangers warned against here.[547] That these admonitions in 4:11 are more specific in character than the general exhortation to increase in brotherly love is hardly evidence of any actual breaches of conduct.[548] In fact, Malherbe has shown that quiet living ($ησυχια$), minding one's own affairs ($πρασσειν τα ιδια$), and manual labour were commonly discussed topics, and that decorum ($ευσχημοσυνη$) and self-sufficiency also were self-evident ideals to most philosophers belonging to the addressees' Hellenistic background.[549]

The question here is whether one must be forced to choose between two extreme alternatives as intimated by H. Koester when he writes that the admonitions of 4:1-12 "are not occasioned by the situation, rather they elaborate a tradition."[550] There is the additional possibility that "the situation" may be addressed by an author, not merely in narrow terms of its specifically unique or concrete problems and needs, but

---

[544] See Plett, 1979a, 59; Lausberg, 1963, 135-6; 1973, 435-7. Harnish (1973, 53) has suggested that 4:9 and 5:1-3 qualify as instances of praeteritio. An example of praeteritio or $παραλειψις$ as a specific device for expressing irony is given in Rhet ad Alex 1434a,17-24 (see 4.4.8.1-4.4.8.2).

[545] E.g., Lightfoot, 1904, 60; Dobschütz, 1909, 182; Frame, 1912, 161-2; Forestell, 1968, 231-2; Best, 1977, 174-7; Marxsen, 1979, 62. Rigaux (1956, 516) is more cautious, but is inclined in the same direction.

[546] Thus, Dibelius, 1937, 23. While Dibelius himself (1931, 216) was faced with the criticism of trying to establish too general a context for parenesis on strict form-critical grounds, in I Thess he argues for the exhortations as not addressing specific situational problems precisely in view of the commendations in 4:1, 9 and the fact that it is reminders of previous instruction that is involved (1937, 19-20, 23).

[547] Donfried's recent arguments (1985-86, 341-2) for seeing a response to concrete failures in 4:1-9 totally ignores the important text-pragmatic remarks in 4:1 to the opposite effect. Also, Jewett's treatment (1984, 16) of the main topics of 4:1-12 under the rubric of "issues" goes too far.

[548] See, e.g., Rigaux (1956, 516) who focuses on this more specific point.

also somewhat more broadly in terms of its belonging to a particular **type of situation** with characteristic needs that can be more or less anticipated.[551] This is not quite the same thing as addressing "the church as a whole for the purpose of general edification."[552]

Thus, one must reckon with the possibility of a mediation between Timothy's reports of more or less concrete or potential needs and Paul's pastoral intuition of a type of situation working in various proportions to motivate the choices of admonitions to be communicated. Paul's experience in establishing new communities of faith would have made him quite aware of the potential dangers not only of eschatological fervor but of the enthusiasm generally characteristic of newly formed religious communities.[553] Such evangelistic-pastoral experience plus only an intimation from Timothy of a possible potentially dangerous trend in Thessalonica would have given occasion enough for such cautions. Furthermore, apart from the possibility of eschatological enthusiasm causing any cessation in mundane labour,[554] Gentile attitudes in general towards manual labour were by no means typically positive.[555]

Consequently, in 4:1-12 Paul is seen as neither **merely** elaborating a tradition nor responding to specific concrete failures, but selectively reminding his addressees of prior admonitions appropriate to the type of situation they were a part of. The selection of topics is quite appropriate to what one would expect to be potential points of danger that would characterize any predominantly Gentile group of people who had responded in faith to Paul's proclamation of the gospel. Furthermore, as shown in 2.1, the use of $\pi\epsilon\rho\iota$ to introduce topical shifts is too general a textual phenomenon to allow this as evidence of answers to explicit questions by the addressees without other substantial indications, as in the case of I Cor 7:1.

4.4.3.2 A Credibility-Enhancing Persuasive Function

The foregoing observations make it possible to recognize another important function of these reminders and admonitions, viz., that of further undergirding the **ethos** of the senders.[556] In ancient rhetoric Aristotle explicitly mentions that the use of maxims

---

[549] Malherbe, 1983, 251-2.

[550] Koester, 1979, 38-9.

[551] Similarly, e.g., Schrage, 1961, 45 ff.

[552] Thus Bradley (1953, 240) who also moves too quickly to see an arbitray connection between parenesis and context on the basis of his study of the parenetic "form" he refers to as the topos. For sound criticisms see Mullins (1980, 541-47) and esp. Brunt (1985, 495-500).

[553] Cf. Rigaux, 1956, 521.

[554] See, e.g., Best, 1977, 174-5.

[555] Cf. Rigaux, 1956, 523.

may serve as an **ethos** type of appeal in that they make the moral purpose of the speaker clear.[557] While maxims and parenesis are not exactly the same thing, they are close enough to justify seeing a parallel here.[558] In **Rhet** 2.21.2 the maxim is described as dealing with what should be chosen or avoided with regard to human actions in general. According to M. Dibelius, it is basically the form of command or summons that distinguishes parenesis from the collection of maxims in a **gnomologium**,[559] although a maxim can also take the form of a command or prohibition.[560]

The persuasive force of maxims is basically realized in their reflection of a general consensus of opinion. In instances and situations where the generality of this consensus is reduced or in conflict, Aristotle observes the need for accompanying supportive arguments.[561] In a similar vein, J.D. Quinn defines parenesis as parenetic speech that does not allow a counter-statement and supports this from Classical, Hellenistic and Jewish-Hellenistic sources,[562] while W. Wolbert distinguishes a similar concept of parenesis from "normative Ethik" where opinions are in conflict and a particular position must be defended.[563] As previously shown by H. Cancik, this common persuasive force of parenesis and other related forms is present in the more general category of "prescriptive" language, and is analogous to the theorem in "descriptive" language.[564] Although this places parenetic language on the more affective side of persuasion, she shows in her analysis of Seneca's letters that "sie die eigenwertige Form eines bestimmten Philosophierens ist."[565]

If Paul had been preoccupied in 4:1-12 with correcting actual instances of failure among the addressees, the **ethos** appeal of this parenesis would be less likely to serve as a preparatory strategy of persuasion. The corrections themselves would then be the main point of the communication. As it is, it is concluded here that 4:1-12 may be seen to serve **directly** as prophylactic and encouraging exhortation in which the focus is on περισσευητε μαλλον (4:1, 10), and **indirectly** as making additional **ethos** ap-

---

[556] The following observations go against Berger (1984, 1077) in this respect. He sees the effects of parenetic sentences as being particularly dependent upon the authority of the teacher, when the contents are general and not accompanied by extensive supporting arguments. Furthermore, Paul explicitly invokes the authority of Christ (4:1-2) and God (4:3, 6-8, 9) here.

[557] Rhet 2.21.16.

[558] See H.D. Betz, 1979, 291 ff.; Wolbert, 1981, 23; Berger, 1984, 1079.

[559] Dibelius/Greeven, 1976, 3.

[560] See Lausberg, 1973, 432; Berger, 1984, 1059-60.

[561] Rhet 2.21.3 ff.

[562] Quinn, 1981, 495-501. See also Perdue (1981, 242-6) summarizing Malherbe (1972).

[563] Wolbert, 1981, 18-19.

[564] Cancik (1967, 16-17, 22-3), who is also referred to by, e.g., H.D. Betz (1974-75, 375; 1979, 254) and Bünker (1984, 96-7).

peals that further bolster the senders' credibility in preparation for the concrete exigence to be treated in 4:13 ff. If the problem in this subsequent passage came about due to some kind of insufficiency in instruction to begin with, the new instruction given in especially 4:14b, 15 ff. (see 2.2.3) could potentially give rise to doubts about the stability and therefore the reliability of Paul's instruction in general. In this situation the hortatory reminders together with the encouraging indications that they were "walking" well and should do so more and more would further serve to establish the senders' pastoral authority so as to confirm present continuity and stability with regard to the past.[566]

4.4.4 The Delimitation and Coherence of 4:13-5:11

Before treating the subsequences 4:13-18 and 5:1-11, a brief survey of the features that speak for seeing them as thematically, formally and functionally building a larger coherent text-sequence is in order.[567] To begin with, both subsequences begin with a statement of the respective themes, accompanied by the vocative αδελφοι, and the transitional connective δε (4:13; 5:1). While the themes in περι των κοιμωμενων and περι...των χρονων και των καιρων are made verbally explicit on the surface level of the text for each text-sequence, a superior cover theme for 4:13-5:11 as a whole such as περι της παρουσιας may be established in the deep structure by inferencing (see 1.2.2) both from these explicit themes and from the apocalyptic contents in each passage.[568] This may be noted here as 4ThInf.

Both subsequences formally close with an admonition beginning with the lexical recurrence of παρακαλειτε αλληλους. Abundant use of apocalyptic motifs is made in both sections in contrast to what precedes and follows and both make use of creedal material, viz., οτι Ιησους απεθανεν και ανεστη (4:14); Ιησου Χριστου του αποθανοντος υπερ ημων (5:9-10).[569] There is also the general conceptual recurrence of συν κυριω εσομεθα (4:17) in αμα συν αυτω ζησωμεν (5:10) with the references to the οι κοιμωμενοι, οι νεκροι/οι ζωντες οι περιλειπομενοι of the former sequence echoed in the word-play in ειτε γρηγορωμεν ειτε καθευδωμεν αμα συν αυτω ζησωμεν in 5:10. Besides this common emphasis at the close of each sequence on being together with the Lord, there is also a common emphasis on not being like

---

[565] Cancik, 1967, 17.

[566] Thus, this parenetic aspect of Paul's apostolic authority is not as independent of the immediate situation as J.L. White (1983, 441) would affirm.

[567] See Plevnik (1979, 71-90) and Collins (1980, 325-43;=1984, 154-72) for perceptive summaries of the more formal evidence for the coherence of 4:13-5:11.

[568] This is what Marxsen (1979, 65) is actually doing when he writes that "Die beiden Stichworte in 4,13 und 5,1 gehören also unmittelbar zusammen: 4,13 nennt einen (für die Thessalonicher akuten) Teilaspekt des 5,1 grundsätzlich formulierten Problems der Zeiten und Stunden , also des Termins der Parusie." Lee/Lee (1975, 34-5, 37) do not observe this higher unity.

[569] See, e.g., Collins, 1980b, 326;=1984, 355.

οι λοιποι who grieve without hope (4:13) and who are spiritually asleep (5:6).

In the text-pragmatic dimension, παρακαλειτε recurs with the SA τοις λογοις τουτοις (4:18) that delimits 4:13-17 and with the SA διο (5:11) that delimits 5:1-10. The occurrence of this expression in 4:18 and its recurrence in 5:11 qualify as SM which together delimit 4:13-5:11 as a functional unit intended to convey consolation and encouragement. They will be noted as 1.2.2.2SM and 1.2.2.2SMit respectively.

4.4.5   The Delimitation and Coherence of 4:13-18

The transition to I Thess 4:13-18 is marked in 4:13 by transitional δε, by the address αδελφοι, and an introductory thematic clause, which may be described here as 4.1ThM: (MBcon) θελομεν (P) ου...υμας αγνοειν...περι των κοιμωμενων. The sequence is explicitly delimited by the SA τοις λογοις τουτοις in the closing admonition (4:18): ωστε παρακαλειτε αλληλους εν τοις λογοις τουτοις. Syntactic-semantic text-coherence is served by lexical-conceptual recurrence in κοιμωμενων/κοιμηθεντας/κοιμηθεντας (4:13, 14, 15) followed by a conceptual recurrence in οι νεκροι εν Χριστω (4:16), by lexical-conceptual recurrence in ανεστη/αναστησονται (4:14, 16) and in ημεις οι ζωντες οι περιλειπομενοι/ ημεις οι ζωντες οι περιλειπομενοι (4:15, 17), and by conceptual recurrence in συν αυτω/συν κυριω (4:14, 17). Furthermore, the text-sequence falls naturally into the following subsequences:[570]

1. 4:13: Thematic clause with motivation.

2. 4:14: First argument introduced by explanatory γαρ and based on the communication partners' common belief in the death and resurrection of Jesus.

3. 4:15-17: Second argument introduced by explanatory γαρ and constituting an appeal to a "word of the Lord" which is summarized in Paul's own words first (4:15b) and then presented directly (4:16-17).

4. 4:18: A concluding exhortation to comfort one another with these words.

4.4.6   The Rhetoric of 4:13-18

In view of the priority of pragmatic considerations, it is important for an interpretation of predominant functions in 4:13-18 to again focus on what is explicitly stated regarding the addressees in relation to the contents and to the types of persuasive appeals as well as on the explicit characterizations the author makes of the text-sequence in terms of its communicative purpose. Such explicit statements are to be found at the beginning (ου θελομεν δε υμας αγνοειν, αδελφοι, περι των κοιμωμενων, ινα μη λυπησθε καθως και οι λοιποι οι μη εχοντες ελπιδα, 4:13) and the end (ωστε παρακαλειτε αλληλους εν τοις λογοις τουτοις, 4:18)

---

[570] On this see, e.g., Collins, 1980, 328-33;=1984, 157-62; Lüdemann, 1984, 213 ff.; and Gillman, 1985, 272-4.

of the passage. Through the reductive, delimiting SA $\tau o\iota\varsigma$ $\lambda o\gamma o\iota\varsigma$ $\tau o\nu\tau o\iota\varsigma$ the admonition $\pi\alpha\rho\alpha\kappa\alpha\lambda\epsilon\iota\tau\epsilon$ becomes an indirect metacommunicative comment by Paul on 4:13 ff. whereby the sequence may be seen as intended to function as $\pi\alpha\rho\alpha\kappa\lambda\eta\sigma\iota\varsigma$ (1.2.2.1SM) in the sense of consolation.

As for the "disclosure formula" ($o\nu$ $\theta\epsilon\lambda o\mu\epsilon\nu$ $\delta\epsilon$ $\nu\mu\alpha\varsigma$ $\alpha\gamma\nu o\epsilon\iota\nu$) in 4:13,[571] it no doubt involves an element of emphasis, but one cannot limit it to this function as W. Harnish does.[572] It not only serves to signal a transition to a different topic but also the introduction of new information, as indicated by $\theta\epsilon\lambda o\mu\epsilon\nu$ together with the noetic verb.[573] This is supported by the distinct contrast between 4:1-12, with its several explicit reminders that the admonitions involved previously given instructions, and 4:13-18, which is without any such explicit remarks.[574] Furthermore, the basically prophylactic admonitions and the encouragements to further growth in conduct pleasing to God in 4:1-12 stand in contrast to Paul's treatment of the problem of deceased believers in 4:13-18. In this latter passage there is a noticeable absence of any comparable reassuring parenthetical remarks (cf. $\kappa\alpha\iota$ $\gamma\alpha\rho$ $\pi o\iota\epsilon\iota\tau\epsilon$ $\alpha\nu\tau o$, 4:10; $\kappa\alpha\theta\omega\varsigma$ $\kappa\alpha\iota$ $\pi\epsilon\rho\iota\pi\alpha\tau\epsilon\iota\tau\epsilon$, 4:1) that they in fact were acting or in this instance reacting appropriately.

Thus, Paul's motivation for his instruction in 4:13, $\iota\nu\alpha$ $\mu\eta$ $\lambda\nu\pi\eta\sigma\theta\epsilon$ $\kappa\alpha\theta\omega\varsigma$ $\kappa\alpha\iota$ $o\iota$ $\lambda o\iota\pi o\iota$ $o\iota$ $\mu\eta$ $\epsilon\chi o\nu\tau\epsilon\varsigma$ $\epsilon\lambda\pi\iota\delta\alpha$, comes across as an indirectly expressed admonition that reflects a concrete deficiency of the addressees rather than merely a prophylactic concern on the part of Paul,[575] especially in view of the comparison to those who do not have hope. These observations together with the persuasive strategies in 4:13-5:11 observed below are taken to indicate that the author perceived the addressees' grief to be of such a nature that it involved a deficiency of faith (cf. 3:10) that posed a serious potential threat to their hope and consequently to their being able to "stand fast in the Lord" (3:8).[576] In other words, it is primarily here that Paul

---

[571] A formula common in Hellenistic letters, see Mullins, 1965, 44-50. Without insisting on their order, the basic elements are $\theta\epsilon\lambda\omega$, a noetic verb in the infinitive, the person addressed ($\sigma\epsilon/\nu\mu\alpha\varsigma$), and the information introduced (usually by $o\tau\iota$ but also by $\pi\epsilon\rho\iota$). Occasionally there is also a vocative address.

[572] Harnish, 1973, 22. Similarly, Rigaux, 1956, 239; Ellingworth/Nida, 1976, 98-9; Reese, 1980, 212-13.

[573] Against Harnish see Lüdemann's arguments (1984, 214) on other instances in Rom 11:25, I Cor 10:1; 12:1. Against Best (1977, 184) even Harnish (1973, 22) accepts Rom 1:13 and II Cor 1:8 as introducing new information and not just emphasizing what is being written.

[574] J.W. Bailey (1955, 301) notes the contrast in general, while Best (1977, 184) notes it more narrowly in regard to 4:9 alone.

[575] It is therefore better to translate $\iota\nu\alpha$ $\mu\eta$ by "that...not" (RSV) or "so that...not" (TEV) rather than "lest" (Weymouth) or "to make sure that" (JB). It is referred to as a prohibition by, e.g., Lightfoot (1904, 63) and Dobschütz (1909, 187). Against Hyldahl's radical view (1980, 123) of open mistrust towards Paul as being reflected here, see 2.2.3.

[576] See esp. Marxsen (1969, 26, 32) and Lüdemann (1984, 214, 220).

comes to grips with a serious, concrete exigence specific to the particular situation of the addressees, a delicate problem needing correction without reproach.

4.4.6.1   I Thess 4:14: The First Argument

In view of the scope of the present analysis, the following observations on the argumentation in 4:14-17 will be selective without attempting to represent all the different exegetical positions that have been taken. After the reference to the addressees' grief-threatened hope, Paul grounds his quasi-logical appeal in their mutually-held basis of hope, their belief in the death and resurrection of Jesus ($ει γαρ πιστευομεν οτι Ιησους απεθανεν και ανεστη$) from which he draws the conclusion $ουτως και ο θεος τους κοιμηθεντας δια του Ιησου αξει συν αυτω$ (4:14). The sentence is full of exegetical problems. Among the various observations and options suggested, the following positions are held to:

1. The first class condition with the indicative allows $ει$ to have a causal sense ("since") reflecting the certitude of faith shared.[577]

2. The use of the "resurrection formula" $ανεστη$, instead of the normal credal "raising formula" ($εγειρειν$), constitutes an adaptation to the context where $αναστησονται$ is used of the resurrection in 4:16.[578]

3. The expression $τους κοιμηθεντας$ is a neutral euphemism for the dead.[579]

4. The prepositional phrase $δια του Ιησου$ does not modify $τους κοιμηθεντας$ but rather the verb.[580]

5. The expression $αξει συν αυτω$ refers to a future event, the "assumption" or "withdrawal" of deceased believers to be with Jesus before God.[581]

---

[577] See, e.g., Marxsen, 1969, 34; Lüdemann, 1984, 219; Holtz, 1986, 190.

[578] Thus Lüdemann (1984, 216) who notes that a comparable adaptation involves the use of $εζησεν$ in Rom 14:9.

[579] An expression also used frequently in pagan funeral inscriptions in general. See, e.g., Rigaux 1956, 529 ff.

[580] Rigaux (1956, 535-6), who takes the opposite view, notes that commentators are fairly equally divided. In favour of this view, since his commentary, see, e.g., Masson (1957, 55-6), Schlier (1972, 77); Harnish (1973, 35); Best (1977, 188-9), Collins (1980, 330;=1984, 159); Cavallin (1983, 60-1); and Holtz (1986, 193). Even if a connection with $τους κοιμηθεντας$ should be accepted, it is doubtful that this would reflect Christian martyrs, against, e.g., Donfried, 1985, 349-51; Pobee, 1985, 113. See Best's arguments (1977, 189) against this view.

[581] See, e.g., Marxsen, 1969, 34-5; Plevnik, 1979, 76; Hyldahl, 1980, 133. Harnish (1973, 34 ff.) takes it too narrowly as a reference to the resurrection. See fur-

This results in the translation "For since we believe that Jesus died and rose again, even so, through Jesus, God will bring with him those who have fallen asleep."[582] It remains to note the stylistic awkwardness involved in both prepositional phrases depending on the same verb and the change of the grammatical subject to "God" in the latter clause.

The brusque change of subject to "God" in the apodosis makes it difficult to evaluate the connection indicated by $ουτως$ $και$. If Paul meant to argue by way of analogy here "as Christ--so the Christians," the change of grammatical subject to "God" in the apodosis does not fit well with $ανεστη$. Furthermore, the use of $αξει$ instead of $εγερει$ shifts the emphasis from resurrection to assumption at the parousia to be with Christ.[583] The fact that it is God who acts in O.T. and Jewish accounts of assumption[584] may help to explain the change of subject and thus strengthen the case for seeing assumption focused upon here. Furthermore, when $δια$ $του$ $Ιησου$ is taken as modifying the verb rather than the participial substantive, one can recognise in this phrase an effort to compensate for this brusque change of the grammatical subject.

In view of Paul's infrequent use of the designation $Ιησους$ by itself, the lexical recurrence of this designation here acquires a significance that goes beyond that of serving textual coherence in general. The $Ιησου$ in the apodosis recalls the $Ιησους$ in the protasis, so as to connect God's future act to the christological ground of this act. G. Lüdemann notes that the preposition, though instrumental, also has a causal nuance reinforced by the causal meaning of $ει$ in the protasis.[585] This indicates that the argument is that of "since--therefore" with a causal connection between the mutually-held creed in 4:14a and the conclusion drawn in 4:14b: "Paul's theological logic is that **because** Jesus died and rose the dead will participate in the parousia. The elpis of the Thessalonians, which is focused on the parousia, need not collapse because of a few deaths."[586]

---

ther Hartman (1966, 186-7) who indicates the strong likelihood that Dan 7:13 (cf. 7:10) or a midrashic usage or exposition thereof informs Paul's thought and usage here. Hyldahl's suggestion (1980, 133) of "gathering" with $επισυναξει/επισυναξουσιν$ (Mark 13:27; Matt 24:31) as parallel to $αξει$ $συν$ $αυτω$ builds on Hartman's observations and takes them a step further. This is a more satisfactory explanation of the whole phrase which avoids the awkward "in fellowship with" as a rendition of $συν$, a common position most recently held by, e.g., Lüdemann, 1984, 214-20.

[582] Thus Lüdemann, 1984, 215, 219.

[583] Thus, e.g., Marxsen, 1969, 33-4; Hyldahl, 1980, 133; Plevnik, 1979, 76; 1984, 276 ff.; Lüdemann, 1984, 219. As Marxsen (1969, 33) and Plevnik (1984, 282) have noted, one should not read I Cor 15:12-28 into this verse. Gillman (1985, 263-81) tends to harmonize these texts too easily on the basis of formal similarities.

[584] See Plevnik (1984, 279-80) with reference to Lohfink (1971, 55-70).

[585] Lüdemann, 1984, 219. See also Cavallin, 1983, 60-1.

[586] Lüdemann, 1984, 220. Elsewhere (251, note 69) he points out that all the refer-

Thus, after the comparison to non-believers who were without hope, Paul proceeds to the credal reference to the death and resurrection of Jesus so as to reassure the addressees' by reiterating the basis of salvation that they already held (1:10). Then he goes immediately on to argue that this salvation also included the deceased believers at the parousia. In other words, his initial strategy of persuasion here is to immediately both reconfirm the kerygma originally preached and reconfirm the addressees' hope as grounded in this kerygma. The particular event of resurrection itself is only presupposed by αξει συν αυτω and is subsequently only given explicit mention in 4:16 (see below).

While this letter reflects a particularly strong focus on salvation in its consumation at the parousia, this is nevertheless firmly grounded in the death and resurrection of Jesus (1:10). The point added here is that deceased believers are included in this salvation.

4.4.6.2   I Thess 4:15-17: The Second Argument

The second response introduced by τουτο γαρ υμιν λεγομεν εν λογω κυριου, constitutes an appeal to authority. The main point of the assumption of the deceased to be with Jesus at the parousia in 4:14 is now explained in terms of both resurrection and assumption. What immediately follows in οτι ημεις οι ζωντες οι περιλειπομενοι εις την παρουσιαν του κυριου ου μη φθασωμεν τους κοιμηθεντας (4:15) is best taken as being Paul's own introductory comment on the "Lord's word" in view of the epistolary style: The contrast between the "we" and the reference to "those who sleep" focuses on the immediate situation.[587] Then comes the quotation itself (4:16-17a):[588] οτι αυτος ο κυριος εν κελευσματι, εν φονη

---

ences to hope in I Thess are related to the expectation of the parousia (1:3; 2:19; 5:8). Cf. Kieffer, 1981, 125-6.

[587] See, e.g., Best, 1977, 193-4; Lüdemann, 1984, 221.

[588] In the absence of the quotation from the gospels some, e.g., Frame (1912, 171) and Vielhauer (1977, 87), suggest that it was an apocryphal word, an agraphon. Lüdemann (1984, 231) sees this as precarious. While observing a consensus in taking it as a word of the risen Christ spoken by a prophet in his name, he modifies this in view of his form-critical analysis by seeing the kernel of 4:16-17 as deriving from a Jewish apocalypse which was understood by Paul as a saying of the Lord. Thus also, e.g., Dibelius, 1937, 25. For a good discussion of the various other options see esp. Best, 1977, 189-93. Hartman (1966, 188-90) presents another more viable solution. He notes that λογος can also mean a "discourse" or parts thereof. The combination of details common to this passage and Matt 24 par. speak for Paul as using a closely-related tradition, viz., a midrash-like combination of Dan 2:44 f.; 7:13 f., 27; 8:25b and 12:1 f. A comparison between this passage and Dan 7:13 and 12:1 f. shows striking parallels in terminology involving "bringing" (αγειν, προσαγειν), "resurrection" (αναστησεσθαι), the dead as "sleeping" (κοιμασθαι, καθευδειν) and the "eternity" of salvation (παντοτε, αιωνιος). Paul is seen as drawing upon his knowledge of a midrash-like structure of a discourse based on Daniel and as applying this to the

αρχαγγελου και εν σαλπιγγι θεου, καταβησεται απ' ουρανου και οι νεκροι εν Χριστῳ αναστησονται πρωτον, επειτα ημεις οι ζωντες οι περιλειπομενοι αμα συν αυτοις αρπαγησομεθα εν νεφελαις εις απαντησιν του κυριου εις αερα. This is rounded off by Paul's summarizing conclusion (4:17b): και ουτως παντοτε συν κυριῳ εσομεθα. While this "word of the Lord" is dominated by the third person, its adaptation to the present situation is immediately apparent in the "we" references, the phrase εν Χριστῳ, the πρωτον/επειτα distinction and the phrase αμα συν αυτοις. At least these are the features that are most commonly agreed upon.[589] However, the separation of redaction and tradition is more useful for a reconstruction of Paul's view or development of Christian apocalyptic than for reconstructing the problem that is being addressed in the communication situation here.[590]

The important question is how this authoritative word relates to the quasi-logical appeal in 4:14 in view of the actual problem experienced by the addressees. The most satisfying explanation appears to be that of N. Hyldahl and especially J. Plevnik, who observe that, if the problem arose from Paul's not having instructed the new community of believers about the resurrection of the dead,[591] this does not explain why it is not the resurrection of the dead that is primarily focused upon in the passage, but rather their "gathering" or "assumption."[592]

Plevnik argues that, given the contemporaneous traditions regarding "assumption" common to both the Jewish and Gentile worlds of thought,[593] and taking the view that Paul had taught the Thessalonian believers about the parousia exclusively in terms of bodily assumption due to expecting this event to occur shortly,[594] their consternation and perplexity over the deaths of believers would be an obvious consequence. Especially so, since assumption was generally conceived of as in-

---

problem in hand.

[589] See, e.g., Marxsen, 1969, 30; Harnish, 1973, 39-46; Best, 1977, 194; Collins, 1980, 332;=1984, 161; Lüdemann, 1984, 232.

[590] Marxsen (1969, 30) and Lüdemann (1984, 221 ff., 232 ff.) find Paul directly redacting Jewish tradition while Harnish (1973, 42-5) and Collins (1980, 331-2;=1984, 160-1) find an intervening pre-Pauline Jewish-Christian stage to be involved in the redaction.

[591] Referring particularly to Marxsen (1969, 23-37) for this view.

[592] Plevnik, 1984, 276 ff. Hyldahl (1980, 121 ff.), however, moves too quickly to generalize that the focus on "gathering" means a focus on the parousia itself as something which Paul must defend, because the addressees had become openly mistrustful of Paul's instruction on both this event and the very gospel itself. Against this view, see under 2.2.1, 2.2.3 and 4.4.6.1.

[593] Plevnik (1984, 280-1), referring to Lohfink (1971, 42-49, 72-74).

[594] Plevnik, 1984, 282. In his second response (4:15-17) Paul expresses himself in a way clearly indicating that more deaths before the parousia are still not seriously considered: επειτα ημεις οι ζωντες οι περιλειπομενοι αμα συν αυτοις

volving the whole person, including the body.[595] Thus, the grounding of the deceased believers' assumption in the death and resurrection of Jesus could only serve as an initial step in Paul's informative-dissuasive response (4:14) and would need to be filled out graphically as to how this would be made possible (4:15-17a).[596]

This makes good sense of the emphasis on the equality of the living and the dead expressed by the living not preceding the dead ($ου$ $μη$ $φθασωμεν$) and by the "dead in Christ"[597] being raised first ($πρωτον$) with both groups then ($επειτα$) able to participate in the assumption ($αρπαγησομεθα$ $εν$ $νεφελαις$ $εις$ $απαντησιν$ $του$ $κυριου$ $εις$ $αερα$· $και$ $ουτως$ $παντοτε$ $συν$ $κυριω$ $εσομεθα$). Thus, over against the other views mentioned in 2.2.3, this view has the advantage of explaining the grief of the addressees (4:13), the focus on assumption in 4:14-17 and the unelaborated reference to the resurrection (4:16) as brought in to explain how the assumption of the deceased was possible.[598] This view also indicates that Paul is addressing a different problem here than in I Cor 15: here it suffices to present the resurrection as a return to life, there it is presented in its aspect of glorious transformation.[599]

Both the focus on being "with" the Lord at the end of 4:14 and of 4:15-17 and the emphasis on the equality between living and deceased believers with regard to their assumption may be seen as aimed at comforting the addressees, especially in view of the explicit indication in 4:18 that this was a major function of the passage: "Comfort one another, therefore, with these words." While it is agreed here with W. Marxsen that the primary function of the passage was to disarm the **potential** threat to the addressees' faith posed by their fellow believers' deaths,[600] one cannot reduce the function of comfort as drastically as he does when he questions the authenticity of this closing admonition.[601]

Nor can one reduce the communicative intent to that of basically providing eschatological instruction as H. Koester does, explained as being due to an effort on Paul's part to transform the conventional genre of the letter into a Christian medium of communication, the drastic expansion of the traditional letter genre being de-

---

$αρπαγησομεθα$ $εν$ $νεφελαις$, $κτλ$. (4:17).

[595] Thus Plevnik (1984, 279) referring to Lohfink (1971, 32, 74) who observes that the contemporaneous views of assumption presupposed the one to be assumed as being bodily alive.

[596] Plevnik, 1984, 281.

[597] See, e.g., Cavallin (1983, 60) and Plevnik (1984, 277) as against the unlikely interpretation of Rigaux (1956, 544) that $οι$ $νεκροι$ $εν$ $Χριστω$ means more than "those who died believing in Christ," viz., that they will be transformed (referring to I Cor 15:51-58).

[598] Thus Plevnik, 1984, 282.

[599] Plevnik, 1984, 282.

[600] Marxsen, 1969, 37; 1979, 67-8.

[601] Marxsen, 1969, 36-7. Such parallel recurrences (4:18; 5:11) are too typical of the letter to use as evidence of interpolation. See ch. 5.

manded by the message of the Christian gospel.[602] Also, Paul is not merely using the occasion of deaths in the community to extend their beliefs on parousia and resurrection so as to strengthen cohesion in the group.[603]

Besides the foregoing observations, further doubt on such positions is cast by A.J. Malherbe's observations of some striking parallel motifs in Hellenistic consolatory speeches, tractates and letters composed by philosophers in particular. Here one finds minimizations of death by making it resemble sleep, calls to cease from grief, which may be followed by recalling a teacher's words, complaints of the deceased having been snatched away ($αναρπαζειν$, $εξαρπαζειν$) followed by comfort that he or she is now dwelling with the gods, and that those now living will soon join the deceased over whom they have no advantage.[604] While such similar features are allowed to carry due weight, he is careful to also point out the differences between 4:13-18 and such consolations. While these urge that reason should keep grief from becoming inordinate, Paul grounds Christian hope and comfort in the death and resurrection of Jesus. Furthermore, the apocalyptic traditions used by Paul are of course foreign to such consolations.[605]

Malherbe, however, goes a little too far in the other direction when he asserts that "Paul is not providing eschatological instruction to inform his readers, but to console those who are grieving."[606] While his observations support the authenticity of the closing exhortation to mutual comfort, the analysis above calls for seeing the situation addressed as having required argumentative-informative dissuasion. In other words, there was a need for both correction and comfort, with the argumentative-instructive dissuasion supporting consolation and the consolation also supporting the dissuasion from a non-Christian type of hope-negating and ultimately faith-negating grief. Thus, while the quasi-logical appeal is prominent in the passage, the conclusion regarding the status of deceased (and living) believers also serves as a powerful **pathos** appeal to confidence.

4.4.7 The Delimitation and Coherence of 5:1-11

The transition to this text-sequence is marked by transitional $δε$, the address $αδελφοι$ and the complex thematic marker 5ThM: (P1) $περι...των χρονων και των καιρων$ (MBref) $ου χρειαν εχετε υμιν γραφεσθαι$, (MBref) $αυτοι γαρ ακριβως οιδατε$ (P1.1) $οτι ημερα κυριου ως κλεπτης εν νυκτι ουτως ερχεται$. A delimitation of the sequence as a whole may be seen in the anaphoric SA $διο$ (5:11) through which the metacommunicative comment $παρακαλειτε$ (1.2.2.2SMit)

---

[602] Koester, 1979, 39-40.

[603] Meeks, 1983a, 227.

[604] See Malherbe (1983, 255) and the references given there. Also Cavallin, 1983, 55-6.

[605] Malherbe, 1983, 256.

[606] Malherbe, 1983, 254.

αλληλους κτλ. indicates the intended communicative function.⁶⁰⁷

Although many critics propose that 5:11 encompasses 4:13-5:10,⁶⁰⁸ Ch. Masson's view is preferred here as more perceptive and correct. While granting a close connection between 4:13-17 and 5:1-10, he observes that the admonitions in 4:18 and 5:11 should be taken as encompassing each passage respectively in view of the parallel character of the admonitions together with the fact that each passage reflects a different emphasis: The former passage focuses on the recipients' anxiety more in relation to their grief and the question of the eschatological status of the deceased, while the latter passage focuses on their anxiety more in relation to their own personal status in face of the imminent parousia (see 4.5.8.2 below).⁶⁰⁹

With regard to coherence on the text-semantic level, as noted above, the text-sequence is initiated by the general topic (P1) of the eschatological consumation in temporal terms: περι δε των χρονων και των καιρων (5:1).⁶¹⁰ This general reference is then subsequently specified (5:2) in terms of "the day of the Lord" (P1.1) which is described in a way that indicates a shift from a temporal focus in 5:1 to that of manner: "as a thief in the night, thus it comes." A further specification follows in 5:3 in terms of "destruction" (ολεθρος), which is described as coming "suddenly" and like "birth pangs" upon those who say "Peace and safety," but for whom there is by no means any escape: οταν λεγωσιν· ειρηνη και ασφαλεια, τοτε αιφνιδιος αυτοις εφισταται ολεθρος ωσπερ η ωδιν τη εν γαστρι εχουσῃ, και ου μη εκφυγωσιν. By way of conceptual and lexical recurrence the theme of "the Day" is continued in terms of not coming upon the addressees like a thief: υμεις...ουκ εστε εν σκοτει, ινα η ημερα υμας ως κλεπτης καταλαβῃ (5:4). Under the influence of this imagery the continuing affirmations regarding the status of addressees and the admonitions to them in the rest of the passage are formulated in "day/night," "light/darkness" and "sleeping/watching" language. Here an associative and allusive play on these words may be seen as rooted in the initial "day" and "night" references in 5:2.⁶¹¹ Partial conceptual recurrence with regard to the escha-

---

607 Against Friedrich's position (1973, 288-315) that 5:1-11 is a later interpolation, I find the arguments by Rigaux (1974-75, 318-40), Plevnik (1979, 71-90) and Collins (1980, 325-43;=1984, 154-72) convincing on the whole.

608 See, e.g., Lightfoot, 1904, 78; Milligan, 1908, 70; Rigaux, 1956, 574; Harnish, 1973, 18; and Marxsen, 1979, 70.

609 Masson, 1957, 70-1. Dobschütz (1909, 214) also limits 5:11 to referring only to 5:1-10.

610 A convincing case is made by Barr (1969, 41) for there being "no significant difference between the two words" combined here. Similarly, e.g., Dobschütz, 1909, 204; Frame, 1912, 180; Masson 1957, 66; Best, 1977, 204, as against, e.g., Trench, 1865, 200-3; Lightfoot, 1904, 70-1; and, though more cautious, also Rigaux, 1956, 553-5. While there are extra-biblical occurrences of this pleonasm (see Rigaux, 1956, 554, who cites Demosthenes, Ep 2.3 among others), it is best to take it as a stock apocalyptic expression taken over by Christian tradition to refer to the eschatological consumation under its prominent temporal aspect. On this see, e.g., Rigaux, 1956, 553-4; Best, 1977, 204; Collins, 1980, 334-5;=1984, 163-4. Cf., e.g., (LXX) Dan 2:21; 7:12; Wis 8:8; and Acts 1:7.

tological aspect of "the Day" also continues in such expressions as $\sigma\omega\tau\eta\rho\iota\alpha\varsigma$ (5:8, 9), $o\rho\gamma\eta\nu$ (5:9) and $\alpha\mu\alpha \; \sigma\upsilon\nu \; \alpha\upsilon\tau\omega \; \zeta\eta\sigma\omega\mu\epsilon\nu$ (5:10).

As for coherence on the text-syntactic level, this is achieved by the lexical recurrence of especially $\eta\mu\epsilon\rho\alpha$ (5:2, 4, 5, 8), $\nu\upsilon\xi$ (5:2, 5, 7), $\kappa\alpha\theta\epsilon\upsilon\delta\epsilon\iota\nu$ (5: 6, 7, 10), $\gamma\rho\eta\gamma\rho\rho\epsilon\iota\nu$ (5:6, 10). For text-pragmatic coherence we may turn to the following rhetorical analysis.

4.4.8 The Rhetoric of 5:1-11

4.4.8.1 The Rhetorical Character of 5:1-3

As for the rhetorical features of the passage, W. Harnish in particular has taken up a previous observation that a general development of the topic of "times and seasons" is avoided by means of the figure **praeteritio**, expressed by $o\upsilon \; \chi\rho\epsilon\iota\alpha\nu \; \epsilon\chi\epsilon\tau\epsilon \; \upsilon\mu\iota\nu \; \gamma\rho\alpha\phi\epsilon\sigma\theta\alpha\iota$ and subsequently explained by the reminder of the addressees' accurate knowledge ($\alpha\upsilon\tau\circ\iota \; \gamma\alpha\rho \; \alpha\kappa\rho\iota\beta\omega\varsigma \; o\iota\delta\alpha\tau\epsilon$) regarding the specific aspect of how "the day of the Lord" would arrive (5:2).[612] He goes further, however, to see this figure as encompassing 5:1-3 with 5:2-3 taken as a variant of the figure **evidentia**, often included in instances of **praeteritio** with the effect of heightening the latent irony in the figure.[613] The modification of $o\iota\delta\alpha\tau\epsilon$ by $\alpha\kappa\rho\iota\beta\omega\varsigma$ is seen as a further possible reflection of such irony.[614]

However, it is questioned here whether irony is a prominent element in this instance and whether the heightening figure of **evidentia** has the function of accentuating this. Instead, its function appears to be to heighten the picture of the day of the Lord in relation to what follows in 5:4 ff. To this end it is worthwhile taking a closer look than Harnish has done at these figures of **praeteritio** and **evidentia**.

The figure **evidentia** is classified as an affective figure and is defined by H. Lausberg as a detailed, essentially static, and vivid description of some state of affairs in a manner that strikes the senses and gives the audience the sense of being present as spectators.[615] In 5:2-3 the description is essentially static, as may be seen in the relation between the more neutral picture of the day of the Lord and the subsequent negative picture where the same event is treated in terms of the destruction it brings. Vividness and detail are achieved by the similes of "a thief in the night" and of "birth pangs." Among the common means of creating a sense of "Gleichzeitigkeit," Lausberg mentions the use of the present tense for either past or future events and the use

---

[611] See, e.g., Koester, 1979, 43; Plevnik, 1979, 79-80.

[612] Harnish (1973, 53), referring to Lausberg (1973, 436 f.). He also (1973, 53, n. 11) cites de Wette (1864, 165) as the earliest commentator to take 5:1 as such a figure, followed by Dobschütz (1909, 203) among others.

[613] Harnish, 1973, 53. See Josephus, Con Ap 2.267-8 for an example of this combination.

[614] Harnish, 1973, 53, n. 8.

[615] Lausberg, 1973, 399 ff.

of direct speech by persons referred to.[616] Both the present tense ($\epsilon\rho\chi\epsilon\tau\alpha\iota/\epsilon\phi\iota\sigma\tau\alpha\mu\alpha\iota$) and direct speech ($\epsilon\iota\rho\eta\nu\eta$ $\kappa\alpha\iota$ $\alpha\sigma\phi\alpha\lambda\epsilon\iota\alpha$) are in evidence here. In the latter case, which involves the use of **sermocinatio**, borderline instances of this figure include the use of an indefinite or a collective person speaking.[617] The use of $\lambda\epsilon\gamma\omega\sigma\iota\nu$ would appear to qualify as such an instance. These observations would then serve to further substantiate the presence of **evidentia** in 5:2-3.

With regard to the **praeteritio** in 3:1, rhetorical theorists give rather disparate descriptions of this figure and its functions. H. Lausberg classifies it under **figurae per detractionem** (a type of **brevitas** figure), which falls in turn under the superior class **figurae sententiae**,[618] whereas H.F. Plett subsumes it simply under **brevitas**.[619] Lausberg observes that the figure, separately or in combination with **percursio/evidentia**, can have the effect of placing the presented topic on a lower, secondary level of importance. On the other hand, Plett notes that with **praeteritio** such a decided direction of attention away from a particular theme can in fact serve to emphasize it.[620] Furthermore, both Lausberg and Plett enumerate several differing motivations for the use of this figure:[621] Lausberg notes the avoidance of something that is unfavourable to the rhetor's own case or which may cause discomfort to the audience, whereas Plett notes the unimportance of the topic, the audience's acquaintance with it, or lack of time to treat it. Both point out the potential function of irony in the figure, which is latent in the tension between the expressed intention of passing over a topic which nevertheless is mentioned.

4.4.8.2 The Rhetorical Functions of 5:1-3

From the foregoing observations, it is clear that irony as consciously directed against the addressee is definitely incompatible with several of the mentioned motivations, so that one cannot take the presence of consciously intended irony for granted in any occurrence of the form. Here, the whole tone of the letter and of the immediately preceding comforting instruction make it quite unlikely that the evidentia constituted by 5:2-3 is meant to heighten any irony aimed at the recipients.[622]

In relation to the preceding co-text in 4:13-18, one may fairly securely conclude that the unexpected deaths of fellow-believers before the parousia would have caused a complex of anxious questions such as when this event would come about,[623]

---

[616] Lausberg, 1973, 404-6.

[617] Lausberg, 1973, 408, 410.

[618] Lausberg, 1973, 375 ff., 435 ff.

[619] Plett, 1979a, 56-9.

[620] Plett, 1979a, 56-9.

[621] Lausberg, 1973, 436-7; Plett 1979, 59.

[622] Against Harnish (1973, 53) and, e.g., Findley (1925, 108).

whether their own personal status in relation to it was secure,[624] etc. Besides such anxiety, it may be added that the need for the additional instruction regarding this problem, now provided in 4:13-17, could also be expected to give rise to a certain degree of insecurity regarding the adequacy of the previous instruction that had been received on the eschatological consumation.[625] Some degree of anxiety regarding the time of the parousia is seen here to be reflected in the choice of the temporal terms ($\chi\rho o\nu o\varsigma$, $\kappa\alpha\iota\rho o\varsigma$) used to introduce the topic in 5:1, while anxiety regarding the adequacy of their instruction is seen as having been anticipated by Paul in the insistence on the accuracy ($\alpha\kappa\rho\iota\beta\omega\varsigma$) of the addressees' knowledge and thereby his earlier instruction on "the day of the Lord" in 5:2.

Thus, $\alpha\kappa\rho\iota\beta\omega\varsigma$ is more adequately explained as reflecting an attempt to reassure rather than to be consciously ironical.[626] Also, insofar as 5:2-3 reflects reliance on traditional material, this would indicate an appeal to authority.[627] The presence of irony could of course be argued for against a background of inordinate attempts to calculate the time of the parousia, but the lack of any extended treatment of this aspect and the character of $\tau\omega\nu$ $\chi\rho o\nu\omega\nu$ $\kappa\alpha\iota$ $\tau\omega\nu$ $\kappa\alpha\iota\rho\omega\nu$ as a general stock expression do not support seeing such an inordinate preoccupation.[628]

Furthermore, though the shift of focus from the temporal perspective in 5:1 to that of manner in 5:2 most likely reflects an implicit **detraction** from some concern with the time of the parousia, there are several reasons for locating the major focus of 5:1-3 in the negative picture arrived at in 5:3:

1. While the element of "unexpectedness" in the simile of "the thief in the night" can imply "incalculability" in relation to the notion of time in 5:1, it more obviously anticipates the emphasis on the "suddenness" of the eschatological destruction as this is elaborated in 5:3.[629]

---

[623] Thus, e.g., Milligan, 1908, 63; Dobschütz, 1909, 202 ff.; Frame, 1912, 178; J.W. Bailey, 1955, 308; Rigaux 1956, 552-3; Masson, 1957, 66-7.

[624] Frame's (1912, 178-9) observations are particularly perceptive here. Similarly, e.g., Milligan, 1908, 63; Rigaux, 1956, 553.

[625] Similarly, Hyldahl, 1980, 122.

[626] Similarly Holtz (1986, 211) as against Harnish, 1973, 53, n. 8.

[627] For the background of 4:2 in Christian apocalyptic see Collins (1980, 335-6;=1984, 164-5) with references, and for arguments regarding a common tradition standing behind 4:3 and Luke 21:34-36 see esp. Hartman (1966, 190-3).

[628] Against, e.g., Collins, 1980a, 342;=1984, 171; Marxsen, 1979, 68-9; Harnish, 1973, 55. Also Best (1977, 203), though he is more cautious.

[629] Harnish's (1973, 52) translation, "dass der Tag des Herrn kommt (gewiss), aber wie ein Dieb in der Nacht," excludes the last part from the addressees' knowledge in a way that is not indicated by the Greek: $o\tau\iota$ $\eta\mu\epsilon\rho\alpha$ $\kappa\upsilon\rho\iota o\upsilon$ $\omega\varsigma$ $\kappa\lambda\epsilon\pi\tau\eta\varsigma$ $\epsilon\nu$ $\nu\upsilon\kappa\tau\iota$ $o\upsilon\tau\omega\varsigma$ $\epsilon\rho\chi\epsilon\tau\alpha\iota$. To be sure, the construction is emphatic, but not in this way which prejudices a stricter contrastive connection with 5:1 than is warranted.

2. There is the emphasis created by the anaphoric connection to the negative picture in 5:3.[630]

3. There is the increased intensity expressed by the suddenness ($αιφνιδιος$), unexpectedness ($ωσπερ η ωδιν τη εν γαστρι εχουση$), and inescapability ($και ου μη εκφυγωσιν$) of eschatological destruction for nonchalant unbelievers.

4. And, most importantly, there is the subsequent emphatic and sustained contrast of the Thessalonian believers in 5:4 ff. to the doomed in 5:3.

Thus, it is proposed here that by means of this strategy of detraction and augmented intensity the negative picture in 5:3 is where the focus lies in order to serve as a contrastive background for the subsequent words of consoling assurance and exhortation.[631] In this there is general agreement with Harnish that in 5:1-3 there is a negative preparation for what Paul has to say positively in 5:4-10,[632] but disagreement in not seeing irony as being expressed by the **praeteritio-evidentia** combination of figures. At the same time, going beyond Harnish, the character of 5:2-3 as an instance of **evidentia** has been given more detailed support.

Also in disagreement with Harnish, it is doubtful that 5:3 ($οταν λεγωσιν·$ $ειρηνη και ασφαλεια, κτλ.$) reflects an attack on external gnostic agitators.[633] This position is rendered highly unlikely by the fact that the contrast in 5:4 ff. is sustained by a general coreference among the references $λεγωσιν$ (5:3), $οι λοιποι$ (5:6, cf. 4:13), and $καθευδοντες/μεθυσκομενοι$ (5:7), where the references in 5:6 and 5:7 can hardly be to a gnosticising faction.[634]

Should one seek a concrete target covered by the indefinite or collective reference $λεγωσιν$ in $οταν λεγωσιν· ειρηνη και ασφαλεια, τοτε αιφνιδιος αυτοις εφισταται ολεθρος κτλ.$, the addressees' persecuting countrymen could easily qualify, since the reference can be quite adequately clarified as directed against appeals to the Roman **pax et securitas**.[635] Such appeals would have been readily found on the lips of the addressees' persecuting fellow countrymen in view of Thessalonica's

---

[630] Westcott/Hort, 1885; Kilpatrick, 1958; Aland et al., 1968; and Nestle/Aland, 1979, are unanimous in preferring the anaphoric reading here.

[631] Similarly Reese (1980, 213) with regard to the function of contrast. But his view of 5:2 as serving "flattery" is not supported here.

[632] Harnish, 1973, 167.

[633] Against Harnish, 1973, 77 ff., 162. See esp. the criticisms of Plevnik, 1979, 75-77; Hyldahl, 1980, 124-26.

[634] This contrast together with the following emphatic assurances in 5:4-5 and 5:9-10 and the fact that the contrast is made to all the addressees in 5:5 strongly discount Jewett's reconstruction (1972, 202; 1984, 32) of a congregation so secure regarding their status due to realised eschatology that they needed to be warned against a false sense of security in 5:3.

[635] Thus, e.g., Bammel, 1960, 837-40; Frend, 1965, 96; Donfried, 1985, 344.

special relation to Rome as a free city.[636] Thus, the threat of eschatological wrath, shown to be implicitly aimed at the addressees' persecutors in 2:14-16 above, may very likely be surfacing again here. The contrast made in 5:4 ff. would consequently have overtones that also serve to strengthen group solidarity and identity in face of the social isolation experienced as a result of adherence to the Christian faith.

To summarize, in the larger consolatory context, the expression of not needing to write on "times and seasons" due to the addressees' knowledge gives the shift of focus from time to manner in 5:1-2 the character of an undramatic indicator to the addressees that the "when" of the parousia is unimportant. Not until one comes to the emphatic contrast made between the eschatological fate of the group in 5:3 and the positive status of the addressees in 5:4 ff. (including the senders in 5:5b ff.) does one see what appears to be the goal of the heightening and affective function of the **evidentia** figure. It is specifically here within 5:1-11 that one finds the strongest textually-embodied evidence of the author relating the audience to a concrete problem with potential to damage their hope and faith, viz., their anxiety over their status in relation to the parousia.

4.4.8.3   The Rhetoric of 5:4-11

As previously noted, the threatening picture of the suddenness of "the Day" and its inescapable destruction for unbelievers, presented in 5:2-3, provides a vivid background against which the eschatological status of the addressees is emphatically contrasted (5:4-5):[637] $υμεις\ δε,\ αδελφοι,\ ουκ\ εστε\ εν\ σκοτει,\ ινα\ η\ ημερα\ υμας\ ως\ κλεπτης\ καταλαβῃ·\ παντες\ γαρ\ υμεις\ υιοι\ φωτος\ εστε\ και\ υιοι\ ημερας.\ ουκ\ εσμεν\ νυκτος\ ουδε\ σκοτους.$ The contrast is not only marked and accentuated by such elements as $υμεις\ δε,\ αδελφοι$ (5:4a), the emphatic position of $υμας$ before the verb that governs it (5:4b) and the emphatic initial position of $παντες$ in 5:5a,[638] but also by the antithesis in the denial of "the Day" coming upon them "as a thief" and by the repetitive insistance on the addressees' positive status. This strongly-marked contrast is sustained in the rest of the passage. It is visible in the initial cohortative admonition not to "sleep like the rest" ($ως\ οι\ λοιποι$, 5:6), in the contrastive comparison between "sleepers/drunks" ($οι\ καθευδοντες/οι\ μεθυσκομενοι$) whose activities belong to the night (5:7) and "we who belong to the day" ($υμεις\ δε\ ημερας\ οντες$, 5:8a), and in the assurance "God has not appointed us to wrath, but to (his own special) possession of salvation" (5:9).[639]

---

[636] On the relation of Thessalonica to Rome see Donfried (1985, 342 ff.) with references.

[637] As Plevnik notes (1979, 78), apart from Harnish (1973, 77 ff.), most other exegetes neglect this contrast. Holtz (1986, 219) is a recent exception.

[638] See, esp. Lightfoot (1904, 73) and Dobschütz (1909, 207-8). The textual sequence of these emphatic expressions in relation to the threatening picture in 5:3 supports a pragmatic explanation of the presence of $παντες$. Thus Plevnik (1979, 85) and Holtz (1986, 220-1) against Harnish (1973, 121) who explains its presence here from a pre-Pauline baptismal parenesis.

In 5:5b the senders are included in the positive description of the addressees (ουκ εσμεν νυκτος ουδε σκοτους) in anticipation of the following cohortative admonitions (5:6, 8). Not only is the exhortation given a particularly gentle pastoral tone due to the hortatory subjunctives used only here in the whole letter,[640] but the continued use of the inclusive "we" in the indicatives in 5:8a, 9-10 also serves to appeal to a common tie of solidarity between the addressors and addressees. The change to "we" in 5:5b is a strong indication that the emphatic αρα ουν relates the exhortation in 5:6 (αρα ουν μη καθευδωμεν ως οι λοιποι αλλα γρηγορωμεν και νηφωμεν) particularly closely to the positive status of the addressees insisted upon in 5:4-5.[641] This is again born out by ημεις δε ημερας οντες ("since we are of the day") introducing the second exhortation in 5:8:[642] νηφωμεν ενδυσαμενοι θωρακα πιστεως και αγαπης και περικεφαλαιαν ελπιδα σωτηριας. The concrete illustration in 5:7 of the nocturnal character of sleepers and drunks appears to focus on νηφωμεν as a parenthetical comment[643] and occasions the renewed affirmation of the addressees' status in 5:8a followed by a renewed νηφωμεν. While there may be a more distant connection between the exhortations and the threatening picture of the "day of the Lord" in 5:2-3 by way of the "day/night" and the "sleeping/watching" imagery, this is only indirect and quite distinctly secondary.[644]

As noted above, the contrasts in 5:4-5 to 5:3 and in 5:8a to 5:7 draw a particularly emphatic distinction between the addressed believers and unbelievers outside the community. In the addressees' concrete situation, the latter group is easily associated with fellow countrymen who not only may have persecuted the believers but also may have tried to dissuade them from their fervent expectation of the parousia through appeals to the Roman peace. These observations together with the foregoing observations of connection, make it unlikely that 5:2 has a prominent threatening function and doubtful that the admonitions in 5:6-8 constitute the basic communicative aim of

---

[639] The sense of περιποιησις in the phrase περιποιησιν σωτηριας is debated. Some, e.g., Dobschütz (1909, 212), Frame (1912, 188); Best (1977, 217) and Marxsen (1979, 70), argue for the sense of "acquisition" followed by an objective genitive. Others, e.g. Lightfoot (1904, 76) and Rigaux (1956, 571), prefer the almost technical sense of this word in both the OT and NT denoting God's act of setting apart a peculiar people for himself with the genitive taken as epexegetical. The latter view is supported here in that it is not the exhortations that are the focus of the passage but rather assurances regarding the status of the addressees as grounded in their election through Jesus Christ.

[640] See, e.g, Frame, 1912, 185; Rigaux, 1956, 563; Laub, 1973, 160; Reese, 1980, 214. This softening of the imperative tone is rather curious, if Paul was intent on countering a position insisting on a type of security characteristic of Gnostic thinking, contra e.g., Harnish, 1973, 132.

[641] Similarly, e.g., Harnish, 1973, 131.

[642] On the possibility of this "light/darkness" terminology as well as the imagery of being clothed with armour (5:8) reflecting a baptismal liturgy or hymn, see Collins' (1980a, 57-62;=1984, 145-53) survey of the relevant literature and his sober conclusions in criticism of the hyperexegesis that tries to establish such fixed liturgical or hymnic elements as informing 5:4-10.

the passage.⁶⁴⁵ The admonitions have more the character of pastoral, prophylactic exhortation and encouragement that find their motivation in the insistence on the believers' positive eschatological status and thereby serve to urge continued vigilance rather than any re-establishment of this status.

This may also be observed in the connection between $νηφωμεν$ and the immediately attached $ενδυσαμενοι\ θωρακα\ πιστεως\ και\ αγαπης\ και\ περικεφαλαιαν\ ελπιδα\ σωτηριας$. The former is best seen as explained by the latter.⁶⁴⁶ It is not any specific course of ethical action that is being enjoined, but rather the need to be sober is explained in terms of bearing the armour of faith, love and hope, viz., in terms of the very character of eschatological existence, of being "sons of the light and the day."⁶⁴⁷ The fact that the faith-love-hope triad surfaces here again with "hope" in the prominent final position (cf. 1:3) may be seen as an indication that it is hope in particular that is being focused upon.⁶⁴⁸ All these observations support seeing dissuasion from incipient doubt as the most prominent aim of the passage with the exhortation playing a supportive role.

With the exhortations grounded in the positive status of the believers, the subsequent reference to God's appointment of believers to salvation through the death of Jesus Christ ($οτι\ ουκ\ εθετο\ ημας\ ο\ θεος\ εις\ οργην\ αλλα\ εις\ περιποιησιν\ σωτηριας\ δια\ του\ κυριου\ ημων\ Ιησου\ Χριστου\ του\ αποθανοντος\ υπερ\ ημων$, 5:9-10a) should not be seen so much as giving the motivation for the exhortations to sober vigilance as giving the theological-christological basis of their status.⁶⁴⁹ Having the "hope of salvation" is obviously one of the primary characteristics of being "sons of the light and the day," and it is particularly to this ($ελπιδα\ σωτηριας$) that the $οτι$ connects the following thought.⁶⁵⁰

---

⁶⁴³ See, e.g., Milligan, 1908, 68; Rigaux, 1956, 565; Harnish, 1973, 131; Marxsen 1979, 69, contra Dobschütz (1909, 209) who takes it as presenting a motivation for the double admonition in 5:6.

⁶⁴⁴ Plevnik (1979, 78) tends to give greater importance to this connection than the textual indications support.

⁶⁴⁵ Disagreement with Plevnik (1979, 78, 87, 89) on the prominence of the elements of threat and admonition here is basically due to my giving the contrasts greater significance against a somewhat more specific background of outside opposition and pressure on the addressees. Apart from this shift of emphasis, his exegesis and judgments are closely shared here, as well as his general conclusion that in 5:1-11 Paul "removes from the life of Christians all speculations and unfounded fears about their future before God" (1979, 90).

⁶⁴⁶ Thus, e.g., Dibelius (1937, 30), Rigaux (1956, 567), Plevnik (1979, 89-90) contra, e.g., Dobschütz (1909, 210-11) and Best (1977, 215) who hold that the participial clause indicates how the Christian should be armed and not how he/she is armed. However, the fact that the addressees were already established in faith, love and hope (1:3), although the last-mentioned element had run into problems, must be allowed to temper such a rigid interpretation of the aorist participle.

⁶⁴⁷ Most forcefully elucidated by Harnish (1973, 134-7), although he seems to elimi-

Thus, a quasi-logical appeal may be observed in 5:4-10. The general position argued for may be seen in the emphatic assertion of the positive eschatological status of both the addressors and addressees (5:4-5, 8a, 10b). This is supported by an explicit premise given in the reference to God's appointment of them to salvation through the death of Jesus Christ (5:9-10a). The premise left implicit here is the addressees' own genuine response (cf. 1:4-10; 2:13-14) to God's call (cf. 2:12; 5:24).

The position regarding their positive eschatological status comes to particularly pointed expression in the reference to life together with Jesus Christ, whether they are living or deceased: ινα ειτε γρηγορωμεν ειτε καθευδωμεν αμα συν αυτω ζησωμεν. While most commentators are content to remark that γρηγορωμεν/καθευδωμεν are used metaphorically of living and dead believers as opposed to the previous literal (5:7) and dissimilar metaphorical (5:6) uses,[651] M. Dibelius goes further to point out that a word-play should be seen as giving rise to a paradox here due to the lack of distinction between sleeping and watching previously found in 5:6-7, a paradox that the reader is forced to solve by connecting these references to 4:17.[652] In this way the close connection between 4:13-18 and 5:1-11 becomes particularly apparent. Both grief and anxiety over deceased believers and a consequent anxiety over the living in relation to the parousia are met with dissuasive argumentation based on the Christ-event of the gospel.

That the parousia was the focus of anxiety with regard to the status of both the living and the dead believers is particularly reflected in the fact that each of the major argumentative-instructive sequences (4:14, 4:15-17 and 5:4-10) culminates climactically in an assuring reference to being "with Christ." The closing metacommunicative utterance διο παρακαλειτε αλληλους και οικοδομειτε εις τον ενα, καθως και ποιειτε once again indicates the comforting-encouraging function of the passage, while the persuasive strategies indicate a continuation of dissuasion from incipient doubt and anxiety. However, the addition of καθως και ποιειτε here and an absence of any such reassurance in 4:13-18 is interpreted to indicate that the more seriously threatening problem is reflected in 4:13-18. Both quasi-logical appeals and the **pathos** type of appeal to confidence may be observed to be particularly prominent in both 4:13-18 and 5:1-11. Finally, from the foregoing analysis it is concluded that

---

nate the ethical dimension entirely and thus goes too far. Thus, Laub, 1973, 159; Plevnik, 1979, 90.

[648] Thus, e.g., Lightfoot, 1904, 10-11; Rigaux, 1956, 569.

[649] Cf. Schrage, 1961, 21, 82 ff.; Harnish, 1973, 143.

[650] Thus, e.g., Lightfoot, 1904, 76; Dobschütz, 1909, 212; Dibelius, 1937, 30, against, e.g., Frame, 1912, 188. Also Rigaux (1956, 369-70), although he includes a connection to the exhortation which is seen as continuing here. A specific indication of the more particular connection is to be seen in the recurrence of σωτηριας in 5:9.

[651] See, e.g., Lightfoot, 1904, 77; Dobschütz, 1909, 213-14; Rigaux, 1956, 571; Masson, 1957, 70; and Marxsen, 1979, 70.

[652] Dibelius, 1937, 30.

5:1-11 is more adequately characterized as persuasion than as parenesis.[653]

4.4.9 The Delimitation and Coherence of 5:12-24

In I Thess 5:12-24 text-semantic coherence is observable in the high density of topics sharing a common religious-ethical reference in the series of admonitions and in the terminating wish-prayer where the topic of "holiness" indicated by $αγιασαι$ may be seen as more or less the covering theme (see below). In the text-pragmatic dimension coherence may be inferred from the dominance of the general conative-exhortational function expressed by the explicit conative verbs ($ερωτωμεν$, $παρακαλουμεν$), the use of the imperative in the series of admonitions and by the petitions in the concluding wish-prayer. In the text-syntactic dimension, coherence is achieved by way of grammatical recurrence evident in the high incidence of asyndeton throughout.[654]

Text-delimitation is achieved indirectly by the the above-mentioned features of coherence in conjunction with the formula-like clause $ερωτωμεν$ $δε$ $υμας$, $αδελφοι$ where the $δε$ is taken as transitional rather than adversative.[655] This is used to open the initial subsequence in 5:12-13 and mark a distinct transition from the preceding text-sequence which is delimited anaphorically by $διο$ $παρακαλειτε$ $κτλ$. (5:11).[656] Near the end of the passage, the wish-prayer in 5:23 contains an instance of a thematic marker that that may be seen as delimiting the text-sequence anaphorically.[657] With the exception of the incipient institutional relations in 5:12, each religious-ethical attitude and act that is enjoined in 5:13-22 may be seen as included under the governing theme of "holiness," viz, that which the God of peace is petitioned to bring about (5:23a).[658] The type of ThM here is that in which the MB and P are fused in the optative verb, viz., $αγιασαι$. It is noted here as 6ThM: (MBcon,P) $αυτος$ $δε$ $ο$ $θεος$ $της$ $ειρηνης$ $αγιασαι$ $υμας$ $ολοτελεις$.

Furthermore, there is the text-syntactic phenomenon of **inclusio** as a delimiting feature in which the motive of "peace" expressed near the beginning of the passage ($ειρηνευετε$ $εν$ $εαυτοις$, 5:13b) is echoed near the close of the passage in the

---

[653] As against, e.g., Laube (1973, 157 ff.), Vielhauer (1975, 50) and most commentators.

[654] See 5:13b, 14b, c, d, 15a, 16-20, 21b, 22, 24.

[655] Thus, e.g., Lightfoot (1904, 78), Dobschütz (1909, 215), Rigaux (1956, 576), Best (1977, 223) and Holtz (1986, 241) as against, e.g., Masson (1957, 71) who takes it adversatively in relation to 5:11.

[656] Roetzel (1972, 368-9) misses this anaphoric reference and mistakenly sees 5:12-22 as specifying 5:11.

[657] See Louw (1982, 116 ff.) who notes that the governing theme of a particular unit of text may be made explicit in initial, medial or final position within the unit. See 1.3.3.

[658] Thus, Marxsen, 1979, 71.

wish-prayer (ο θεος της ειρηνης, 5:23a).⁶⁵⁹ Also, the petition to keep the addressees blameless εν τη παρουσια του κυριου ημων Ιησου Χριστου serves as a concluding eschatological climax. Finally, as noted in 3.1.4 above, there is a perceptible shift from a generally conative-exhortational focus to a conative-phatic focus in 5:25 ff.

The smaller subsequences within the passage are fairly easy to isolate on the basis of text-syntactic and text-semantic features. First there is the subsequence of 5:12-13: ερωτωμεν δε υμας, αδελφοι, ειδεναι τους κοπιωντας εν υμιν και προιοταμενους υμων εν κυριω και νουθετουντας υμας και ηγεισθαι αυτους υπερεκπερισσου εν αγαπη δια το εργον αυτων. ειρηνευετε εν εαυτοις. It is clearly delimited by the formulation ερωτωμεν δε υμας, αδελφοι that opens it, and by the formulation παρακαλουμεν δε υμας, αδελφοι in 5:14a that introduces the next subsequence. Reference is made here basically to the disposition of esteem towards those carrying out a more distinct ministry within the community, on the one hand (5:12-13a),⁶⁶⁰ and to peaceful behaviour among the members in general, on the other hand (5:13b): ειρηνευετε εν εαυτοις. The sense of this last admonition is not altogether clear due to the variant readings εαυτοις/αυτοις. Since the variant αυτοις can have either a rough or smooth breathing mark, the external evidence of manuscripts is not of much help here. The proximity of this admonition to those in 5:12-13a could favour seeing it as enjoining the members in general to be at peace with those holding more prominent positions of service. This would speak in favour of αυτοις taken with **spiritus lenis**.⁶⁶¹ However, in that case one would expect μετ' αυτων instead.⁶⁶² This observation, together with the asyndetic connection and the change to the grammatical imperative, speaks more strongly for a reference to relations among the members in general, and thus for the formulation εν εαυτοις or εν αυτοις with the rough breathing mark.⁶⁶³ The connection between this admoni-

---

659 See II Cor 13:11 where the admonition ειρηνευετε occasions the immediately subsequent reference to God as ο θεος της αγαπης και ειρηνης.

660 In view of its position between κοπιωντας and νουθετουντας it is preferable to take προισταμενους in the sense of "protect, care for" rather than "preside, lead, direct." Nevertheless, one cannot deny that there is some distinction between members in general and an emerging group of leaders here. Some, e.g., Milligan (1908, 71), Dobschütz (1909, 215), Dibelius (1937, 30), Best (1977, 221), Holmberg (1978, 116) and Marxsen (1979, 71), see the line between laity and an emerging clergy as still more or less fluid, while others, e.g., Lightfoot (1904, 79), Rigaux, (1956, 576-9). Masson (1957, 72) and Meeks (1983a, 134), see a more fixed distinction as already present. The evidence really does not take one beyond the former position. See esp. Best's arguments.

661 Thus, e.g., Milligan (1908,72-3), but who translates "find your peace through them," viz., "through their leadership." This rendering, however, presupposes a more clearly fixed institutional leadership which is hardly in evidence. As a more general admonition, Mark 9:50 provides the striking parallel ειρηνευετε εν αλληλοις.

662 Thus, e.g., Best, 1977, 228. Cf. Rom 12:18: μετα παντων ανθρωπων ειρηνευοντες.

tion and the preceding one is thus quite general: the more specific relation of esteem to members with a special ministry leads quite naturally to the general relation of peace between all members.

The next subsequence is taken here to be 5:14-15. Following upon the introductory appeal παρακαλουμεν δε υμας, αδελφοι with transitional δε, a more particular unity of the admonitions in 5:14 is obvious. The first three more specific admonitions,[664] νουθετειτε τους ατακτους, παραμυθεισθε τους ολιγοψυχους, αντεχεσθε των ασθενων, culminate in the general admonition μακροθυμειτε προς παντας. This topic of "longsuffering" or "patience" is then further developed, first negatively (ορατε μη τις κακον αντι κακου τινι αποδω) and then positively (αλλα παντοτε το αγαθον διωκετε (και) εις αλληλους και εις παντας) in 5:15.[665] At the same time, the inclusive reference παντας in 5:14e, referring internally to fellow-believers, is given a universal expansion in 5:15b, εις αλληλους και εις παντας, which creates a concluding climax.[666] The focus here is primarily on concrete acts of admonishing, encouraging and helping various internal groups, and of not returning evil for evil but eagerly pursuing the good for believers and all people. The patience urged in 5:14e presents the basic disposition from which all such behaviour should proceed.

The unity of the subsequence 5:16-18 is quite obvious: παντοτε χαιρετε, αδιαλειπτως προσευχεσθε, εν παντι ευχαριστειτε· τουτο γαρ θελημα θεου εν Χριστω Ιησου εις υμας. Text-syntactic coherence is created by the three adverbial expressions respectively followed by three imperatival verbs. Text-semantically, coherence is served by the references of the verbs to intimately related dispositions of believers in their spiritual life.[667] Thus, it is most likely that τουτο, as a delimiting SA, relates all three admonitions to God's will rather than just the last one

---

[663] Thus, e.g., Lightfoot (1904, 80), Dobschütz (1909, 219-20), Best (1977, 228). However, others such as Frame (1912, 195) and Masson (1957, 73), although accepting εν εαυτοις, nevertheless see a reflection here of conflict between members and leaders. Against this, see esp. Best's arguments.

[664] The occurrence of the verb νουθετειν both here and in 5:12 is taken to support the view, held by, e.g., Masson (1957, 73) and Friedrich (1976, 248) following some of the church Fathers, that in 5:14 the author turns from addressing members in general to addressing the leaders specifically. However, the repeated general address made to υμας, αδελφοι beginning both 5:12-13 and 5:14 and the above-mentioned fluid distinction between members and emerging leaders discounts this. See esp. Best's arguments (1977, 228-9).

[665] Thus, e.g., Best, 1977, 233; Holtz, 1986, 254.

[666] Thus, Best (1977, 233-4) who rightly rejects the variant reading of the additional και and notes that it destroys the climactic effect. Those who take 5:15 as a separate sequence on a par with 5:14 (e.g. Dobschütz, 1909, 215, 221-2), miss the connection with 5:14d.

[667] Evidence for the intimate interrelation of these three dispositions lies close at hand in 1:1-3 and 3:9-10.

in 5:18a.[668] This analysis indicates that 5:15 is not an integral part of the unit.[669]

The next basically-coherent subsequence is 5:19-22. A more particular unity of the first two admonitions (5:19-20) is apparent from formal parallelism: το πνευμα μη σβεννυτε, προφητειας μη εξουθενειτε. Apart from the negated imperative verbs each preceded by a modifying adverbial expression, there is the close referential connection between το πνευμα as the source of spiritual gifts and προφητεια as a specific instance of such gifts.[670] The focus on spiritual gifts, however, does not stop here but continues in 5:21-22:[671] παντα δε δοκιμαζετε, το καλον κατεχετε, απο παντος ειδους πονηρου απεχεσθε. This interpretation follows from the adversative connective δε in 5:21.[672] Consequently, παντα should be taken as coreferring with what precedes in 5:19-20, and therefore as referring relatively to the totality of spiritual manifestations and not absolutely to everything whatsoever.[673] As for το καλον this should be taken as "what is good" in accordance with God's will relative to spiritual manifestations as a test of their validity, rather than absolutely as "the good,"[674] and also the following phrase απο παντος ειδους πονηρου as "from every evil kind/form" relative to spiritual manifestations rather than purely ethically and absolutely as "from every form of evil."[675] These observations show that groupings of admonitions fall naturally together in somewhat larger units than C. Roetzel has suggested by his division of them into 5:12-13a, 5:13b, 5:14, 5:15 and the single admonitions in 5:16-22.[676]

The fact of 5:23-24 as a coherent unit hardly needs comment: αυτος δε ο θεος της ειρηνης αγιασαι υμας ολοτελεις, και ολοκληρον υμων το πνευμα και η ψυχη και το σωμα αμεμπτως εν τη παρουσια του κυριου ημων Ιησου Χριστου τηρηθειη. πιστος ο καλων υμας, ος και ποιησει. Formally the wish-prayer (5:23) is a close parallel of the terminating/transitional wish-prayer in 3:11-13, opening with αυτος δε ο θεος and expressing the petitions in the optative. The final

---

[668] Similarly, e.g., Lightfoot, 1904, 82; Milligan, 1908, 75; Rigaux, 1956, 589; Masson, 1957, 74; Best, 1977, 234; Holtz, 1986, 258.

[669] Against, e.g., Dibelius (1937. 31) and Marxsen (1977, 72), who see 5:15-18 as a unit, and Friedrich (1976, 249), who sees 5:15 and 5:16 as closely connected in form and content.

[670] Thus, e.g., Dobschütz, 1909, 225; Frame, 1912, 204; Dibelius, 1937, 31; Rigaux, 1956, 591; Best, 1977, 240; and Marxsen, 1979, 72. Less likely is Lightfoot's suggestion (1904, 83) that a reference to spiritual gifts need not be seen for το πνευμα, but rather a more general reference to not quenching the Spirit by way of carelessness, hardness of heart or immorality.

[671] Thus, e.g., Dobschütz, 1909, 226; Frame, 1912, 208; Masson 1957, 76; Forestell, 1968, 233; Best, 1977, 240-1; Marxsen, 1979, 72; Holtz, 1986, 258.

[672] The omission in some important mss. is explained either by assimilation to the first syllable of the following δοκιμαζετε, or by some scribes simply not seeing the connection with what precedes. On this, see, e.g., Lightfoot, 1904, 84; Dobschütz, 1909, Metzger, 1971, 633; Best, 1977, 240.

[673] Thus, e.g., Dobschütz (1909, 226), Frame (1912, 208), Rigaux (1956, 592); and Best (1977, 240) as against Lightfoot (1904, 84) who takes it as "all things

encouraging promise (5:24) is connected climactically by way of asyndeton. The o $καλων$ corefers with $o\ θεος$ and the pro-verb $ποιησει$ (with the ellipsis of $αυτο$, cf. 4:10a) substitutes for $αγιασαι\ υμας/ολοκληρον...τηρηθειη$ and thus qualifies as a SA delimiting the subsequence 5:23-24.

In conclusion of these observations on the coherence and delimitation of the smaller units, it should be pointed out that they may be seen as combining into two basic unities on a level just below that of 5:12-24 as a whole, viz., the admonitions in 5:12-22 and the wish-prayer and closing assurance in 5:23-24. This is obvious from the fact that the former are admonitions addressed to the addressees, while the latter is primarily made up of petitions addressed to God, although indirectly via the optative.

4.4.10 The Rhetoric of 5:12-24

The form of parenesis consisting of summons that are loosely strung together is fairly closely exemplified here.[677] Also, it has been pointed out that the passage has a rythmical character that sets it apart from the general texture of the rest of the letter[678] and that, as in Rom 12:9 ff., traditional material from a Semitic environment is being drawn upon here.[679] While these formal observations warn against reading any urgent problems from these utterances,[680] they do not necessitate the conclusion that they do not reflect selections of admonitions that were more or less relevant to the community's needs.[681] Formal support for this middle position may be seen from the larger groupings of the admonitions in 5:12-22, as analysed above.

---

whatsoever."

[674] Thus, Holtz, 1986, 262. See also Best (1977, 240) as against Lightfoot (1904, 86).

[675] This relative sense indicates the preferability of taking $πονηρου$ as an adjective rather than as a substantive, something not brought out so clearly by Best (1977, 240-1). Lightfoot (1904, 87) gives a concise and clear discussion of the possible meanings of $ειδους$: 1) "the outward form" without the notion of unreality; 2) "appearance, semblance"; and 3) "sort, kind, species" without the technical sense of "species" as opposed to "genus." He prefers the first meaning, while Best is followed here in preferring the third meaning in view of co-textual relations.

[676] Roetzel, 1972, 368.

[677] As is well known, parenesis as a literary genre was particularly defined and related to N.T. material by Dibelius (1961, 239; 1976, 3). The criteria he isolated for identifying the genre may be summarized here under their syntactic, semantic and pragmatic text-semiotic aspects: 1) Syntactic: Single admonitions, usually in the form of commands or summons, are loosely strung together or follow one after the other without explicit connection. 2) Semantic: The admonitions are of a general, ethical content. 3) Pragmatic: a) The admonitions are directed to a specific audience, real or fictional; b) they are not directly addressed to a specific

Thus, with the difference of not constituting reminders of previous instruction, the admonitions in 5:12-22 appear to function similarly to those in 4:1-12 (see 4.4.3.1). Directly they serve as generally relevant, prophylactic and encouraging exhortation; indirectly they serve as further means of **ethos** appeal that would have the effect of reinforcing the reliable and authoritative status of Paul and company (see 4.4.3.2). Besides this latter function being generally realized through the urging of the religious-ethical precepts, it may be seen in particular in the urging of "God's will" (5:18b) and in the petition that God should "sanctify" the addressees wholly (5:23a). As noted above, $αγιασαι$ more or less summarizes the acts and dispositions previously enjoined. At the same time it presents the divine source of the process by which the addressees may be kept blameless in the event of the parousia. An **ethos** appeal is observable in this utterance of righteous concern made by the author. Furthermore, as a reference to blamelessness at the parousia, one observes once more an instance of **pathos** appeal (cf. 3:13).

Another reason why it is doubtful that any serious problems are being addressed in 5:12-22 is that these admonitions, together with the wish-prayer and affirmation in 5:23-24, constitute the text-sequence that closes the letter-body, a most unlikely place to take up any problems of appreciable seriousness. To refer to 5:12-24 as a **peroratio** in accordance with what was normally regarded as such in ancient oratory would not be strictly appropriate (see under 1.7.6) in view of the use of parenesis here. Previously, R. Jewett has classified 5:23-28 as the **peroratio**, whereas G. A. Kennedy has seen 5:23-24 as "the epilogue" and 5:25-28 as "the closure."[682] The delimitation of 5:12-24 from 5:25 ff. and the integral relation of 5:23-24 with 5:12-22 arrived at above advises against this inclusion of 5:25 ff. and against the strict limitation and classification of 5:23-24 as a **peroratio**. It is more appropriate to see 5:23-24 as the culmination of a process of winding-down already started in 5:12 ff.

Taking these cautions into consideration, it may nevertheless be observed that besides 5:12-24 occurring at the end of the body-proper of this act of communication, there are several points of contact with characteristic features noted for the **peroratio** in ancient rhetoric (see 1.7.6). Aristotle notes that the style of the **peroratio** should be characterized by asyndeton with short sentences.[683] Whereas the asyndeton and short sentences in 5:12-22 should be seen primarily as reflecting parenetic style, especially in view of Rom 12:9 ff., there is nevertheless something more appropriate to

---

aspect of the immediate situational context of the addressee(s).

[678] Rigaux, 1962, 184.

[679] See Best, 1977, 241-2.

[680] Similarly, e.g., Dobschütz, 1909, 220; Rigaux, 1956, 576; 1962, 184; Best, 1977, 227, against, e.g., Frame, 1912, 191 ff.; Masson, 1957, 73; Schmithals, 1965, 121-6; Friedrich, 1976, 247-50.

[681] Against, e.g., Rigaux, 1962, 184.

[682] Jewett, 1984, 17; Kennedy, 1984, 144.

[683] Aristotle, Rhet 3.19.6.

this occurring here at the close of the letter than, e.g., in 4:1-12.[684] Also, a certain sonority is affected by the admonitions beginning with words with initial π and ending with verbs in 5:16-22 leading up to the wish-prayer.[685] Reading the text aloud makes these observations particularly appreciable. As for the characteristic of appeal to goodwill and playing upon the emotions of the audience, there are the **ethos/pathos** appeals noted above.

Whereas recapitulation of the main points of a discourse is also a characteristic feature of the **peroratio**, there is nothing that can strictly qualify as such here. However, something similar to this may be seen in the recurrence of some important topics and motifs treated previously. Without pressing too direct a connection as some exegetes do,[686] we may see some connection between the reference to the $\alpha\tau\alpha\kappa\tau\text{o}\upsilon\varsigma$ (5:14b) and the admonitions to quiet living, minding one's own affairs, manual labour and decorous behaviour in 4:11-12,[687] and the reference $\text{o}\lambda\iota\gamma\text{o}\psi\upsilon\chi\text{o}\upsilon\varsigma$ (5:14c) as reflecting the anxiety occasioned by persecution (2:14, 3:2-5) and the deaths of fellow believers (4:13 ff.).[688] There is also the final assurance of salvation at the parousia expressed in 5:23-24 by $\pi\iota\sigma\tau\text{o}\varsigma\ \text{o}\ \kappa\alpha\lambda\omega\nu\ \upsilon\mu\alpha\varsigma,\ \text{o}\varsigma\ \kappa\alpha\iota\ \pi\text{o}\iota\eta\sigma\epsilon\iota$ (5:24) which can be seen as reflecting the sentiments in 5:1-11: The "Day" cannot surprise the addressees like a thief in the night (5:4) since they are sons of light and day (5:5) who are destined by God for the possession of salvation (5:9-10).[689] Also, the admonitions to rejoicing always, unceasing prayer and thanksgiving in all circumstances constitute an echo of these important motives in 1:2-3, 6; 2:13, 19-20 and 3:9-10.

While these observations do not qualify 5:12-24 as a **peroratio** characteristic of orations as such, there are nevertheless sufficient peroration-like characteristics to justify taking 5:12-24 as a whole to function as the conclusion not merely of the text-sequence of 4:1-5:24, but of the whole letter-body (1:2-5:24).

---

[684] This text-sequence has parallels in I Cor 16:13-18, II Cor 13:5-11 and Phil 4:2-9. Cf. Hurd, 1972, 33.

[685] Martin's observation (1964, 135-6) of this in support of seeing "headings of a Church service" is too speculative.

[686] For a criticism of Frame (1912, 196-200) in this respect see Best (1977, 231-2).

[687] See esp. Spicq (1956, 1-13, esp. 11) who cogently argues for the sense "the disorderly" as opposed to "idlers" so as to relate this admonition generally to 4:11-12 as a whole and not specifically to the admonition on manual labour in 4:11c.

[688] Thus, e.g. Best, 1977, 228-32; Marxsen, 1979, 71-2.

[689] Similarly, e.g., Marxsen, 1979, 73.

4.4.11 Some Concluding Observations on I Thess 4:1-5:24

From the foregoing analysis one may observe a further and final example of the same strategy of ring-composition in 4:1-5:24 as observed for 1:2-2:16 and 2:17-3:13 above (see 4.1.5 and 4.2.6): A=4:1-12, B=4:13-5:11 and A'=5:12-24. This may be seen generally from the text-semantic and text-pragmatic dimensions in the specific concentrations of religious-ethical topics in sequences of admonitions in 4:1-12 and 5:12-24, in contrast to the more sustained treatment of eschatological topics in 4:13-5:11 aimed at informing, consoling and encouraging the addressees.

There are particularly striking formal features of a complex of recurring words and phrases which recur as a complex only in 4:1-12 and 5:12-24: there is the recurrence of the performative verbs ερωτωμεν (4:1; 5:12) and παρακαλουμεν (4:1, 10; 5:14) and the recurrence of τουτο γαρ εστιν θελημα του θεου (4:3; 5:18) together with the lexical and partial lexical recurrences to be seen in πνευμα (4:8; 5:19), απεχεσθε (4:3; 5:22), αγιασμος/αγιασμω/αγιασαι (4:3, 7; 5:23), εκαλεσεν υμας/καλων υμας (4:7; 5:24). While the recurrences of πνευμα and απεχεσθε may be accidental here, the combination of the use of the performative verbs, the reference to the will of God and the closely related references to election and sanctification (cf. 4:7; 5:23-24) can hardly be so.[690]

Finally, while this overall pattern is shared with the text-sequences 1:2-2:16 and 2:17-3:13, it is not established here on the fifth ranking level but on the fourth one. This is hardly surprising, since ring-composition and other patterns of compositional organization have been shown to inform any unit from very small text-sequences up to whole works (see 6.1). On the other hand, this observation of ring-composition once again gives general support to the delimitations arrived at more directly by way of explicit delimitation markers and more indirectly by text-linguistic features of coherence in 4:1-5:24. Thus, together with the third sequential-hierarchical level of the sequence 4:1-5:24 previously established (see ch. 3), fourth and fifth levels may be represented as follows in Figure 7:

---

[690] This conclusion is given firm support in ch. 5 below.

LEVEL III

I Thess 4:1-5:24

1.2.2SM; C; Predominance of Explicit Conative Function.

LEVEL IV

4:1-12	4:13-5:11	5:12-24
1.2.2.1SMind; 3ThM; SA; C Prominence of Religious-Ethical Material with a Hortatory Function. Prominence of Ethos Appeals.	1.2.2.2SM; 4ThInf; C Prominence of Eschatological Material with Dissuasive and Consolatory Functions. Prominence of Pathos/Quasi-Logical Appeals.	5ThM; C Prominence of Religious-Ethical Material with a Hortatory Function. Prominence of Ethos Appeals.

LEVEL V

4:13-18	5:1-11
4.1ThM; SA; C	4.2ThM; SA; C

Figure 7

Chapter 5

AN ANALYSIS OF MACROSTYLISTIC SYMMETRY IN THE
LETTER-BODY

5.1   TEXTUAL SYMMETRY: BACKGROUND, METHOD, FUNCTIONS

Besides the symmetrical structures that have been long observed in stylistic analysis for such smaller verbal units as phrases, clauses and sentences,[691] there is the steadily increasing documentation of symmetrical structures of composition informing larger textual units from paragraphs to entire works in different kinds of texts and in different languages and cultures.[692] A perusal through the relevant literature shows that criteria for warranting the discovery of compositional symmetry have been constituted singly or in combination (1) by parallel numbers of syllables or of words or by roughly equal numbers of lines, (2) by patterned recurrences of grammatical formulations, words, phrases or clauses or by complexes of such elements; (3) by patterned recurrences of motives, themes or thought-sequences, and (4) by patterned recurrences created by the symmetrical use of forms (similes, proverbs, etc.), genres (prayers, hymns, etc.) or predominances of text-types (narrative, descriptive, directive, etc.).

The use of terminology for describing the various patterns is not always the same among those carrying out this type of analysis, nor is it always sufficiently clear and consistent.[693] Consequently, it is desireable to make explicit some of the simpler,

---

[691] See, e.g., Denniston 1952, 70-98; Lausberg, 1973, 310-32; Plett, 1979a, 33-42. On the N.T. see, e.g., Duncan, 1926, 129-43; Jeremias, 1958, 145-56.

[692] Only a selective documentation of this can be given here: Classical and Hellenistic Greek texts (e.g., van Otterlo, 1944; Myres, 1953, 89-134, 151, 217; Whitman, 1958, 87 ff.; Niles, 1979, 36-9; Welch, 1981, 250-258); Latin texts (e.g., Welch, 1981, 258-64; Traill, 1981, 232-41; Maskalew, 1982, 116-22); Sumero-Akkadian texts (e.g., Smith, 1981, 17-35); Ugaritic texts (e.g., Welch, 1981b, 36-49); Hebrew texts (e.g., Lund, 1942, 51-136; Thiering, 1963, 189-209; Fishbane, 1975, 15-38; Bar-Efrat, 1980, 154-73; Radday, 1981, 50-117; W.G.E., Watson, 1981, 118-68; Lichtenstein, 1982, 202-11; Magonet, 1982; 365-76); NT Greek texts (e.g., Lund, 1942, 139-411; Vanhoye, 1963; 1974, 49-380; Sibinga, 1970, 194-208; Chevallier, 1971, 129-42; Swetnam, 1972, 368-85; 1974, 333-48; Malatesta, 1973; Lamarche, 1975, 453-63; K. E. Bailey, 1976; Welch, 1981a, 211-49); Patristic Latin texts (e.g., Sider, 1973, 405-23) Old French (e.g., Niles, 1973, 4-12); Old English (e.g., Bartlett, 1935; Hieatt, 1975, 249-65; Niles, 1979a, 924-35), etc.

[693] See Welch (1981c, 9-10) for a summary of various terms used for chiasmus. However, Welch himself does not give a satisfactory typology of patterns when he

more common patterns and their designations which include those that are relevant for the present analysis:[694] 1) **Simple** parallels (A A'); 2) **alternating** pattern (A B A' B'); 3) **ring** pattern (A B A' or A B C B' A'); 4) **chiasmus** (A B B' A'); and 5) **inclusio** (A B C, etc., A').

In the following analysis we shall follow S. Bar-Efrat's important methodological observation that whereas patterns established on more than one criterion separately, e.g., verbal as well as thematic elements, serve to strengthen the validity of seeing a particular pattern's presence, one should avoid establishing a pattern by mixing miscellaneous elements.[695] There is good reason for this caution, since the mixing of miscellaneous elements (e.g., A=theme, B=word, C=gramatical formulation, D=simile, etc.) appreciably increases the danger of subjectively imposing a patterned structure that can actually be quite foreign to a particular text. In other instances such a procedure can make the evidence for a pattern appear to be more explicit or sophisticated than it actually is.

Such symmetrical structures appear to not only have served esthetic functions, but also afforded a means of internal organization in ancient writing which did not make extensive use of punctuation, not to speak of paragraphs, capitalization and other devices for indicating unity and transition of thought.[696] The audio-oral character of ancient literature[697] makes this explanation particularly viable in the many instances where repetitions of sound patterns, words, phrases, etc., serve as an important indication of structure.[698] However, since these particular explicit indications of structure are not everywhere evident in ancient literature, such practical functions cannot be taken as universal practice but rather as a tendency encouraged by such general circumstances of textual production and reception.

Where symmetrical structures are clearly in evidence, this may be taken to indicate the particular care with which a text has been composed[699] and may serve as evidence regarding the delimitation and unity of the particular text involved.[700] Whether or not a particular symmetrical structure has any semantic or pragmatic function beyond that of macro-syntactically organizing a text or subordinate text-sequence must obviously involve a more subjective level of interpretation where parallel

---

extends the chiasmus pattern (A B B' A') to cover other similar patterns that can be more suitably distinguished as ring or concentric patterns.

[694] Cf., e.g., Bar-Efrat, 1980, 170. For variations of ring and chiastic patterns see Watson, 1981, 123 ff.

[695] Bar-Efrat, 1980, 172.

[696] Welch, 1981c, 12. On punctuation see Metzger, 1964, 26-7.

[697] See Kennedy, 1963, 4. Cf. Augustine (Conf 6.3) who found it strange that Ambrose "eyes glanced over the pages" while "his voice and tongue were silent."

[698] Welch (1981c, 12) also notes that such explicitly patterned elements would be a helpful tool in memorization.

[699] Sider, 1973, 408.

[700] Bar-Efrat, 1980, 172; Welch, 1981, 12.

or concentric patterns may be seen as in some way expressing or accentuating meaning or focussing on that which is of primary importance.[701] Establishing the viability of the presence of such functions will depend very much on being able to establish a tangible relation of such formal features to the contents and/or rhetorical functions of the text.[702]

5.2   TEXT-SYNTACTIC SYMMETRY IN I THESS 1:2-5:24

In the preceding text-linguistic and rhetorical analyses, the use of such text-stylistic devices as **inclusio** and circular composition have been repeatedly observed as supportive features of text-delimitation and coherence. The observations of the circular composition informing 1:2-2:16, 2:17-3:13 and 4:1-5:24 have been made primarily on criteria drawn from the text-pragmatic and text-semantic dimensions, with some supporting evidence taken from the text-syntactic dimension in terms of groupings of verbal recurrences.[703] The following analysis will now concentrate entirely on the text-syntactic dimension with regard to patterned verbal elements such as lexical, partial lexical and lexical-grammatical recurrences, not only in terms of single words, but also loose clusters of closely recurring words, as well as recurrences of whole phrases and clauses.

Whereas such elements of verbal recurrence are accounted for in text-linguistics as a common text-syntactic means of creating text-coherence, the patterned recurrences of such elements in modern texts appears to be confined for the most part to highly formalized poetry.[704] In ancient texts the accentuation of this general characteristic of textual coherence by way of patterned recurrences was extended to prose texts as well.[705]

Regarding previous analyses of the structure of I Thess along these lines, the work of K. Thieme rests solely on the recurrences of key words at the beginning and end of text-sequences.[706] This basis must be judged as inadequate, being too narrow and involving too great a degree of arbitrary selectivity. On the other hand, J. C. Hurd arrived at an identical pattern of ring-composition for 1:2-2:16 and 2:17-3:13 as estab-

---

[701] Sider, 1973, 406 ff.; Bar-Efrat, 1980, 172-73; Welch, 1981, 12.

[702] See Sider, 1973, 406-23.

[703] See 4.1.5, 4.2.6 and 4.5.11 above.

[704] de Beaugrande/Dressler, 1981, 54 ff.

[705] E.g., see the speech of Hushai in II Sam 17:8-13 as analysed by Bar-Efrat, 1980, 170-72.

[706] Thieme, 1963, 450-58. He arrives at the following structure of superior and subordinate text-sequences after the prescript: 1) I Thess 1:2-2:16 subdivided into 1:2-10, 2:1-13 and 2:14-16; 2) 2:17-3:13 subdivided into 2:17-20, 3:1-5 and 3:6-13; 3) 4:1-12 subdivided into 4:1-2, 4:3-8 and 4:9-12; 4) 4:13-5:11 subdivided into 4:13-18, 5:1-3 and 5:4-11; 5) 5:12-28 subdivided into 5:12-13, 5:14-22 and 5:23-28.

lished in this study with 2:1-12 and 3:1-8 as the central panels respectively.[707] However, his method of mixing thematic and lexical elements in establishing parallel elements is unsatisfactory.[708] Furthermore, while he observed that 4:13-5:11 was a central panel within 4:1-5:22, he was unable to demonstrate this in the same way as for the other units.[709]

As mentioned above, the analysis of patterned verbal elements falls exclusively within the text-syntactic dimension. Such evidence should not be seen as decisive in itself,[710] but as intercorroborative with the circular pattern of composition already established above from text-semantic and text-pragmatic criteria. Also, in order to safeguard the selection of verbal elements from becoming the means of an arbitrary imposition of structures foreign to the text, the selection of verbal elements and formulations will be almost totally restricted to those that occur not more than twice within the respective text-sequences where a pattern is established. An exception is made for χαρα, χαιρω in 3:19-20 and 3:9 where the parallelism is obvious.

Following these prescriptions, one comes to some rather striking results that corroborate previous evidence for the recurring circular pattern of composition in I Thess 1:2-2:16, 2:17-3:13 and 4:1-5:24 respectively and strengthen this evidence appreciably for the unity of these three text-sequences. The verbal elements in the following Figures 8-10 have been arranged as far as possible in accordance with their natural sequential occurrence in the text. The numerical entries within parentheses after each verbal entry indicate in which verse the verbal entry is found within the respective subsections.

---

[707] Hurd, 1972, 25-7.

[708] Hurd's analysis of 4:15-18 (1972, 22) provides a striking sample of this weakness.

[709] Hurd, 1972, 29.

[710] See esp. Swetnam's criticisms (1972, 368-85; 1974, 333-48) of Vanhoye's use (1963) of such formal criteria for text-delimitation and organization.

I THESSALONIANS 1:2-2:16

CHIASTIC PATTERN	ALTERNATING PATTERN
1:2-10 (A)	(a)
ευχαριστουμεν τῳ θεῳ (2) μιμηται...εγενηθητε (6) δεξαμενοι...λογον (6) οργης (10)	μνημονευοντες...κοπου (3)
2:1-8 (B)	(b)
υμας το ευαγγελιον του θεου (2) παρακλησις (3) θεος μαρτυς (5) ως...εαυτης τεκνα (7)	ουχ...ανθρωποις αρεσκοντες... θεῳ (4)
2:9-12 (B')	(a')
υμας το ευαγγελιον του θεου (9) μαρτυρες...θεος (10) ως...τεκνα εαυτου (11) παρακαλουντες (12)	μνυμονευετε...κοπον (9)
2:13-16 (A')	(b')
ευχαριστουμεν τῳ θεῳ εδεξασθε...λογον (13) μιμηται εγενηθητε (14) οργη (16)	θεῳ μη αρεσκοντων... ανθρωποις (15)

Figure 8

I THESSALONIANS 2:17-3:13

CHIASTIC PATTERN	ALTERNATING PATTERN
2:17-20 (A)	(a)
καρδια (17) το προσωπον υμων ιδειν (17) του κυριου ημων Ιησου εν τη...παρουσια (19) χαρα...χαρα (19, 20)	ελθειν προς υμας (18)
3:1-5 (B)	(b)
Τιμοθεον (2) ευαγγελιω (2) παρακαλεσαι (2)	εις το στηριξαι (2)
3:6-8 (B')	(a')
Τιμοθεου (6) ευαγγελισαμενου (6) παρεκληθημεν (7)	ελθοντος...προς ημας (6)
3:9-13 (A')	(b')
χαρα...χαιρομεν (9) ιδειν υμων το προσωπον (10) καρδιας (13) εν τη παρουσια του κυριου ημων Ιησου (13)	εις το στηριξαι (13)

Figure 9

I THESSALONIANS 4:1-5:24

CHIASTIC PATTERN	ALTERNATING PATTERN
4:1-12 (A)	(a)
αδελφοι, ερωτωμεν υμας (1) τουτο γαρ...θελημα...θεου (3) απεχεσθαι (3) παρακαλουμεν δε υμας, αδελφοι (10)	περι δε...ου χρειαν εχετε γραφειν υμιν, αυτοι γαρ (9)
4:13-18 (B)	(b)
μη...καθως...οι λοιποι (13) Ιησους απεθανεν (14) αμα συν αυτοις (17) παρακαλειτε αλληλους (18)	την παρουσιαν του κυριου (15)
5:1-11 (B')	(a')
μη...ως οι λοιποι (6) Ιησου...αποθανοντος (9-10) αμα συν αυτω (10) παρακαλειτε αλληλους (11)	περι δε...ου χρειαν εχετε υμιν γραφεσθαι, αυτοι γαρ (1-2)
5:12-24 (A')	(b')
ερωτωμεν δε υμας, αδελφοι (12) παρακαλουμεν δε υμας, αδελφοι (14) τουτο γαρ θελημα θεου (18) απεχεσθε (22)	τῃ παρουσιᾳ του κυριου (23)

Figure 10

5.3 TEXT-SYMMETRY AND MACROSTRUCTURE: SOME OBSERVATIONS

It may be observed that the various text-sequences marked by the clusters of verbal elements or formulations constituting the units of the chiastic and alternating patterns above regularly coincide with text-sequences and subsequences previously delimited by delimitation markers and/or other semantic-pragmatic textual criteria in the foregoing text-linguistic and rhetorical analysis. This consideration touches upon the relation of symmetrical structure to the macrostructure established on text-linguistic and rhetorical criteria and merits further comment.

As a purely formal, text-syntactic and stylistic phenomenon, it should come as no surprise that one and the same symmetrical structure of composition can delimit and unify text-sequences that have different ranks and different contents and communicative functions. In other words, symmetrical structures may be referred to as empty, non-generic forms. This also allows for two or more types of symmetrical structure to co-occur in a particular text-sequence. As already noted, that which gives such compositional structures their validity is basically their objective justification by way of recurring features in the text, the safeguarding restriction of evidence limited to only twice-recurring elements, and the consistency of patterning within the particular unit of text involved.

It has already been observed that the recurring pattern of ring-composition (A B A'), as based primarily on elements belonging to the semantic and pragmatic textual dimensions, delimits and unifies 1:2-2:16 and 2:17-3:13 on the fifth-ranking level and 4:1-5:24 on the fourth-ranking level of the macrostructure.[711] Regarding text-syntactic, concrete verbal elements alone (words, word-clusters, phrases, etc.), one arrives at the recurring chiastic pattern where the A A' units lie on the fifth (1:2-2:16; 2:17-3:13) and fourth-ranking (4:1-5:24) levels and the B B' units lie on the sixth (2:1-12; 3:1-8) and fifth-ranking (4:13-5:11) levels respectively.[712] In addition, the alternating verbal elements in the a b a' b' pattern also fall in text-sequences of different ranks.

Thus, purely formal symmetrical structures may obviously involve units of text that lie on different-ranking levels of a text's macrostructure, since such symmetrical structures are indeed empty, non-generic forms. This indicates that N.W. Lund's reference to such patterns as "chiasmus" in terms of "Formgeschichte" was hardly appropriate.[713] Furthermore, the presence of such text-symmetrical phenomena (see under 5.1) in ancient Greek and Latin texts, besides Old English and Old French texts, indicate that this was not a peculiar Semitic "form" but more likely lies on the general level of "faculté de langage."[714] By contrast, a text's macrostructure is closely tied up with its generic identity as involving a more or less typical combination of features from the syntactic, semantic and above all the pragmatic textual dimensions which, apart from certain types of poetry, do not include textual symmetry as a dis-

---

[711] See 4.5.11 above.

[712] See 4.1.5, 4.2.6 and 4.5.11 above.

[713] Lund, 1942, 17 ff., 25 ff.

[714] As against Lund (1942, 25 ff.). For a correlation of this level of linguistic generality with those of "Gattungstheorie" and "Formgeschichte" see Hellholm (1980, 74).

tinctive ingredient.[715]

It is important to note that although the chiastic and alternating symmetrical structures do not respect the various levels of rank to which the text-sequences belong in the macrostructure, they nevertheless regularly coincide with both the larger and smaller delimitations of these text-sequences. Thus, apart from the levels of rank, they give corroborative support to the various delimitations previously arrived at by other text-linguistic and rhetorical criteria. The chiastic pattern displayed above can also be seen as corroborating the ring-pattern on the various levels insofar as the B B' units may be taken as simple parallels within the central sections of 2:1-12, 3:1-8 and 4:13-5:11. Thus, one can speak of an obvious, general strategy of circular composition in each section which is based on criteria from the syntactic, semantic and pragmatic textual dimensions.[716] Finally, the consistent co-occurrence and recurrence of the ring, chiastic and alternating patterns in each section provide intercorroborative evidence for the closely-knit unity of each one respectively. The relevance of these observations of symmetrical structures for the question regarding the integrity of I Thess and for the interpretation of its communicative function(s) will be taken up below in chs. 6 and 7.

---

[715] For the relation of these three text-semiotic dimensions to the question of genre, see esp. Hellholm, 1980, 62-95; 1986, 25-6, 33 ff., and the literature referred to there.

[716] In view of this consistent, tightly woven macrostylistic symmetry, Bahr's position (1968, 36) that Paul's own hand takes up the pen in 4:1 ff. by way of an authenticating subscription after an amanuensis' composition of 1:1-3:13 is most dubious.

PART III

THE INTERPRETATION OF I THESSALONIANS AS AN ACT OF COMMUNICATION

Chapter 6

I THESS: PERSUASIVE ACT OCCASIONED BY A RHETORICAL EXIGENCE

In the preceding analyses the primary focus has been on establishing textual coherence and delimitation as well as making explicit the various appeals made to the emotions, to credibility and to reason relatively understood, although aspects of functional relations between the major text-sequences have also been touched upon to some extent. What follows is an attempt to use these text-centered observations and the insights of persuasive strategies as conceptualized in rhetoric in interpreting the functional relations holding between the major text-sequences and how these functional relations assist in disclosing the rhetorical exigence occasioning the letter as a whole.

6.1 I THESS 1:2-3:13: ITS FUNCTION OF CAPTATIO BENEVOLENTIAE

From the analyses in 3.2.1 and 4.1.4 above it may be observed that the letter-conventions of **philophronesis** in 1:2-3:13 have been expanded by a schematic sequence of recollective narrative events (see 3.2.3.1) accompanied by more or less extensive comments serving rhetorical strategies typically associated with **exordium** and **narratio** in ancient rhetoric (see 1.7.6.2).

The initial thanksgiving/prayer-report (1:2-3) introduces the general subject of the letter, viz., the practical outworking of the addressees' faith, love and hope. Following this, the recollective narrative sequence begins already in 1:4 with the reference to the event of their "election" which is thematically expanded in 1:5 ff. in terms of its historical realization in the gospel-event shared by the addressors and addressees. It was shown that the repeated references to this gospel-event in the thematic subsequence 1:2-2:16 alternate between a prominence of focus on the addressees' reception of the word in 1:2-10 and 2:13-16 and on the addressors' mediation of the word in 2:1-12. The repeated references to these aspects provide the bases in particular for addressee-laudatory (1:6-8, 9b-10); 2:13-14), addressor-apologetic (1:5, 9a; 2:1-12) and opposition-vituperative (2:14-16) strategies of persuasion, among various other credibility and affective appeals. Together with the reiterated topics of thanksgiving, reception of the word and imitation, the related exordial strategies of praise and vituperation strikingly frame the apologetic sequence (2:1-12), with the vituperation serving as a terminating climax to 1:2-2:16 as a whole.

The conventional epistolary "visit" theme (see 3.2.1.2), was also shown to be expanded variously in the next thematic subsequence of 2:17-3:13 (see 4.2). Following the absolute spatial marker in 1:5 and subsequent iterations (see 3.2.3.1), relative temporal and spatial markers signal a shift from the initial gospel-event to the events of departure and unsuccessful attempts to return (2:17-18), to the sending of Timothy (3:1 ff.), to his return (3:6) and to the addressors's present desire to visit the addressees again (3:8, 9-13). The mention of each of these narrative events is not only expressed in emotionally charged language but also occasions more extensive comments that take the form of intense expressions of affection, concern and goodwill (2:19-20; 3:6b-8, 9-13) and a short, pointed treatment of the destined character of Christian suffering (3:3-4) argued in such a way as to enhance the addressors' credibility. Particularly striking are the "joy" expressions (2:19-20; 3:9), together with the reminder of past desire and the expression of present desire to make a return visit (2:17-18; 3:10-11), which frame the report of Timothy's visit (3:1-8).

With regard to the delimitation of the subsequences 1:2-2:16 and 2:17-3:13 it is important to note that they are distinguished by criteria from the text-semantic and text-syntactic dimensions. In the former subsequence there is the expansion of the "election" theme in terms of the initial gospel-event with a spatial focus on "presence" with the addressees, and in the latter there is the expansion of the "visit" theme with a spatial focus on "absence" from the addressees. In the text-pragmatic dimension, however, the two subsequences share basically common persuasive strategies. This commonality is especially obvious from the ring-compositional feature of the prominent **pathos/ethos** appeals of thanksgiving/prayer-reports, praise, blame, expressions of joy and wish-prayer petitions occurring variously in initial and final panels that respectively frame central panels characterized by relatively more prominent quasi-logical appeals (see 4.1.8 and 4.2.6). The majority of these appeals have been shown to be aimed implicitly or explicitly at strengthening goodwill and credibility.[717] Furthermore, this general **pragmatic** coherence and delimitation of 1:2-3:13 as a whole is supported by the further observation of the framing, letter-conventional thanksgiving/prayer-reports in 1:2-3 and 3:9-10 together with the iterated thanksgiving-report in 2:13 (see 3.2.1.1). These were interpreted as having the function of indirect SM (see 3.2.1). Also, as noted by Kl. Berger, the typical function of such expressions of thanksgiving in relation to the addressee is primarily that of **captatio benevolentiae.**[718]

It is important to observe that all of the references to past events are not specifically informative but for the most part recollective, with the exception of Timothy's return (3:6).[719] This is an indication that the primary communicative intention is to be found, not in the references to the events themselves, but in other functions realized by the extended, explicit comments which they occasion. In the reception process such a schematic recollection of events would no doubt activate the addressees' memories, while the various comments would serve to induce them to re-live their recent experience of entry into and life in the faith as being successful and genuine and the addressors' mediation of this experience as being divinely approved, genuine and responsible. Both inspite of the prolonged stretches of persuasive comments and, at

---

[717] In view of the continuation of philophronetic expressions of joy and thanksgiving and the focus on the arguments regarding tribulations in 3:3-4, Moffat's characterization (1910, 5) of apologia pro absentia sua as the main function of 2:17-3:13 is seen as going too far. On his characterization of 2:1-12 as apologia pro vita et labore suo (1910, 5 and 26) see below.

[718] Berger, 1974, 219-24.

[719] The fact that all of the narrative information up to 3:6 was available to the addressees through Timothy questions the appropriateness of Lyons' description (1985, 208) of 2:17-3:13 as "autobiographical update."

the same time, by means of them, it is possible to discern such general narrative features as tension and climax in the progression of events. Such features constitute a specific "reportable" quality of narrative communication that serves to hold the attention of the audience.[720] Following the initial gospel event, the tensions of separation, of unsuccessful attempts to return, and of having to remain behind when sending Timothy may be seen as culminating in a climax in the report of his return with goodnews of their faith, love and continued goodwill.[721]

This does not mean, however, that all is now perfectly well with the Thessalonian believers. In the concluding thanksgiving/prayer-report the "deficiencies of faith" (3:10) referred to are obviously part of the motivation of the addressors' intensely expressed desire to make a future visit. Insofar as the letter itself must be judged as a substitute for the contact of such a future visit, it is most likely that the unusually long exordial/narrative-like character of 1:2-3:13 and this reference to deficiencies prepare for a treatment of such in the following subsequence of 4:1-5:24 (see 4.3).

An important consequence of these observations is that, although there is a denser sequence of narrated events in 2:17-3:13, narrative and exordial characteristics are so closely integrated in realizing the persuasive strategies of **captatio benevolentiae** in 1:2-3:13 as a whole that any attempt to divide it into the discrete functional text-sequences of **exordium** and **narratio** must be judged as artificial and inappropriate.

Indirect support for this is to be seen in the fact that previous attempts to impose these two units of rhetorical disposition on 1:2-3:13 have issued in quite disparate delimitational schemes: 1) F.W. Hughes has delimited 1:1-10 as the **exordium** (including the prescript), 2:1-3:10 as the **narratio**, and 3:11-13 as a **partitio**,[722] 2) R. Jewett has 1:1-5 as the **exordium** (including the prescript) and 1:6-3:13 as the **narratio**,[723] and 3) G.A. Kennedy has 1:2-10 as the "proem" (**exordium** without the prescript), 2:1-8 as a "refutation of charges against Paul, anticipating objections to his authority and thus important for his ethos in the letter," and 2:9-3:13 seen to "recast the materials of a narration in striking ethical and pathetical terms."[724]

Kennedy's delimitation is less susceptible to the charge of a mechanical, organic application of rhetorical **dispositio** than the former two, but is nevertheless insufficiently motivated from the perspective of text-specific features of coherence and delimitation. From the perspective of ancient rhetoric, the close integration of the features and functions of **exordium** and **narratio** may be noted as being quite within the bounds of good rhetorical strategy, both in theory[725] and in practice.[726] Intertextual

---

[720] See Quastoff, 1980, 52 ff., 86.

[721] See the supporting observations of temporal-spatial features in 3.2.3.1.

[722] For references to Hughes' conclusions see Jewett, 1984, 12, n. 47, and 17.

[723] Jewett, 1984, 15-17.

[724] Kennedy, 1984, 142-3.

[725] Rhet ad Alex 1438b,15-28; 1442b,28-32 (see 1.7.6.2).

[726] See Goldstein's analysis (1968, 134) of Demosthenes, Ep 3.1-10. As in I Thess 1:2-3:13, the facts to be narrated by Demosthenes are already familiar to the addressees and only need to be referred to in summary form.

support may also be seen in the exordium-like functions of "antecedent histories" in O.T.-Jewish exhortatory discourse as analysed under 8.2.2 below.

Finally, Jewett's observation of 3:11-13 as having the character of a **transitus**, in objection to Hughs' classification of it as a **partitio**, is certainly more appropriate (see 4.3).[727] These interpretive conclusions in general, apart from finer distinctions based on a more adequate text-centered and dynamical-rhetorical approach, lie closer to the position of such exegetes as Ph. Vielhauer and H. Koester who have described the passage very generally as a **proem**.[728]

6.2 THE EXORDIUM-LIKE RELATION OF 1:2-3:13 TO 4:1-5:24

Returning now to briefly consider a common dispositional characteristic of private and official Hellenistic letters, C.J. Bjerkelund has shown that a significant number of these are basically structured by a thanksgiving/request succession of major functional text-sequences with the thanksgiving part functioning as either a general introduction or a specific preparation for the subsequent request part which introduces the main point of the letter.[729] Apart from the criticisms directed at his form-critical analysis (see 3.2.2.1) and disagreement with his conclusion that the main point of the letter lies precisely in the encouragement to "abound more and more" (4:1, 10), Bjerkelund is broadly correct in seeing I Thess as being informed by this particular schematic sequence.[730]

Thus, this common strategy of letter-disposition, the fact that the thanksgiving part in I Thess has been expanded by types of strategies typical of the **exordium/narratio** of ancient rhetoric, and the fact that these strategies lead up to the reference to something that is not as it should be, viz., the "deficiencies of faith" (3:10) followed by the terminal/transitional wish-prayer in 3:11-13, all these factors are strong indications that the main "point" of the communication lies in the following major text-sequence of 4:1-5:24.

---

[727] Jewett, 1984, 16-19.

[728] Vielhauer, 1975, 84; Koester, 1982, vol. II, 55.

[729] See Bjerkelund, 1967, 44-50, 60-66.

[730] Bjerkelund, 1967, 133-5.

6.3   I THESS 4:1-5:24: EXHORTATION, ARGUMENTATIO AND PERORATIO

Under 3.2.2 and 3.2.3.2 above it was shown that 4:1-5:24 constitutes a coherent and delimited functional text-sequence on the same level with 1:2-3:13. A predominant, explicitly conative function is realized by the various, recurrent imperative expressions on the surface level of the text. Among these, the conative, performative $\epsilon\rho\omega\tau\omega/\pi\alpha\rho\alpha\kappa\alpha\lambda\omega$ expressions (4:1, 10; 5:12, 14) were shown to have the particular delimiting function of iterative SM. As more specific subtypes of this overall conative function, general exhortation predominates in the subsequences 4:1-12 and 5:12-24 and consolation-dissuasion predominates in 4:13-5:11 (see 4.4).

In 4.4.2-4.4.3 the text-sequence of 4:1-12 was shown to be a subordinate unit, delimited in particular by the $\pi\alpha\rho\alpha\gamma\gamma\epsilon\lambda\iota\alpha/\pi\alpha\rho\alpha\gamma\gamma\epsilon\lambda\lambda\omega$ expressions (4:2, 11) functioning as subordinate, indirect, iterative SM. Attention to the predominantly text-pragmatic features in the passage indicates that the admonitions are repeatedly characterized as reminders of previously given instructions (4:1, 2, 6, 11). This "reminding" element and the explicit assurances recognizing the addressees' fulfillment of these instructions ($\kappa\alpha\theta\omega\varsigma$ $\kappa\alpha\iota$ $\pi\epsilon\rho\iota\pi\alpha\tau\epsilon\iota\tau\epsilon$, 4:1; $\kappa\alpha\iota$ $\gamma\alpha\rho$ $\pi\omicron\iota\epsilon\iota\tau\epsilon$ $\alpha\upsilon\tau\omicron$, 4:10) indicate that the admonitions, though generally relevant, are not remedial but rather prophylactic and meant to encourage further growth.

Consequently, one cannot reasonably locate the "deficiencies of faith" (3:10) in 4:1-12. In fact, several factors combine to strengthen an interpretation of 4:1-12 as also realizing an **ethos** appeal serving to strengthen the credibility and authority of the addressors in preparation for dealing with the actual "deficiencies of faith" that are located specifically in 4:13-5:11.[731] These factors may be summarized as follows:

1.   There is the lack of a corrective function in 4:1-12.

2.   There is the contrast of old information in 4:1-12 with the new information signalled in 4:13.

3.   There is the seriousness of the addressees' grief and anxiety reflected in the dissuasive appeals and the comforting instruction in 4:13-5:11.

4.   There is the greater need to obtain conviction reflected in the prominence of quasi-logical arguments in 4:13-5:11.

5.   And there is the focus that 4:13-5:11 obtains by way of the ring-compositional strategy observed in 4.4.11 and Fig. 10 under 5.2.

Among the various interpretations made of the arguments and appeals in 4:13-5:11 (see 2.2.3, 4.4.6 and 4.4.8) the most probable reconstruction of the background is that the addressees had been previously instructed about the parousia primarily if not exclusively in terms of their bodily assumption, since it was regarded to be imminent. As a result, the circumstance of unexpected deaths in the community appears to have caused a fair degree of grief and anxious perplexity (4:13, 18) over the departed. This grief and perplexity with its serious potential threat to hope and faith

---

[731] A fairly recent view of the "deficiencies" (3:10) being located specifically in 4:13-5:11 has been forwarded by Reese (1980, 215), but without the arguments presented here.

is met with in 4:13-17 by the comforting instruction of the assumption of the dead as grounded in the death and resurrection of Jesus and accomplished through their resurrection at the parousia (see 4.4.6).

The analysis of the persuasive strategies in 5:1-10 (see 4.4.8) is taken to support seeing a reflection of the addressees' anxiety over their own eschatological status, most likely also related to the deaths in the community in view of 5:10 in particular. This potential threat to hope and faith is met with by assertions and arguments emphatically insisting on their positive status of election to salvation in contrast to complacent unbelievers.

Both sequences of theological-eschatological reasoning in 4:13-17 and 5:1-10 are given a Christological basis (4:14; 5:9-10) and both are concluded by parallel admonitions to comfort one another in 4:18 and 5:11. These admonitions were shown to be subordinate, recurrent SM that together delimit 4:13-5:11 as a whole and also incorporate it into the overall conative function of 4:13-5:24. While they explicitly indicate **consolatio** as a major function of the passage, the related function of **dissuasio** is implicitly present in 4:13 ($\iota\nu\alpha$ $\mu\eta$ $\lambda\upsilon\pi\eta\sigma\theta\epsilon$ $\kappa\alpha\theta\omega\varsigma$ $\kappa\alpha\iota$ $o\iota$ $\lambda o\iota\pi o\iota$ $o\iota$ $\mu\eta$ $\epsilon\chi o\nu\tau\epsilon\varsigma$ $\epsilon\lambda\pi\iota\delta\alpha$), in the emphatic contrast between the positive eschatological status of the addressees (5:4-5, 8a, 9-10) to complacent outsiders (5:3, 6-7), and in the quasi-logical persuasive character of the material in 4:14-17 and 5:4-10. The addition of $\kappa\alpha\theta\omega\varsigma$ $\kappa\alpha\iota$ $\pi o\iota\epsilon\iota\tau\epsilon$ in 5:11 in relation to 5:1-10 and the absence of any such acknowledgement in 4:13-18 is interpreted to indicate that the more seriously threatening problem is reflected in 4:13-18.

In the analyses of 4.4.9-4.4.11 it was shown that, in the ring-compositional return to explicit religious-ethical exhortation in 5:12 ff., the general parenesis not only serves a general **ethos** appeal, as in 4:1-12, but 5:12-24 as a whole is also characterized by a peroration-like function. This is indicated by the asyndetic style (shared with parenesis) with progressively shorter utterances in 4:12-22, the recurrence of various important themes and motifs of the letter-body as a whole, and the **pathos** appeal located in the terminating wish-prayer. As such, 5:12-24 is interpreted to have a text-concluding function both in the text-sequence 4:1-5:24 and in relation to the letter-body as a whole. Besides the clear thematic shift between 5:1-11 and 5:12 ff., the delimitation of the section is realized for the most part indirectly by features of text-semantic and text-syntactic coherence. This is indicated by an anaphoric ThM in 5:23 more or less subsuming the preceding religious-ethical topics (5:12 ff.) under the theme of "holiness," by the grammatical recurrence of imperatives and asyndeton, and by the recurrence of the references to "peace" (5:13, 23) as a delimiting **inclusio**.

These text-centered observations, with due attention given to the pragmatic dimension in terms of dynamical-rhetorical strategies, indicate that there is an integration of typical epistolary, exhortatory and rhetorical features of discourse which make it difficult if not inappropriate to delimit and classify the major part of 4:1-5:24 **strictly** in terms of **argumentatio** with some part at the end as **peroratio** as defined in the rhetorical handbooks. The specific **argumentatio** (4:13-5:11) is sandwiched between panels of general religious-ethical exhortation with the latter panel combining general parenesis with peroration-like functions.

Furthermore, in contrast to 4:1-12 and 5:12-24 it has been shown that it is only 4:13-5:11 which reflects a rhetorical exigence, i.e. something not as it should be, a "divergence with regard to experience, opinion and understanding" which calls for resolution by means of persuasive speech.[732] As for 4:1-12 and 5:12-24, the religious-

---

[732] Fafner, 1977, 42. See 1.7.1 above.

ethical admonitions have a "response-reinforcing" function urging adherence to what is already accepted. While this sort of "persuasion" is typical of moral discourse and sermons, not accounted for in classical rhetoric, it was possible to show that it also served an accessory **ethos**, authority-enhancing function in relation to the main rhetorical exigence (see under 4.4.3).

These conclusions may be contrasted with previous rhetorical-dispositional analyses. F.W. Hughes' would classify 4:1-5:5 as **probatio**, 5:4-11 as **peroratio**, 5:12-22 as "exhortation," and 5:23-28 as "conclusion," whereas R. Jewett takes 4:1-5:22 as **probatio** and 5:23-28 as **peroratio**.[733] On the other hand, G.A. Kennedy is more circumspect in describing 4:1-5:22 as "headings" that "open with a proposition in general terms (4:1)," 5:23-24 as the "epilogue" and 5:25-28 as the "closure." He also refers to the "chiastic return to other injunctions" in 5:12-22.[734] However, both his and the other analyses lack the delimitational precision afforded by text-linguistic analysis. More seriously, they are insufficiently dynamical in giving appropriate attention and priority to the pragmatic signals that indicate the functional relations that hold between the major subsequences within 4:1-5:24 and that help to locate the rhetorical exigence in 4:13 ff.

6.4 INTERPRETING THE RHETORICAL SITUATION OF THE LETTER

6.4.1 The Persuasive Coherence of I Thess as a Whole

In view of these observations it is concluded that the immediate, primary exigence occasioning the persuasive strategies of I Thess as a whole is to be identified in the deaths of fellow believers and the addressees' reactions of grief, perplexity and anxiety in the context of their expectation of direct assumption at the imminent parousia.

While the addressees' faith and their goodwill towards the addressors were still basically intact (3:6), the admixture of grief, perplexity and anxiety and what may have been seen as an apparent incongruence between previous instruction and present reality would call for a particularly delicate handling of the situation. As noted in 2.2.1 and 2.2.3, such a situation presented a **serious potential** for questioning not merely the sincerity of Paul and his co-workers and the reliability of their instruction concerning the parousia, and the eschatological sufferings, but even the very reliability of the gospel itself. In view of this, the unusual length of the so-called "thanksgiving" section, with its narrative/exordium-like character, finds an eminently good explanation.[735]

Furthermore, within the general rhetorical-functional relation between 1:2-3:13 and 4:1-5:24, the ring-composition of 1:2-2:16, 2:17-3:13 and 4:1-5:24 significantly serves to specify where the major persuasive concerns of the letter lie.[736] Here the

---

[733] See Jewett, 1984, 15-17.

[734] Kennedy, 1984, 142-44.

[735] Similarly regarding Demosthenes Ep 1.1-4, Goldstein (1968, 178) observes that a long captatio benevolentiae is just what one expects when the situation addressed is a delicate one.

relative prominence of quasi-logical appeals in each of the central panels (2:1-12; 3:1-8; 4:13-5:11) reflects a need to achieve a relatively greater degree of conviction regarding personal integrity, the nature of the addressees' tribulations and the problems of grief and anxiety raised by the unexpected decease of fellow-believers. From a text-internal perspective the position of the first two elements in the exordial-like part of the letter and the third one in the probatio-like part indicates that it is the third concern which constitutes the central problem. Also, from a text-external perspective of relative probabilities, the kind of apparent incongruence between instruction and reality noted above would obviously call the instructor's credibility into question; and a potential threat to the eschatological hope that had thus far given meaning to the endurance of severe tribulations would not only endanger morale but also call into question the actual nature of such tribulations. These combined factors provide powerful arguments in favour of seeing anticipative, prophylactic strategies in 2:1-12 and 3:3-4 with the problem reflected in 4:13 ff. as being the primary exigence.

One may narrow down the matter of this rhetorical exigence even further by asking for the **stasis** or **quaestio**.[737] From the position taken under 4.4.6 it follows that this was primarily perplexity and doubt over the eschatological status of deceased believers, while under 4.4.8 it was argued that this also led to the related anxious question of the eschatological status of those who remained. It is here that one finds the rhetorically significant divergence in understanding and experience to which the various rhetorical strategies of the letter as a whole are directed.

6.4.2   The Particular Question of I Thess 2:1-12

Regarding the debated character of 2:1-12, the foregoing interpretation together with observations made in 2.2.1 and 4.1.3.2 above indicate that this passage has an **anticipative apologetic function**. The fit with exordial strategies described in ancient rhetoric is striking. Besides such exordial strategies as praise (cf. 1:6-10) and vituperation (cf. 2:15-16), reference is made to an exordial apologetic strategy in general wherein the speaker should try to dispel any disagreeable suspicion, whether openly expressed or not (see 1.7.6.2).

Within the wider perspective of this rhetorical convention A.J. Malherbe's observation of parallels in 2:1-12 to specifically Cynic conventions of anticipative apologetic probably casts more light on how the addressees' would interpret the passage than on Paul's singular dependence on such a more specific socio-cultural convention (see 8.2.2.2). There are indeed some striking parallels. Besides a number of verbal connections, e.g., κολακευειν, δοξα, κενος, παρρησια, παρακαλειν, ηπιος, βαρος, etc., there are such features as an insistance on divine commission and comparisons of the Cynic propagandist to a "father" or a "nurse."[738]

---

[736] See 4.1.8, 4.2.6, 4.4.11 and Figures 8, 9 and 10 under 5.2.

[737] On this see, e.g., Lausberg, 1973, 61 ff.; Kennedy, 1963, 306 ff.

[738] Thus, Malherbe (1970, 203-22) focusing particularly on Dio Chrysostom, Orat 32, besides drawing on other material.

However, besides the use of a common language, the question is whether these parallels would not arise somewhat naturally due to a common type of situation in which the authority and responsibility of a preacher/teacher is expressed in relation to actual or potential followers. In favour of this broader human connection, one finds the Jewish Teacher of Righteousness from Qumran in the thanksgiving hymn of 1QH vii.6-25 not only insisting on his divine commission (vii.10, 19-20) in a context of external antagonism but also connecting this with his being like both a "father" and a "nurse" in relation the community (vii.19-22).[739]

While concrete accusations could be quite naturally expected from the addressees' persecuting fellow-countrymen as well as unbelieving Jews (2:14-16), even this presupposition is not necessary to explain 2:1-12, although such accusations are quite likely to have occurred. At the same time, the foregoing rhetorical interpretation does not allow the apologetic character of 2:1-12 to disappear behind implicit parenetic and philophronetic functions that are obviously also present.[740] Nor should the specific contours of the authority/credibility-enhancing function loose their sharpness as in W. Marxsen's discernment of the ultimate function of "ein **Apologie des Evangeliums.**"[741]

6.4.3 The Question of Rhetorical Genre

The foregoing interpretation raises the question of rhetorical genre, which is taken up here with the reservations made in 1.7.4 well in mind. The prominence of **consolation** as a primary function in what most closely resembles a rhetorical **probatio** in the text, viz., 4:13-5:11, would appear to provide an important indication of the rhetorical genre to which I Thess stands the closest. However, a survey of views on **consolatio** itself in this regard turns up widely divergent opinions.

In ancient rhetoric consolations were usually one component among others of funeral speeches,[742] although they also appear to have been regarded as a class of speech ranged in general beside deliberative, epideictic, forensic speeches, etc., by Cicero (**Orat** 3.55.210) and Quintilian (**Inst Orat** 10.1.47; 11.3.153). While A.J. Malherbe notes that Theon's treatment (**Progym** 3.117) of consolation implies that he considered it a major example of protreptic,[743] G.A. Kennedy points to Menander

---

[739] The context supports taking אוֹמֵן to mean "nurse." See (loc. cit.) Maier (1960), Vermes (1962), Lohse (1971) and Gaster (1976), as against Holm-Nielsen (1960, 130) who has "foster father."

[740] Supporting, e.g., Moffat (1910, 5) and Best (1977, 16, 22), and going against, e.g., Malherbe (1977, 23; 1983, 240 ff.), and more recently Lyons (1985, 191 ff.) who refers to "Paul's exemplary ethos" in 2:1-12.

[741] Marxsen, 1979, 25.

[742] See Kassel, 1958, 40 ff.

[743] Malherbe, 1983, 254, n. 73. Since he classifies consolation as a type of parenesis, he adds here that parenesis and protreptic were not as yet distinguished at that time.

the rhetor's treatment (2.9) of the consolatory speech under epideictic.[744] Also, without relying explicitly on ancient authorities, Kl. Berger classifies consolation as epideictic,[745] while H. Lausberg assigns it to the deliberative category as an instance of **privata concilia**.[746] From the perspective of types of ancient letters, there is an example of a consolatory letter given by Pseudo Demetrius where the deliberative character of consolation as an instance of **privata concilia** may be seen to be reflected in the following remarks: επει μη παρων τετυχηκα παρακαλειν σε, δι' επιστολης εκρινα τουτο ποιησαι. φερε γουν το γεγονος ως δυνη κουφοτατα και καθως αλλω παρηνεσας, σεαυτω παραινεσον (**Ep Typ**, 5).[747]

In view of all these divergent opinions it is questionable as to whether either epideictic or deliberative categories can be taken to give an adequate account of consolation. The question would call for a lengthy investigation in its own right. For our purposes, it is sufficient to focus on I Thess in terms of a relative prominence of rhetorical generic affinities in general. The following affinities, relatively speaking, indicate a closer relation to the deliberative genre than to the other possibilities.

To begin with, there is the future-oriented focus in the response-changing function of dissuasion from grief and incipient doubt, besides in the response-reinforcing, more general admonitions to advance in leading a life pleasing to God. Also, typical means of "deliberative argumentation" are particularly prominent in the Christological proofs (4:14; 5:9-10) in what has been identified as the **argumentatio** (4:13-5:11).[748]

Furthermore, Aristotle's remarks on **narratio** in deliberative oratory (**Rhet** 3.16.11) reveal striking parallels and a pragmatic flexibility relevant to the exordial-narrative character of I Thess 1-3. After stating that narrative is very rare in deliberative speeches, he goes on to note that, if there is narrative, it will refer to past things so that the hearers, being reminded of them, may take better counsel about the future. He adds that this narration may be characterized by vituperation or praise, in which case the speaker is noted to depart from the typical function of a deliberative orator. In view of the rhetorical observations made above, the striking fit of this description with major features in I Thess 1-3 need not be elaborated upon here. At the same time, besides these commonalities and differences from what is typical of the deliberative genre, there is the basic difference of the type of addressor and addressee who were not concerned with the mundane questions of what is politically expedient, but rather with the spiritual questions of truth and salvation.

---

[744] Kennedy, 1984, 76.

[745] Berger, 1984, 1199-201.

[746] Lausberg (1973, 896) referring generally to Kassel (1958).

[747] This is provided with an English translation by Malherbe (1977, 32-3): "Since I did not happen to be present to comfort you, I decided to do so by letter. Bear, then, what has happened as light as you can, and exhort yourself just as you would exhort someone else."

[748] On these and other characteristics of deliberative argumentation in N.T. letters see Berger, 1984, 1148.

G.A. Kennedy's classification of I Thess as "basically deliberative" is arrived at in a more loose and general way. He regards it as "an exhortation to stand fast in the Lord (3:8) with specific advice for Christian life, given in chapters 4-5."[749] In this way he overlooks the rhetorical exigence in 4:13 ff. By contrast, R. Jewett sees the rhetorical genre most closely associated with I Thess as being epideictic, "because it concentrates on praise and blame with a prominent traditional subject being thanksgiving to the gods.[750] He goes on to assert that "the main argument of the letter is an extended narration of the grounds for giving thanks to God in 1:6-3:13" on the basis of which "the concrete issues in the congregation are expressed as reminders of the pattern of praiseworthy and blameworthy behaviour suitable to the new age."[751] Against this, 4:13 ff. is obviously not a "reminder" and in view of the "reported" character of the thanksgivings one has to do with a sustained exordial strategy of **captatio benevolentiae** rather than with a traditional thanksgiving to God.

6.4.4 Some General Concluding Observations

Although many exegetes do not assign any one of the problems they discern to be addressed in the letter a relatively greater degree of urgency than the others,[752] the general position that the primary concrete problem addressed by I Thess is reflected in 4:13 ff. is itself not new (see 1.1.2).[753] What is new in this study is the greater precision and the wholistic text-centered observations and arguments afforded by a text-linguistic and dynamical-rhetorical approach in delimiting the major functional text-sequences and interpreting their text-internal and addressee-oriented functions in relation to those references in the text that reflect an exigence or exigences in the communicative situation. Furthermore, while giving recognition to the multiplicity of co-occurring functions in the text, this approach provides a more adequate basis for interpreting their relative weights of importance.

The extreme opposite to the conclusions thus arrived at is expressed by G. Lyons in the rather categorical assertion that "the parenetic remarks that occupy the last two chapters of the letter do not suggest that Paul's praise is a subtle means of approaching a serious problem in Thessalonica needing correction."[754] This assertion

---

[749] Kennedy, 1984, 142.

[750] Jewett (1984, 14) referring to Lausberg (1973, 131 f.).

[751] Jewett, 1984, 14.

[752] See, e.g., Lightfoot, 1904, 51, 62; Zahn, 1906, Vol. I, 154-5; McNeile, 1953, 126-7; Masson, 1957, 7-8; Robert/Feuillet, 1959, Vol. II, 394-5; Guthrie, 1961, 180-1; Schlier, 1972, 11-13; Wikenhauser/Schmid, 1973, 401; Best, 1977, 15, 180 ff.; Klijn, 1980, 120-1; Koester, 1980, Vol. II, 112-14; Ragnarsson, 1983, 131-5; L. Morris, 1984, 24-6; Holtz, 1986, 29-31.

[753] See, e.g., Baur, 1867, Vol. II, 99; Gregory, 1909, 658; Jülicher, 1931, 59; Knopf/Lietzmann/Weinel, 1949, 80-1; Meinertz, 1950, 83; Marxsen, 1963, 32-3; 1969, 26, 32; 1979, 28-9; Reese, 1980, 215; Lüdemann, 1984, 214, 220.

simply hangs in the air in the absence of a wholistic text-centered, rhetorical analysis of the letter and the neglect of 4:13-18 apart from three fleeting references.[755] By contrast, the wholistic analysis and interpretation of the present study pass a negative judgment on all those views which see the primary communicative intention and/or the primary occasion of the letter as being located in 1:2-3:13 (see 1.1.2).[756]

As E. Best points out, although strictly speaking the occasion is Timothy's return with news (3:6), it is the content of his report that actually occasions the letter.[757] While the contents of his report are no doubt reflected throughout the letter, the present rhetorical analysis and interpretation would indicate that 4:13 ff. is where one finds the primary occasioning exigence anticipated in the reference to "deficiencies of faith" (3:10). As a delicate problem of grief and perplexity with serious destructive potential, it called for correction without reproof and give rise to an extraordinary expenditure of pastoral encouragement and prophylactic strategies of persuasive appeals.

In connection with the validity of the foregoing interpretation, some important observations are appropriate here regarding the consequences of this textual and rhetorical analysis and interpretation for the question of integrity (ch. 7). Also, a closer look needs to be taken at the complex intertextuality of I Thess in terms of worship-appropriate and exhortatory features of O.T.-Jewish discourse in particular. This is necessary in order to do justice to the congruence of multiple structures and functions that are discernible and to be able to more adequately show that the rhetorical set of such features is predominant from the perspective of the text's initial context (ch. 8).

---

[754] Lyons, 1985, 177.

[755] Lyons, 1985, 186, 201, and 208.

[756] As against, e.g., Dobschütz, 1909, 62; Schubert, 1939, 26; Funk, 1966, 264; Boers, 1975-76, 153. While Rigaux (1956, 57) does not neglect the importance of I Thess 4-5, he nevertheless finds that the present condition addressed is that of affliction (3:3-4) and that the letter could well have ended at 3:13 (493).

[757] Best, 1977, 13-14.

Chapter 7

I THESS: A SINGLE, INTEGRAL, COHERENT ACT OF COMMUNICATION

In taking up the question of the integrity of I Thess, the scope here is limited to that of indicating the specific contribution made to this from the foregoing text-centered, rhetorical conclusions. An exhaustive survey of the various interpolation and compilation theories has been provided by R. F. Collins,[758] so that we can concentrate on the more prominent issues of the debate in relation to text-coherence.

In general his survey indicates that, with the exception of a significant opinion questioning the authenticity of 2:13-16, there is considerable lack of agreement among the scholars who dispute the integrity of the letter, whether in terms of interpolation or compilation.[759] Furthermore, each of these two main types of theories questioning the integrity of I Thess are dominated by what turns out to be untenable presuppositions: 1) a somewhat rigid norm of Pauline consistency in the use of language and expression of thought is presupposed in interpolation theories, and 2) a specific, rather inflexible, normative epistolary form for the composition of Paul's letters involving a smooth flow of thought free of repetitions or doublets is assumed in compilation theories.[760]

7.1 THE CONSISTENCY PRESUPPOSITION AND INTERPOLATION IN I THESS

The presupposition of Paul's conceptual and stylistic consistency will not be addressed at length here. The most recent formulation of serious arguments put forward by B. A. Pearson primarily on this basis against the authenticity of 2:13-16[761] has been rather decisively disarmed by J. Coppens, with the exception of the apparent inconsistency of Paul's attitude towards the Jews.[762] The classical issue here is the

---

[758] Collins, 1979, 67-106;=1984, 96-135. Since his survey another compilation theory has appeared written by Pesch (1984) in which he reconstructs a letter from Athens (2:13-16; 2:1-12; 2:17-3:5; 4:1-8; 3:11-13) dated 49 A.D. and a later one from Corinth (1:1-10; 3:6-10; 4:9-5:28) dated 50 A.D. With regard to criteria, this turns out to be a new variation on an old melody.

[759] Collins, 1979, 97;=1984, 126.

[760] Collins, 1979, 97, 104;=1984, 126, 133.

[761] Pearson, 1971, 79-94. See Collins, 1979, 75-6;=1984, 104-5.

apparent uncharacteristic anti-Judaism in 2:14-16 compared to Gal 1-2, Rom 9-11 and Phil 3:5-6.[763]

In general, the rigid norm of consistency that this is based on is disqualified by Collins in view of the occasional character of Paul's letters and the fact that his thought "proceeds dialectically and in almost quantum leaps."[764] In particular, the analysis in 4.1.4.2 underlines the fact that there is not a reflexion of general "anti-Judaism" as such in 2:14-16, but rather the vituperation is aimed at those Jews in particular who specifically opposed and hindered the gospel. As implied by the comparison in 2:14, the Gentile addressees' persecuting countrymen were also included in the condemnation.

Finally, just as the observation of Paul's use of traditional materials in 1:9-10, 4:13-18 and 5:1-11 have served to discount G. Friedrich's rejection of the authenticity of 5:1-11, so also in 2:13-16 Collins can show traditional material mingled with distinct features of Pauline style.[765]

7.2 THE EVIDENCE OF TEXTUAL AND RHETORICAL COHERENCE

As for the second presupposition regarding a fixed epistolary form and the redactional evidence of repetitions, this is roundly refuted by the text-linguistic and rhetorical analyses and interpretation of the present study.

To begin with, intercorroborative criteria observed in the text-syntactic, text-semantic and text-pragmatic dimensions of I Thess prove beyond a shadow of doubt that repetition, indeed, patterned repetition is of the very essence of the compositional style of the letter.[766] The ring-compositional character of 1:2-2:16, 2:17-3:13 and 4:1-5:24 was shown to be so thoroughly consistent that a later interpolation of 2:13-16 would be highly improbable purely on formal grounds.[767] Furthermore, Pearson's proposal that, after deleting 2:13-16, the unit of 2:11-12 provides a more natural, formal introduction to the so-called "apostolic parousia" of 2:17-3:13 must be judged as textually untenable. For one thing, a characteristic signal of transition such as $\gamma\alpha\rho$,

---

[762] Coppens, 1975, 90-95. More recent contributions contesting Pearson's position are represented by, e.g., Okeke, 1980-81, 127-36; Lüdemann, 1983, 25-7; Broer, 1983, 59-91; and Donfried, 1984, 242-53.

[763] On this see Pearson, 1971, 85-6.

[764] Collins (1979, 99;=1984, 128) supporting this observation from Noack's study of Rom (1965, 155-66) in particular. Cf. Okeke, 1979-80, 127-36.

[765] Collins (1979, 100-4;=1984, 129-33) referring to Bornkamm (1969, 32) on 1:9-10, among others, and to Rigaux (1974-75, 318-40) as against Friedrich (1973, 288-315) on 5:1-11. See also Collins (1980, 325-43;=1984, 154-72) on 4:13-5:11 in this respect.

[766] See under 4.1.8, 4.2.6, and 4.4.11, as well as Figures 8, 9, and 10 under 5.2 above.

[767] See Figure 5 under 4.1.8 and Figure 8 under 5.2 above.

δε, etc., is absent in 2:11. For another, the coherence and delimitation of 2:1-12 is thoroughly established under 4.1.3 above. Suffice it to note here that the topic of the addressers' ministry of the word and the eschatological climax bind these verses intimately to 2:1-12 as the concluding part.[768]

There is also the fact that the central panels, i.e. 2:1-12, 3:1-8 and 4:13-5:11, of the ring-pattern were shown to consistently subdivide further on specifically text-syntactic and text-semantic criteria into parallel panels, i.e. 2:1-8/2:9-12, 3:1-5/3:6-8 and 4:13-18/5:1-11, so as to indicate a more complex chiastic pattern (A B B' A') within the general ring pattern (A B A'). This adds a further argument on the formal side against G. Friedrich's view that 5:1-11 is interpolated.

In sum, the following combination of considerations provide a powerful, predominantly formal argument both in favour of integrity and against the presupposition that repetitions are significant criteria for discerning redactional activity: 1) the complete, text-semiotic base (syntactic, semantic and pragmatic) of textually intercorroborative criteria and the consistency of the general, recurring ring-compositional pattern that emerges; 2) the stringency of criteria used in isolating the lexical evidence of the text-syntactic patterned recurrences (see 5.2) and the consistency and congruity of the more specific chiastic and alternating patterns that emerge.

Turning now to focus on pragmatic, rhetorical considerations, in 4.1.4.2 above the second thanksgiving-report (2:13 ff.) was shown to provide a springboard for opposition-directed vituperation. In concert with the more formal parallels, this strategy of blame functions as a rhetorically related and balancing **pathos** appeal in relation to the praise of the addressees introduced by the initial thanksgiving-report (1:2 ff.). Not only are such affective appeals typical exordial strategies of ancient rhetoric, but vituperation is typically realized by way of a digression. Against, e.g., B. A. Pearson and H. Boers, these observations explain the unexpected character of the passage and support its appropriateness from rhetorical convention.[769] At the same time, these features of the pragmatic text-dimension serve to underline the inadequacy of D. Schmidt's "linguistic evidence for an interpolation."[770] Not only is his linguistic evidence drawn purely from the syntactic level, but it is also limited to the level of sentences rather than that of text.[771] The greater degree of embedment (i.e., the longer chains of successively dependent clauses) of sentences and the greater number of such embedments in 2:13-16 relative to the rest of 1:2-3:10 is taken to indicate an aberration in Pauline style that supports the theory of interpolation. However, such an aberration finds a most adequate explanation in the text-pragmatic dimension, particularly so in view of the rhetorical typicality of vituperation realized by way of digression.[772]

---

[768] Similarly, Lüdemann, 1983, 26-7.

[769] Pearson, 1971, 89; Boers, 1975-76, 152.

[770] D. Schmidt (1983, 269-79) in support of Pearson (1971).

[771] D. Schmidt, 1983, 271.

[772] In a forth-coming article the present author can show that the vituperation of 2:15-16 is realized by the typical form of a woe-oracle, apart from the introductory ουαι, as this form occurs in the O.T., later Jewish and also early Christian literature. As indicated in 8.2.1, the wish-prayers (3:11-13; 5:23-24) also have

Finally, with regard to both interpolation and compilation theories in general, these have all been too easily argued for primarily on the basis of syntactic and semantic criteria, the pragmatic aspect being largely neglected. As noted in 1.1.3.3, it is the pragmatic dimension that is ultimately decisive in determining whether a text is coherent or not, since shared contextual knowledge for filling in the pragmatic gaps is usually assumed in varying degrees in situation-dependent communication. Also, as noted under 1.2.4.2, for persuasive texts rhetoric is an indispensable tool in accessing this shared contextual knowledge through the typical persuasive strategies discernable in the text in relation to some exigence. Thus, before an occasional text like I Thess is judged to lack original coherence, either in terms of interpolation or compilation, it is methodologically imperative that its pragmatic coherence should receive a thorough and concerted investigation. Only after such an investigation proves unable to provide an adequate and reasonable explanation of the various textual elements in relation to the text as a whole is it reasonable to proceed to an examination of some kind of redactional activity.[773]

Thus, in view of the foregoing evidence of textual coherence and, above all, in view of the basic rhetorical coherence of I Thess (see ch 6), the various compilation theories should be seen as lacking fundamental grounds of motivation.[774] The unusal length of the so-called thanksgiving section of I Thess 1-3 is shown to be rhetorically appropriate. Also, the feature of repetitions must be judged as not merely characteristic of parenesis and prevalent in Pauline style[775] it is the very norm of the style of this letter. Furthermore, the approach of what may be called the Funk school of epistolary form-criticism must be judged to be inadequate to an interpretation of I Thess (see under 3.1.3). Apart from the fact that this approach cannot account for the shape of Rom,[776] this judgment is established not only on the basis of the foregoing text-linguistic and rhetorical analysis, but also in view of the following analysis which indicates how intertextual features of O.T.-Jewish exhortatory discourse, besides those of rhetoric, are used by Paul to expand the epistolary features of thanksgiving-report, visit theme and petition. Finally, if I Thess is the work of a redactor, the foregoing observations indicate that he has worked with such skill and thoroughness that any attempt to distinguish what was from what finally came to be must be regarded as a futile exercise in subjective guess-work.

---

distinct O.T.-Jewish formal precedents.

[773] Similarly, Collins, 1979, 96;=1984, 125.

[774] This goes against each of the main theories put forward, which include Eckart (1961), Schmithals (1964; 1965, 89-157; 1972, 123-218), Refshauge (1971) and Pesch (1984). See Kümmel (1962) for a thorough criticism of Eckart, and Suhl (1975, 96-102) for one of Schmithals, besides the general criticisms given by Collins (1979, 85-107;=1984, 114-35).

[775] Thus, Kümmel, 1962, 217-18.

[776] Collins (1979, 104;=1984, 133) also adds Phil.

Chapter 8

I THESS: CREATIVE ACT IN A PRACTICAL PROCESS OF COMMUNICATION

8.1 "THE CHRISTIAN LETTER IN THE MAKING"

In an article on I Thess as an "experiment in Christian writing" H. Koester has treated Paul's production of this letter as "the creative moment" of "the Christian letter in the making."[777] Of particular importance are his observations that 1) the approach of establishing typicalities through comparison with Pauline and other Christian letters obscures the creative process manifested in I Thess and that 2) the literary composition of I Thess should not be described as **sui generis**, since in the process of producing something new there is always some balance of continuity with discontinuity; various old forms and traditional elements are used, modified and pressed into new combinations.[778]

The foregoing rhetorical interpretation, however, exposes serious inadequacies in his rather communication-abstract concept of the letter as an "experiment" as well as in his explanations of the expansions and adaptations of private letter conventions as occasioned almost exclusively by "the message of the Christian gospel" and Paul's new "experience" to the exclusion of a specific occasioning exigence in the communicative context.[779] Furthermore, I Thess can only be regarded as the earliest extant letter of Paul to which we have access and not necessarily as the very first one he wrote as an apostle of the gospel.

Consequently, when treating intertextuality,[780] it is preferred here to refer to the letter as **one** important, early, creative act in the practical communicative process of forging a type of letter suited to not only the Christian message and Paul's experience, but also to important aspects of text-reception involved in the communicative context.

---

[777] Koester, 1979, 33, 33-44.

[778] Koester, 1979, 34-5. In general see, e.g., Wellek/Warren, 1963, 234-5; Fowler, 1970-71, 199-216.

[779] Koester, 1979, 35, 40.

[780] The particular type of intertextuality meant here is that which is involved in the evolution of genres or classes of text types with typical patterns of characteristics and not the narrower sense involving the ways people use or refer to well-known texts. See Jenny, 1976, 264; de Beaugrande/Dressler, 1981, 10-11, 182 ff.

One such feature of reception is the major exigence of grief and perplexity over deceased believers focused on in the preceding analyses and interpretation. Besides this, the general apostle-neophyte roles of the communicators would account for the appropriateness of the general religious-ethical exhortation explicitly expressed in 4:1-12 and 5:12-22. Also, the inclusion of wish-prayers (3:11-13; 5:23-24) and the use of blessing (1:1; 5:28) and thanksgiving expressions, etc., has suggested to some exegetes an anticipation of a worship-setting of reception (see below).

In what follows, we shall focus on intertextuality with regard to worship-appropriate features of discourse in conjunction with features of religious-ethical exhortatory discourse. The reason for this double focus is that an important background of intertextuality is provided by O.T.-Jewish discourse in which such exhortatory discourse, besides prayers and psalms sharing similar features, is closely connected with cultic contexts. The observation of this aspect of intertextuality will not only serve to strengthen the probability of an anticipated worship-setting of reception for the letter, but also to give a more adequate account of the intertextual features of exhortatory discourse than provided by the previous sporadic references to this aspect.

In particular, these observations will serve to balance A.J. Malherbe's relevant but one-sided observations of specifically Cynic hortatory conventions informing the implicit exhortation he observes in I Thess 1-3. Especially so in view of O.T.-Jewish counterparts to his proposed Cynic pattern of such motives and topics as imitation, reminding, divine commission of the speaker, and his comparison to a father and/or a nurse in relation to the addressee being exhorted and instructed.[781] On the basis of such Cynic and other Hellenistic conventions Malherbe has argued that the primary intention of the letter is that of exhortation in general.[782] On the one hand, the Cynic parallels are made to highlight the implicit parenesis in the first major part of the letter.[783] On the other hand, while recognizing the consolatory character and function of 4:13-18, he appeals to Hellenistic authors in support of classifying consolation as a form of parenesis.[784] Consequently, this passage is lumped together with the other material in chs 4-5 without attributing to it any appreciable degree of greater urgency.

Malherbe's intertextual observations appear to be more relevant for elucidating the Thessalonian addressees' horizon of generic codes with compatible features than for establishing Paul's singular dependence on such Cynic conventions, although as a Hellenistic Jew he must have had some acquaintance with them. However, both in view of textual theory and practice as demonstrated above, all such general observations of intertextual parallels only have interpretive validity when made relative to a concerted textual and contextual, rhetorical analysis and interpretation. Significantly, important intertextual features of O.T.-Jewish hortatory discourse in I Thess can be shown to be congruous with the rhetorical features elucidated above, i.e., as both dispositionally and persuasively relevant to the occasioning exigence in 4:13 ff.

---

[781] Malherbe, 1970, 203-22; 1983, 240-49.

[782] Malherbe, 1972; 1983.

[783] Malherbe, 1970; 1983, 240-49.

[784] Malherbe, 1983, 254-56.

8.2   INTERTEXTUALITY AND A WORSHIP-SETTING OF RECEPTION

R.F. Collins has suggested that the probable novelty of reading Christian texts in the early Christian worship service provides a likely explanation for the strongly worded adjuration in the letter-closing "that this letter be read to all the brethren" ($\varepsilon\nu o\rho\kappa\iota\zeta\omega$ $\upsilon\mu\alpha\varsigma$ $\tau o\nu$ $\kappa\upsilon\rho\iota o\nu$ $\alpha\nu\alpha\gamma\nu\omega\sigma\theta\eta\nu\alpha\iota$ $\tau\eta\nu$ $\varepsilon\pi\iota\sigma\tau o\lambda\eta\nu$ $\pi\alpha\sigma\iota\nu$ $\tau o\iota\varsigma$ $\alpha\delta\varepsilon\lambda\phi o\iota\varsigma$, 5:27).[785] Apart from the fact that worship would constitute the most likely concrete setting when "all the brethren" would be gathered for such a reading, a fairly strong argument can also be made for the anticipation of this particular setting from features of intertextuality for which the constraint of "appropriateness" plays a powerful roll.[786]

For our purposes it is sufficient to establish a general connection with a worship setting without entering into the highly subjective attempt to establish the particular place a reading of the letter would have been likely to occur at within such a service. Furthermore, the focus here is ultimately on appropriateness although the origins of the features observed are also of accessory importance.

8.2.1   The More Obvious Worship-Appropriate Features in I Thess

To begin with there are the following more obvious worship-oriented features, already noted by previous exegetes, which are cumulatively significant.

First of all, there is the replacement of the common epistolary conventions of the opening ($\chi\alpha\iota\rho\varepsilon\iota\nu$) and closing ($\varepsilon\rho\rho\omega\sigma\theta\varepsilon$) greetings by the "grace and peace" blessings (1:1; 5:28). While a complex background of epistolary greetings, Christian commissionings, and Jewish prayers and salutations[787] indicate a pre-Pauline origin, a worship-appropriate usage here is strengthened by the fact that the closest and most natural model for early Christian worship was Jewish worship which significantly was opened and closed by an analogous **beracha**.[788]

Secondly, there are the reports of thanksgiving (1:2-3; 2:13; 3:9-10) which, although being specifically epistolary due to their reported character (see 3.2.1), have distinct liturgical associations especially in O.T. (e.g., Ps 9; 106) and Jewish (e.g., 1QH ii.20; vii.6) literature.[789]

---

[785] Collins (1982-83, 122-7;=1984, 365-70) referring to Col 4:16 among other relevant texts. Likewise Marshall (1983, 165) who explains the force of the command as due to Paul himself taking up the pen after an amanuensis had written the body of the letter. See Hartman (1986, 137 ff.) on Paul's letters in general as being intended for reading and rereading.

[786] On the relation of intertextuality and appropriateness see, e.g., de Beaugrande/Dressler (1981, 183).

[787] See Wiles, 1974, 111.

[788] See, e.g., Berger, 1974, 191-207; and Collins, 1980a, 53;=1984, 139-40.

[789] See Audet, 1958, 371-99; 1959, 643-62; Robinson 1963, 124-58; 1964, 194-235; Berger, 1974; 219-24. Schubert (1939, 184-5) himself recognized a liturgical as-

Thirdly, there are the striking wish-prayers (3:11-13; 5:23-34) concluding the two major text-sequences of the letter-body. While recognizing their expressive, parenetic and instructional functions, G.P. Wiles has correctly emphasized their "liturgically oriented" function.[790] R. Jewett had previously charactered them as "homiletic benedictions" developed "in Hellenistic rather than Hebraic circles" of the early Church in view of the flexibility of the contents to fit the particular co-texts of occurrence and the consistent stylized use of δε and the optative.[791] However, without denying the possibility of a "homiletic" usage here, Jewett's so-called Hellenistic-Christian background of development is hardly credible in view of the O.T. parallels Wiles discovers in Gen 27:28, Ps 20, Ps 122:7, I Kgs 8:57-61, and II Chr 30:18-19 and an epistolary occurrence in II Macc 1:2-6.[792] To these examples we may add I Sam 2:20, Gen 48:15-16 and Sir 50:23-24. Not only is the optative used in most of these instances, but the connective δε in the Pauline instances has a most adequate text-connective explanation. It is noteworthy that the wish-prayers in I Kgs 8:57-61 and Sir 50:23-24 are presented as occuring in the context of worship and are both preceded by a **beracha** in which God is blessed for his salvific relation to Israel.

As for the expansion of the conventional ασπασασθε greeting by the "holy kiss" (5:26), a liturgical background is possible but difficult to establish.[793] And as for the various theories regarding the presence of a baptismal catechism, liturgy or hymn in the letter or parts of it, none of these have proved convincing.[794]

8.2.2 Other Worship-Oriented, O.T.-Jewish Features of Discourse

Besides these observations, it is possible to see in the narrative characteristics outlined above for 1:2-3:13 (see 3.2.3 and 6.1) and the subsequent explicit exhortation in 4:1-5:24 important indications of intertextuality specific to O.T.-Jewish exhortatory discourse which has close associations with contexts of worship. Very generally this involves a common strategy of form and content where an initial dogmatic and/or narrative part presenting God's attributes and/or his activity in "salvation history" prepares for a subsequent exhortatory sequence with implicit or explicit religious-ethical contents in which the addressee is urged to live in a way pleasing to God.

---

sociation.

[790] Wiles, 1974, 52-68.

[791] Jewett, 1969, 18-34.

[792] Wiles, 1974, 26-9. In II Macc 1:2-6 the wish-prayer expands the common epistolary proskynema.

[793] See Collins (1980a, 51-53;=1984, 137-39) who cites Mullins (1968, 426) and Threade (1968-69, 125-43) in favour of a general epistolary directive as against, e.g., Wiles (174, 51-2), Cuming (1975-76, 110-13) and Gibbs (1977-78, 545-47) who see a liturgical directive here.

[794] See Collins (1980a, 55-62;=1984, 142-53) for a survey of the literature and for balanced judgments in this respect.

This schema with typical types of contents regularly appears in speeches that are intimately connected with the covenant formulary and Israel's peculiar sense of "salvation history" as elucidated by Kl. Baltzer.[795] Apart from a "preamble" and an "invocation of witness," he identifies the main parts of the covenant formulary as "(1) 'antecedent history,' (2) statement of substance concerning the mutual relationship of the parties to the covenant, (3) the individual stipulations of the covenant, and (4) blessings and curses."[796] On a higher level of generality the last three constituents may be subsumed under what was previously designated as the more explicitly "exhortative" part, with "exhortative" taken in a very broad religious-ethical sense. Furthermore, the recollective narrative has a basically ethos, authority-enhancing function in preparation for the subsequent exhortation.[797] Also, a common connective introducing the exhortative part is וְעַתָּה rendered by καὶ νῦν in the LXX and usually followed by a conative expression and some title of address thus: καὶ νῦν, Ισραηλ, ακουε των δικαιωματων κτλ. (Deut 4:1).[798] This, however, may be absent as in Josh 23:6 where the LXX has ουν signalling the transition.

These features not only characterize what may be classified as "covenant speeches" in, e.g., Deut 1-4; 28:69-30:20 and Josh 24 and in Jahweh's discourse to Moses in Exod 34 in the context of covenant renewal,[799] but also other speech genres as, e.g., the "farewell" or "testament" speech in Josh 23 and the "transfer of office" speech in I Sam 12 in the context of covenant ratification.[800]

While there is obvious development and change, Baltzer is able to trace the basic features of the covenant formulary in such Jewish texts as the **Manual of Discipline** (1QS) and the **Damascus Document** (CD), where the recollective narrative becomes overshadowed by "dogmatic" considerations,[801] in testament speeches such as Abraham's last words to Isaac in **Jub 21** and the **Testaments of the Twelve Patriarchs**, where the element of Israel's salvation history is replaced by "biographical confessions or examples for admonition,"[802] and on down into early Christian literature,

---

[795] See Baltzer, 1971, 19-38, 90-91.

[796] Baltzer, 1971, 97.

[797] Thus Kennedy, 1980, 123.

[798] Cf. Exod 19:5; Deut 10:12; Josh 24:14; I Sam 12:13. See Baltzer, 1971, 32 and n. 65.

[799] With Kennedy, 1980, 123-4. Cf. Baltzer, 1971, 19-36.

[800] See Baltzer, 1971, 65, 68, 81-3.

[801] Baltzer 1971, 99-122.

[802] Baltzer, 1971, 137 ff., esp. 144-6. See also Thyen (1955, 111 ff.) on this development, although he does not refer to the Test 12 Patr in this respect. See also the testament of Tobit in Tob 14:3-11. In most of these testaments the sections of religious-ethical exhortation are introduced by καὶ νῦν with a conative expression and address. In favour of a Jewish origin of the Test 12 Patr, see, e.g., Hultgård (1981, 53-80). De Jonge (1959, 556), who has defended a Christian origin and dated them between ca. 150-190 A.D., has more recently (1980)

viz., the **Epistle of Barnabas**, the **Didache**, the so-called **Second Epistle of Clement** as the earliest extant Christian sermon, and the "parenetic sermon" in the apocryphal **Acts of John** 106-107.[803]

As an explanation of the remarkable stability of this schema with typical types of contents shared by texts in this range of literature, Baltzer suggests worship as the most likely common type of setting.[804] The arguments for such a common context have been subsequently substantially strengthened by L. Hartman.[805]

Furthermore, on a somewhat broader textual base and with particular reference to the works of both Kl. Baltzer and A. Jaubert, Hartman has outlined a pattern of covenant-related topics and motives (i.e., text-semantic features) which occur or recur in what he refers to as the dogmatic, ethical and blessing/curse schema (i.e., text-semantic and syntactic features) of the covenant formulary.[806] Together, these features inform what he calls a "covenant ideology" defined as "eine Sammlung von Vorstellungen, die ein zusammenhängendes Muster bilden, und deren Kerngedanke es ist, dass Gott dadurch, dass er mit den Menschen in Verbindung getreten ist, eine Beziehung errichtet hat, die gegenseitige Gelübde und Verpflichtungen für die Bundespartner, Gott und sein Volk, bedeutet."[807] While noting points in common with W.D. Davies, W.C. van Unnik and E.P. Sanders, Hartman differentiates his approach as aimed at isolating a coherent pattern of covenant ideology in coherent texts, at avoiding the treatment of such a pattern as stiff and unvariable, and at dealing with a thought pattern of covenantal ideas that covers a broader conceptual field.[808]

In what Hartman refers to as the "dogmatic" section the covenant-related topics and motives found to be prominent are constituted by references to God as creator, ruler and judge of the world, as being righteous. merciful, and impartial, and as having elected Israel in mercy and love, made a covenant with her (beginning with the fathers), revealed himself to her and given promises to her to which he remained faithful. Furthermore, this faithfulness and his salvation are witnessed to by Israel's history.[809]

---

backed away from such a radical hypothesis.

[803] Baltzer, 1971, 123-36, 172-5.

[804] Baltzer (1971, 167 ff.) with special reference to the liturgical structure of IQS i. 18-ii. 18.

[805] Hartman, 1979, 101 ff.

[806] Hartman, 1980, 106-7. See Baltzer (1971) and Jaubert (1963). Besides some of the texts referred to above he refers to Exod 19-34; Lev 26; Deut 32; Ezra 9; Neh 9; Jer 31; Ezek 36; Dan 9; Wis 10-19; Jub 1; 22; CD i-ii; Test Levi 8-18; Test Jud 18-25.

[807] Hartman, 1980, 103.

[808] Hartman (1980, 103-5) referring to Davies (1955, 259 f.), van Unnik (1960, 109-26) and Sanders (1977).

[809] Hartman, 1980, 106.

In the "ethical" section the prominent covenant-related aspects involve the covenantal obligations of both parties, what God has promised to do and what Israel was obligated to do or refrain from doing. That which is essential here is the relationship of the Jewish people as being God's people and he their Lord; often described as a close father/sons (children) relationship in which they "know" him. On the positive side, when they are faithful to the covenant, take it upon themselves to do God's commandments, keep his word, etc., God will dwell among them, give them peace, security and favourable circumstances and allow them to inherit and live in the promised land. On the negative side, the people are above all commanded to avoid every kind of idolatry and are often warned of the ethical confusion of heathens.[810]

The third part of the covenant ideology involves the blessings and curses attendant upon observance or disobedience to the covenant obligations. To blessing belongs life; to acknowledge God is to choose life, to receive God's protection, peace, mercy, forgiveness and a bountiful and blessed life in the promised land. Failure to keep the obligations due to being stiff-necked, hardhearted or blasphemously proud brings about the wrath of God, judgment, strife, misfortune, deformity, exile and death.

These features may obtain an eschatological colouring where the promised land becomes a heavenly Canaan or the kingdom of God, with judgment and exile as the counterparts. Or the thought may be developed in terms of a new covenant or a time of restoration when God's people will be gathered and the promises, gifts and obligations renewed, a time of forgiveness and purification, of receiving God's Spirit and being God's children in holiness and righteousness with his law written in their hearts, a time when circumcision is not merely the outer sign of the covenant, but the faithful are also circumcised in heart.[811]

Hartman's interest is basically theological in his demonstration of this covenant ideology in and behind I Thessalonians, besides Galatians and Romans (not taken up below). In so doing, he establishes a fundamental resonating board against which he is able to gain insights into Paul's thought regarding the inclusion of Gentile believers as members of God's chosen people as he interacts in various communicative situations.[812] For our present purpose, however, his observations of such distinctive features of O.T.-Jewish discourse informing the intertextuality of I Thess is seen as adding to the evidence of typical features called forth by the appropriateness constraints of an anticipated worship-setting of reception, besides being relevant to the occasioning rhetorical exigence.

Before taking up these considerations, however, a brief look at Acts 13:16-41 strengthens the evidence for the impact of this O.T.-Jewish heritage on early N.T. discourse in a setting of worship.

---

[810] Hartman, 1980, 106. He adds that, although most of the references are made to the covenant of Sinai, the obligations are similar even when the covenants of Abraham or Noah are invoked.

[811] Hartman, 1980, 106-7.

[812] Hartman, 1980, 108-18.

8.2.2.1 The Sermon in Acts 13 and O.T.-Jewish Exhortatory Discourse

It is instructive to observe how some of these elements of O.T.-Jewish exhortatory discourse have been exploited in Paul's sermon in Acts 13:16-41, viz., the λογος παρακλησεως he was invited to give after the Scripture reading in the worship service of a synagogue at Antioch of Pisidia. In this respect, G. A. Kennedy's recent proposal that this particular sermon, besides the other "missionary sermons" in Acts, is a Christian counterpart of the Jewish "covenant speech" needs some qualifications.[813] For one thing, there appears to be a mediation here of O.T. forms and contents by Jewish-synagogal homiletic tradition.[814] For another, these features plus those of typically Jewish scriptural interpretation are pressed into the service of persuasion to acceptance of something new rather than exhortation to adherence to what is basically already shared.

We may note that the schematic recital of salvation history (13:16-22), with the covenant-related topics of "election" and "deliverance" (13:17) in relation to the promised land (13:19), is expanded by the Christian kerygma (13:24 ff.). This corresponds roughly to the **narratio** of classical rhetoric.[815] Also, the messianic, midrashic **argumentatio** (13:32-37) from Scripture[816] is introduced by the covenant-related topics of "what God promised to the fathers" being fulfilled "to us their children" (13:32-33), although now through the resurrection of Jesus. The transitional clause introducing the "exhortation" is realized here by ουν plus conative expression and address (13:38a): γνωστον ουν εστω υμιν, ανδρες αδελφοι, οτι κτλ. What is thus introduced, however, is not religious-ethical exhortation to adhere to what is generally accepted covenantal behaviour. Rather, it is exhortation to acceptance of the gospel implicit in the application of the significance of Jesus Christ to the addressees regarding the forgiveness of sins (13:38-40) and in the Scriptural warning (Hab 1:5) of destruction for unbelieving scoffers (13:40-41). Both forgiveness of sins and destruction are covenant-related motives particular to the blessing/curse part of the covenant formulary, so that one is able to detect promising/warning functions analo-

---

[813] See Kennedy, 1980, 129-30.

[814] Besides noting the typical initial narrative, Hartman (1963-64, 117-34) goes beyond Doeve (1954, 172 ff.) in establishing that II Sam 7:6-16 is connected not only with Acts 13:16-23 but also 13:32 ff. by midrashic techniques whereby Is 55:3 and Ps 16:10 are used to elucidate II Sam 7:12 ff. in proving that the Messiah will be raised from the dead without seeing corruption (cf. Goldsmith, 1968, 321-4). These and other arguments of his establish an earlier provenance for this type of Christian sermon than that of the time of the composition of the Acts, as, e.g., against Dibelius (1951, 120 ff.). For a survey of other literature and arguments in this debate see Bruce (1985, 1582-88). On the recollective narrative feature as an element of the Synagogue's homiletic tradition in Paul's sermon here and in Acts 7:2-47 see, e.g., Wright, 1952, 76; Bultmann, 1952, 96; Thyen, 1955, 110; Wilckens, 1963, 50; and Scroggs, 1976, 292, with cited literature.

[815] Similarly, Berger, 1984, 1368.

[816] On the midrashic character see Hartman (1963-64, 117-34), and on the description as argumentatio, see Berger (1985, 1368).

gous to those of the explicit covenantal blessings and curses.[817]

Such similarities and differences indicate how the old was expanded by the new, how features of exhortatory discourse that usually urge adherence to what is shared were exploited to urge acceptance of something new, the gospel of Jesus Christ. The context is significantly that of worship.

8.2.2.2 The Intertextuality of O.T.-Jewish Discourse in I Thess

With regard to I Thess, L. Hartman identifies the following significant representation of features of this covenant ideology.[818] In the initial section of the letter there is the particularly striking element of divine love and election in 1:4,[819] ειδοτες, αδελφοι ηγαπημενοι υπο (του) θεου, την εκλογην ημων. There is also the addressees' reception of the God's word (1:5-6, 8) in connection with the Holy Spirit and their abandonment of idols to serve the true and living God (1:9).[820] Regarding the Holy Spirit in this connection, **Jub** 1:23 is cited: "they will turn to me...and I will circumcise the foreskin of their heart...and I will create in them a holy spirit."

As for specifically covenant-related features in what is refered to as the parenetic section, there is the important topic of God's requirement of "holiness" (4:3, 7).[821] Furthermore, there is the exclusive knowledge of God by his people in the acknowledgment that they are leading a life pleasing to God (4:1) and in their juxtaposition to the heathen who do not know God (4:5). Departure from their special relation to God who gives them his Holy Spirit (4:8) entails God's departure from this relation (understood). This reference to the Holy Spirit is taken to reflect Ezekiel's prophecy (Ezek 36:27; 37:14) that it would be given in the renewal of the covenant. Thus, implicitly behind the text one hears the classical covenant promise "I will dwell among them."[822] Related to this is the unusual reference to the addressees' being divinely instructed (θεοδιδακτοι, 4:9) regarding mutual brotherly love. This is supported by Jer 31:33 f. with the references to God's law being placed in the heart and men not needing to be taught.[823] Another point of contact is seen in περιποιησις σωτηριας

---

[817] Berger's categorization (1984, 1368) of 13:38-41 as peroratio is more appropriate for the warning in 13:40-41 alone, with the additional ουν marking the transition.

[818] See Hartman, 1980, 108-9.

[819] See Deut 4:37; Josh 24:3; cf. Deut 7:6 ff.

[820] Regarding idols, Hartman (1980, 108, n. 17) refers to Deut 30:2 (see also Deut 29:17-18).

[821] Hartman (1980, 108) refers here to Deut 28:9. See also, e.g., Exod 19:6; Deut 7:6; 26:16-19.

[822] Hartman (1980, 108) referring to Exod 25:8; 29:45, etc.

[823] Following, e.g., Rigaux, 1956, 517. As Malherbe admits (1983, 253), his own suggestion that θεοδιδακτοι reflects a tacitly shared Stoic criticism of the Epicurian concept of friendship is a rather remote possibility. As Malherbe also

(5:9) which, with the first noun not given an unusual active sense (see under 4.4.8.3), reflects Exod 19:5: "you shall be my own possession." Here it is contrasted with "wrath." This together with the following reference to life "together with him" (5:10) reflects the covenant-related features of the gift of life and the hope of fellowship with God.[824]

Besides these observations we may add that such covenant-related features as deliverance from hostile nations and encouragement to take the promised land[825] find an eschatological counterpart in the references to the addressees' salvation from the eschatological "wrath" (1:10), which comes upon their opponents who oppose the gospel (2:14-16), and in the reference to God's call "into his kingdom and glory" (2:12). Besides the references to the requirement of "holiness" in 4:3, 7, there are the additional references to this in eschatological contexts in both the wish-prayers concluding the two major text-sequences (3:13; 5:23). The latter wish-prayer concludes by another reference to election and asserts God's faithfulness (5:24) in accomplishing this holiness. There is also the warning of God's judgment for non-compliance in 4:6. Finally, the motive of "standing fast" in relation to the Lord in $\sigma\tau\eta\kappa\epsilon\tau\epsilon\ \epsilon\nu\ \tau\omega\ \kappa\upsilon\rho\iota\omega$ (3:8) also appears to have a distinctly covenant-related background. Besides such expressions as $\kappa\alpha\iota\ \epsilon\sigma\tau\eta\ \pi\alpha\varsigma\ o\ \lambda\alpha o\varsigma\ \epsilon\nu\ \tau\eta\ \delta\iota\alpha\theta\eta\kappa\eta$ (II Kgs 23:3) and $\epsilon\nu\ \tau\alpha\iota\varsigma\ \delta\iota\alpha\theta\eta\kappa\alpha\iota\varsigma\ \epsilon\sigma\tau\eta\ \tau o\ \sigma\pi\epsilon\rho\mu\alpha\ \alpha\upsilon\tau\omega\nu$ (Sir 44:12; cf. 45:23-24), this motive is prominent in the **hodayoth** and **berakoth** texts of Qumran in the pervasive covenant-centered references to "standing" or having a "standing place" in relation to God.[826]

These and other related features of intertextuality may be brought into a somewhat sharper focus in the following observations. The particular connection, however, with worship-appropriate features will be kept on a fairly high level of generality of worship-oriented discourse without an attempt to establish a closer tie with any more specific genre as such. One reason for this is that the general two-part doctrinal-narrative/ethical-exhortative schema of general exhortatory discourse may be observed to characterize not only whole, discrete speeches of related but different genres[827] and summarizing instructions for such speeches (Exod 19:4/5-6), but also shorter subsequences within them.[828] Another reason is that the introductory doctrinal-narrative sequence may be observed to also characterize various benedictory, thanksgiving and confessional prayers and psalms where it does not precede ethical exhortation but rather a petitionary sequence addressed to God.[829]

---

notes, the repeated reminders of Paul's previous instruction in 4:1-12 renders unlikely Koester's suggestion (1979, 39) that Paul coined this term to indicate that the addressees were independent of his authority.

[824] Hartman, 1980, 108-9.

[825] See Deut 3:21-22; Josh 23:3-5; 24:8-13; I Sam 12:7 ff.; Deut 7:8.

[826] See, e.g., 1QH vii.19 f.; xviii.6 ff., 28 f. See further Grundmann, 1971, 645-6.

[827] See, e.g., Deut 1:6-3:29/4:1-40; Josh 24:2-13/14-17; Test Iss 1-3/4-7. See 8.2.2 above.

[828] See, e.g., Deut 4:9-14/15-20; 4:32-39/40; 10:1-11/12 and Test Zeb 1-4/5; 6-7/8-10. See further Berger, 1974, 207 ff.

As previously observed (6.1), the basis of the extensive comments serving exordial functions in I Thess 1-3 is constituted by a schematic series of recollected events (see 3.2.3.1) in which one can recognize the essentials of an "antecedent history."[830] To this we may add the observation that there is the striking parallel sequence of "thanksgiving," "remembrance" and "election" motives in the opening lines of both I Thess 1:2-4 and thanksgiving psalms in Ps 105:1-6 and Ps 106:1-5 leading up to "antecedent histories" in each case.[831] Also, at the close of the latter psalm (106:47) there is the additional parallel to I Thess 3:9-13 of a closing petitionary sequence in which a renewed reference to thanksgiving forms a delimiting **inclusio**. A very general precedent for this recollective narrative followed by a sequence of prayer petitions is illustrated by the numerous texts just cited above. More particularly in I Kgs 8:56-61 and Sir 50:22-24, two of the closest formal parallels to Paul's wish-prayers in 3:11-13 and 5:23-24[832] may be noted to be preceded by **berakoth** with a short recollection of past divine mercy and salvation for which God is blessed.

The difference in I Thess is that the recollective account specifically involves a recent Christian "salvation history" shared by the addressors and addressees so as to have somewhat of an autobiographical character. Even though the focus on the senders is more prominent here, this autobiographical aspect must not be allowed to totally overshadow the fact that there is a primary focus on the addressees in a significant portion of the passage (1:2-4, 6-10; 2:13-14; 3:2b-3a, 5, 6, 9).[833] Furthermore, the focus on the addressors is always in their relation to the addressees. Such a double focus in reminders of a common past serves to enhance a sense of solidarity between the communicating parties. This particularly comes to expression in the use of the inclusive "we" in 1:9a, 10c and in 3:3b, 4a besides the prevelent occurrence of 1st and 2nd person references. A similar combination of features is also to be observed, e.g., in the "antecedent history" in Deut 29:2-8. Furthermore, the features of "reminding" ($\kappa\alpha\theta\omega\varsigma$ $o\iota\delta\alpha\tau\epsilon$, 1:5, etc.) and "imitation" ($\upsilon\mu\epsilon\iota\varsigma$ $\mu\iota\mu\eta\tau\alpha\iota$ $\eta\mu\omega\nu$ $\epsilon\gamma\epsilon\nu\eta\theta\eta\tau\epsilon$, 1:6) are also paralleled in the (pseudepigraphical) autobiographical recollections in the **Test 12 Patr**. While these elements are for the most part implicitly present in such autobiographical reminders of the patriarchs' behaviour, they can also come to explicit expression, as in **Test Zeb** 5:4 ($\omega\varsigma$ $o\iota\delta\alpha\tau\epsilon$) and in **Test Ben** 3:1 ($\mu\iota\mu o\upsilon\mu\epsilon\nu o\iota\ldots I\omega\sigma\eta\phi$, cf. 4:1).

---

[829] See, e.g., II Sam 7:18-24/25-29; I Kgs 8:23-24/25-53; Ps 44:1-22/23-26; 106:1-46/47-48; Dan (LXX: 3:26-33/34-45); 9:4-16/17-19; Tob 8:5-6/7; I Macc 4:30/31-33; and Acts 4:24-28/29-30 among other instances. On these and other texts see, e.g., Audet, 1958, 371-99; 1959, 643-62; Robinson 1963, 124-58; 1964, 194-235; and esp. Giraudo, 1981, 81-260.

[830] This particular aspect is not specifically taken up by Hartman (1980, 106, 108) who refers to a "dogmatic" section in general without explicitly describing I Thess 1-3 in such terms.

[831] Cf. Ps 111:1-5 where a reference to "covenant" replaces the "election" motive.

[832] See also, e.g., Rom 15:5-6 and 15:13. See under 8.2.1.

[833] There is a tendency to neglect this aspect by Lyons (1985, 177-221).

Taking the analysis further, as in O.T.-Jewish exhortatory discourse, there is the major transitional clause that opens the exhortatory section. This feature is realized in 4:1 by λοιπον ουν plus address and conative expressions introducing the explicitly religious-ethical admonitions and eschatological material in 4:1-5:24. Here the feature of religious-ethical exhortation interspersed by or combined with eschatological instruction is shared with the **Test 12 Patr** and other exhortatory literature noted by H. Thyen to reveal traits most likely characteristic of the synagogal homiletic tradition.[834]

Very generally, the **Test 12 Patr** have been noted to be characterized by a more or less typical schema of 1) (pseudepigrpahical) autobiographical retrospect, 2) ethical exhortation typically introduced by "and now my children" followed by a conative expression, and 3) an eschatological section looking to the future and typically introduced by some such phrase as "I know that in the last times."[835] In the **Testament of Dan** in particular, one may observe in the exhortatory part (5:1-6:11) an instance of ring-composition roughly analogous to that in I Thess 4:1-5:24: an initial sequence of strictly religious-ethical exhortation (**Test Dan** 5:1-3) leads to strictly eschatological instruction (5:4-13) with a return to more general religious-ethical exhortation (6:1 ff.) mingled with further eschatological references.

Apart from similar parallels in the other testaments, there are also a striking number of similar general admonitions, expressions and motives scattered variously in the framing exhortatory panels in both texts. These may be compared as follows, with each example from the **Test Dan** followed by one from I Thess: 1) εσεσθε εν ειρηνῃ (5:2), ειρηνευετε εν εαυτοις, (5:18); 2) τον θεον της ειρηνης (5:2), ο θεος της ειρηνης (5:23); 3) αληθειαν φθεγγεσθε εκαστος προς τον πλησιον αυτου (4:6), το μη υπερβαινειν και πλεονεκτειν...τον αδελφον αυτου (4:6) 4) αγαπατε...αλληλους (5:3), το αγαπαν αλληλους (4:9); 5) διατηρησατε...απο παντος εργου πονηρου (6:8), απο παντος ειδους πονηρου απεχεσθε (5:22); 6) αγαπησατε...την μακροθυμιαν (6:8), μακροθυμειτε προς παντας (5:14).

Also, as in I Thess 4:13 (ου θελομεν δε υμας αγνοειν, αδελφοι, κτλ.), the transition from general exhortation to eschatological instruction is signalled by an introductory clause with a noetic verb (οιδα γαρ οτι εν εσχαταις ημεραις κτλ., 5:4) that has a similar "disclosure" function.[836]

Some striking parallels may also be observed between I Thess 1:2-3:16 and the thanksgiving of the Teacher of Righteousness in 1QH vii.6-25, already touched upon above under 6.4. Granted the far-reaching differences in the prose and poetic texttypes and the explicit direction of address, the former to a community and the latter to God, the following parallels may be observed:[837]

---

[834] Thyen, 1955, 106 ff.

[835] See, e.g., Becker, 1970,172-77; Baltzer, 1971, 144-63; Weimar, 1973, 160-62. Cf. Aschermann, 1955, 8-10.

[836] Elsewhere this same feature occurs in Test Iss 6:1 (οιδα, τεκνα μου, οτι εν εσχατοις καιροις κτλ.) and Test Zeb 9:5 (εγνων εν γραφῃ πατερων μου, οτι εν εσχαταις ημεραις κτλ.).

[837] The English translation of the quotations from 1QH vii are taken from Gaster (1976, 172-4).

1. Both texts open with expressions of thanksgiving to God, although in I Thess 1:2 this is reported and in 1QH vii.6 it is addressed directly: "I give thanks unto Thee, O Lord."

2. Both addressors subsequently refer to the support of God's "power" and "holy spirit," the former in relation to his gospel ministry in Thess 1:5 and the latter in relation to his spiritual stability in 1QH vii.6b-7a: "for by Thine own strength hast Thou stayed me, and has wafted o'er me Thy holy spirit that I cannot be moved."

3. Further common features are combined in the assertion of the genuine character (I Thess 1:5b, 9a; 2:1-12) and the divine commission (I Thess 1:5a; 2:4) of both addressors as spiritual authorities in relation to their specific communities of faith, as in 1QH vii.8b-10: "Thou has made me like a strong tower upon a lofty wall,....a tower which Thou has provided, O my God, for (this) holy community...Words flow free on my tongue, as it were trained by Thee" (see further vii.17-20).

4. In connection with the foregoing features both addressors liken themselves to both a "father" and a "nurse" in relation to the communities for which they stand as spiritual authorities, as in I Thess 2:7, 11 and 1QH vii.20-21: "Thou hast...set me as a father to them Thou holdest dear, and as a nurse unto them whom Thou hast made exemplars of men. They open their mouths for my words, like sucklings...and like as a babe that plays on the bosom of its nurse."[838]

5. Finally, the opponents of both addressors are depicted as standing under divine condemnation, as in I Thess 2:15-16 and in 1QH vii.12: "All them that challenge me Thou makest to stand condemned" (see also vii.22-23).

It is rather unlikely that these parallels may be taken as evidence of a direct intertextual dependence on the part of Paul. Besides sharing a common O.T.-Jewish heritage, both authors belonged to a basically common type of general situational context as spiritual leaders for minority, externally threatened, religious communities. Thus, the parallels may be seen as indicating how in two historically different situations that shared very general common characteristics, among which worship was a significant element,[839] two different authors drew on common motifs in which spiritual, cultic and practical concerns became united in a similar pattern.

Finally, from the perspective of style, there is a somewhat sonorous, worship-appropriate quality achieved in I Thess by the patterned recurrences of especially the thanksgiving and joy clauses in I Thess 1-3 and the beseeching and exhorting clauses in I Thess 4-5, besides the other recurring words and phrases demonstrated in 5.2 above.

---

[838] On this parallel see already, e.g., O. Betz (1956-57, 320-22). See also Braun (1966, Vol. I, 234).

[839] For an extended discussion of the major arguments for and against the cultic purpose of the hodayoth and berakoth of 1QH, see, e.g., Holm-Nielsen (1960, 332-48) who comes out in favour of the cultic purpose.

8.2.3 Conclusions on O.T.-Jewish Intertextuality

To sum up, while giving the distinctly epistolary and persuasive-rhetorical textual and contextual features of I Thess their due recognition, due weight must also be given to the integration of features of O.T.-Jewish discourse of a type which strengthens the probability of an anticipated worship-setting of reception. What is essential in this respect for the letter as a whole is the general schematic features of O.T.-Jewish exhortatory discourse as accompanied by typical types of contents including covenant-related topics and motives and the expressions of blessing and the wish-prayers. As for the thanksgiving section in 1:2-3:13, some striking features of intertextuality establish the influence of O.T.-Jewish **hodayoth** and **berakoth** in the form of psalms, hymns and prayers.

The various specific and general parallels adduced are by no means intended to indicate a direct intertextual dependency between I Thess and the above mentioned texts, although this is not impossible in some instances in view of Paul's likely intimate acquaintance with many if not most of them. Rather, by virtue of the various parallels indicated, the texts presented above are meant to illustrate features that he for the most part was quite certainly used to hearing week after week in the worship services of the synagogue, both in the reading of Scripture and in synagogal sermons. In other words, features that more or less represent part of a rich linguistic code of worship-related language from which he could select elements either consciously or subconsciously for combination with other literary conventions as the immediate constraints of appropriateness required.

As previously noted, from the perspective of Hellenistic Cynic literature, A.J. Malherbe in particular has drawn attention to parallels in I Thess 1-3 of "imitation" motifs as well as "reminding" expressions, besides other typical hortatory features as comparisons to a "father" and "nurse" and claims of "divine commission."[840] However, in view of the preceding O.T.-Jewish parallels his observations should not be taken to indicate Paul's singular indebtedness to Cynic-Hellenistic conventions so much as to a commonality of exhortatory features bridging the horizons of Cynic-Hellenistic and O.T.-Jewish exhortatory traditions. Besides Paul's likely acquaintance with both these traditions through his close contact with both Greek and Jewish environments, the common features would also naturally come to expression due to a common general type of communicative situation.

In this preacher/teacher and hearer/community-of-faith type of situation, exhortation appears to have a typical "response-reinforcing" function urging adherence to that which one already for the most part accepts in principle but needs reminding of with regard to practice (see 4.4.3.2).[841] In W. Wolbert's distinction between **parenesis**, where a generality of consensus is presupposed, and **normative ethics**, where opinions conflict so that a particular position must be defended with concerted argumentation, one finds a general parallel to a relative distinction held here between exhortatory discourse and persuasive discourse.[842] The former lies closer to "coercive" and

---

[840] Malherbe, 1970, 203-22; 1983, 238-56.

[841] Relevant Hellenistic authors in this regard are Isocrates, Ad Nic, 40-41; Seneca, Ep, 13.15; 94.21, 25; Dio Chrysostom, Orat, 17. 2, 5. These are quoted by Perdue (1981, 242-4) with reference to Malherbe (1972).

[842] Wolbert, 1981, 18-19. Parenesis had a most peripheral place in ancient rhetoric.

"rogative" subtypes of the general conative function in which the addressees' co-operation may be more reliably presupposed (see 1.7.1).

Finally, the foregoing intertextual features of exhortatory discourse in particular are not merely compatible with the specific rhetorical situation argued for above, but in fact actually reflect supportive appeals eminently appropriate to the occasioning exigence. From the rich reflection of covenant ideology observed in I Thess, L. Hartman draws the theological implication that "man dahinter eine Betrachtungsweise vermuten muss, nach der die Heidenchristen als Mitglieder des Eigentumsvolkes Gottes betrachtet wurden."[843] Against the background of the main exigence of the addressees' grief, anxiety, and incipient doubt, as interpreted above, these combined indications of their inclusion as members of God's special possession (5:9) obtain a heightened degree of appropriateness. This is particularly underlined by the fact that the reminder of their divine election stands not only at the beginning (1:4), but also recurs within (2:12; 4:7; 5:9) and concludes the letter-body (5:24) with the insistence on God's faithfulness in accomplishing complete sanctification commensurate with their election in preparation for the parousia (5:23-24). Furthermore, there is the congruence of the rhetorical exordial-narrative functions observed in I Thess 1-3 and the "antecedent history" typical of O.T.-Jewish exhortatory discourse.

8.3 GENERAL SUMMARY AND CONCLUSIONS

The complex intertextuality of I Thess as indicated in the foregoing analyses helps to explain why each individual category of letter or exhortatory conventions of discourse or even the traditional rhetorical **genera** and **dispositio** are not entirely adequate for the classification of the text nor for its strict delimitation into and classification of functional textual subsequences.

As for disposition, we may summarize the following general conclusions. The general two-part schema of the letter-body is distinctly informed by the integrated conventions of Greek letters and O.T.-Jewish exhortatory discourse, with the former expanded by the latter. The expansion of the "thanksgiving" part (1:2-3:13) is also contributed to by the typical rhetorical strategies of an integrated **exordium/narratio**. Its unusual length also is justified by these strategies as a sensitive preparation for the treatment of a delicate exigence. In the wish-prayer (3:11-13) concluding this section one finds what corresponds to a **transitus** in cultic language. Unlike the orations envisaged in the ancient rhetorical handbooks, the subsequent specific **argumentatio** dealing with the occasioning rhetorical exigence (4:13-5:11) is sandwiched between two panels of religious-ethical exhortation (4:1-12 and 5:12-24). Both these panels of exhortation were shown to have a general prophylactic, parenetic function as well as a more particular **ethos**, authority-enhancing function relative to the occasioning exi-

---

See, e.g., Berger, 1984, 1075.

[843] Hartman, 1980, 117. He goes on to note that there is, nevertheless, a problem on the part of the Jews who persecuted the apostles and hindered the gospel so as to bring down judgment on themselves (2:15-16). In Gal this problem is manifested in Paul's heavy attack on those who continue to insist on circumcision as a requirement for inclusion, while in Rom the problem of inclusion receives a calmer more systematic treatment.

gence. Furthermore, the complex integration of intertextual features continues in the latter panel (5:12-24) which was shown to combine general parenesis and a wish-prayer with peroration-like functions. Finally, the general "message" part of the text (1:2-5:24), combining epistolary, rhetorical and exhortational, worship-oriented features of discourse, is framed by a prescript (1:1) and letter-closing (5:25-28) in which the greeting elements ("grace and peace") in particular deviate from current Hellenistic letter conventions so as to be more appropriate to religious, worship-oriented discourse.

This complex integration of various generic features witnesses to a high degree of authorial creativity and precludes the adequateness of a simple generic classification. Since the text represents a basically practical act of communication, rather than a consciously literary one (see 1.3.2.2), the creativity must be seen as primarily motivated by sensitive attention to the appropriateness constraints of a complex communication situation in which epistolary, rhetorical-persuasive, and exhortatory **types of situations** as well as an anticipated worship-setting of reception all coincided. In observing such a phenomenon of more than one set of typical structures and functions, motives, topics, phraseology, etc., informing one and the same text, the decisive question, as indicated by R. Knierim in general, is how such elements interact and which of them dominates over the others.[844] Furthermore, as Knierim also observes, "there is reason to believe that individual texts are dependent not only on typical settings, but at least as much on the specific situations to which they owe their existence."[845]

On the basis of the foregoing research, the conclusion drawn here is that it is the rhetorical situation and the rhetorical features of persuasion in the text, as presented in ch. 6 above, that dominate over the other sets of generic features when it comes to the question of the initial, immediate communicative goal or intention of the text. The reconstruction of the rhetorical situation, as centered on the exigence reflected in 4:13-5:11 and on the various explicit and implicit persuasive strategies relating to this exigence, is able to give the most coherent account of both the single, more explicit references reflecting various aspects of the situation as well as of the functional relations holding between the various text-sequences in relation to the whole text as an integral act of communication.

The general epistolary function of achieving "contact" between spatially separate communicators (see 1.7.5) is distinctly present and important,[846] but cannot give an adequate account of the presence or the need for the complex intertextuality we have observed. Also, as observed under 7.2 above, those of a more puristic form-critical bent are happy to follow B.A. Pearson in eliminating 2:13-16 as an interpolation so as to be able to recognize a more "normal" epistolary form.[847] But to try to force any such more "normal" epistolary form on the text does violence to its complex intertextuality which is closely linked to its situationality. Furthermore, the foregoing obser-

---

[844] Knierim, 1973, 162 ff.

[845] Knierim, 1973, 165.

[846] This description of the primary function or intention of I Thess is represented by, e.g., Vielhauer, 1975, 87.

[847] See Pearson (1971) followed by, e.g., Boers (1975-76, 152) and Koester, 1979, 38.

vations on the tightly woven symmetrical structure of the text render this position as most dubious.

As for the combination of typical epistolary features and functions with those of exhortatory discourse, this goes a long way in identifying the philophronetic and implicit exhortatory functions of I Thess 1-3 and the explicit religious-ethical exhortation of I Thess 4-5. But, with epistolary philophronesis and general pastoral exhortation taken as the primary communicative functions (see under 3.1.3.1), neither the unusual length of the exordium-like "thanksgiving" section in 1:2-3:13 nor the particular urgency indicated by the argumentative character of especially 4:13-5:11 are adequately accounted for.

By contrast, the present study not only indicates that both the epistolary and exhortatory features in the text are appropriate to the complex situation, but also shows how these are integrated with typical persuasive features of rhetorical discourse so as to explicitly and implicitly serve persuasive strategies that are **dominated** by the rhetorical exigence reflected in 4:13-5:11. As argued above, this exigence is anticipated at the end of the exordial-narrative section in the reference to the "deficiencies of faith" (3:10) and is constituted by the unexpected decease of fellow believers prior to the parousia. The reference to the addressees' non-Christian type of grief (4:13) and the direction of argumentation point to incipient doubt and anxious perplexity on the part of the addressees. To be more specific, the **quaestio** concerns the eschatological status of the deceased (4:13-17), as well as the eschatological status of those who remained (5:1-10). The occasion of the addressees' budding doubts and non-Christian type of grief must have involved what was interpreted to be an apparent inconsistency between Paul's previous eschatological instruction on the immanently expected parousia given primarily in terms of bodily assumption on the one hand, and the unexpected reality of their recent experience of believers' deaths prior to this event, on the other hand.

Such a situation called for a delicate combination of consolation and correction without reproof. While consolation was obviously a major aim of the informative and argumentative features of the passage, the simultaneous presence of **dissuasion** from the insipient doubts and perplexity occasioning the non-Christian type of grief reflected in 4:13 indicates that the main aim could not have been only consolation (4:18; 5:11) pure and simple. There was more at stake here than the provision of fuller understanding and the assuagement of human grief over their dead. The apparent incongruence between prior instruction and present reality would not only jeopardize Paul's credibility, but even more seriously the resulting incipient doubt and grief would pose a serious potential threat to adherence to the gospel itself. From this perspective, the intended consolation itself, as grounded in Christian hope (4:14; 5:9-10), may be seen as a means of strengthening Paul's dissuasion aimed at hindering budding doubt from coming to full bloom.

As for the rhetorical genre, the one to which I Thess would have the closest resemblance is the deliberative one. And with regard to letter classification, the foregoing observations would generally indicate that it should be located roughly at the center in W.G. Doty's "spectrum of private, intimate letters and open, public letters" and as combining parenetic and consolatory features with the primary dissuasive concerns made explicit above.[848] To look at this complex intertextuality from a more general perspective, one may observe an apparent tension between the more specifically occasional epistolary and rhetorical-persuasive features and the more general features of

---

[848] See Doty, 1969, 196-8.

exhortatory discourse that are quite appropriate to the ongoing life of Christian communities at large. Such a tension finds a most likely resolution in the assumption that I Thess (and probably most of Paul's letters) was not intended to be **purely** occasional, but 'to be read and reread.'[849]

Thus, while the general religious-ethical exhortatory features and the instructive aspects on eschatology in the text would tend to attain greater prominence in later, more general contexts of reading in the ongoing life of the church, it is the concrete rhetorical situation as reconstructed for the initial context of reception that gives the most coherent account of the letter as an integral act of communication.

In brief, within the broader response-reinforcing function with the **ultimate** intention of increasing adherence to the Christian gospel, an overall coherence of text-oriented and user-oriented rhetorical features indicate that the primary **immediate** intention of the letter is informed by the response-changing function of persuasive discourse aimed at resolving the specific rhetorical exigence reflected in 4:13-5:11. While the epistolary function of contact and the sermonic functions of religious-ethical and worship-appropriate exhortation are present, it is the rhetorical-persuasive function that predominates.

From the analyses and interpretations carried out, no simple generic classification is seen to be entirely adequate for a description of I Thess. It is a creative act in a practical process of communication combining 1) the warmth of a private letter providing contact between "brethren," 2) the pastoral, gospel-centered, religious-ethical concern and the worship-appropriate features of Christian exhortatory discourse, and 3) the sensitive use of rhetorical strategies aimed at dissuading the addressees from incipient doubts, grief and anxiety that posed a serious potential threat to adherence to the gospel.

No doubt, this rich intertextual complexity is an important feature that satisfies appropriateness constraints not only for an initial meaningful reading "to all the brethren" in Thessalonica but also for subsequent meaningful readings both within and outside of the ongoing life of the Christian community of faith.

---

[849] Thus, recently Hartman (1986, 137-39) regarding Paul's letters in general.

LIST OF ABBREVIATIONS
The More Common
Dictionaries, Encyclopædias, Journals, Series and Translations

AGJU	Arbeiten zur Geschichte des antiken Judentums und des Urchristentums
AGSU	Arbeiten zur Geschichte des Spätjudentums und des Urchristentums
ATANT	Abhandlungen zur Theologie des Alten und Neuen Testaments
ATR	Anglican Theological Review
BETL	Bibliotheca ephemeridum theologicarum lovaniensium
BEvT	Beiträge zur evangelischen Theologie
BFCT	Beiträge zur Förderung christlicher Theologie
Bib	Biblica
BNTC	Black's New Testament Commentary
BSac	Bibliotheca Sacra
BT	The Bible Translator
BTB	Biblical Theology Bulletin
BU	Biblische Untersuchungen
BWANT	Beiträge zur Wissenschaft vom Alten und Neuen Testament
BZNW	Beihefte zur ZNW
CBQ	Catholic Biblical Quarterly
CGT	Cambridge Greek Testament
CNT	Commentaire du Nouveau Testament
ConBNT	Coniectanea biblica, New Testament
ConBOT	Coniectanea biblica, Old Testament
DTT	Dansk teologisk tidsskrift
EBib	Etude biblique
EGT	Expositor's Greek Testament
EKKNT	Evangelisch-katholischer Kommentar zum Neuen Testament
EncyBrMacr	The New Encyclopædia Britannica, Macropædia, 15th ed., 1979.
ETL	Ephemerides theologicae lovanienses
FRLANT	Forschungen zur Religion und Literatur des Alten und Neuen Testaments
FS	Festschrift
HeyJ	Heythrop Journal
HNT	Handbuch zum Neuen Testament
HTR	Harvard Theological Review
IB	Interpreter's Bible
ICC	International Critical Commentary

IDB	Interpreter's Dictionary of the Bible
IDBSup	IDB Supplementary Volume
Int	Interpretation
JB	The Jerusalem Bible
JBC	The Jerome Biblical Commentary
JBL	Journal of Biblical Literature
JJS	Journal of Jewish Studies
JR	Journal of Religion
JRH	Journal of Religious History
JSNTSup	Journal for the Study of the New Testament-Supplement Series
JSS	Journal of Semitic Studies
JTS	Journal of Theological Studies
KJV	The King James (Authorized) Version of the Bible
LB	Linguistica biblica
LCL	Loeb Classical Library
LLL	Longman Linguistic Library
LS	Louvain Studies
Luth	Die Bible nach der Übersetzung Martin Luthers
MeyerK	H.A.W. Meyer, Kritisch-exegetischer Kommentar über das Neue Testament
MNTC	Moffatt New Testament Commentary
NCBC	New Century Bible Commentary
Neot	Neotestamentica
NovT	Novum Testamentum
NovTSup	Novum Testamentum, Supplements
NTD	Das Neue Testament Deutsch
NTF	Neutestamentliche Forschungen
NTS	New Testament Studies
NTTS	New Testament Tools and Studies
PRE	Paulys Real-Encyklopädie der classischen Altertumswissenschaft
PVTG	Pseudepigrapha Veteris Testamenti graece
RB	Revue biblique
RechBib	Recherches bibliques
RHPR	Revue d'histoire et de philosophie religieuses
RSV	Revised Standard Version of the Bible
RV	Revised Version of the Bible
SANT	Studien zum Alten und Neuen Testament
SBL	Society of Biblical Literature
SBLDS	SBL Dissertation Series
SBLSBS	SBL Sources for Biblical Study
SBS	Stuttgarter Bibelstudien
SBT	Studies in Biblical Theology

SEÅ	Svensk exegetisk årsbok
SNT	Studien zum Neuen Testament
SNTSMS	Society for New Testament Studies Monograph Series
ST	Studie theologica
STK	Svensk teologisk kvartalskrift
StudNeot	Studia neotestamentica
SUNT	Studien zur Umwelt des Neuen Testaments
TDNT	Theological Dictionary of the New Testament
TEV	The New Testament in Today's English Version
TF	Theologische Forschung
TLZ	Theologische Literaturzeitung
TRu	Theologische Rundschau
UTB	Uni-Taschenbücher
VT	Vetus Testamentum
Weymouth	Weymouth's New Testament in Modern Speech
WMANT	Wissenschaftliche Monographien zum Alten und Neuen Testament
WUNT	Wissenschaftliche Untersuchungen zum Neuen Testament
ZNW	Zeitschrift für die neutestamentliche Wissenschaft
ZTK	Zeitschrift für Theologie und Kirche

BIBLIOGRAPHY

TEXTS AND TRANSLATIONS

1) Ancient Texts Belonging to the World of Jewish and Christian Origins and Traditions.

Apocrypha and Pseudepigraph of the Old Testament in English.
    Vols. I-II. Ed. by R.H. Charles. Oxford, 1913.
The Apostolic Fathers.
    Vols. I-II. Trans. by K. Lake. (LCL) Cambridge, Mass., 1912-1913.
Die Apostolischen Väter.
    Ed. by F.X. Funk and K. Bihlmeyer. (Sammlung ausgewählter kirchen- und dogmengeschichtliche Quellenschriften, 2.1.1) 2nd ed. Tübingen, 1956.
Augustine.
    Confessions. Vols I-II. Trans. by W. Watts. (LCL) Cambridge, Mass., 1912.
----------.
    Confessions and Enchiridion. Library of Christian Classics. Vol. VII. Ed. by A.C. Outler. Philadelphia and London, 1955.
Die Bible (Luth).
    Oder die Ganze Heilige Schrift des alten und neuen Testaments nach der Übersetzung Martin Luthers. Stuttgart, 1972.
Biblia Hebraica.
    Ed. by R. Kittel. 7th ed. by P. Kahle, A. Alt and O. Eissfeldt. Stuttgart, 1951.
The Dead Sea Scriptures.
    In English Translation with Introduction and Notes by T.H. Gaster. 3rd ed. New York, 1976.
The Dead Sea Scrolls in English.
    Trans. by G. Vermes. Penguin Books, 1962.
Good News for Modern Man (TEV).
    The New Testament in Today's English Version. Trans. by R.G. Bratcher. New York, 1966.
The Greek New Testament.
    Ed. by K. Aland et al. 3rd ed. Stuttgart, 1968.
The Greek Versions of the Testaments of the Twelve Patriarchs.
    Ed. by R.H. Charles. Oxford, 1908.
The Jerusalem Bible (JB).
    With Abridged Introductions and Notes. Gen. ed. A. Jones. London, 1966.
Josephus.
    The Life. Against Apion (Vol. I). Jewish Wars (Vols. II-III). Jewish Antiquities (Vols. IV-X). Vol.I-IV trans. by H. St. J. Thackeray; Vol. V by H. St. J Thackeray and R. Marcus; Vols. VI-VII by R. Marcus; Vol. VIII by R. Marcus and A. Wikgren, and Vol. IX by L. H. Feldman. (LCL) Cambridge, Mass., 1926-1965.
Η ΚΑΙΝΗ ΔΙΑΘΗΚΗ.
    Ed. by G.D. Kilpatric. 2nd ed. London, 1958.
The King James Version (KJV).
    The Holy Bible. 1611.
The New English Bible (NEB).
    O.T. 1970, N.T. (2nd ed.) 1970. Oxford, 1970.

New Testament Apocrypha.
> Vols. I-II. Ed. by E. Hennecke, W. Schneemelcher and R.McL. Wilson. SCM Press Ltd., 1963-65.

The New Testament in the Original Greek.
> Ed. by B.F. Westcott and F.J.A. Hort. London, 1885.

Novum Testamentum Graece.
> Ed. by K. Aland, et al. 26th ed. (25th ed. by E. Nestle and K. Aland, 1963) Stuttgart, 1979.

The Old Testament Pseudepigrapha.
> Vol. 1. Apocalyptic Literature and Testaments. Ed. by J.H. Charlesworth. London, 1983.

The Old Testament Pseudepigrapha.
> Vol. 2. Expansions of the "Old Testament" and Legends, Wisdom and Philosophical Literature, Prayers, Psalms, and Odes, Fragments of Lost Judeo-Hellenistic Works. Ed. by J.H. Charlesworth. Garden City, N.Y., 1985.

Revised Standard Version (RSV).
> The Bible. O.T. 1952, Apocr. 1957, N.T. (2nd ed.) 1971. New York, 1952-71.

Revised Version (RV).
> Holy Bible with Apocrypha. N.T. 1880, O.T. 1884, Apocr. 1895. Oxford, 1880-95.

Septuaginta.
> Vols. I-II. Ed. by A. Rahlfs. 7th ed. Stuttgart, 1962.

Testamenta XII Patriarcharum.
> Ed. by M. de Jonge. (PTVG, 1) Leiden, 1964.

The Testaments of the Twelve Patriarchs.
> A Critical Edition of the Greek Text. Ed. by M. de Jonge. (PVTG, 1/2) Leiden, 1978.

Die Texte aus Qumran.
> Hebraisch und Deutsch. Ed. by E. Lohse. München, 1964.

Die Texte vom Toten Meer.
> Trans. by J. Maier. München and Basel, 1960.

Weymouth's New Testament in Modern Speech (Weymouth).
> Trans. by R.F. Weymouth. Rev. by J.A. Robertson. London, 1924.

2) Ancient Texts Belonging to the Greek and Roman World outside Jewish and Christian Origins and Traditions.

Anaximenes.
> See Rhetorica ad Alexandrum.

Theon.
> Aphthonii Progymnasmata. Rhetores. Graeci. Vol. I. Ed. by H. Rabe. (Teubner) Lipsiae, 1926.

Aristotle.
> The "Art" of Rhetoric. Vol. XXII. Trans. by J.H. Freese. (LCL) Cambridge, Mass., 1926.

----------.
> The Poetics. Vol. XXIII. Trans. by W.H. Fyfe (LCL) Rev. ed. Cambridge, Mass., 1932.

Cicero.
> De Oratore. Vol. III. Trans. by E.W. Sutton and H. Rackham. (LCL) Rev. ed. Cambridge, Mass., 1948.

----------.
> Letters to His Friends. Vols. XXV-XXVI trans. W.G. Williams; Vol. XXVII trans. by W.G. Williams and M. Cary. (LCL) Cambridge, Mass., 1927-29.

The Cynic Epistles.
> A Study Edition by A.J. Malherbe. (SBLSBS, 12) Missoula, Mont., 1977.

Demetrius.
> On Style. Trans. by W.R. Roberts. (In vol. XXIII of Aristotle, LCL) Rev. ed. Cambridge, Mass., 1932.

Demosthenes.
> Letters. In vol. VII. Trans. by N.W. De Witt and N.J. De Witt. (LCL) Cambridge, Mass., 1949.

Dio Chrysostom.
> Vols I-V. Trans. by J.W. Cohoon and H.L. Crosby. (LCL) Cambridge, Mass., 1932-51.

Diogenes Laertius.
> Lives of Eminent Philosophers. Vols. I-II. Trans. by R.D. Hicks. (LCL) Cambridge, Mass., 1925.

Epictetus.
> The Discourses as Reported by Arrian, The Manual, and Fragments. Vols. I-II. Trans. by W.A. Oldfather. (LCL) Cambridge, Mass., 1925.

Isocrates.
> Vols. I-II trans. by G. Norlin; Vol. III trans. by La Rue Van Hook. (LCL) Cambridge, Mass., 1928-45.

Menander Rhetor.
> Ed. with trans. and comm. by D.A. Russell and N.G. Wilson. Oxford, 1981.

Pseudo Demetrius.
> Demetrii et Libanii qui feruntur ΤΥΠΟΙ ΕΠΙΣΤΟΛΙΚΟΙ et ΕΠΙΣΤΟΛΙΜΑΙΟΙ ΧΑΡΑΚΤΗΡΕΣ. Ed. by V. Weichert. (Teubner) Lipsiae, 1910.

----------.
> Epistolary Types. Text with Trans. by A.J. Malherbe in "Ancient Epistolary Types," Ohio Journal of Religious Studies 5 (1977) 28-39.

Quintilian.
> Institutio Oratoria. Vols. I-IV. Trans. by H.E. Butler. (LCL) Cambridge, Mass., 1920-22.

Rhetorica ad Alexandrum.
> Trans. by H. Rackham (In vol. XVI of Aristotle, LCL) Rev. ed. Cambridge, Mass., 1957.

Seneca.
> Epistulae Morales. Vols. IV-VI. Trans. by R.M. Gummere. (LCL) Cambridge, Mass., 1917-25.

LITERATURE

Aland et al., 1968.
    See **The Greek New Testament** under Texts and Translations.
Aschermann, H., 1955.
    Die paränetischen Formen der Testamente der zwölf Patriarchen und ihr Nachwirken in der frühchristlichen Mahnung. Eine formgeschichtliche Untersuchung. (Diss.) Berlin, 1955.
Audet, J.P., 1958.
    "Esquisse Historique du Genre Littéraire de la "Bénédiction" Juive et de l'"Eucharistie" Chrétienne (1)," **RB** 65 (1958) 371-99.
----------, 1959.
    "Literary Forms and Contents of a Normal Εὐχαριστία in the First Century," **SE** 1 (1959) 643-62.
Aune, D.E., 1983.
    Prophecy in Early Christianity and the Ancient Mediterranean World. Grand Rapids, Mich., 1983.
Austin, J.L., 1975.
    How to Do Things with Words. Ed. by J.O. Urmson and M. Sbisà. 2nd ed. (1st ed., 1962) Oxford, 1975.
Bahr, G.J., 1968.
    "The Subscriptions in the Pauline Letters," **JBL** 87 (1968) 27-41.
Bailey, J.W., 1955.
    I and II Thessalonians. (IB, vol. XI) Ed. by B.A. Buttrick et al. New York and Nashville, 1955.
Bailey, K.E., 1976.
    Poet and Peasant. A Literary Cultural Approach to the Parables in Luke. Grand Rapids, 1976.
Baltzer, Kl., 1971.
    The Covenant Formulary in Old Testament, Jewish, and Early Christian Writings. Trans. by D.E. Green. Oxford, 1971. (Ger. ed.: **Das Bundesformular**. (WMANT, 4) 2nd rev. ed. Neukirchen-Vluyn, 1964)
Bammel, E., 1960.
    "Ein Beitrag zur paulinischen Staatsanschauung," **TLZ** 85 (1960) 837-40.
----------, 1981.
    "Preparation for the perils of the last days: I Thessalonians 3:3," **Suffering and Martyrdom in the New Testament**. (FS for G.M. Styler) Ed. by W. Horbury and B. McNeil. Cambridge - Sydney, 1981, 91-100.
Bar-Efrat, S., 1980.
    "Some Observations on the Analysis of Structure in Biblical Narrative," **VT** 30 (1980) 154-73.
Barr, J., 1969.
    Biblical Words for Time. (SBT, f.s., 33) 2nd ed. (1st ed., 1962) London, 1969.
Bartlett, A.C., 1935.
    The Larger Rhetorical Patterns in Anglo-Saxon Poetry. (Columbia University Studies in English and Comparative Literature, 122) Morningside Heights, N.Y., 1935.
Bauer, W., 1979.
    A Greek-English Lexicon of the New Testament and Other Early Christian Literature. Trans. and ed. by W.F. Arndt, F.W. Gingrich and F.W. Danker. Chicago and London, 1979.

Baur, F.C., 1866-67.
Paulus, Der Apostel Jesu Christi. Sein Leben und Wirken, seine Briefe und seine Lehre. Ein Beitrag zu einer Kritischen Geschichte des Urchristenthums. Vols. I (1866), Vol. II (1867). 2nd ed. (1st ed., 1845) Leipzig, 1866-67.

de Beaugrande, R.-A., and W.U. Dressler, 1981.
Introduction to Text Linguistics. (LLL, 26) London, 1981.

Becker, J., 1970.
Untersuchungen zur Entstehungsgeschichte der Testamente der zwölf Patriarchen. (AGJU, 8) Leiden, 1970.

----------, 1976.
Auferstehung der Toten im Urchristentum. (SBS, 82) Stuttgart, 1976.

Berger, Kl., 1974.
"Apostelbrief und apostolische Rede. Zum Formular frühchristlicher Briefe," **ZNW** 65 (1974) 190-231.

----------, 1977.
Exegese des Neuen Testaments. (UTB, 658) Heidelberg, 1977.

----------, 1984.
"Hellenistische Gattungen im Neuen Testament," **Aufstieg und Niedergang der römischen Welt.** Geschichte und Kultur Roms im Spiegel der neueren Forschung, II. Ed. by H. Temporini and W. Haase. **Principat.** Bd. 25.2. Ed. by W. Haase. Berlin and New York, 1984, 1031-1432.

Best, E., 1977.
A Commentary on the First and Second Epistles to the Thessalonians. (BNTC) 2nd ed. (1st ed., 1972) London, 1977.

Betz, H.D., 1974-75.
"The Literary Composition and Function of Paul's Letter to the Galations," **NTS** 21 (1974-75) 353-79.

----------, 1979.
Galations. A Commentary on Paul's Letter to the Churches in Galatia. (Hermeneia) Philadelphia, 1979.

Betz, O., 1956-57.
"Die Geburt der Gemeinde durch den Lehrer," **NTS** 3 (1956-57) 116-37.

Bitzer, L.F., 1968.
"The Rhetorical Situation," **Philosophy and Rhetoric** 1 (1968) 1-14.

----------, 1980.
"Functional Communication: A Situational Perspective," **Rhetoric in Transition.** Studies in the Nature and Uses of Rhetoric. Ed. by E.E. White. University Park, Pa., and London, 1980, 21-38.

Bjerkelund, C.J., 1967.
Parakalô. Form, Function und Sinn der parakalô-Sätze in den paulinischen Briefen. (Bibliotheca Theologica Norvegica, 1) Oslo, 1967.

Black, E., 1965.
Rhetorical Criticism. A Study in Method. New York and London, 1965.

Blass, F., and A. Debrunner, 1961.
A Greek Grammar of the New Testament and Other Early Christian Literature. Trans. and rev. by R.W. Funk. Chicago and London, 1961.

----------, 1979.
Grammatik des neutestamentlichen Griechisch. Rev. by F. Rehkopf. 15th ed. Göttingen, 1979.

Bleich, D., 1978.
Subjective Criticism. Baltimore and London, 1978.

Boers, H., 1975-76.
   "The Form-Critical Study of Paul's Letters: 1 Thessalonians as a Case Study," **NTS** 22 (1975-76) 140-58.
Booth, W.C., 1983.
   The Rhetoric of Fiction. 2nd ed. (1st ed., 1960) Chicago and London, 1983.
Bornemann, W., 1894.
   Die Thessalonischerbriefe. (MeyerK, 10) 6th ed. Göttingen, 1894.
Bornkamm, G., 1969.
   Early Christian Experience. Trans. by P.L. Hammer. London, 1969.
---------, 1971.
   Paul. Trans. by D.M.G. Stalker. London - Toronto, 1971.
Bradley, D.G., 1953.
   "The **Topos** as a Form in the Pauline Paraenesis," **JBL** 72 (1953) 238-46.
Braun, H., 1966.
   Qumran und das Neue Testament. Vols. I-II. Tübingen, 1966.
Breuer, D., 1974.
   Einführung in die pragmatische Tesxttheorie. (UTB, 106) München, 1974.
---------, 1977.
   "Die Bedeutung der Rhetorik für die Textinterpretation," **Rhetorik. Kritische Positionen zum Stand der Forschung.** Ed. by H.F. Plett. München, 1977, 23-44.
Brinker, K., 1983.
   "Textfunction. Ansätze zu ihrer Beschreibung," **Zeitschrift für germanistische Linguistik** 11 (1983) 127-48.
Brinton, A., 1981.
   "Situation in the Theory of Rhetoric," **Philosophy and Rhetoric** 14 (1981) 234-48.
Broer, I., 1983.
   "<<Antisemitismus>> und Judenpolemik im Neuen Testament. Ein Beitrag zum besseren Verständnis von 1 Thess 2,14-16," **Biblische Notizen** 20 (1983) 59-91.
Brooks, C., and R.P. Warren, 1979.
   Modern Rhetoric. 4th ed. (1st ed., 1972) New York - Atlanta, 1979.
Brown, G., and G. Yule, 1983.
   Discourse Analysis. (Cambridge Textbooks in Linguistics) Cambridge - Sydney, 1983.
Bruce, F.F., 1952.
   The Acts of the Apostles. The Greek Text with Introduction and Commentary. 2nd ed. (1st ed., 1951) Grand Rapids, 1952.
---------, 1985.
   "The Acts of the Apostles: Historical Record or Theological Reconstruction?," **Aufstieg und Niedergang der römischen Welt.** Geschichte und Kultur Roms im Spiegel der neueren Forschung, II. Ed. by H. Temporini and W. Haase. **Principat.** Bd. 25.3. Ed. by W. Haase. Berlin and New York, 1985, 2570-2602.
Brunt, J.C., 1985.
   "More on the **Topos** as a New Testament Form," **JBL** 104 (1985) 495-500.
Bühler, K., 1926.
   "Die Krise der Psychologie," **Kant-Studien** 31 (1926) 455-526.
---------, 1933.
   "Die Axiomatik der Sprachwissenschaften," **Kant-Studien** 38 (1933) 19-90. (ET: "The Axiomatization of Language Sciences," in Innis, 1982, 91-164)
---------, 1934.
   Sprachtheorie. Die Darstellungsfunction der Sprache. Jena, 1934.

----------, 1982.
    "The Axiomatization of the Language Sciences," Trans. of Bühler, 1933, by R.E. Innis in Innis, 1982, 91-164.
Bull, W.E., 1960.
    Time, Tense, and the Verb. A Study in Theoretical and Applied Linguistics, with Particular Attention to Spanish. (University of California Publications in Linguistics, 19) Berkley and Los Angeles, 1960.
Bultmann, R., 1910.
    Der Stil der paulinischen Predigt und die kynisch-stoische Diatribe. (FRLANT, 13) Göttingen, 1910.
----------, 1951.
    Theology of the New Testament. Vol. I. Trans. by K. Grobel. New York, 1951.
Bünker, M., 1984.
    Briefformular und rhetorische Disposition im 1.Korintherbrief. (Göttinger Theologische Arbeiten, 28) Göttingen, 1984.
Burgoon, M., and E.P. Bettinghaus, 1980.
    "Persuasive Message Strategies," **Persuasion: New Directions in Theory and Research.** Ed. by M.E. Roloff and G.R. Miller. (Sage Annual Reviews of Communication Research, 8) Beverly Hills and London, 1980, 141-69.
Burke, K., 1950.
    A Rhetoric of Motives. Englewood Cliffs, N.J., 1950.
Cadbury, H.J., 1955.
    The Book of Acts in History. New York and London, 1955.
Caffi, Cl., 1984.
    "Some Remarks on Illocution and Metacommunication," **Journal of Pragmatics** 8 (1984) 449-67.
Cancik, H., 1967.
    Untersuchungen zu Senecas Epistulae morales. (Spudasmata, 18) Hildesheim, 1967.
Cavallin, H.C., 1983.
    "Parusi och uppståndelse," **STK** 59 (1983) 54-63.
Chadwick, H., 1950.
    "I Thess. 3:3: σαινεσθαι," **JTS** 1 (1950) 156-58.
Charolles, M., 1983.
    "Coherence as a principle in the interpretation of discourse," **Text** 3 (1983) 71-97.
Chatman, S., 1978.
    Story and Discourse: Narrative Structure in Fiction and Film. Ithica and London, 1978.
Chevallier, M.-A., 1971.
    "I Pierre 1/1 à 2/10. Structure Littéraire et Conséquences Exégétiques," **RHPR** 51 (1971) 129-42.
Church, F.F., 1978.
    "Rhetorical Structure and Design in Paul's Letter to Philemon," **HTR** 71 (1978) 17-33.
Collins, R.F., 1974-75.
    "The Church of the Thessalonians," **LS** 5 (1974-75) 336-49. (=Collins, 1984, 285-96)
----------, 1978-79.
    "The Faith of the Thessalonians," **LS** 7 (1978-79) 249-69. (=Collins, 1984, 209-29)

----------, 1979.
"A propos the Integrity of 1 Thess," **ETL** 55 (1979) 67-106. (=Collins, 1984, 96-135)
----------, 1980.
"Tradition, Redaction, and Exhortation in 1 Thess 4,13-5,11," **L'Apocalypse johannique et l'Apocalyptique dans le Nouveau Testament.** Ed. by J. Lambrecht. (BETL, 53) Louvain, 1980, 325-43. (=Collins, 1984, 154-72)
----------, 1980a.
"1 Thess and the Liturgy of the Early Church," **BTB** 10 (1980) 51-64. (=Collins, 1984, 136-53)
----------, 1980-81.
Paul As Seen through His Own Eyes. A Reflection on the First Letter to the Thessalonians," **LS** 8 (1981-82) 348-81. (=Collins, 1984, 175-208)
----------, 1982-83.
"<<...that this letter be read to all the brethren>>. A New Testament Note," **LS** 9 (1982-83) 122-27. (=Collins, 1984, 365-70)
----------, 1982-83a.
"The Unity of Paul's Paraenesis in 1 Thess 4,3-8. 1 Cor 7,1-7 a Significant Parallel," **NTS** 29 (1982-83) 420-29. (=Collins, 1984, 326-35)
----------, 1984.
Studies on the First Letter to the Thessalonians. (BETL, 66) Leuven, 1984.

Combrink, H.J.B., 1984.
"Multiple meaning and/or multiple interpretation of a text," **Neot** 18 (1984) 26-37.

Conzelmann, H., 1975.
1 Corinthians. A Commentary on the First Epistle to the Corinthians. Trans. by J.W. Leitch. Bib. and ref. by J.W. Dunkly. Ed. by G.W. MacRae. (Hermeneia) Philadelphia, 1975.

Conzelmann, H., and A. Lindemann, 1980.
Arbeitsbuch zum Neuen Testament. (UTB, 52) 5th ed. (1st ed., 1975) Tübingen, 1980.

Cope, E.M., 1877.
The Rhetoric of Aristotle, with a Commentary. Vols. I-III. Rev. and ed. by J.E. Sandys. (1st ed., 1867) Cambridge, Eng., 1877.

Coppens, J., 1975.
"Miscellanées bibliques. LXXX. Une diatribe antijuive dans I Thess., II, 13-16," **ETL** 51 (1975) 90-95.

Coseriu, E., 1980.
Textlinguistik. Eine Einfürung. Ed. and rev. by J. Albrecht. (Tübinger Beiträge zur Linguistik, 109) Tübingen, 1980.

Cuming, G.J., 1975-76.
"Service-Endings in the Epistles," **NTS** 22 (1975-76) 110-13

Davies, W.D., 1955.
Paul and Rabbinic Judaism. Rev. ed. (1st ed., 1948) London, 1955.

Denis, A.-M., 1957.
"L'Apôtre Paul, prophète <<messianique>> des Gentils. Étude thématique de 1 Thess, II, 1-6," **ETL** 33 (1957) 245-318.

Denniston, J.D., 1952.
Greek Prose Style. Oxford, 1952.
----------, 1954.
The Greek Particles. 2nd ed. (1st ed., 1934) Oxford, 1954.

Dibelius, M., 1931.
"Zur Formgeschichte des Neuen Testaments (ausserhalb der Evangelien)," **TRu** N.F., 3 (1931) 207-42.
----------, 1937.
An die Thessalonicher I II. An die Philipper. (HNT, 11) 3rd. ed. Tübingen, 1937.
----------, 1961.
Die Formgeschichte des Evangeliums. 4th ed. with introduction by G. Iber. Ed. by G. Bornkamm. (1st ed., 1919) Tübingen, 1961. (ET: **From Tradition to Gospel.** Trans. by B.L. Woolf (from the 2nd ed., 1933). New York, 1933)
----------, 1976.
James. A Commentary on the Epistle of James. Rev. by H. Greeven. Trans. by M.A. Williams. Ed. by H. Koester. (Hermeneia) Philadelphia, 1976.
van Dijk, T., 1977.
Text and Context. Explorations in the Semantics and Pragmatics of Discourse. (LLL, 21) London, 1977.
----------, 1980.
Macrostructures. An Interdisciplinary Study of Global Structures in Discourse, Interaction, and Cognition. Hillsdale, N.J., 1980.
----------, 1981.
Studies in the Pragmatics of Discourse. (Janua Linguarum, Series Maior, 101) The Hague, 1981.
van Dijk, T., and J.S. Petöfi (eds), 1977.
Grammars and Descriptions. Studies in Text Theory and Text Analysis. (Research in Text Theory/Untersuchungen in Texttheorie, 1) Berlin and New York, 1977.
Dimter, M., 1981.
Textklassenkonzepte heutiger Alltagssprache: Kommunikationssituation, Textfunktion und Textinhalt als Kategorien alltagssprachlicher Textklassifikation. Tübingen, 1981.
von Dobschütz, D.E., 1909.
Die Thessalonicher-Briefe. (MeyerK) 7th ed. Göttingen, 1909.
Dockhorn, K., 1977.
"Kritische Rhetorik?," **Rhetorik.** Kritische Positionen zum Stand der Forschung. Ed. by H.F. Plett. München, 1977, 252-75.
Doeve, J.W., 1954.
Jewish Hermeneutics in the Synoptic Gospels and Acts. Assen, 1954.
Donfried, K.P., 1984.
"Paul and Judaism. I Thessalonians 2:13-16 as a Test Case," **Int** 38 (1984) 242-53.
----------, 1985-86.
"The Cults of Thessalonica and the Thessalonian Correspondence," **NTS** 31 (1985-86) 336-56.
Doty, W.G., 1969.
"The Classification of Epistolary Literature," **CBQ** 31 (1969) 183-99.
----------, 1973.
Letters in Primitive Christianity. (Guides to Biblical Scholarship, N.T. Series) Philadelphia, 1973.
Dressler, W. (ed.) 1978.
Current Trends in Textlinguistics. (Research in Text Theory, 2) Berlin, 1978.

Duncan, T.S., 1926.
"The Style and Language of Saint Paul in his First Letter to the Corinthians," **BSac** 83 (1926) 129-43.

Eckart, K.-G., 1961.
"Der zweite echte Brief des Apostels Paulus an die Thessalonicher," **ZTK** 58 (1961) 30-44.

Eco, U., 1976.
A Theory of Semiotics. (Advances in Semiotics) Bloomington, 1976.

----------, 1979.
The Role of the Reader. Explorations in the semiotics of texts. London - Johannesburg, 1979.

----------, 1984.
Semiotics and the Philosophy of Language. London, 1984.

Ellingworth, P., and E.A. Nida, 1975.
A Translator's Handbook on Paul's Letters to the Thessalonians. (Helps for Translators, 17) Stuttgart, 1975.

Enkvist, N.E., 1983.
"Rhetorical Aspects of Text Linguistics," **Adjoining Cultures as Reflected in Literature and Language.** Ed by J.X. Evans. (Proceedings of the XVth Triennial Congress of the Fédération Internationale des Langues et Littératures Modernes, Tempe, Arizona, Aug. 28-Sept. 9, 1981) Tempe, 1983, 65-79.

Exler, F.X.J., 1923.
The Form of the Ancient Greek Letter. A Study in Greek Epistolography. (Diss., Catholic Univ. of America) Washington, D.C., 1923.

Fafner, J., 1977.
Retorik. Klassisk og moderne. Indføring i nogle grundbegreber. København, 1977.

Faw, E., 1952.
"On the Writing of First Thessalonians," **JBL** 71 (1952) 217-25.

Findley, G.G., 1925.
The Epistles of Paul the Apostle to the Thessalonians. (CGT) Cambridge, Eng., 1925.

Fish, S., 1980.
Is There a Text in This Class? The Authority of Interpretive Communities. Cambridge, Mass., and London, 1980.

Fishbane, M., 1975.
"Composition and Structure in the Jacob Cycle (Gen. 25:19-35:22)," **JJS** 36 (1975) 15-38.

Føllesdal, D., and L. Walløe, 1977.
Argumentatsjonsteori og vitenskapsfilosofi. Oslo, 1977.

Forestell, J.T., 1968.
"The Letters to the Thessalonians," (JBC) Ed. by R.E. Brown, et al. London, 1968.

Fowler, A., 1970-71.
"The Life and Death of Literary Forms," **New Literary History** 2 (1970-71) 199-216.

Fowler, R.M., 1985.
"Who is "the Reader" in Reader Response Criticism?" **Semeia** 31 (1985) 5-23.

Frame, J.E., 1912.
A Critical and Exegetical Commentary on the Epistles of St. Paul to the Thessalonians. (ICC) Edinburgh, 1912.

Francis, F.O., 1970.
"The Form and Function of the Opening and Closing Paragraphs of James and I John," **ZNW** 61 (1970) 110-26.

Franck, E., 1985.
Revelation Taught. The Paraclete in the Gospel of John. (ConBNT, 14) Malmö, 1985.

Frend, W.H.C., 1965.
Martyrdom and Persecution in the Early Church. A study of a Conflict from the Maccabees to Donatus. Oxford, 1965.

Friedrich, G., 1964.
"$\varepsilon\dot{\upsilon}\alpha\gamma\gamma\acute{\varepsilon}\lambda\iota o\nu$," **TDNT** 2 (1964) 721-35.

----------, 1973.
"1. Thessalonicher 5,1-11, der apologetische Einschub eines Späteren," **ZTK** 70 (1973) 288-315.

----------, 1976.
"Der erste Brief an die Thessalonicher," **Die Briefe an die Galater, Epheser, Philipper, Kolosser, Thessalonicher und Philemon.** Trans. and comm. by J. Becker, H. Conzelmann, and G. Friedrich. (NTD, 8) Göttingen, 1976.

Funk, R.W., 1966.
Language, Hermeneutic, and Word of God. The Problem of Language in the New Testament and Contemporary Theology. New York - London, 1966.

----------, 1967.
"The Apostolic <<Parousia>>. Form and Significance," **Christian History and Interpretation: Studies Presented to John Knox.** Ed. by W.R. Farmer, et al. Cambridge, Eng., 1967, 249-68.

Furnish, V.P., 1968.
Theology and Ethics in Paul. Nashville and New York, 1968.

Gaster, T.H., 1976.
See **The Dead Sea Scriptures** under Texts and Translations.

Gibbs, J.M., 1977-78.
"Canon Cuming's 'Service-Endings in the Epistles'. A Rejoinder," **NTS** 24 (1977-78) 545-7.

Gillman, J., 1985.
"Signals of Transformation in 1 Thessalonians 4:13-18," **CBQ** 47 (1985) 263-81.

Giraudo, C., 1981.
La Struttura Letteraria Della Preghiera Eucaristica. Saggio sulla genesi letteraria di una forma. (Analecta Biblica. Investigationes Scientificæ in Res Biblicas, 92) Rome, 1981.

Goldsmith, D., 1968.
"Acts 13:33-37: A Pesher on II Samuel 7," **JBL** 87 (1968) 321-24.

Goldstein, J.A., 1968.
The Letters of Demosthenes. New York and London, 1968.

Graumann, C.F., 1984.
"Wundt - Mead - Bühler. Zur Sozialität und Sprachlichkeit menschlichen Handelns," **Karl Bühlers Axiomatik.** Fünfzig Jahre Axiomatik der Sprachwissenschaften. Ed. by C.F. Graumann and T. Herrmann. Frankfurt am Main, 1984, 217-47.

Gregory, C.R., 1909.
Einleitung in das Neue Testament. Leipzig, 1909.

Grice, H.P., 1975.
"Logic and Conversation," **Syntax and Semantics. Vol. 3: Speech Acts.** Ed. by P. Cole and J.L. Morgan. New York, 1975, 41-58.

Grosse, E.U., 1976.
Text und Kommunikation. Eine linguistische Einführung in die Functionen der Texte. Stuttgart, 1976.

Grundmann, W., 1971.
"στήκω, ἵστημι," **TDNT** 7 (1971) 636-53.

Gülich, E., 1970.
Makrosyntax der Gliederungssignale im gesprochenen Französisch. München, 1970.

Gülich, E., Kl. Heger and W. Raible, 1979.
Linguistische Textanalyse. Überlegungen zur Gliederung von Texten. (Papiere zur Textlinguistik/Papers in Textlinguistics, 8) 2nd ed. (1st ed., 1974) Hamburg, 1979.

Gülich, E., and W. Raible, 1977.
Linguistische Textmodelle. Grundlagen und Möglichkeiten. (UTB, 130) München, 1977.

----------, 1977a.
"Überlegungen zu einer makrostrukturellen Textanalyse: J. Thurber, The Lover and his Lass," **Grammars and Descriptions.** Studies in Text Theory and Text Analysis. Ed. by T. van Dijk and J.S. Petöfi. (Research in Text Theory, 1) Berlin, 1977, 132-75. (=Gülich/Heger/Raible, 1979, 73-149)

Guthrie, D., 1961.
New Testament Introduction. The Pauline Epistles. London, 1961.

Güttgemanns, E., 1976.
"Generative Poetics," **Semeia** 6 (1976) 1-181.

Hallbäck, G., 1980.
"Teksten mellem betydning og virkelighed. Om forholdet mellem strukturel analyse og historisk kritik," **DTT** 43 (1980) 251-70.

Halliday, M.A.K., 1973.
Explorations in the Functions of Language. London, 1973.

Halloran, S.M., 1976.
"Tradition and Theory in Rhetoric," **Quarterly Journal of Speech** 62 (1976) 234-41.

Harder, G., 1936.
Paulus und das Gebet. (NTF) Gütersloh, 1936.

Hardmeier, Ch., 1978.
Texttheorie und biblische Exegese. zur rhetorischen Funktion der Trauermetaphorik in der Prophetie. (BEvT, 79) München, 1978.

Harnish, W., 1973.
Eschatologische Existenz. Ein exegetischer Beitrag zum Sachanliegen von 1 Thessalonicher 4, 13-5,11. (FRLANT, 110) Göttingen, 1973.

Harris, R., 1898.
"A Study in Letter-Writing," **The Expositor,** 5th ser., 8 (1898) 161-80.

Hartman, L., 1963-64.
"Davids son. Apropå Acta 13, 16-41," **SEÅ** 28-29 (1963-64) 117-34.

----------, 1966.
Prophecy Interpreted. The Formation of some Jewish Apocalyptic Texts and of the Eschatological Discourse. Mark 13 Par. (ConBNT, 1) Lund, 1966.

----------, 1979.
Asking for a Meaning. A Study of 1 Enoch 1-5. (ConBNT, 12) Lund, 1979.

----------, 1979a.
"Att förstå en nytestamentlig text. Undersökningsmetoder och tolkningsresultat," **SEÅ** 44 (1979) 115-21.
----------, 1980.
"Bundesideologie in und hinter einigen paulinischen Texten," **Die paulinische Literatur und Theologie. The Pauline Literature and Theology.** Ed. by S. Pedersen. Århus and Göttingen, 1980, 103-18.
----------, 1983.
"Survey of the Problem of Apocalyptic Genre," **Apocalypticism in the Mediterranean World and the Near East.** Ed. by D. Hellholm. (Proceedings of the International Colloquium on Apocalypticism, Uppsala, Aug. 12-17, 1979) Tübingen, 1983, 329-43.
----------, 1985.
Kolosserbrevet. (Kommentar till Nya Testamentet, 12) Uppsala, 1985.
----------, 1986.
"On Reading Others' Letters," **Christians among Jews and Gentiles.** (FS for K. Stendahl) Ed. by G.W.E. Nickelsburg and G.W. MacRae. Philadelphia, 1986, 137-46.

Harweg, R., 1980.
"Meta-assertorische, Meta-propositionale und Meta-ontologische Aussagen. Ein Beitrag zur Typo- und Textologie Metakommunikativer Rede," **Folia Linguistica** 14 (1980) 283-328.

Hellholm, D., 1980.
Das Visionenbuch des Hermas als Apokalypse. Formgeschichtliche und texttheoretische Studien zu einer literarischen Gattung. Vol. 1: Methodologische Vorüberlegungen und makrostrukturelle Textanalyse. (ConBNT, 13:1) Lund, 1980.
----------, 1986.
"The Problem of Apocalyptic Genre and the Apocalypse of John," **Semeia** 36 (1986) 13-64. (A previous version appeared in **Society of Biblical Literature 1982 Seminar Papers.** Ed. by K.H. Richards. Chico, Calif., 1982, 157-98)
----------, 1986-87.
"En textgrammatisk konstruktion i Matteusevangeliet," **SEÅ** 51-52 (1986-87) 80-89.

Hempfer, Kl.W., 1973.
Gattungstheorie. Information und Synthese. (UTB, 133) München, 1973.

Henneken, B., 1969.
Verkündigung und Prophetie im 1. Thessalonicherbrief. (SBS, 29) Stuttgart, 1969.

Hernandi, P., 1976.
"Literary Theory: A Compass for Critics," **Critical Inquiry** 3 (1976) 369-86.

Hester, J.D., 1984.
"The Rhetorical Structure of Galations 1:11-2:14," **JBL** 103 (1984) 223-33.

Hieatt, C.B., 1975.
"Envelope Patterns and the Structure of **Beowulf**," **English Studies in Canada** 1 (1975) 249-65.

Hinks, D.A.G., 1936.
"Tria Genera Causarum," **The Classical Quarterly** 30 (1936) 170-76.

Hirsch, E.D., 1967.
Validity in Interpretation. New Haven, Conn., 1967.
----------, 1975.
"Current Issues in Theory of Interpretation," **JR** 55 (1975) 298-312.

Hoek, L.H., 1981.
> La marque du titre. Dispositifs sémiotiques d'une pratique textuelle. (Approaches to Semiotics, 60) The Hague - New York, 1981.

Hoey, M., 1983.
> On the Surface of Discourse. London, 1983.

Holmberg, B., 1978.
> Paul and Power. The Structure of Authority in the Primitive Church as Reflected in the Pauline Epistles. (ConBNT, 11) Lund, 1978.

Holm-Nielsen, S., 1960.
> Hodayot. Psalms from Qumran. (Acta Theologica Danica, 2) Aarhus, 1960.

Holtz, T., 1986.
> Der Erste Brief an die Thessalonicher. (EKKNT, 13) Zürich - Neykirchen-Vluyn, 1986.

Horbury, W., 1982.
> "1 Thessalonians ii. 3 as Rebutting the Charge of False Prophecy," **JTS** 33 (1982) 492-508.

Hübner, H., 1984.
> "Der Galaterbrief und das Verhältnis von Antiker Rhetorik und Epistolographie," **TLZ** 109 (1984) 241-50.

Hughes, F.W., 1983.
> The Literary Rhetoric of II Thessalonians. (Unpub. Diss., Northwestern University) 1983.

Hultgård, A., 1981.
> L'eschatologie des Testaments des Douze Patriarches. II: Composition de l'ouvrage; textes et traductions. (Acta Universitatis Upsaliensis, Historia Religionum, 7) Stockholm, 1981.

Hunter, A.M., 1961.
> Paul and His Predecessors. 2nd ed. (1st ed., 1940) London, 1961.

Hurd, J.C., 1965.
> The Origin of I Corinthians. London, 1965.

----------, 1972.
> "Concerning the Structure of 1 Thessalonians," (Unpublished paper presented at the SBL Annual Meeting, Los Angeles, Sept. 1-5, 1972) 1-49.

----------, 1976.
> "First Letter to the Thessalonians," **IDBSup** (1976) 900.

Husserl, E., 1970.
> "Zur Logik der Zeichen (Semiotik)," E. Husserl, Philosophie der Arithmetik. Logische und psychologische Untersuchungen. Mit ergänzenden Texten (1890-1901). Ed. by L. Eley. (Husserliana. Gesammelte Werke, 12) The Hague, 1970, 340-73.

Hyldahl, N., 1972-73.
> "Jesus og jøderne ifølge 1 Tess 2,14-16," **SEÅ** 37-38 (1972-73) 238-54.

----------, 1980.
> "Auferstehung Christi, Auferstehung der Toten (1 Thess 4,13-18)," **Die paulinische Literatur und Theologie. The Pauline Literature and Theology.** Ed. by S. Pedersen. Århus and Göttingen, 1980, 119-35.

Hymes, D.H., 1968.
> "The Ethnography of Speaking," **Readings in the Sociology of Language.** Ed. J.A. Fishman. The Hague and Paris, 1968, 99-138.

Innis, R.E., 1982.
  Karl Bühler: Semiotic foundations of language theory. (Topics in Contemporary Semiotics) New York, 1982.
Iser, W., 1972.
  "The Reading Process: A Phenomenological Approach," **New Literary History** 3 (1972) 279-99. (=Iser, 1974, 274-94)
----------, 1974.
  The Implied Reader: Patterns of Communication in Prose Fiction from Bunyan to Beckett. Baltimore and London, 1974.
Jakobson, R., 1960.
  "Closing Statement: Linguistics and Poetics," **Style in Language.** Ed. by T.A. Sebeok. Cambridge, Mass., 1960, 350-77.
Jannaris, A.N., 1898.
  "Misreadings and Misrenderings in the New Testament," **The Expositor,** 5th ser., 8 (1898) 429-31.
Jaubert, A., 1963.
  La notion d'alliance dans le judaisme aux abords de l'ère chrétienne. (Patristica Sorbonensia, 6) Paris, 1963.
Jenny, L., 1976.
  "La stratégie de la forme," **Poetique** 7 (1976) 257-81.
Jeremias, J., 1958.
  "Chiasmus in den Paulusbriefen," **ZNW** 49 (1958) 145-56.
Jewett, R., 1969.
  "The Form and Function of the Homiletic Benediction," **ATR** 51 (1969) 18-34.
----------, 1972.
  "Enthusiastic Radicalism and the Thessalonian Correspondence," **Society of Biblical Literature 1972 Proceedings.** Vol. 1. Ed. by L.C. McGaughy, 1972, 181-245.
----------, 1984.
  "The Thessalonian Church as a Millenarian Movement," (Unpublished paper presented at the SBL Annual Meeting, Chicago, Dec. 8-11, 1984) 1-53.
----------, 1986.
  The Thessalonian Correspondence. Pauline Rhetoric and Millinarian Piety. (Foundations and Facets: New Testament) Philadelphia, 1986. (Unfortunately became available to me after my book was already in the press)
de Jonge, M., 1959.
  "The Testaments of the Twelve Patriarchs and the New Testament," **SE** 1 (1959) 546-56.
----------, 1980.
  "The Main Issues in the Study of the Testaments of the Twelve Patriarchs," **NTS** 26 (1980-81) 508-24.
Judge, E.A., 1980.
  "The Social Identity of the First Christians: A Question of Method in Religious History," **JRH** 20 (1980) 201-17.
Jülicher, D.A., 1931.
  Einleitung in das Neue Testament. (Grundriss der Theologischen Wissenschaften, 7) Tübingen, 1931.
Kallmeyer et al., 1974.
  Lektürekolleg zur Textlinguistik. Band 1: Einführung. Band 2: Reader. Frankfurt am Main, 1974.

Kassel, R., 1958.
>   Untersuchungen zur griechischen und römischen Konsolationsliteratur. (Zetemata, 18) München, 1958.

Kennedy, G.A., 1963.
>   The Art of Persuasion in Greece. Princeton, 1963.

----------, 1980.
>   Classical Rhetoric and Its Christian and Secular Tradition from Ancient to Modern Times. London, 1980.

----------, 1984.
>   New Testament Interpretation through Rhetorical Criticism. Chapel Hill and London, 1984.

Kieffer, R., 1972.
>   Essais de méthodologie néo-testamentaire. (ConBNT, 4) Lund, 1972.

Kilpatrick, 1958.
>   See Η ΚΑΙΝΗ ΔΙΑΘΗΚΗ under Texts and Translations.

Kinneavy, J.L., 1971.
>   A Theory of Discourse. The Aims of Discourse. Englewood Cliffs, N.J., 1971.

Kittang, A., 1975.
>   Litteraturkritiske problem. Teorie og Analyse. Bergen, 1975.

Klijn, A.F.J., 1980.
>   An Introduction to the New Testament. Trans. by M. van der Vathorst-Smit. Rev. ed. (1st ed., 1967) Leiden, 1980.

Knierim, R., 1973.
>   "Old Testament Form Criticism Reconsidered," Int 27 (1973) 435-68.

Knopf, R., H. Lietzmann, and H. Weinel, 1949.
>   Einführung in das Neue Testament. (Die Theologie in Abriss, 2) Berlin, 1949.

Koerner, K., 1984.
>   "Karl Bühler's Theory of Language and Ferdinand de Saussure's Cours," Lingua 62 (1984) 3-24.

Koester, H., 1979.
>   "I Thessalonians. Experiment in Christian Writing," Continuity and Discontinuity in Church History. (FS for G.H. Williams) Ed. by F.F. Church and T. George. (Studies in the History of Christian Thought, 19) Leiden, 1979, 33-44.

----------, 1982.
>   Introduction to the New Testament. Volume Two: History and Literature of Early Christianity. (Hermeneia: Foundations and Facets) Philadelphia - New York, 1982.

Koskenniemi, H., 1956.
>   Studien zur Idee und Phraseologie des griechischen Briefes bis 400 n. Chr. (Annales Academiæ Scientiarum Fennicæ, Ser. B., 102,2) Helsinki, 1956.

Kubczak, H., 1984.
>   "Bühlers Symptomfunktion," Zeitschrift für Romanische Philologie 100 (1984) 1-25.

Kümmel, W.G., 1962.
>   "Das literarische und geschichtliche Problem des ersten Thessalonicherbriefes," Neotestamentica et Patristica. FS for O. Cullmann. (NovTSup, 6) Leiden, 1962, 213-27.

----------, 1973.
>   Einleitung in das Neue Testament. 17th ed. (Completely rev. ed. of the Einleitung in das Neue Testament by P. Feine and J. Behm) Heidelberg, 1973. (ET: Introduction to the New Testament. Trans. by H.C. Kee. Rev. ed. (1st ed., 1966) Nashville, 1975)

Lamarche, P., 1975.
"Structure de l'épitre aux Colossiens," **Bib** 56 (1975) 453-63.
Lategan, B.C., 1984.
"Current issues in the hermeneutical debate," **Neot** 18 (1984) 1-17.
----------, 1985.
"Reference: Reception, Redescription and Reality," **Text and Reality**. Aspects of Reference in Biblical Texts. By B.C. Lategan and W.S. Vorster. (SBL Semeia Studies) Philadelphia and Atlanta, 1985, 67-93.
Latte, K., 1941.
"Phyle," **PRE** 20 (1941) 994-1011.
Laub, F., 1973.
Eschatologische Verkündigung und Lebensgestaltung nach Paulus. Eine Untersuchung zum Wirken des Apostels beim Aufbau der Gemeinde in Thessalonike. (BU, 10) München, 1973.
Lausberg, H., 1973.
Handbuch der Literarischen Rhetorik. Eine Grundlegung der Literaturwissenschaft. 2nd ed. (1st ed., 1960) München, 1973.
----------, 1979.
Elemente der Literarischen Rhetorik. Eine Einführung für Studierende der klassischen, romanischen, englischen und deutschen Philologie. 6th ed. (1st ed., 1963) München, 1979.
Lee, R., and C. Lee, 1975.
"An Analysis of the Larger Semantic Units of 1 Thessalonians," **Notes on Translation** 56 (1975) 28-42.
Leech, G.N., 1983.
Principles of Pragmatics. (LLL, 30) London, 1983.
Lichtenstein, M.H., 1982.
"Chiasm and Symmetry in Proverbs 31," **CBQ** 44 (1982) 202-11.
Lightfoot, J.B., 1904.
Notes on Epistles of St Paul from Unpublished Commentaries. London, 1904.
Lohfink, G., 1971.
Die Himmelfahrt Jesu. Untersuchungen zu den Himmelfahrts- und Erhöhungstexten bei Lukas. (SANT, 26) München, 1971.
Lohse, 1971.
See **Die Texte aus Qumran** under Texts and Translations.
Longenecker, R.N., 1984-85.
"The Nature of Paul's Early Eschatology," NTS 31 (1984-85) 85-95.
Louw, J.P., 1973.
"Discourse Analysis and the Greek New Testament," **BT** 24 (1973) 101-18.
----------, 1982.
Semantics of New Testament Greek. (SBL Semeia Studies) Philadelphia and Chico, Calif., 1982.
----------, 1984.
"Primary and secondary reading of a text," **Neot** 18 (1984) 18-25.
Lüdemann, G., 1983.
Paulus und das Judentum. (Theologische Existenz heute, 215) München, 1983.
----------, 1984.
Paul, Apostle to the Gentiles. Studies in Chronology. Trans. by F.S. Jones. Philadelphia, 1984.
Lund, N.W., 1942.
Chiasmus in the New Testament. A Study in Formgeschichte. Chapel Hill, N.C., 1942.

Lütgert, W., 1909.
    Die Vollkommenen in Philippi und die Enthusiasten in Thessalonich. (BFCT, 12.6) Gütersloh, 1909.
Luz, U., 1968.
    Das Geschichtsverständnis des Paulus. (BEvT, 49) München, 1968.
Lyons, G., 1985.
    Pauline Autobiography. Toward a New Understanding. (SBLDS) Atlanta, 1985.
Magonet, J., 1982.
    "Some Concentric Structures in Psalms," **HeyJ** 23 (1982) 365-76.
Maier, 1960.
    See **Die Texte vom Toten Meer** under Texts and Translations.
Malatesta, E., 1973.
    The Epistles of St. John. Greek Text and English Translation Schematically Arranged. Rome, 1973.
Malbon, E.S., 1983.
    "<<No Need to Have Any One Write>>? A Structural Exegesis of 1 Thessalonians," **Semeia** 26 (1983) 57-83.
Malherbe, A.J., 1970.
    "<<Gentle as a Nurse>>.The Cynic Background to 1 Thess ii," **NovT** 12 (1970) 203-17.
----------, 1977.
    Social Aspects of Early Christianity. Baton Rouge.
----------, 1977a.
    See **The Cynic Epistles** under Texts and Translations.
----------, 1983.
    "Exhortation in First Thessalonians," **NovT** 25 (1983) 238-56.
Malinowski, B., 1953.
    "The Problem of Meaning in Primitive Languages," **The Meaning of Meaning.** Ed. by C.K. Ogden and I.A. Richards. 9th ed. (1st ed. 1923) New York and London, 1953, 296-336.
Marshall, I.H., 1983.
    1 and 2 Thessalonians. (NCBC) Grand Rapids, Mich. - London, 1983.
Martin, R.M., 1959.
    Toward a Systematic Pragmatics. (Studies in Logic) Amsterdam, 1959.
Marxsen, W., 1963.
    Einleitung in das Neue Testament. Eine Einführung in ihre Probleme. Gütersloh, 1963.
----------, 1969.
    "Auslegung von 1 Thess 4,13-18," **ZTK** 66 (1969) 22-37.
Maskalew, W., 1982.
    Formular Language and Poetic Design in the Aeneid. (Mnemosyne. Bibleotheca Classica Batava, 73) Leiden, 1982.
Masson, C., 1957.
    Les Deux Épitres de Saint Paul aux Thessaloniciens. (CNT, 11a) Neuchâtel and Paris, 1957.
McKnight, E.V., 1985.
    The Bible and the Reader. An Introduction to Literary Criticism. Philadelphia, 1985.
McNeile, A.H., 1953.
    An Introduction to the Study of the New Testament. Oxford, 1953.

Mearns, C.L., 1980-81.
"Early Eschatological Development in Paul. The Evidence of I and II Thess," **NTS** 27 (1980-81) 137-57.

Meeks, W.A., 1983.
"Social Functions of Apocalyptic Language in Pauline Christianity," **Apocalypticism in the Mediterranean World and the Near East.** Ed. by D. Hellholm. (Proceedings of the International Colloquium on Apocalypticism, Uppsala, Aug. 12-17, 1979) Tübingen, 1983, 687-705.

----------, 1983a.
The First Urban Christians. The Social World of the Apostle Paul. New Haven, Conn., and London, 1983.

Meinertz, M., 1950.
Einleitung in das Neue Testament. 5th ed. (1st ed. by A. Schaefer, 1898) Paderborn, 1950.

Metzger, B.M., 1964.
The Text of the New Testament. Its Transmission, Corruption, and Restoration. New York and London, 1964.

----------, 1971.
A Textual Commentary on the Greek New Testament. A Companion Volume to the United Bible Societies' Greek New Testament (third edition). Stuttgart, 1971.

Miller, G.R., 1980.
"On Being Persuaded: Some Basic Distinctions," **Persuasion: New Directions in Theory and Research.** Ed. by M.E. Roloff and G.R. Miller. (Sage Annual Reviews of Communication Research, 8) Beverly Hills and London, 1980, 11-28.

Milligan, G., 1908.
St Paul's Epistles to the Thessalonians. The Greek Text with Introduction and Notes. London, 1908.

Moffatt, J., 1910.
The First and Second Epistles of Paul the Apostle to the Thessalonians. (EGT, Vol. IV) London, 1910.

Morris, Ch.W., 1938.
Foundations of the Theory of Signs. (International Encyclopedia of Unified Science) Chicago, 1938.

Morris, L., 1984.
The Epistles of Paul to the Thessalonians. An Introduction and Commentary. 3rd ed. (1st ed., 1956) Leicester - Grand Rapids, Mich., 1984.

Moule, C.F.D., 1959.
An Idiom Book of New Testament Greek. 2nd ed. (1st ed., 1953) Cambridge, Eng., 1959.

Moulton, J.H., 1908.
A Grammar of New Testament Greek. Vol. I. Prolegomena. 3rd ed. (1st ed., 1906) Edinburgh, 1908.

Moulton, J.H., and N. Turner, 1963.
A Grammar of New Testament Greek. Vol. III. Syntax. By N. Turner. Edinburgh, 1963.

Mullins, T.Y., 1965.
"Disclosure, A Literary Form in the New Testament," **NovT** 7 (1965) 44-50.

----------, 1968.
"Greeting as a New Testament Form," **JBL** 87 (1968) 418-26.

----------, 1972.
"Formulas in New Testament Epistles," **JBL** 91 (1972) 380-90.

----------, 1973.
> "Visit Talk in New Testament Letters," **CBQ** 35 (1973) 350-58.

Myres, J.L., 1953.
> **Herodotus, Father of History.** Oxford, 1953.

Nestle/Aland, 1963, 1979.
> See **Novum Testamentum Graece** under Texts and Translations.

Nida, E.A., 1964.
> **Toward a Science of Translating.** Leiden, 1964.

Nida, E.A., and W.D. Reyburn, 1981.
> **Meaning across Cultures.** (American Society of Missiology Series, 4) Maryknoll, 1981.

Nida, E.A., and Ch.R. Taber, 1969.
> **The Theory and Practice of Translation.** (Helps for Translators, 8) Leiden, 1969.

Niel, W., 1950.
> **The Epistle of Paul to the Thessalonians.** (MNTC) London, 1950.

Niles, J.D., 1973.
> "Ring-Composition in La Chanson de Roland and La Chançun de Williame," **Olifant** 1 (1973) 4-12.

----------, 1979.
> "On the Design of the **Hymn to Delian Apollo**," The Classical Journal 75 (1979) 36-9.

----------, 1979a.
> "Ring Composition and the Structure of **Beowulf**," Publications of the Modern Language Association 94 (1979) 924-35.

Nock, A.D., 1933.
> **Conversion.** The Old and the New in Religion from Alexander the Great to Augustine of Hippo. London - New York, 1933.

O'Brien, P.T., 1977.
> **Introductory Thanksgivings in the Letters of Paul.** (NovTSup, 49) Leiden, 1977.

Oepke, A., 1953.
> **Die Briefe an die Thessalonicher.** (NTD, 8) Göttingen, 1953.

Okeke, G.E., 1980-81.
> "I Thess ii. 13-16. The Fate of the Unbelieving Jews," **NTS** 27 (1980-81) 127-36.

Olsson, B., 1974.
> **Structure and Meaning in the Fourth Gospel.** A Text-Linguistic Analysis of John 2:1-11 and 4:1-42. (ConBNT, 6) Lund, 1974.

----------, 1985.
> "A Decade of Text-Linguistic Analyses of Biblical Texts at Uppsala," **ST** 39 (1985) 107-26.

----------, 1986.
> "Structural Analyses in Handbooks for Translators," **BT** 37 (1986) 117-27.

van Otterlo, W.A.A., 1944.
> **Untersuchungen über Begriff, Anwendung und Entstehung der griechischen Ringkomposition.** (Mededelingen der Nederlandsche Akademie van Wetenschappen, Afdeling Letterkunde, n.s. 7, 3) Amsterdam, 1944.

Partridge, J.G., 1982.
> **Semantic, Pragmatic and Syntactic Correlates.** An Analysis of Performative Verbs based on English Data. (Tübinger Beiträge zur Linguistik, 143) Tübingen, 182.

Patte, D., 1976.
> What is Structural Exegesis? (Guides to Biblical Scholarship, New Testament Series) Philadelphia, 1976.

----------, 1983.
> "Method for a Structural Exegesis of Didactic Discourse. Analysis of 1 Thessalonians," Semeia 26 (1983) 85-129.

----------, 1983a.
> Paul's Faith and the Power of the Gospel. A Structural Introduction to the Pauline Letters," Philadelphia, 1983.

Pearson, B.A., 1971.
> "1 Thessalonians 2:13-16: A Deutero-Pauline Interpolation," **HTR** 64 (1971) 79-94.

Perdue, L.G., 1981.
> "Paraenesis and the Epistle of James," **ZNW** 72 (1981) 241-56.

Perelman, Ch., and L. Olbrechts-Tyteca, 1969. **The New Rhetoric: A Treatise on Argumentation.** Trans. by J. Wilkens and P. Weaver from the 1st French ed. Notre Dame and London, 1969.

----------, 1970.
> La Nouvelle Rhétorique. Traité de l'Argumentation. 2nd ed. (1st ed., 1958) Paris, 1970.

Pesch, R., 1984.
> **Die Entdeckung des ältesten Paulus-Briefes. Paulus--neugesehen. Die Briefe an die Gemeinde der Thessalonicher.** Freiburg - Vienna, 1984.

Petersen, N.R., 1984.
> "The reader in the gospel," Neot 18 (1984) 38-51.

Piaget, J., 1954.
> **The Construction of Reality in the Child.** Trans. by M. Cook. New York, 1954.

du Plessis, J.G., 1984.
> "Some aspects of extralingual reality and the interpretation of texts," **Neot** 18 (1984) 80-93.

Plett, H.F., 1977.
> **Rhetorik.** Kritische Positionen zum Stand der Forschung. (Kritische Information, 50) München, 1977.

----------, 1979.
> Textwissenschaft und Textanalyse. Semiotik, Linguistik, Rhetorik. (UTB, 328) 2nd ed. (1st ed., 1975) Heidelberg, 1979.

----------, 1979a.
> **Einführung in die rhetorische Textanalyse.** 4th ed. (1st ed., 1971) Hamburg, 1979.

Plevnik, J., 1979.
> "1 Thess 5,1-11: Its Authenticity, Intention and Message," **Bib** 60 (1979) 71-90.

----------, 1984.
> "The Taking Up of the Faithful and the Resurrection of the Dead in 1 Thessalonians 4:13-18," **CBQ** 46 (1984) 274-83.

Plümacher, E., 1972.
> **Lukas als hellenistischer Schriftsteller.** Studien zur Apostelgeschichte. (SUNT, 9) Göttingen, 1972.

Pobee, J.S., 1985.
> **Persecution and Martyrdom in the Theology of Paul.** (JSNTSup, 6) Sheffield, 1985.

Quastoff, U.M., 1980.
> Erzählen in Gesprächen. Linguistische Untersuchungen zu Strukturen und Funktionen am Beispiel einer kommunikationsform des Alltags. (Kommunikation und Institution, 1) Tübingen, 1980.

Quinn, J.D., 1981.
> "Parenesis and the Pastoral Epistles," De la Torah au Messie. (FS for H. Cazelles) Ed. by M. Carrez, et al. Paris, 1981, 495-501.

Radday, Y.T., 1981.
> "Chiasmus in Hebrew Biblical Narrative," Chiasmus in Antiquity. Structures, Analyses, Exegesis. Ed. by J.W. Welch. Hildesheim, 1981.

Ragnarsson, P.-E., 1983.
> Thessalonikerbreven. (Kommentar till Nya Testamentet, 13) Stockholm, 1983.

Raible, W., 1972.
> Satz und Text. Untersuchungen zu vier romanischen Sprachen. (Beihefte zur Zeitschrift für Romanische Philologie, 132) Tübingen, 1972.

----------, 1980.
> "Was sind Gattungen? Eine Antwort aus semiotischer und textlinguistischer Sicht," Poetica 12 (1980) 320-49.

Reddick, R.J., 1986.
> "Textlinguistics, text theory, and language users," Word 37 (1986) 31-43.

Reese, J.M., 1980.
> "A Linguistic Approach to Paul's Exhortation in 1 Thess 3:13-5:11," Society of Biblical Literature 1980 Seminar Papers. Ed. by P.J. Achtemeier. Chico, Calif., 1980, 209-18.

Refshauge, E., 1971.
> "Literaerkritiske overvejelser til de to Thessalonikerbreve," DTT 34 (1971) 1-19.

Richards, I.A., 1965.
> The Philosophy of Rhétoric. New York, 1965.

Rigaux, B., 1956.
> Saint Paul: Les Épitres aux Thessaloniciens. (EBib) Paris and Gembloux, 1956.

----------, 1974-75.
> "Tradition et redaction dans 1 Th. v. 1-10," NTS 21 (1974-75) 318-40.

Robert, A., and A. Feuillet, 1959.
> Introduction à la Bible. Tome II. Nouveau Testament. Tournai, 1959.

Robertson, A.T., 1934.
> A Grammar of the Greek New Testament in the Light of Historical Research. Nashville, 1934.

Robinson, J.M., 1963.
> "The Historicality of Biblical Language," The Old Testament and Christian Faith. Essays by Rudolf Bultmann and Others. Ed. by B.W. Anderson. London, 1963, 124-58.

----------, 1964.
> "Die Hodajot-Formel in Gebet und Hymnus des Frühchristentums," Apophoreta (FS for E. Haenchen) Ed. by W. Eltester and F.H. Kettler. Berlin 1964.

Roetzel, C., 1972.
> "I Thess 5:12-28: A Case Study," Society of Biblical Literature 1972 Proceedings. Vol. II. Ed. by L.C. McGaughy, 1972, 367-83.

Roller, O., 1933.
> Das Formular der paulinischen Briefe. (BWANT, 4th ser., 6) Stuttgart, 1933.

Roloff, M., 1985.
"Zur Kontaktfunktion der sprachlichen Kommunikation," **Zeitschrift für Phonetik, Sprachwissenschaft und Kommunikationsforschung** 38 (1985) 239-50.
Rosenfield, L.W., 1980.
"The Practical Celebration of Epideictic," **Rhetoric in Transition: Studies in the Nature and Uses of Rhetoric**. Ed. by E.E. White. University Park, Pa., and London, 1980, 131-55.
Ryan, M.-L., 1979.
"Toward a Competence Theory of Genre," **Poetics** 8 (1979) 307-37.
Sanders, J.T., 1962.
"The Transition from Opening Epistolary Thanksgiving to Body in the Letters of the Pauline Corpus," **JBL** 81 (1962) 348-62.
Sattler, W.M., 1947.
"Conceptions of Ethos in Ancient Rhetoric," **Speech Monographs** 14 (1947) 55-65.
Schenk, W., 1984.
Die Philipperbriefe des Paulus. Kommentar. Stuttgart - Mainz, 1984.
Schlier, H., 1972.
Der Apostel und seine Gemeinde. Auslegung des ersten Briefes an die Thessalonicher. Freiburn - Wien, 1972.
Schmidt, D., 1983.
"1 Thess 2:13-16: Linguistic Evidence for an Interpolation," **JBL** 102 (1983) 269-79.
Schmidt, S.J., 1971.
"Das kommunikative Handlungsspiel als Kategorie der Wirklichkeitskonstitution," **Grammatik, Kybernetik, Kommunikation**. (FS for A. Hoppe) Ed. by K.G. Schweisthal. Bonn, 1971, 215-27.
----------, 1976.
Texttheorie. Probleme einer Linguistik der sprachlichen Kommunikation. (UTB, 202) 2nd ed. (1st ed., 1973) München, 1976.
----------, 1980.
Grundriss der empirischen Literaturwissenschaft. Teilbd. 1: Der gesellschaftliche Handlungsbereich Literatur. Wiesbaden, 1980.
----------, 1982.
Grundriss der empirischen Literaturwissenschaft. Teilbd. 2: Zur Rekonstruktion literaturwissenschaftlicher Fragestellungen in einer empirischer Theorie der Literature. Wiesbaden, 1982.
Schmithals, W., 1964.
"Die Thessalonicherbriefe als Briefkomposition," **Zeit und Geschichte**. (FS for R. Bultmann) Ed. by E. Dinkler. Tübingen, 1964, 295-315.
----------, 1965.
Paulus und die Gnostiker. Untersuchungen zu den Kleinen Paulusbriefen. (TF, 35) Heidelberg - Bergstedt, 1965.
----------, 1972.
Paul and the Gnostics. Trans. by J.E. Steely. Nashville, 1972.
Schmitz, O., 1968.
"$\pi\alpha\rho\alpha\kappa\alpha\lambda\acute{\epsilon}\omega$ and $\pi\alpha\rho\acute{\alpha}\kappa\lambda\eta\sigma\iota\varsigma$ in the NT," **TWNT** 5 (1968) 793-99.
Schnackenburg, R., 1970.
"Apostles before and during Paul's Time," **Apostolic History and the Gospel**. (FS for F.F. Bruce) Ed. by W.W. Gasque and R.P. Martin. The Paternoster Press, 1970, 297-303.

Schrage, W., 1961.
> Die konkreten Einzelgebote in der paulinischen Paränese. Ein Beitrag zur neutestamentlichen Ethik. Gerd Mohn, 1961.

Schubert, P., 1939.
> Form and Function of the Pauline Thanksgivings. (BZNW, 20) Berlin, 1939.

Schweitzer, A., 1953.
> The Mysticism of Paul the Apostle. Trans. by W. Montgomery. 2nd ed. (1st ed., 1931) London, 1953.

Scott, R.L., 1980.
> "Intentionality in the Rhetorical Process," Rhetoric in Transition: Studies in the Nature and Uses of Rhetoric. Ed. E.E. White. University Park, Pa., and London, 1980, 39-60.

Scroggs, R., 1976.
> "Paul as Rhetorician," Jews, Greeks and Christians, Essays in Honor of W.D. Davies. Ed. by R. Hamerton-Kelly and R. Scroggs. Leiden, 1976, 271-98.

Searle, J.R., 1975.
> "Indirect Speech Acts," Syntax and Semantics. Vol.3: Speech Acts. Ed. by P. Cole and J.L. Morgan. New York, 1975, 59-82. (Republished in J.R. Searle, Expression and Meaning. Cambridge, Eng., 1979, 30-57)

----------, 1975a.
> "A Taxonomy of Illocutionary Acts," Language, Mind, and Knowledge. Ed. by K. Gunderson. Minneapolis, 1975, 334-69. (Republished in J.R. Searle, Expression and Meaning. Cambridge, Eng., 1979, 1-29)

Sellin, G., 1983-84.
> "Textlinguistische und Semiotische Erwagüngen zu Mk. 4.1:34," NTS 29 (1983-84) 508-30.

Sibinga, J.S., 1970.
> "A Study in I John," Studies in John. (FS for J.N. Sevenster; NovTSup, 24) Leiden, 1970, 194-208.

Sider, R.D.; 1973.
> "On Symmetrical Composition in Tertullian," JTS 24 (1973) 405-23.

Siegert, F., 1985.
> Argumentation bei Paulus gezeigt an Röm 9-11. (WUNT, 34) Tübingen, 1985.

Sloan, T.O., and Ch. Perelman, 1979.
> "Rhetoric," EncyBrMacr 15 (1979) 798-805.

Smith, R.F., 1981.
> "Chiasm in Sumero-Akkadian," Chiasmus in Antiquity. Structures, Analyses, Exegesis. Ed. by J.W. Welch. Hildesheim, 1981, 17-35.

Snyman, A.H., 1984.
> "Style and meaning in Romans 8:31-9," Neot 18 (1984) 94-103.

Spicq, C., 1956.
> "Les Thessaloniciens <<inquiets>> étaient-ils des paresseux?," ST 10 (1956) 1-13.

Spillner, B., 1977.
> "Das Interesse der Linguistik an Rhetorik. (Kritische Information, 50) München, 1977, 93-108.

Steen, A.H., 1938.
> "Les Clichés Épistolaires dans les Lettres sur Papyrus Grecque," Classica et Mediaevalia 1 (1938) 119-76.

Stubbs, M., 1983.
> Discourse Analysis. The Sociological Analysis of Natural Language. Oxford, 1983.

Suhl, A., 1975.
Paulus und seine Briefe. Ein Beitrag zur paulinischen Chronologie. (SNT, 11) Gütersloh, 1975.
Suleiman, S.R., 1980.
"Introduction. Varieties of Audience-Oriented Criticism," **The Reader in the Text. Essays on Audience and Interpretation.** Ed. by S.R. Suleiman and I Crosman. Princeton, 1980, 3-45.
Swetnam, J., 1972.
"Form and Content in Hebrews 1 - 6," **Bib** 53 (1972) 368-85.
----------, 1974.
"Form and Content in Hebrews 7 - 13," **Bib** 55 (1974) 333-48.
Sykytris, J., 1931.
"Epistolographie," **PRE** Supp. vol. 5 (1931) 185-220.
Theissen, G., 1974.
"Soziale Schichtung in der korinthischen Gemeinde: Ein Beitrag zur Soziologie des hellenistischen Urchristentums," **ZNW** 65 (1974) 232-72.
Thieme, K., 1963.
"Die Struktur des ersten Thessalonicher-Briefes," **Abraham unser Vater. Juden und Christen im Gespräch über die Bibel.** (FS for O. Michel) Ed. by O. Betz, M. Hengel, and P. Schmidt. (AGSU, 5) Leiden, 1963, 450-58.
Thiering, B., 1963.
"The Poetic Forms of the Hodayot," **JSS** 8 (1963) 189-209.
Thraede, Kl., 1968-69.
"Ursprünge und Formen des 'Heiligen Kusses' im Frühen Christentum," **Jahrbuch für Antike und Christentum** 11-12 (1968-69) 124-180.
----------, 1970.
Grundzüge griechisch-römischer Brieftopik. (Zetemata, 48) München, 1970.
Thrall, M.E., 1962.
Greek Particles in the New Testament. Linguistic and Exegetical Studies. (NTTS, 3) Leiden, 1962.
Thyen, H., 1955.
Der Stil der Jüdisch-Hellenistischen Homilie. (FRLANT, 47) Göttingen, 1955.
du Toit, H.C., 1984.
"Presuppositions of source and receptor," Neot 18 (1984) 52-65.
Traill, D.A., 1981.
"Ring-Composition in Catullus 64," **The Classical Journal** 76 (1981) 232-41.
Traugott, E.C., and M.L. Pratt, 1980.
Linguistics for Students of Literature. New York - Toronto, 1980.
Trench, R.C., 1880.
Synonyms of the New Testament. London, 1880.
van Unnik, W.C., 1960.
"La conception paulinienne de la nouvelle alliance," **Littérature et theologie pauliniennes.** Ed. by A. Deschamps et al. (RechBib, 5) Bruges and Paris, 1960, 109-26.
Vanhoye, A., 1974.
"Discussions sur la structure de l'Épitre aux Hébreux," **Bib** 55 (1974) 349-80.
----------, 1976.
La Structure Littéraire de l'Épitre aux Hebreux. (StudNeot, 1) 2nd ed. (1st ed., 1963) Paris and Bruges, 1976.
Vermes, 1962.
See **The Dead Sea Scrolls in English** under Texts and Translations.

Vielhauer, Ph., 1975.
>	**Geschichte der urchristlichen Literature.** Einleitung in das Neue Testament, die Apokryphen und die Apostolischen Väter. Berlin and New York, 1975.

de Villiers, P.G.R., 1984.
>	"The interpretation of a text in the light of its socio-cultural setting," **Neot** 18 (1984) 66-79.

Vorster, W.S., 1984.
>	"The historical paradigm - Its possibilities and limitations," **Neot** 18 (1984) 104-23.

Watson, F., 1986.
>	Review of Lüdemann (1984). **Theology** 89 (1986) 58-60.

Watson, W.G.E., 1981.
>	"Chiastic Patterns in Biblical Hebrew Poetry," **Chiasmus in Antiquity.** Structures, Analyses, Exegesis. Ed. by J.W. Welch. Hildesheim, 1981, 118-68.

Watzlawik, P., J.H. Beavin and D.D. Jackson, 1967.
>	**Pragmatics of Human Communication.** A Study of Interactional Patterns, Pathologies, and Paradoxes. New York, 1967.

Weimar, P., 1973.
>	"Formen früjüdischer Literatur. Eine Skizze," **Literatur und Religion des Früjudentums.** Eine Einführung. Ed. by J. Maier and J. Schreiner. Würzburg and Gerd Mohn, 1973, 123-62.

Welch, J.W., 1981.
>	"Chiasmus in Ancient Greek and Latin Literatures," **Chiasmus in Antiquity.** Structures, Analyses, Exegesis. Ed by J.W. Welch. Hildesheim, 1981, 250-68.

----------, 1981a.
>	"Chiasmus in the New Testament," **Chiasmus in Antiquity.** Structures, Analyses, Exegesis. Ed by J.W. Welch. Hildesheim, 1981, 211-49.

----------, 1981b.
>	"Chiasmus in Ugaritic," **Chiasmus in Antiquity.** Structures, Analyses, Exegesis. Ed by J.W. Welch. Hildesheim, 1981, 36-49.

----------, 1981c.
>	"Introduction," **Chiasmus in Antiquity.** Structures, Analyses, Exegesis. Ed. by J.W. Welch. Hildesheim, 1981, 9-16.

Wellek, R., and A. Warren, 1963.
>	**Theory of Literature.** 3rd ed. (1st ed., 1949) Penguin Books, 1963.

Wendland, P., 1905.
>	**Anaximenes von Lampsakos.** Studien zur ältesten Gechichte der Rhetorik. Berlin, 1905.

Werlich, E., 1979.
>	**Typologie der Texte.** Entwurf eines textlinguistischen Modells zur Grundlegung einer Textgrammatik. (UTB, 450) 2nd ed. (1st ed., 1975) Heidelberg, 1979.

----------, 1982.
>	**A Text Grammar of English.** (UTB, 597) 2nd ed. (1st ed., 1976) Heidelberg, 1982.

Westcott/Hort, 1885.
>	See **The New Testament in the Original Greek** under Texts and Translations.

White, E.E., 1980.
>	"Rhetoric as Historical Configuration," **Rhetoric in Transition: Studies in the Nature and Uses of Rhetoric.** Ed. by E.E. White. University Park, Pa, and London, 1980. 7-20.

White, J.L., 1972.
>   The Form and Function of the Body of the Greek Letter. A Study of the Letter-Body in the Non-Literary Papyri and in Paul the Apostle. (SBLDS, 2) Missoula, Mont., 1972.

----------, 1983.
>   "Saint Paul and the Apostolic Letter Tradition," **CBQ** 45 (1983) 433-44.

Whitman, C.H., 1958.
>   **Homer and the Heroic Tradition.** Cambridge, Mass., 1958.

Wienold, G., 1983.
>   "Narrative Texts and Models of Hierarchical and Sequential Structure," **Allgemeine Sprachwissenschaft, Sprachtypologie** und **Textlinguistik.** (FS for P. Hartmann) Ed. by M. Faust. Tübingen, 1983, 417-30.

Wikenhauser, A., and J. Schmid, 1973.
>   **Einleitung in das Neue Testament.** 6th ed. (1st ed., 1953) Freiburg - Wien, 1973.

Wiklander, B., 1984.
>   **Prophecy as Literature.** A Text-Linguistic and Rhetorical Approach to Isaiah 2-4. (ConBOT, 22) Malmö, 1984.

Wiles, G.P., 1974.
>   **Paul's Intercessory Prayers.** The Significance of the Intercessory Prayer Passages in the Letters of St Paul. (SNTSMS, 24) Cambridge, England, 1974.

Wilcke, H.-A., 1967.
>   **Das Problem eines messianischen Zwischenreichs bei Paulus.** (ATANT, 51) Stuttgart, 1967.

Wimsatt, W.K., and M. Beardsley, 1954.
>   **The Verbal Icon.** Lexington, 1954.

Wolbert, W., 1981.
>   **Ethische Argumentation und Paränese in 1 Kor 7.** (Moraltheologische Studien, 8) Düsseldorf, 1981.

Wörner, M.H., 1981.
>   "'Pathos' als Uberzeugungsmittel in der Rhetorik des Aristoteles," **Pathos, Affekt, Gefuhl.** Ed. by I. Craemer-Ruegenberg. München, 1981, 53-78.

----------, 1984.
>   "Selbstrepräsentation im Ethos des Redners. Ein Beitrag der aristotelischen Rhetorik zur Untersuchung der Grundlagen sprachlichen Handelns," **Zeitschrift für Sprachwissenschaft** 3 (1984) 43-64.

Wright, G.E., 1952.
>   **God Who Acts.** London, 1952.

Wuellner, W.H., 1976.
>   "Paul's Rhetoric of Argumentation in Romans: An Alternative to the Donfried-Karris Debate over Romens," **CBQ** 38 (1976) 330-51.

----------, 1978.
>   "Der Jakobusbrief im Licht der Rhetorik und Textpragmatik," **LB** 43 (1983) 5-66.

----------, 1979.
>   "Greek Rhetoric and Pauline Argumentation," **Early Christian Literature and the Classical Intellectual Tradition.** (FS for R.M. Grant) Ed. by W.R. Schoedel and R.L. Wilken. (Théologie Historique, 53) Paris, 1979, 177-88.

Zahn, Th., 1906.
>   **Einleitung in das Neue Testament.** Vol. I. 3rd ed. (1st ed., 1897-99) Leipzig, 1906.

AUTHOR INDEX

Aland et. al. ... 87, 131
Aschermann ... 184
Audet ... 68-69, 175, 183
Aune ... 105
Austin ... 68

Bahr ... 153
Bailey, J.W. ... 120, 130
Bailey, K. E. ... 145
Baltzer ... 177-178, 184
Bammel ... 104, 131
Bar-Efrat ... 145-147
Barr ... 127
Bartlett ... 145
Bauer ... 57, 87, 110
Baur ... 5, 53, 167
Beaugrande, de/Dressler ... 7-10, 23, 39, 147, 173, 175
Becker ... 5, 55, 184
Berger ... 21, 24, 38-39, 41-43, 71, 116-117, 158, 166, 175, 180, 182, 187
Best ... 3, 50, 52-54, 56-57, 65, 82-85, 87, 92, 95-97, 101-107, 110-111, 115-116, 120-121, 123-124, 127, 130, 132, 134, 136-142, 167-168
Betz, H.D. ... 34, 36, 41, 43, 117
Betz, O. ... 185
Bitzer ... 35, 39
Bjerkelund ... 4-5, 62-63, 69, 72-75, 112-113, 160
Black ... 21, 23, 41-42
Blass/Debrunner ... 60, 90, 105, 107
Bleich ... 18
Boers ... 4, 62-63, 69, 71, 94-95, 111, 168, 171, 188
Booth ... 22
Bornemann ... 55
Bornkamm ... 53, 170
Bradley ... 51, 63, 116
Braun ... 185
Breuer ... 8, 19, 36, 39
Brinker ... 13, 21, 30
Brinton ... 35
Broer ... 170
Brooks/Warren ... 35-36
Brown/Yule ... 7, 14, 19, 21, 52
Bruce ... 50
Brunt ... 116
Bühler ... 12-13
Bull ... 76

Bultmann ... 111, 180
Bünker ... 43-44, 117
Burgoon/Bettinghaus ... 37
Burke ... 36

Cadbury ... 51
Caffi ... 16
Cancik ... 117-118
Cavallin ... 55, 121-122, 125-126
Chadwick ... 104
Charolles ... 8
Chatman ... 22
Chevallier ... 145
Church ... 43
Collins ... 51, 58, 70, 87, 101-102, 104, 106, 114, 118-119, 121, 124, 127, 130, 169-170, 172, 175-176
Combrink ... 17-18
Conzelmann ... 60, 82
Conzelmann/Lindemann ... 55, 69
Cope ... 38
Coppens ... 170
Coseriu ... 14-15
Cuming ... 176

Davies ... 34, 178
Denis ... 53
Denniston ... 93, 145
Dibelius ... 53, 65, 70, 83, 85, 91, 94, 96, 115, 123, 134-135, 137, 139-140
Dibelius/Greeven ... 117
Dijk, van ... 7, 9, 14, 24-25, 28-29
Dijk, van/Petöfi ... 7
Dimter ... 14
Dobschütz ... 52-53, 55, 65, 83-85, 90-91, 94-95, 98, 101-107, 110-111, 115, 120, 127-128, 130, 132, 134-139, 141, 168
Dockhorn ... 36, 38
Doeve ... 180
Donfried ... 97, 114-115, 121, 131, 170
Doty ... 43, 61-64, 66-67, 110, 189
Dressler ... 7
Duncan ... 145

Eckart ... 172
Eco ... 18
Ellingworth/Nida ... 78, 89, 94-95, 100-102, 106, 111, 120
Enkvist ... 6, 39
Exler ... 61, 64

Fafner ... 34-38
Faw ... 3, 51
Findley ... 129
Fish ... 18
Fishbane ... 145
Follesdal/Walloe ... 19-20
Forestell ... 139
Fowler, A ... 173
Fowler, R.M. ... 22
Frame ... 4, 52-53, 55, 83, 89, 92, 94-95, 101, 106-108, 111, 115, 123, 127, 130, 132-133, 135, 137, 139, 141-142
Francis ... 70
Franck ... 91
Frend ... 131
Friedrich ... 55, 65, 83, 127, 138-139, 141, 170
Funk ... 4-5, 61-62, 64, 71, 168
Furnish ... 115

Gaster ... 165, 184
Gibbs ... 176
Gillman ... 119, 122
Giraudo ... 183
Goldsmith ... 180
Goldstein ... 43-44, 65, 159, 163
Graumann ... 13
Gregory ... 5, 167
Grice ... 23, 52
Grosse ... 13, 28-30
Grundmann ... 182
Gülich ... 25
Gülich/Raible ... 7, 16, 24-29, 31-32
Guthrie ... 3, 167
Güttgemanns ... 7

Hallbäck ... 17
Halliday ... 12, 14
Halloran ... 36
Harder ... 67
Hardmeier ... 7
Harnish ... 55, 115, 120-121, 124, 127-135
Harris ... 94
Hartman ... 17, 21, 42, 67, 122-123, 130, 175, 178-183, 187, 190
Harweg ... 16
Hellholm ... 7-11, 14, 20, 24, 26-28, 31-32, 42, 152-153
Hempfer ... 7, 15-16, 20
Henneken ... 53, 55, 91

Hernandi ... 15
Hester ... 44
Hieatt ... 145
Hinks ... 40-41
Hirsch ... 8, 18-19, 21
Hoek ... 60
Hoey ... 7
Holm-Nielsen ... 165
Holmberg ... 110, 137
Holtz ... 3, 55, 57, 84-85, 89-90, 92-93, 96-98, 107, 111, 114, 121, 130, 132, 136, 138-140, 167
Horbury ... 53
Hübner ... 34, 43-44
Hughes ... 44
Hultgård ... 177
Hunter ... 82
Hurd ... 3, 51, 56, 142, 147-148
Husserl ... 9
Hyldahl ... 5, 54, 56, 120-122, 124, 130-131
Hymes ... 12, 17, 19, 21

Innis ... 13
Iser ... 17, 22

Jakobson ... 12, 14-16
Jannaris ... 111
Jaubert ... 178
Jenny ... 173
Jeremias ... 145
Jewett ... 5-6, 53, 55, 115, 141, 159, 163, 167, 176
Jonge, de ... 177
Judge ... 50
Jülicher ... 5, 167

Kallmeyer et al. ... 7, 24
Kassel ... 165-166
Kennedy ... 5-6, 23, 34, 36-44, 46, 83, 90, 102, 114, 141, 146, 159, 163-164, 166-167, 177, 180
Kieffer ... 17, 20, 123
Kilpatrick ... 87, 131
Kinneavy ... 11-14, 17, 21, 23, 34, 36-38, 40
Kittang ... 19
Klijn ... 3, 55, 167
Knierim ... 6, 42, 188
Knopf/Lietzmann/Weinel ... 5, 167
Koerner ... 13

Koester ... 3-5, 63, 69, 114-116, 126, 128, 160, 167, 173, 182, 188
Koskenniemi ... 43, 60-61, 64-66, 68, 71, 81
Kubczak ... 13, 17
Kümmel ... 3, 65, 107, 172

Lamarche ... 145
Lategan ... 17-19, 21-22
Latte ... 98
Laub ... 133-135
Lausberg ... 23, 36, 40, 42, 44, 85, 89, 97, 115, 117, 128-129, 145, 164, 166-167
Lee/Lee ... 83, 86, 88-89, 97, 100, 107, 112, 118
Leech ... 14, 17, 19, 21-23, 52, 68, 74
Lichtenstein ... 145
Lightfoot ... 3, 65, 81, 83-84, 87, 89-90, 92, 94-96, 102-103, 105-108, 111, 120, 127, 132-133, 135-137, 139-140, 167
Lohfink ... 56, 122, 124
Lohse ... 165
Longenecker ... 111
Louw ... 7, 18-19, 21, 29, 136
Lüdemann ... 5, 50, 55, 119-124, 167, 170-171
Lund ... 145, 152
Lütgert ... 53, 55
Luz ... 55
Lyons ... 52, 54. 83, 89, 97, 158, 165, 167, 183

Magonet ... 145
Maier ... 165
Malatesta ... 145
Malbon ... 17
Malherbe ... 4, 51, 53, 63, 65, 85, 92-93, 114, 116-117, 126, 164-166, 174, 181, 186
Malinowski ... 15
Marshall ... 4, 89, 98, 175
Martin ... 13, 23
Marxsen ... 5, 50, 52, 55, 65, 78, 83, 94, 97-98, 101, 110-112, 114-115, 118, 121-122, 124, 127, 130, 132, 134-135, 137, 139, 142, 165, 167
Maskalew ... 145
Masson ... 3, 83, 91, 121, 127, 130, 135-139, 141, 167
McKnight ... 19-20
McNeile ... 3, 167
Mearns ... 56

Meeks ... 57, 96, 98, 126, 137
Meinertz ... 5, 167
Metzger ... 66, 114, 139, 146
Miller ... 35
Milligan ... 4, 53, 92, 96, 98, 106, 127, 130, 134, 137, 139
Moffat ... 4, 158, 165
Morris, Ch.W. ... 7
Morris, L. ... 101, 167
Moule ... 100, 106
Moulton ... 60
Moulton/Turner ... 90, 105
Mullins ... 62, 64, 71, 116, 120, 176
Myres ... 145

Nestle/Aland ... 87, 131
Nida ... 24
Nida/Reyburn ... 20
Nida/Tabor ... 24
Niel ... 55
Niles ... 145
Nock ... 114

O'Brian ... 67, 95
Oepke ... 55
Okeke ... 170
Olsson ... 7-8, 17, 24, 31, 39
Otterlo, van ... 145

Partridge ... 68, 74
Patte ... 17
Pearson ... 62, 94-95, 169, 171, 188
Perdue ... 117, 186
Perelman/Olbrechts-Tyteca ... 23, 36, 38, 40-41, 90-92, 97
Pesch ... 70, 169, 172
Petersen ... 18-19, 22
Piaget ... 19
Plessis, du ... 17, 22
Plett ... 7-11, 15, 18, 24, 36, 39, 44, 82, 89, 115, 129, 145
Plevnik ... 5, 56, 118, 122, 124-125, 127-128, 131-132, 134
Plümacher ... 51
Pobee ... 82, 96, 121

Quastoff ... 159
Quinn ... 115, 117

Radday ... 145
Ragnarsson ... 167
Raible ... 9, 25, 27

Reddick ... 19
Reese ... 120, 131, 133, 167
Refshauge ... 172
Richards ... 36
Rigaux ... 4, 49-51, 60, 65, 78, 81, 83-84, 87, 89-96, 98, 101-108, 110-116, 120-121, 125, 127, 130, 133-136, 139, 141, 168, 170, 181
Robert/Feuillet ... 3, 167
Robertson ... 60, 105-106
Robinson ... 68-69, 175, 183
Roetzel ... 136, 139
Roller ... 60-61, 64-65
Roloff ... 16
Rosenfield ... 40-41
Ryan ... 7

Sanders ... 61-62, 64, 178
Sattler ... 36-37
Schenk ... 7-8, 20, 60
Schlier ... 3, 107, 167
Schmidt, D. ... 171
Schmidt, S.J. ... 7, 18, 24
Schmithals ... 53, 55, 70, 141, 172
Schmitz ... 91
Schnackenburg ... 50
Schrage ... 116, 135
Schubert ... 4-5, 32, 61, 63, 67-69, 83, 111, 168, 175
Schweitzer ... 55
Scott ... 35
Scroggs ... 34
Searle ... 14, 74
Sellin ... 7
Sibinga ... 145
Sider ... 146-147
Siegert ... 90-92
Sloan/Perelman ... 23-24
Smith ... 145
Snyman ... 39
Spicq ... 142
Spillner ... 39
Steen ... 72-73
Stubbs ... 7, 16
Suhl ... 50, 172
Suleiman ... 22
Swetnam ... 145, 148
Sykytris ... 43

Theissen ... 51
Thieme ... 147
Thiering ... 145
Thraede ... 71, 176
Thrall ... 111-112
Thyen ... 180, 184
Toit, du ... 20
Traill ... 145
Traugott/Pratt ... 14, 76
Trench ... 127

Unnik, van ... 178

Vanhoye ... 145, 148
Vermes ... 165
Vielhauer ... 3, 50, 61, 65, 69, 107, 123, 135, 160, 188
Villiers, de ... 18-19, 21
Vorster ... 17-19, 21-22

Watson, F. ... 50
Watson, W.G.E. ... 145-146
Watzlawick/Beavin/Jackson ... 16
Weimar ... 184
Welch ... 145-147
Wellek/Warren ... 173
Wendland ... 44
Werlich ... 9, 21
Westcott/Hort ... 87, 131
Wette, de ... 128
White, E.E. ... 35
White, J.L. ... 4-5, 61-62, 64-65, 69, 111, 118
Whitman ... 145
Wienold ... 25
Wikenhauser/Schmid ... 3, 65, 167
Wiklander ... 7-8, 10, 19-20, 24, 36, 39
Wiles ... 65-67, 81, 108-109, 175-176
Wilke ... 55
Wimsatt/Beardsley ... 13
Wolbert ... 115, 117, 186
Wörner ... 37-38, 86
Wright ... 180
Wuellner ... 19, 34, 39, 41, 43, 63, 97

Zahn ... 3, 167

GREEK AND LATIN REFERENCES

Anaximenes
  Rhet ad Alex
    1434a,17-24 ... 115
    1436a,31-38 ... 44
    1436a,33-39 ... 45
    1437a,1 ff. ... 45
    1438a,3 ff. ... 45
    1438b,15-28 ... 45, 159
    1439a,7-10 ... 46
    1439a,20-40 ... 43
    1440b,13 ... 40
    1442b,28-32 ... 45, 159
    1442b,33 ff. ... 45
    1444b,21-30 ... 45

Aristotle
  Poet
    6.1 ... 51
    15.1 ... 51
    19.7 ... 51
    23.1 ... 51
    25.1 ... 51
    25.15 ... 51
  Rhet
    1.1.11 ... 38
    1.2.2 ... 89
    1.2.3 ff. ... 36-37
    1.2.8 ff. ... 38
    1.2.14 ... 90
    1.2.14 ff. ... 91
    1.3.1-5 ... 40
    2.1.5 ... 37
    2.1.7 ... 37
    2.1.8 ... 37
    2.1.9 ... 37
    2.4 ff. ... 37
    2.4.1 ... 37
    2.4.2 ff. ... 93
    2.11.1-7 ... 85
    2.18.1 ... 40
    2.21.2 ... 117
    2.21.3 ff. ... 117
    2.21.16 ... 117
    2.22.3 ... 89
    2.23.21 ... 90
    2.25.8 ff. ... 90
    3.6.9 ... 90
    3.13.1-4 ... 42
    3.13.4 ... 44
    3.14.4 ... 45
    3.14.5 ... 44
    3.14.6 ... 44
    3.14.7 ... 45
    3.14.12 ... 44
    3.15.1 ... 45
    3.16.5 ... 85
    3.16.8-10 ... 45
    3.16.11 ... 45, 166
    3.17.1 ff. ... 46
    3.17.5 ... 46
    3.17.16 ...85
    3.19.1 ... 46
    3.19.1 ff. ... 46
    3.19.6 ... 142

Cicero
  Fam
    15.16.2 ... 71
  Orat
    3.55.210 ... 165

Demetrius
  De eloc
    4.225 ... 43
    4.229 ... 43
    4.229-31 ... 43
    4.232 ... 43

Demosthenes
  Ep
    1.1-4 ... 163
    2.3 ... 127
    3.1-10 ... 159

Dio Chrysostom
  Orat
    17.2, 5 ... 186
    32 ... 164

Diogenes Leartius
  1.116 ... 51
  2.12 ... 51
  3.78 ... 51
  8.41 ... 51
  8.67 ... 51
  8.74 ... 51
  10.117 ... 51

Epictetus
  Dss
    1.18.21 ... 112
    1.30.5 ... 112
    2.1.8 ... 112
    2.8.15 ... 112
    2.14.9 ... 112

2.19.33 ... 112
3.24.88 ... 112
Isocrates
  Ad Nic
    40-41 ... 186
  Panath
    33 ... 51
    35 ... 51
    70 ... 51
    105 ... 51
    119 ... 51
    126 ... 51
    130 ... 51
    191 ... 51
  Panegy ... 40
    15 ... 51
    34 ... 51
    66 ... 51
    157 ... 51
Josephus
  Ant
    8.50-54 ... 70
  Bell
    2.390 ... 112
  Cont Ap
    1.47 ... 51
    1.57 ... 51

1.69 ... 51
1.145 ... 51
1.251 ... 51
1.279 ... 51
2.1 ... 51
2.199 ... 51
2.262 ... 51
2.267-8 ... 128
2.276 ... 51
2.287 ... 51
2.291 ... 51
Menander Rhetor
  2.9 ... 166
Pseudo Demetrius
  Ep typ
    5 ... 166
Quintilian
  Inst Orat
    10.1.47 ... 165
    11.3.153 ... 165
Seneca
  Ep
    13.15 ... 186
    94.21, 25 ... 186
Theon
  Progym
    3.117 ... 165

OLD TESTAMENT

Genesis
  27:28 ... 176
  48:15-16 ... 176
Exodus
  19:4-6 ... 182
  19:5 ... 177, 182
  19:6 ... 181
  19-34 ... 178
  25:8 ... 181
  29:45 ... 181
  34 ... 177
Leviticus
  26 ... 178
Deuteronomy
  1-4 ... 177
  1:6-4:40 ... 182
  3:21-22 ... 182

4:9-20 ... 182
4:32-40 ... 182
4:37 ... 181
7:6 ... 181
7:6 ff. ... 181
7:8 ... 182
10:1-12 ... 182
10:12 ... 177
18:22 ... 105
26:16-19 ... 181
28:9 ... 181
28:69-30:20 ... 177
29:2-8 ... 183
29:17-18 ... 181
30:2 ... 181
32 ... 178

Joshua
  23 ... 177
  23:3-5 ... 182
  23:6 ... 177
  24 ... 177
  24:2-17 ... 182
  24:3 ... 181
  24:8-13 ... 182
  24:14 ... 177
I Samual
  2:20 ... 176
  12 ... 177
  12:7 ff. ... 182
  12:13 ... 177
II Samual
  7:6-16 ... 180
  7:18-29 ... 183
I Kings
  8:23-53 ... 183
  8:56-61 ... 183
  8:57-61 ... 176
II Kings
  23:3 ... 182
II Chronicles
  30:18-19 ... 176
Ezra
  9 ... 178
Nehemiah
  9 ... 178
Psalms
  9 ... 175
  16:10 ... 180
  20 ... 176
  44 ... 183
  105:1-6 ... 183
  106 ... 175, 182
  106:1-5 ... 183
  106:47 ... 183
  111:1-5 ... 183
  116:12 ... 110
  122:7 ... 176
Isaiah
  55:3 ... 180
Jeremiah
  31 ... 178
  31:33 f. ... 181
Ezekiel
  36 ... 178
  36:27 ... 181
  37:14 ... 181
Daniel
  2:21 ... 127
  2:44 f. ... 123
  3:26-45 (LXX) ... 183
  7:12 ... 127
  7:13 ... 122, 123
  7:27 ... 123
  8:25b ... 123
  9 ... 178
  9:4-19 ... 183
  12:1 ... 57
  12:1 f. ... 123
Habakkuk
  1:5 ... 180

O.T. APOCRYPHA AND PSEUDEPIGRAPHA

II Baruch
  70:2 f. ... 57
  70:5 ... 57
  70:8-10 ... 57
IV Ezra
  5:1-12 ... 57
  13:30 f. ... 57
  14:16 f. ... 57
Jubilees
  1 ... 178
  1:23 ... 181
  21 ... 177
  22 ... 178
  23:13 f. ... 57
I Maccabees
  4:30-33 ... 183
II Maccabees
  1:2-6 ... 176
  1:11-17 ... 70
Sirach
  44:12 ... 182
  45:23-24 ... 182
  50:22-24 ... 183
  50:23-24 ... 176
Testaments of the
Twelve Patriarchs
  Benjamin
    3:1 ... 183

    4:1 ... 183
Dan
    4:6 ... 184
    5:1-3 ... 184
    5:1-6:11 ... 184
    5:2 ... 184
    5:3 ... 184
    5:4 ... 184
    5:4-13 ... 184
    6:1 ff. ... 184
    6:8 ... 184
Issachar
    1-7 ... 182
    6:1 ... 184
Judah
    18-25 ... 178

Levi
    8-18 ... 178
Zebulon
    1-5 ... 182
    5:4 ... 183
    6-10 ... 182
    9:5 ... 184
Tobit
    8:5-7 ... 182
    14:3-11 ... 177
Wisdom
    8:8 ... 127
    10-19 ... 178

QUMRAN

CD ... 177
    i-ii ... 178
1QH
    ii.20 ... 175
    vii.6 ... 175, 185
    vii.6b-7a ... 185
    vii.6-25 ... 165, 184
    vii.8b-10 ... 185
    vii.10 ... 165
    vii.12 ... 185

    vii.17-20 ... 185
    vii.19 f. ... 182
    vii.19-20 ... 165
    vii.20-21 ... 185
    vii.22-23 ... 185
    xviii.28 f. ... 182
    xviii.6 ff. ... 182
1QS ... 177
    i.18-ii.18 ... 178

NEW TESTAMENT

Matthew
    9:18 ... 103
    24:31 ... 122
Mark
    9:50 ... 137
    13:7 f. ... 57
    13:27 ... 122
Luke
    3:8 ... 91
Acts
    1:7 ... 127
    2:20 ... 91
    4:24-30 ... 183
    7:2-47 ... 180
    13:16-41 ... 180
    17:2 ... 50
    17:4-5 ... 50
    17:5-10 ... 50

    20:23 ... 105
    21:4 ... 105
    21:10-11 ... 105
Romans ... 32, 43
    1:8 ... 67
    1:8 ff. ... 67
    1:13 ... 120
    1:26 ... 95
    4:16 ... 95
    5:12 ... 95
    11:25 ... 84, 120
    11:30 ... 95
    12:1 ... 74
    12:9 ff. ... 141
    12:18 ... 137
    13:6 ... 95
    13:11 ... 84
    13:13 ... 84

15:5-6 ... 183
15:9 ... 95
15:13 ... 183
I Corinthians
  1:4 ff. ... 67
  1-4 ... 43
  1:26 ... 84
  2:13 ... 113
  4:17 ... 95
  7:1 ... 51
  7:25 ... 51
  8:1 ... 51
  10:1 ... 120
  11:10 ... 95
  12:1 ... 51, 120
  13 ... 41
  15 ... 43
  15:51-58 ... 125
  16:1 ... 51
  16:13-18 ... 142
  16:15 ... 84
  16:17 ... 111
II Corinthians
  1:3 ... 69
  1:8 ... 120
  2:13 ... 89
  4:1 ... 95
  5:20 ... 91
  7:13 ... 95
  8:2 ... 50
  8:9 ... 84
  9:12 ... 111
  11:9 ... 111
  11:25 ... 89
  12:3-4 ... 84
  12:17 ... 90
  13:5-11 ... 142
  13:10 ... 95
  13:11 ... 137
Galations ... 44
  1:1-2 ... 60
  1:3-5 ... 60

1:6 ... 69
2:1 ... 50
3:1-14 ... 43
5:12 ... 98
5:26 ... 84
Ephesians
  1:15 ... 67, 95
  5:17 ... 95
  6:13 ... 95
Philippians
  1:3 ff. ... 67
  2:22 ... 84
  2:30 ... 111
  3:2 ... 98
  4:2-9 ... 142
Colossians
  1:3 ff. ... 67
  1:9 ... 95
  4:16 ... 175
II Thessalonians ... 44
  2:11 ... 95
I Timothy
  2:1 ... 73
  6:2 ... 73
Philemon
  4 ... 68
  4 ff. ... 67
  4-7 ... 70
  8-9 ... 74
  15 ... 95
Hebrews
  13:22 ... 91
I Peter
  1:2 ... 60
II Peter
  1:2 ... 60
Jude
  2 ... 60
Revelation ... 57
  12:10 ... 103

OTHER EARLY CHRISTIAN TEXTS - CHURCH FATHERS

Acts of John
  106-107 ... 178
Augustine
  Conf
    6.3 ... 146

Barnabas ... 178
II Clement ... 178
Didache ... 178